The Banshee

A new, updated edition

'Dr Patricia Lysaght's book *The Banshee* is arguably the best book-length study of Irish folklore to have come out in the postwar period. It is exhaustive in its coverage of the data (ancient and modern), magisterial in its handling of secondary sources, and innovative in the application of theoretical models of folkloristics to the material at hand. What is more, the book is gracefully and compellingly written, with much to say both to the professional folklorist/Celticist and to a more general audience of intelligent readers about a truly fascinating subject. I have learned a great deal from *The Banshee* and consult it often. I have also found it to be a very usable text in classes on Celtic folklore or on folklore in general.'

Professor Joseph Falaky Nagy
Folklore and Mythology Program UCLA
February 1996

Patricia Lysaght

Patricia Lysaght is a native of county Clare, in the west of Ireland. Her academic background is in Law and the Classics, as well as Irish Language and Literature, and Irish and Comparative Folklore and Ethnology. Her doctoral thesis was first published in book form as *The Banshee, The Irish Supernatural Death Messenger* in 1986. She is a lecturer in the Department of Irish Folklore, University College Dublin. Dr Lysaght's work has appeared in major international publications, and she has lectured widely at academic conferences and institutions in Europe, the USA and Canada, as well as parts of Asia. She is a member of the International Society for the Study of European Ideas and the International Society for Folk Narrative Research. She is Irish representative of Société Internationale D'Ethnologie et de Folklore, the International Commission for the Study of Religion in Everyday Life, and the European Ethnocartographic Working Group. She is currently President of the International Commission for Ethnological Food Research. She organised the bi-annual congress of the Commission in Ireland in 1994 and edited the proceedings, entitled *Milk and Milk Products, from Medieval to Modern Times* (Edinburgh 1996). Dr Lysaght was an Alexander von Humboldt scholar at Westfälische Wilhelms-Universität, Münster, Germany, in 1987-8. She was guest international scholar at The Hungarian Academy of Sciences in 1995, and Guest Professor of Folklore at Seminar für Volkskunde, Georg-August-Universität, Göttingen, Germany, in 1996-7.

THE IRISH DEATH MESSENGER

PATRICIA LYSAGHT

Roberts Rinehart Publishers

Published by Roberts Rinehart Publishers
5455 Spine Road
Boulder, Colorado 80301

Distributed to the trade by Publishers Group West

ISBN 1-57098-138-8

Library of Congress Card Catalog Number 97-66386

First published by The O'Brien Press Ltd.
20 Victoria Road
Dublin, Ireland

Copyright © 1986 Patricia Lysaght

10 9 8 7 6 5 4 3 2 1

Jacket design: Ann W. Douden

Cover illustration: From an original etching by Margaret Arthur, Bangor, Co.
Down; entitled "... Endlessly through aeons" a quotation from John Hewitt's
'Retreaded Rhymes," courtesy of the Graphic Gallery, Dublin

Printed in the United States of America

For Liam T., Édaín and Liam P.E.

Foreword to Second Edition

In the course of the past decade I have travelled to many parts of Ireland, both urban and rural, at the invitation of various local societies and groups to talk about the banshee. On each occasion I have been impressed by people's deep-seated interest in the banshee, by the understanding which people have of the underlying functions of such a belief, and by the respect they demand for those who hold the belief.

It has also been gratifying for me to realise that my knowledge and views of the tradition have been essentially in harmony with those of my audiences. The effect of experiences shared and discussed on such occasions, as well as numerous other communications and personal fieldwork in the years since the initial publication of *The Banshee*, has been to substantiate rather than alter the conclusions of the book. The original text has been left largely unchanged for the present edition, apart from a small number of minor adjustments and revisions. A new Introduction has been provided and the Bibliography brought up to date.

The first edition of this work, published in 1986, was welcomed in both folklore and other academic circles. It also inspired a number of poetic compositions, and was well received by the general public. For these reasons, and also in gratitude to the numerous tradition-bearers throughout Ireland who so willingly shared their knowledge and experiences, I am glad that the O'Brien Press are making the study available again, and I would like to thank them for doing so.

Once more I wish to acknowledge the assistance of my colleagues in the Department of Irish Folklore, and also Sylvie Muller, Paris, in the preparation of this edition. I also thank my family, to whom this work is once again dedicated.

Patrica Lysaght
4 July 1996

Acknowledgements

The author wishes to thank the staff of the Department of Irish Folklore, University College Dublin, in particular Professor Bo Almqvist, for their help in producing the doctoral thesis on which this work is based.

She also thanks Dr. Risteard B. Breathnach, Professor Tomás de Bhaldraithe, Dr. Yolande de Pontfarcy-Sexton, Mary Finlay, Professor P.L.Henry, Dr. Ian Mac Aonghais, Frances Morrissey, Patrick J. Morrissey, Tomás Ó Cathasaigh, Pádraig Ó Cearbhaill, Professor Tomás Ó Concheanainn, Anne O'Connor, Donncha Ó Cróinín, Seán Ó Curraoin, Niall Ó Dónaill, Anne O'Dowd, Professor Pádraig Ó Fiannachta, Diarmuid Ó Giolláin, Dr. Éamonn Ó hÓgáin, Aindrias Ó Muimhneacháin, Dr. Seán Ó Súilleabháin, Dr. Patrick C. Power and Pádraig Ua Maoileoin.

Grateful thanks is also given to the numerous tradition-bearers throughout Ireland, and to the collectors, whose dedication to the task of preserving the traditions of the Irish people has made this work possible.

The author also thanks the staff of the audio-visual centre, University College, Dublin, Professor Seóirse Bodley for permission to print extracts from his poetic composition for music, *The Banshee*, Ursula Mattenberger for line drawings, Gerardine Meaney for editorial work.

Finally she extends her personal gratitude to her family.

Contents

List of Appendices

> Distribution and frequency of terms denoting the connection between the death-messenger and certain families; families reputed to be followed by the supernatural death-messenger; questionnaire replies dealing with the position of members of families followed by the banshee, *badhb*, etc.

> A breakdown of the records in the archival and printed source material dealing with the manifestations of the supernatural death-messenger according to *genre*; aural manifestations; visual manifestations; manifestation situations; times of manifestations; places of manifestations; experiencers (in connection with deaths)

> The Comb Legend; The Imprint of the Banshee's Five Fingers Legend; The Shirt Legend

> Traditional material of definitive provenance in the manuscript material in the Department of Irish Folklore (1928-1981), and printed works (c. 1800-1981); American and Canadian sources (questionnaire replies, letters and printed sources); traditional material of indefinite provenance in printed works

Maps and Illustrations

The baronies of Ireland

The provinces and counties of Ireland

Introduction

I

The subject of this study is a supernatural being who figures prominently in Irish folk belief, and who is popularly known as the banshee (Irish: *an bhean sí*). The aim of the study is to ascertain the profile of this supernatural being in Irish folk tradition, to establish the social contexts and functions of belief in such a being, and to trace its age and origin insofar as this is possible.

In certain areas of Ireland this supernatural being is, in addition to the name banshee, also called the *badhb* or the *babha* (*badhbh*), and a number of less common names are also found. Some of these names have implications for the nature of the tradition in certain areas, and in this study, therefore, the term 'supernatural death-messenger' – or sometimes simply 'death-messenger' – is used whenever it is necessary to stress that the tradition in general is under discussion. This generic term emphasises the activity which stands out as central to the traditions of the supernatural being – that of proclaiming deaths which are imminent or have just occurred. The various manifestations of the being will be investigated later, and the results will not be anticipated here. It is immediately obvious in the vast majority of the sources, however, that the being is understood to be a woman, and consequently the pronoun 'she' is used when referring to the supernatural death-messenger.

II

Since the banshee is so closely associated with Ireland and Irish tradition in general opinion, and since the traditions about her concern such central issues as attitudes to life and death, it is not surprising that she has figured in publications of different kinds in the nineteenth and twentieth centuries. Most of these accounts, however, are popular, generalised descriptions of her, such as Elliot O'Donnell's book, *The Banshee* (c. 1920), which is based on a few, not very reliable, sources. There is little to be gleaned either from the few pages that nineteenth-century Irish antiquarian writers such as T. Crofton Croker, John O'Donovan, Nicholas O'Kearney and others have devoted to the subject. None of these writers were professional folklorists; their knowledge of the genuine death-messenger tradition was limited and their accounts contain unwarranted generalisations. Interpretations, if they are found at all, are based on outmoded antiquarian theories or are influenced by personal idiosyncrasies. Similar defects are also evident in the treatment of the banshee in magazines such as *Ireland's Own*, and in a variety of other popular publications which have appeared during the past two decades. It is only in relatively recent times that the death-messenger has received scholarly attention, most notably the work of Lysaght and Sorlin.[1]

Because of the absence of basic research in relation to the supernatural death-messenger in Irish folk tradition until recently, it is not surprising that some handbooks and surveys contain information of dubious value or which is directly misleading. A lack of knowledge of the Irish language has also debarred many writers from much of the available source material. Yet, even with regard to sources in English, it is hardly unfair to say that most treatments of the death-messenger give the impression that the writers are unaware that an enormous body of folklore has been collected in Ireland since the days of W.B. Yeats and Lady Wilde. As a result, many important aspects of the death-messenger tradition remained uninvestigated or even unnoticed. One of the main reasons for this has been that only a relatively small proportion of the oral source material in relation to the death-messenger which is preserved in the Irish Folklore Collections in manuscript form,[2] or as sound records or audio visual tapes, has appeared in print. In this study, therefore, a broad selection of the various tradition types is given, together with liberal quotations from the material collected from the oral tradition. In the case of English quotations from the folklore manuscripts, the originals have been followed closely: only obvious spelling mistakes have been corrected, and punctuation somewhat normalised. In the Irish-language accounts, including transcriptions from tapes, the quotations follow the official standard orthography insofar as this does not intrude upon grammar forms and other distinctive traits in the respective dialects. Full English translations of the Irish-language accounts are given, and these, together with transcriptions of English-language accounts from tapes, are as faithful as possible to the original without deviating too much from normal English usage.

III

PRIMARY SOURCES

Reliable description and analysis of a folklore subject depends on the quantity and quality of the source material. The present study is based on a very large and representative body of oral traditions collected throughout Ireland over a period of some sixty years, and found mainly in archival collections dating from the 1920s to the 1980s, in recent questionnaire replies, and in material resulting from personal fieldwork. For convenience of reference and for mapping purposes, this traditional material is often referred to as 'archival sources' throughout this work.

The folklore material preserved in manuscript form in the archive of the Department of Irish Folklore, University College, Dublin, constitutes the main part of the Irish Folklore Collections and is the richest and primary

coimisiún béaloideasa éireann

conntae... *na Zaillime*,... barúntact *Cill Tártan*
paróiste... *O na Berize*
Ainm an Sgríobnóra... *Seán Ó Flanagan*
Seoladh an Sgríobnóra... *na Cartrín Bearga*
Do repíobar ríor an... *Seancas*... ro ap an... *22ᵃᵈ Lugnas* 1937
ó béal-aicrir... *Bridín Ní Mupas*
aor... 85 (87)... gairm-beata... *bean fuirióga* acá in a comnuí
i mbaile Feapainn... *Tóin Rosmzl*
agur a raoluiod agur a tógad i... *D Tóin Rosmzl*
Do cuala ré (rí) an... *Seancas* ro... blian ó fin ó
... (aor an uair rin...) a bí in a cumnuí an uair rin
i

An bean síde

*Tamall do blianta ó som bíos
tap a eu ag daoine
muinteapdée liom m sa Cillín op
cuapt - az tiz Seán Uí Máirín
op cuapt. bí Seán zo (zo)
h- an-Dorm tínn i n- Osbondeál
na Zaillime, 7 yua mé mise
Sap a cup a tuapisze zo*

Plate 1

source available for virtually any investigation of Irish folklore.[3] The manuscripts are in two series – the so-called Main Manuscripts dating from the late 1920s onwards, and the Schools' Manuscripts (1937-8), amounting to 1127 volumes. The main manuscripts consist, for the most part, of the collectors' handwritten large notebooks bound into volumes, as well as a considerable body of questionnaire replies accumulated over the past six decades. They are thus almost exclusively the work of adult collectors and contributors.[4] More than two hundred substantial accounts of the supernatural death-messenger belief from almost every county in Ireland came to light from these manuscripts (Connaught: 44; Leinster: 52; Munster: 55; Ulster: 71). These accounts are mostly in English and their geographical distribution is shown on Map 1.[5] An excerpt from a main manuscript account from Co. Galway about the banshee (IFC 389: 481) dating from 1937 is shown in Plate 1, above.

The Schools' Manuscripts, consisting of over eleven hundred volumes of folklore material, are the result of a folklore collecting scheme in the Primary Schools of the Republic of Ireland during the years 1937-38. This large collection of folk tradition yielded almost four hundred items of direct relevance to the supernatural death-messenger tradition (Connaught: 83; Leinster: 134; Munster: 135; Ulster (3 counties: 40)) and their distribution is shown on Map 1.[6] In attempting to get as representative a distribution pattern as possible throughout Ireland, death-messenger traditions in the archives of The Ulster Folk and Transport Museum were sought. Just eight manuscript references – from adult correspondents and dating from the nineteen fifties and sixties – were obtained from this source [7] (Antrim 7, 8; Down 3, 7, 8, 26; Fermanagh 2; Tyrone 1); their geographical distribution is also shown on Map 1. Further information from parts of the northeast, from adults as well as schoolchildren, was obtained by means of a questionnaire on the banshee circulated in the late 1970s, as described below (cf. Down 18-25; Tyrone 8, and Map 1).[8]

On the basis of a survey of the material in the Main and Schools Manuscripts, which established most of the principal elements of the death-messenger tradition, a detailed questionnaire about the banshee and related supernatural beings was formulated and circulated by the Department of Irish Folklore, University College Dublin, in May 1976, to regular questionnaire correspondents throughout Ireland and to some people outside Ireland who had requested a copy.[9] The purpose of the questionnaire was to gather further up-to-date information about the death-messenger throughout Ireland and to find out the contemporary status of the belief. There were almost one hundred and forty replies in all, four of which came from the United States (USA 2, 4, 5, 6), one from Wales (information here referred to Wexford (Wexford 17)), and the remainder were from Ireland (Connaught: 20; Leinster: 40; Munster: 31; Ulster: 41) – see map 1.[10] The full text of the questionnaire in Irish and English is contained in Appendix 1, pp. 247-54.

Arising from a radio programme in August 1976, twenty-three letters from people in Ireland, dealing with the banshee and related beings, were received in 1976-77 and their distribution is shown on Map 1. Five further letters came from the United States as a result of a short item on the banshee in the July-August 1977 issue of *Dúchas,* an Irish-American publication (Appendix 5.2, p. 362).[11]

I myself have been familiar with the banshee belief in my native west Clare and in many other parts of the west of Ireland since childhood. However, as a result of my survey of the archival material, I became aware of the added diversity of the death-messenger belief in the midlands and the eastern part of Ireland, and in order to explore and understand this

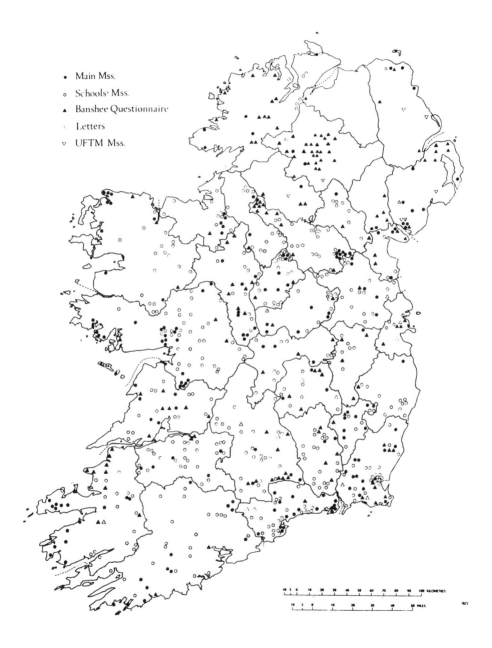

- • Main Mss.
- ○ Schools' Mss.
- ▲ Banshee Questionnaire
- ⌇ Letters
- ▽ UFTM Mss.

1. The types and provenance of the archival sources on which the analysis of the Irish supernatural death-messenger tradition is based

situation more fully, I carried out intensive fieldwork in 1976 and 1978 (see
Laois 14, 15, 16, 17, 18, 19 and Kildare 13) in specific parts of these
regions with which I was familiar and where I had already established
contacts. I conducted many in-depth and extended taped interviews based
on the Banshee questionnaire, and the considerable amount of
contemporary information on the banshee and related beings thus
collected, is transcribed in two substantial volumes (1840 and 2114) of the
Main Manuscripts' collection of the Department of Irish Folklore. Further
material which I collected in Dublin in 1982 constitutes something of a
special case and will be referred to later.

VALUE OF THE SOURCES

The source value of the material relating to the death-messenger found in
the Main Manuscripts' collection must be rated highly. The vast majority
(188) of these accounts were taken down by professional field collectors,
including full-time and special collectors,[12] of the Irish Folklore Commission
or the Department of Irish Folklore, or by experienced and reliable
part-time collectors.[13] Much of the rest, though contributed by occasional
collectors or amateurs, compares favourably with the abovementioned
categories. While the geographical distribution of the Main Manuscripts'
material can be uneven, as it tends to reflect only those areas in which
collectors have worked, it is, in the case of the death-messenger belief,
admirably complemented by the material in the Schools' Manuscripts'
collection, which has a much wider distribution, and also by the
questionnaire replies and by other detailed communications as already
mentioned.

Most of the material in the Schools' Manuscripts was written down by
children in the senior classes of the primary schools who were, not
surprisingly, unfamiliar with any of the stringent guidelines for folklore
collecting and transcription, as, most likely, were many of their teachers. It
is to be expected, therefore, that their accounts are not normally as full, or
as lengthy, as those in the Main Manuscripts,[14] and while the children's
informants are generally mentioned, the background information about
them of the type usually found in the Main Manuscripts, is not always
given. Nevertheless, most of the death-messenger material in the Schools'
Manuscripts' collection is of considerable value, especially in helping to
establish distribution patterns. Additionally, the volume of material is
surprisingly large considering that no direct questions about the banshee
or related beings were asked in the guideline booklet prepared by Seán Ó
Súilleabháin and distributed by the Department of Education to the schools
participating in the folklore collection scheme.[15] It may well be that the
somewhat eerie subject appealed to the children. Also, much of the

The Banshee.

A great number of people in this locality believe in the Banshee or the Bou as it is generally called. The Banshee follows certain families and when one of the family is about to die she is seen crying and combing her long hair. She is said to be like an old woman with long grey hair. When the person dies she disappears.

It is said that on one occasion, that a man in this locality succeeded in taking the comb from the Banshee and that night she came and sat on his window sill, and she was crying bitterly, and the man had to give it back with a hot tongs. It is also believed that if you gave it back with your naked hand you would run the risk of instant death.

The following are some of the families which she is supposed to follow:–

The O'Connors, Browns, Keegans,

death-messenger material consists of short belief statements and legends, and these genres are more easily handled by children than longer and more complex categories. Certain aspects of the tradition – for example, the belief that a comb left lying around should not be picked up – were especially relevant to children and this may be why The Comb Legend figures so prominently in the Schools' Manuscripts. Most of all, the prevalence of the death-messenger belief in the Schools' Manuscripts is, no doubt, an indication of just how strong and immediate the belief was for young and old at the time. The above extract from the Schools' Manuscripts (IPCS 889: 73-4; Plate 2) was written by Maggie Kinsella, a schoolchild in Monaseed National School, Co. Wexford (1937).

On re-assessing the results of the Banshee Questionnaire, it must be said that the quantity and quality of the replies are most striking. Almost one hundred and forty adult correspondents throughout most of Ireland, answered the questionnaire, which consisted of twenty-four detailed questions, in a most painstaking fashion, and the replies are, for the most part, rich and varied, and can be considered trustworthy. Comprising four large manuscript volumes (2110-2113) of the Main Manuscripts' collection, these replies provide a virtually incomparable contemporary statement of the nature and status of the death-messenger belief. Additionally, as is evident from Map 1, they are, geographically speaking, broadly based, and many are from areas not already represented in other sources, thus providing a more complete pattern of distribution of the tradition over the whole geographical area under study. Another important aspect of the questionnaire was that it was possible thereby to get additional information on certain aspects of the tradition which needed clarification. Not all of these were obvious when the questionnaire was being formulated; in a country like Ireland, however, where so many aspects of folk tradition – especially as far as the banshee is concerned – are still so immediate, it was possible to redress this situation in a variety of ways – by means of correspondence, telephone conversations or fieldwork, for example.

As to the American questionnaire replies, while they generally lack the detail of their Irish counterparts, they are, nevertheless, important as records of the perceptions of the death-messenger belief in the early decades of the century among some descendants of nineteenth-century Irish emigrants. The same can be said of the letters from America.

The letters received from various parts of Ireland are also valuable sources in that many of them are quite detailed, and they all happen to be from areas where no death-messenger traditions appear to have been previously recorded (cf. Map 1).

Finally, personal fieldwork contributed significantly to an elucidation of the death-messenger belief, both past and present. All of the people interviewed had had personal experience of the death-messenger, some over a period of several decades, and were, therefore, an important contemporary source of information about the nature, social context, function, and status of the belief throughout most of the twentieth century. In Co. Kildare, I interviewed an excellent informant, a farmer who was in his late fifties at the time, and in Dublin a woman called Anne Hill, who represented the vigorous urban traditions of the banshee. Extracts from her detailed personal experience narrative are given in Chapter 13.

My main and most important informant, however, was Mrs Jenny McGlynn (Co. Laois) who was in her late thirties at the time and who has a virtual 'theology' of the banshee. I also interviewed her mother, now deceased, who had experienced the banshee over many decades, including on an occasion shortly before the interview, when a neighbour had died. Jenny's accounts, including many personal experiences, must rank among the best collected. In fact, it was possible to almost observe the belief 'in operation' during my first collecting visit to Jenny – a man who had lived in the immediate vicinity of her home died in hospital and Jenny claimed to have heard the banshee the night before he died. An extract from her account of the experience is given in Chapter 13. Over the years since my initial interviews with her in the 1970s, Jenny has told me that she has experienced the banshee at the deaths of neighbours and relatives – including her own mother's death. Her personal experience narratives bear witness to the continuing relevance of the banshee tradition for some people in Ireland as the twentieth century draws to a close.

By any standards, the corpus of source material described and evaluated above – almost eight hundred accounts, collected from almost as many informants, throughout the length and breadth of Ireland since the early part of the present century – constitutes a vital and basic resource, for any indepth analysis of the death-messenger traditions in Ireland over the past century and a half. The material undoubtedly has implications also for an assessment of the profile of the tradition in earlier periods, including its possible age and origin. The material also offers the best indication as to which elements of the death-messenger tradition belong to Ireland as a whole, which elements belong only to particular parts of the country, and, importantly, which elements appear to be extraneous and to have been attracted to the death-messenger complex from elsewhere over the course of time. These collections also provide a yardstick for an evaluation of the miscellaneous material on the death-messenger in a variety of printed sources from the nineteenth and twentieth centuries. This material will now be assessed.

SECONDARY SOURCES

In addition to the primary oral sources just discussed – which include material published in *Béaloideas*, The Journal of the Folklore of Ireland Society – use has also been made of material on the death-messenger which has appeared in printed works from the nineteenth- and twentieth-centuries in cases where its source value seems reliable.[16] About a hundred and fifty such references came to light – only six of which are in Irish[17] – and the provenance of only about half of them can be determined accurately (see Map 2).[18]

The influence of printed material on the oral traditions of the death-messenger appears to be negligible. Most of the books and journals in which such material appeared were not intended for, and probably never reached, the majority of the ordinary people. Even literary compositions in

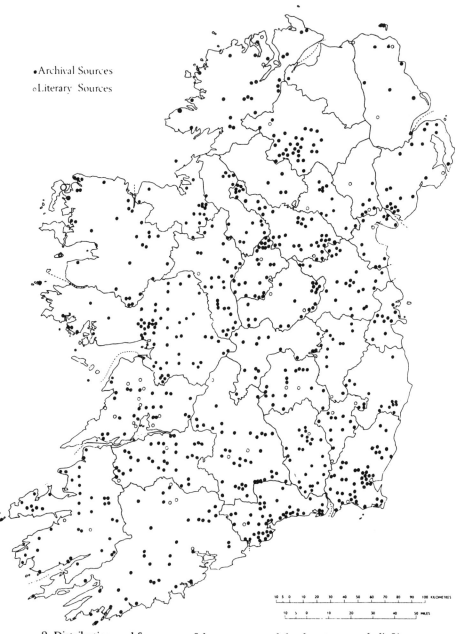

•Archival Sources
○Literary Sources

2. Distribution and frequency of the supernatural death-messenger belief in
Ireland on the basis of the archival (1928-1981) and printed (c.1800-1981)
sources

fairly popular magazines such as *Ireland's Own*, based on re-worked oral source material, do not appear to have entered the oral stream. Most of the printed accounts lack the detail of the oral records and some of them contain material which is obviously totally untraditional.

The firmest proof of the occurrence of a certain phenomenon before a particular date, however, is the evidence embedded in literary sources, if these are reliable. But since such sources have often been tampered with, as already stated, for a variety of possible reasons (artistic, moral, religious, ideological and so on), they can be used only with the greatest caution, and only where their evidence is corroborated by genuine recent folk tradition. In some instances they have been totally rejected.

The printed sources occasionally provide information from areas not already represented in the archival material. However, since they constitute only fifteen per cent of the total source material used here, and because they suffer from the shortcomings mentioned, it is the evidence of the archival records, including personal fieldwork, which is mainly relied on and the printed records must be regarded as subsidiary.[19] A full list of the archival and printed sources on which this work is based is given in Appendix 5, pp. 321-64.

IV

THE DISTRIBUTION OF THE
DEATH-MESSENGER TRADITION

The general distribution of the death-messenger belief as indicated in the twentieth-century archival sources and the nineteenth- and twentieth-century printed sources, is shown on Map 2. From this, it is obvious that the belief has been widespread throughout mainland Ireland and has also existed on off-shore islands such as Rathlin off the Antrim coast (Antrim 1, 2), Clare Island and Inishbofin off Mayo (Mayo 31), south-Inishturk off Galway (Galway 12), the Great Blasket off Kerry (Kerry 15), Dursey Island (Cork 6) and Clear Island off the coast of Cork (Cork 39).

The apparent absence of the tradition in some areas may result simply from insufficient collecting. This is the likely reason for the relatively smaller quantity of records from some of the north-eastern counties compared to most of the rest of Ireland, indicating in particular lack of participation in the Schools' Scheme 1937-8 (cf. above, p. 18). The apparent lack, however, of any genuine record for Tory Island off the northwest coast of Donegal, where some collecting has been done, and also for the Aran Islands of Galway, where collecting has been fairly intensive and where recent inquiries have been made (Galway 1, 2, 3, 4, 5), indicate that the tradition might not have existed there. A former north-Inishturk

26   The Banshee

(Mayo) islander now living on the mainland states that the banshee was unknown on the island.[20] The belief also apparently lacked importance in Scattery Island off the south coast of Clare.[21] However, even if these exceptions are real – and not merely apparent – they are relatively insignificant and one may for practical purposes say that the death-messenger belief is encountered all over Ireland.

V

The sources, extensive and varied as they are, allow for sustained analysis of all important aspects of the death-messenger tradition. The first eleven chapters of this study survey and establish the various constituent elements in the tradition. In Chapter 12, an attempt is made to assess the age and origin of the death-messenger belief, and also to find solutions to certain problems arising out of the survey in the earlier chapters. The final chapter is devoted to an analysis of continuity and change in the death-messenger traditions in the twentieth century.

In the presentation and analysis of the material, the distribution of the various beliefs and legends is first established in order to ascertain what elements of the tradition are found throughout Ireland or only in particular parts of it. On the basis of their distribution and frequency attempts have then been made to determine the manner of dissemination and the age of the respective traditions. Because genre is an important clue to the different distribution patterns appearing in connection with various death-messenger traditions, special treatment is given to certain legends which have developed around the nucleus of death-messenger beliefs and which cannot be properly understood unless they are analysed separately. On the other hand, such legends – even though they have grown out of folk beliefs – have also given rise to beliefs and belief statements. Consequently, genre analysis is supplemented by cross-genre analysis. The terminology used here – for example, memorate, belief statement, legend and fabulate – has been developed by C.W. von Sydow and by the Finnish folklorists Lauri Honko and Juha Pentikäinen.[22] The now well-known methods developed and employed of Honko (1962, 1964) and Pentikäinen (1968, 1978) in relation to analysing complex traditional material, are here adapted to specifically Irish material. In Chapter 12, where the age and origin of the belief and its various components is assessed, literary source material in Irish, ranging from the Old to the Modern Irish periods, has been surveyed and source criticism has also been applied to it.

The names by which the death-messenger is known can be an important indication of her characteristics and origin and of the regional variations in the traditions concerning her. A survey of these names will, therefore, be the starting point for our investigation of the material.

1

Names

Many names may be used for one and the same supernatural being in different areas or even within one area. A study of such names may help us to understand the origin, dissemination, morphology and function of the beliefs about the being in question. The distribution of dialect forms of a name may provide a key to the direction in which the particular term spread, possibly also to the dissemination channels and to the probable age of the belief. Aspects of the word formation and phonology of the respective names may provide *termini ante quem* and *termini post quem* not only for the names themselves but also for the beliefs implied in them. Etymologies, in so far as they have been correctly understood by the people who held the beliefs, may account for prominent traits in, for example, the appearance and role behaviour of the respective beings. False etymologies — whether originally supplied by 'the folk' or by scholars or pseudo-scholars — may also influence beliefs and legends.

The terminology attached to supernatural beings in Ireland is apparently less varied than that found in many countries.[1] There are surprisingly few names for the supernatural death-messenger. Nevertheless, they are worthy of attention for several of the reasons outlined above. It is obviously necessary to survey these names before entering upon a detailed analysis of other traits. The present state of knowledge of Irish dialects will only allow tentative conclusions to be drawn: only future research will enable certain sound changes to be dated with greater accuracy. It is possible, however, to point to facts and probabilities of importance in interpreting the traditions under discussion[2] relying upon the best authorities on dialectology and etymology.

Names for the supernatural death-messenger in Irish tradition may conveniently be divided into three groups: 1) *bean síl*

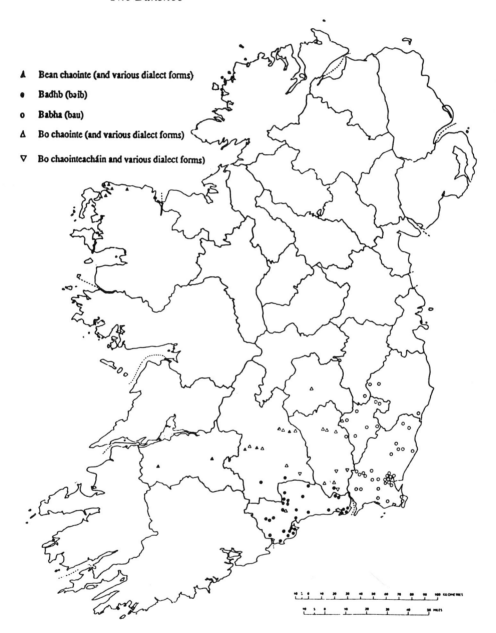

A   Bean chaointe (and various dialect forms)

●   Badhb (bəib)

o   Babha (bau)

Δ   Bo chaointe (and various dialect forms)

▽   Bo chaointeacháin and various dialect forms)

3. Names other than *bean sí*/banshee

banshee, 2) *bean chaointe* (and similar forms) and 3) what we may refer to as *badhbh*-appellations. The distribution of the term *bean sí/banshee* corresponds to the distribution of the death-messenger belief shown on Map 2, while that of the other names for the death-messenger is shown on Map 3.

II

Undoubtedly, the most common name is *bean sí*, or, as it is commonly anglicised, *banshee*. The term is found over the whole distribution area of the supernatural death-messenger belief gleaned from the archival and printed records listed in Appendix 5 (Map 2). This area covers most of Ireland. The few blank areas on Map 2 are no doubt due more to insufficient collecting rather than to the absence of the name or tradition. However, the fact that apparently neither *bean sí* nor any other term has been recorded from such western islands as Tory, north-Inishturk or Achill, and the ambiguous nature of the evidence from the Aran Islands, may in fact be due to the absence of the tradition there.[3] The wide distribution of *bean sí/*banshee and its occurrence in areas where other names are also found (Map 3) owes something to literary influence. Often used in books, magazines and newspapers, *banshee* is likely to have been regarded as the 'standard' form. Statements such as the following indicate that local terms have been superseded fairly recently in certain places:

> The *bean chaointe* we used to call her. The *bean sí* they call her now (Limerick 20).

Nevertheless it is reasonable to assume that the name *bean sí/ banshee* has for centuries been the most common and most widespread.

A *terminus ante quem* for the name in the sense of super-natural death-messenger is afforded by Piaras Feiritéir's lament for the death in Flanders (c. 1642)[4] of Muiris Mac Gearailt mac Ridire Chiarraí[5]:

> Ins an Daingean níor chaigil an ceol-ghol,
> Gur ghlac eagla ceannaidhthe an chnósta,
> Dá n-eagla féin níor bhaoghal dóibh sin,
> Ní chaoinid mná sidhe an sórt soin.

[In Dingle the crying did not grow faint,
And the hoarding merchants grew afraid,
But they need not fear for themselves,
Banshees do not bewail their sort.]
(Ua Duinnín 1934, p. 74, lines 29-32).

Because of the paucity of references to it in the literary records, it is not possible to get a clear indication of how widespread the term *bean sí* 'supernatural death-messenger' may have been in the seventeenth and eighteenth centuries. One must not, however, conclude that this appellation was much more uncommon then, or even in earlier centuries, than it is at present, or was at the turn of the century. In fact, on the basis of an early Irish text it seems that *bean sí* in the meaning 'supernatural death-messenger' may be traced to about the middle of the eighth century.[6]

Bean sí has a venerable pedigree in another sense. In early Irish sources, words such as *ben síde* or *ben a sídib, banshídaige*, 'a female dweller in a *síd*', 'a fairy woman' (*Dictionary of the Irish Language s.v. ben, síd, síth, sídaige*) occur. The original meaning of *síd* (gen. *síde*) is disputed; usually the word is translated 'fairy hill' or 'fairy mound'. Tomás Ó Cathasaigh, who recently dealt with this problem,[7] might well be right in assuming that the word originally meant '(the) Otherworld'. Even if that was so, it seems indisputable that *ben síde* occurring in early Irish texts is a 'fairy woman', and in Modern Irish, *bean sí* is also sometimes used in this sense, synonymously with *bean an leasa* 'the woman of the fairy fort', 'a fairy woman'. This is the case in Scottish Gaelic where *Bean-Shìthe*, 'a fairy woman' is found.[8]

There can be no doubt that *bean sí*, 'fairy woman' and *bean sí*, 'supernatural female death-messenger' are one and the same expression. Are there reasons to object, then, to the statement sometimes found in printed sources as well as in material taken down orally, that the death-announcing *bean sí* 'is a fairy woman'? This question will be dealt with in greater detail later, but it must be emphasised here that it is difficult to regard the death-announcing *bean sí* as a fairy in the ordinary sense of that expression. Fairies are imagined to be social beings, living in communities. Often depicted as married and having children, they may have friendly as well as unfriendly relations with humans, and may even be engaged in love affairs with them.[9]

The death-announcing *bean sí* is a solitary being *par préférence*; one never hears of *bean sí* communities and the being is never said to be married (indeed, no male counterpart is imagined to exist). There are no tales about a *bean sí* doing a friendly turn for human beings. In most respects, then, the fairy beliefs and the belief in the death-announcing *bean sí* are as different as two sets of beliefs in supernatural beings can be. It is also puzzling that *bean sí/banshee* appears never to have been used about a 'fairy woman' in the ordinary sense in genuine material in the English language. Tomás Ó Cathasaigh[10] is of the opinion that the word *síd* originally meant '(the) Otherworld' and indeed 'woman of the Otherworld' would be an apt description of the *bean sí* 'supernatural death-messenger' while 'fairy woman' in the ordinary sense, would be off the mark even if it were correct from an etymological point of view.[11]

The knowledge shared by all native Irish-speakers and by many people with minimal Irish, that *bean sí* meant 'fairy woman', is likely to have coloured beliefs and narratives about the death-messenger, though it would seem that it is the shell rather than the core of the tradition that has been affected. The name may, for instance, have helped to attract certain legends originally attached to the fairies to the *bean sí* complex. Certain traits in the description of the appearance and behaviour of the *bean sí* – though by no means the most common traits – may also be best understood as borrowings from fairy lore.

Only one false etymology appears to have been attached to *bean sí/banshee*, namely that the meaning would be 'white fairy'. This explanation is found, for example, in John Keegan's *Legends and Tales of the Queen's County Peasantry*[12] and it also turns up in a reply to the questionnaire in 1976 (Kerry 45). The assumption here is that the first part of the word is Irish *bán* 'white' and that *sí* means 'fairy' (though, of course, adjectives do not usually precede nouns in Irish, and though *sí* is an attributive genitive (genitive singular of *sí*) which can only be taken to mean fairy when following a noun, as in *aois sí*, 'inhabitants of a fairy mound', 'fairies', *an slua sí*, 'the fairy host', or, indeed, in *bean sí*). In support of the false etymology Keegan adds, 'this spirit is so named, probably from its being said to make its appearance generally in white garments.' This is, of course, putting the cart before the horse. The being did not get its name from its appearance in white, but the idea that *ban* in *banshee* was Irish *bán*, 'white' arose because people were familiar with the existing belief that the being appeared in garments of that colour. The false etymology may in turn have strengthened the belief that the *bean sí* was dressed in white, but it would hardly have had much influence since not only all native Irish speakers but even people with a rudimentary knowledge of Irish would regard it as absurd.

Whatever specific meaning is allotted to *sí* in *bean sí* here, it may be taken for granted that it refers to a mystic quality – the supernatural character of the being. The basic word, *bean*, clearly indicates this supernatural being was imagined as a woman. A possible explanation of why beings of this kind are so often imagined to be women in Ireland may be found in those Irish tales which represent the Otherworld as 'The Land of Women' *Tír inna mBan*.[13] It is obvious, however, that once an appellation like *bean sí* had become traditional and dominant, the very name gave the stamp of authority to the femininity and made it difficult for the belief to develop in another direction.

III

The supernatural death-messenger is called *bean chaointe* (or similar) in parts of Tipperary and Limerick in east Munster and of Mayo in Connaught (Map 3). In Tipperary *bean chaointe* is reported from Twomileborris (Tipperary 4) and Cappaghwhite (Tipperary 30)[14] and *bean chaointe cháinte* from Ballagh (Tipperary 27), in Limerick *bean chaointe* is reported from Garryduff (Limerick 20) and *bean a' chaointe* from Bruff (oral communication from Dr Dáithí Ó hÓgain). In four examples from north-west Mayo (Mayo 6, 7, 8, 29) the term is spelled *bean chaointe*, no doubt representing a pronunciation, *bean chaoint'* [b'an 'xi:nt'], while another example from Killgaligan in the same area (oral communication from Dr. Séamus Ó Catháin) has the form *bean chaoint'* [b'an 'xi:nt'].

As already seen (p. 29) there are indictions the term *bean chaointe* was formerly more common in Limerick. There is no evidence to show it existed in earlier times outside the counties where it is now found. It is also difficult to explain satisfactorily its strange distribution, in particular the wide gap between the northern and the southern areas. It is noteworthy the term *bo*

(< *bodhbh*) *chaointe* (see p. 35) is found in the same part of Tipperary as *bean chaointe*. It would be tempting, and possibly correct, to consider the latter form to be a hybrid of *bo chaointe* and *bean sí*. Assuming this to be so — and assuming there is a connection between the Tipperary-Limerick area on one hand and the Mayo area on the other — one would be inclined to think the Mayo tradition was an importation from the south. It is not possible to say when and why this might have happened and it would seem no other specific resemblances between Tipperary-Limerick and north-Mayo have been noted. Alternatively, one could surmise the term arose independently in the two areas.

Etymologically, there is no problem. *Bean chaointe/bean a' chaointe/bean chaoint'* means simply 'a keening woman'. The usual meaning of the word *cáineadh*, appearing in *bean chaointe cháinte*, is 'condemnation', 'blame', or the like,[15] but it seems probable the word carries no specific meaning in the context of the name; it is likely to be merely ornamental assonance.

Bean chaointe — like *bean sí* — tells us that the being is female. The attributive genitive 'caointe' in *bean-chaointe*, however, does not, like that in *bean sí*, refer to the origin or dwelling-place of the being but to her activity or role behaviour — her keening. That this is a supernatural being is thus not expressed in the name *bean chaointe*; an ordinary human keening woman is referred to by the same term. Since the name would as a rule be preceded by the definite article — *an bhean chaointe* — the implication one has to do with no ordinary keening woman is usually clear. Such women would usually be referred to in the plural as *mná caointe*. As will be seen the keen or wail is one of the most prominent traits in the traditions about the female supernatural death-messenger.[16] Hence *bean chaointe* is a very apt name for her. Many traits in the traditions of the being are best explained by assuming the supernatural death-messenger's appearance and actions mirror to some some extent those of human keening women. For these reasons the suggestion made above that *bean chaointe* might have developed independently in Tipperary-Limerick and in Mayo is perhaps more likely than it may appear at first glance. However that may be, *bean chaointe* gave further authority to the collective belief that the death-messenger was a woman and possessed some traits of a human keening woman.

IV

The group of terms referred to as *badhbh*-appellations (Map 3) consists of either a dialect form of the word given in standard Irish dictionaries as *badhbh* or of that word followed by an attributive genitive singular of dialect forms of the words *caoineadh* or *caointeachán*. Though the spelling *badhbh*, which one would expect to represent a pronunciation [baiv], occurs occasionally in the folklore manuscripts (e. g. Waterford 36, 37, 38, all from the same collector), it seems likely the word, in the meaning under discussion, was not pronounced in that way and the spelling is due to the influence of standard Irish.[17] Instead, the two main forms of the word are *badhb* [bəib] and *babha* [bau]. In English language sources the former is frequently spelled *bibe*, and the latter form — which now occurs exclusively in areas where Irish is extinct — *bow*, or, more seldom, *bough* (cf. Henry 1957-8, pp. 408-9). The forms *bo* [bo] and *bó* [bo:] only occur before an attributive adjective.

The *badhb*-area, i.e. the area in which the pronunciation [bəib] is to be found (not to be confused with the *badhbh*-area where all the terms which may be derived from standard Irish *badhbh* are found) consists mainly of Waterford, but the form has seeped into Kilkenny (Kilkenny 16) and Tipperary (Tipperary 7, 21), areas with close dialectical affinity to Waterford Irish, commonly termed the *Déise* dialect.[18] The term does not appear to have penetrated Cork. P.L. Henry[19] states it is also found in 'South Kerry Ir. as a local term for the more general *banshee*' according to 'accounts in the Folklore Archives' from that area. (Henry does not refer to any particular manuscript and in view of the distinct distribution patterns for the *badhbh* names which the examination of the source material reveals, this reference is dubious.)[20] Apart from the examples in the archival material, the term *badhb* is found in dialect studies and topographical works relating to Waterford. R.B. Breatnach[21] notes the term from the parish of Ringagonagh, and in *The Place-Names of Decies* there are references to such places as *Bóithrín na Baidhbe*, *Bóthar na Baidhbe*, *Tobar na Baidhbe* and *Bán na mBadhb*.[22] In John O'Brien's *Focalóir Gaoidhilge-Sax-Bhéarla* published in 1768 *badhb* is glossed as '*Bean-Síghe*, a fairy woman vulgarly supposed to belong to particular families'. No source is stated.[23]

The *babha*-area consists mainly of Wexford[24] and Carlow,[25] but the form has also penetrated north-east Kilkenny (Kilkenny 8), south Kildare (Kildare 8)[26] and Wicklow (Wicklow 1, 12, 13). Here, too, the archival sources can be complemented by dialect studies from Wexford[27] and from Carlow.[28] The form is also attested in an eighteenth-century manuscript from Wexford.[29] P.L. Henry[30] refers to *bow* from Wexford and Carlow with the meaning 'banshee' but his information is derived from the IFC manuscripts.

The term *bo* (or *bó*) *chaointe* is found in the manuscripts in a variety of spellings such as *bohaíonta, boheanter, bohinkey*, mainly in Kilkenny and in mid-Tipperary.[31] There is also an isolated example from Carlow (Carlow 12) in the vicinity of Kilkenny examples. According to P.L. Henry[32] 'A Laois (Trumera, Mountrath) informant offered 'bó chaointe'', for the *banshee*. The occurrence of the term in mid-Laois is surprising; one would expect to find it nearer the Kilkenny examples. In word-lists and in dialect studies the term is noted from Kilkenny in *Irisleabhar na Gaedhilge* XI, 1901, p. 93, by R.A. Breatnach[33] and by E. Ó Ceallaigh.[34] In his *Linguistic Atlas and Survey of Irish Dialects*[35] H. Wagner gives the word as '*bé? chaointe*' [be 'xiːn't'ə] for north Kilkenny but this is probably a misreading of his source, Professor Breatnach's thesis, which has the form *bo chaointe*.[36]

Among older literary sources referring to the *bo chaointe* special mention should be made of Michael Banim's novel 'Crohoore of the Bill-Hook' (1825). The use of the term *bocheentha* (p. 64)[37] probably reflected the practice of his native Kilkenny.[38] The Gaelic scholar John O'Donovan[39] is not too specific in stating: 'In the eastern counties of Ireland this fabled female spright is called *Bodhbh chaointe* (Bowe Keentè) . . . ' but since he was a native of Attateemore,[40] it seems possible that he, too, had mainly Kilkenny in mind. More problematic is a reference in Nicholas O'Kearney's introduction to *Feis Tighe Chonáin*:[41]

> In the Parish of Modeligo, and townland of Mountain Castle, in the county of Waterford, so late as the beginning of the present century, a Badhbh, Bo Chaointe, or Bean Sighe, was in the habit of appearing . . .

From this quotation one might get the impression the term *bo chaointe* was current in Waterford in the eighteenth century.

As already seen — and as will appear even more clearly below — one would not expect the form *bo* in this area. It is more probable that O'Kearney heard the term in counties Kilkenny or Tipperary, and simply included it as a synonym for *badhb* without due regard for the locality he was describing. Finally, it may be mentioned that James Murphy from Glynn, south-Carlow,[42] refers to *Bogheentheath* in his novel *The House in the Rath*.[43] This might be intended to represent *bo chaointe*, but in view of the fact that the same writer also spells the word *Bogheentheagh*[44] it would appear he had in mind *bo chaointeach*, which one may perhaps regard as a variant form of *bo chaointeacháin*. The term *bo chaointeach* seems to have gone out of use as a name for the supernatural death-messenger, but a questionnaire answer from Kilcash, Clonmel, Tipperary (Tipperary 16), states a pouting child (male or female) was referred to as a *boheentach*, and the term might formerly have been found in certain parts of the margin of the *badhbh*-area synonymously with *banshee*.[45]

The form *bo chaointeacháin*, spelled *bocaoideachán*, *boheentacán*, is a form which has been recorded mainly in south-Kilkenny (Kilkenny 14, 16). The example adduced by Henry[46] is also from this area.

It may be said, by way of summing up, that the *badhbh*-area consists of a clearly distinguishable *badhb*-area (Waterford, south-Tipperary and south-Kilkenny) and an equally clearly distinguishable *babha*-area (mainly Wexford and Carlow). The 'derivatory' terms — *bo* (*bó*) *chaointe* and *bo chaointeacháin* — occur on the outskirts of these areas, as though there was specific need there to clarify what kind of a *badhb* or *babha* is being dealt with. These terms, whatever their age, are likely to be more recent than *badhb* and *babha*. Another impression given by the distribution map — one unlikely to be erroneous — is that the names have spread mainly from the south towards the north. This is especially noticeable as regards *babha*. Although the fact that little collecting has been undertaken in Wicklow and Laois would make it unwise to assert the form was not previously found further north in these counties, it seems likely the map shows the distribution essentially as it was several centuries ago. A further indication in that direction is afforded by the fact that the term *babha* is found in areas where the percentage of Irish speakers was small by about 1800.[47] It can be assumed the spread of the term took place mainly when Irish was the dominant language there. The problem of the age of the *badhbh*-names would be partially solved if it was possible to date the sound-changes involved in the different dialect forms of the word.[48] Unfortunately, it is not yet possible to date with any accuracy either the hardening of the *bh* in this word as found in *badhb*, or the development of the diphthong as in *babha*,[49] but the distinct borderline between the *badhb*-area and the *babha*-area indicates the distinction is old. The problem cannot be solved without taking into account the pronunciation of the word in meanings other than that of 'supernatural death-messenger', found outside the *badhb*- and *babha*-areas as demarcated above. In this connection it may also be mentioned that the occurrence of the word *badhb(h)* in meanings other than 'supernatural death-messenger' – such as 'a scold', 'a scolding woman' or 'a bogey' – in many areas of Ireland, including Cork and Kerry, may offer at least part of the solution to the enigmatic problem of why *badhb* 'supernatural death-messenger' has not penetrated further south-west.[50] If one were in doubt as to what was meant by *badhb*, one would perhaps be more inclined to adhere to an unequivocal term, such as *bean sí*.

Whatever the date of the sound changes it cannot be doubted that *badhb*, *babha* and *bo* (*bó*) are derived from the word *badb* (earlier *bodb*) appearing in early Irish sources;[51] according to Breatnach and Henry, it is the latter form (*bodb*) which has given rise to *bó* (*bo*).[52] In *DIL*, *Badb* is glossed 'Name of a wargoddess'; 'scald-crow (in which form the goddess appeared).' As an attributive genitive singular it occurs in the sense 'deadly', 'dangerous', 'ill-fated', and it is also used as a derogatory term about human beings (*a bhaidhbh!* 'thou witch'!). The word has relations in other Indo-European languages being cognate with Gaulish *boduo-*, OE *beadu*, ON *bǫð* 'battle', Mod. W. *Bod(a)* ('mountain kite', and also Cornish *bodu* 'hawk').[53] The etymology of the word is thus clear in its main outlines. It would appear Modern Irish *badhb(h)* — in all its meanings — denotes a dangerous, frightening and aggressive being, mainly — if not exclusively — of the female sex. These connotations may have helped to preserve and strengthen these aspects in the 'supernatural death-messenger', even though the word was gradually becoming unintelligible, especially in the forms *babha* and *bo* (*bó*) in areas where Irish was no longer spoken.

The early Irish *Badb* (*Bodb*) presents another problem somewhat similar to that raised by the term *bean sí*. How exactly is *Badb* of early Irish literature related to the *badhb/babha* 'supernatural death-messenger' of nineteenth- and twentieth-century folk tradition in the south-east of Ireland?

This question will be discussed in some detail in subsequent chapters, but a number of points may be outlined here.

The *Badb (Bodb)* in the literature from the medieval period onwards resembles the *badhb/babha* of later folk tradition in many respects but differs from her in others.[54] The *Badb* is almost exclusively connected with battles, while the *badhb/babha* is mainly attached to non-violent deaths. Though the *Badb* sometimes foretells slaughter and in this respect is a kind of death-messenger, she is also depicted as appearing after death rejoicing over the slain, a role in which the *badbh/babha* is not found. While the *Badb* is often depicted as washing bloodstained garments or limbs, the *badhb/babha*, while associated with water, does not appear to be engaged in washing.[55] Unlike *Badb*, the *badhb/babha* combs her hair. The *Badb* is also represented as a goddess with a spouse — the war god Nét — while the *badhb/babha* is a being of a lower order and, like the *bean sí*, without a male partner. In the old sources *Badb* is connected with heroic individuals (e.g., Cú Chulainn, Cormac Conloingeas etc.),[56] while the *badhb/babha*, like the *bean sí*, is ostensibly attached to families.

A special problem is connected with the form in which the respective beings appear. As mentioned, the *Badb* frequently takes the shape of a crow. If it can be said the *badhb/babha* is found in bird-shape at all, this shape is certainly uncommon and not that of a crow in particular. The translation of *badhbh* in Dinneen's dictionary (with reference to Peter O'Connell's Ms. *Irish-English Dictionary*) 'a female fairy or phantom said to be attached to certain families, appearing as a scald-crow or royston-crow' is not borne out by folk tradition. In this connection it may be mentioned that the meanings 'a royston-crow', 'a vulture or other ravenous bird', 'a carrion-crow', given to *badhbh* in Dinneen's and Ó Dónaill's dictionaries are apparently not found anywhere in living speech in Ireland, and it would appear they derive from the old literary texts.

One may ask, of course, whether some of the differences between the *Badb* of literature and the *badhb/babha* of later folk tradition are merely apparent. The early Irish texts in which the *Badb* appears are of a mythological and heroic nature, and it may be that motifs already found in folk tradition on a lower level have been changed and elevated to fit this aristocratic and martial context. On the other hand it is also possible these differences — or some of them — are as a result of a later euhemerisation and popularisation of the beliefs as they are found in the old literary sources. In any case one can hardly doubt that the *badhb/babha*, not only from the point of view of etymology but also from the point of view of the contents of the beliefs, is to some extent a descendant of the *Badb* in the older sources.[57] The *badhbh*-names see the being in terms of her female sex and her frightening and threatening appearance. This concept is complemented in the terms *bo (bó) chaointe* and *bo chaointeacháin* which make reference to her main activity, that of keening or crying for the dead.

V

From the analysis of the names for the supernatural death-messenger in Irish folk tradition a number of conclusions may be drawn.

All the names are in Irish, and there can be no doubt the beliefs, whatever their ultimate origin, were fully developed in Gaelic Ireland.

The distribution pattern of those names, as found in twentieth-century folklore sources, is on the whole confirmed and corroborated by existing source material from the seventeenth, eighteenth and nineteenth centuries. In a few instances where this is not the case one has reason to doubt the authenticity or accuracy of the early sources.

The term *bean sí* for the female death-messenger is certain to have been used before the middle of the seventeenth century and it seems possible to date it to around the eighth century or so.[58] It also appears that *bean sí* in the sense of 'a woman of the Otherworld' is a more apt description of the *bean sí* 'supernatural death-messenger' than 'fairy woman' in the ordinary sense of the expression.

The distribution pattern and the varying dialect forms of *badhbh* point to a considerable age for these terms in the area where they are now found. The term *babha* is also found in its present area and meaning in the eighteenth century,[59] while *badhb* is found in its present meaning in the same century.[60] Furthermore the similarities between the *Badb/Bodb* in early Irish sources and the *badhb/babha* of modern folk tradition again indicate that at least some forms of the belief were current in ancient Ireland — a matter which is dealt with in detail in Chapter 12.[61]

All the names state or imply the being in question is feminine. In other instances too, the etymologies — in so far as they have been understood — would seem not only to reflect the beliefs about the being and her appearance and behaviour but also to have strengthened the beliefs.

False etymologies seem to have played a negligible part in the development of the death-messenger belief, though it is possible the misunderstanding of *bean* 'woman' as *bán*, 'white' has contributed to the fairly frequent idea that the *bean sí* was dressed in that colour.

2

Folk Views of the Origin of the Supernatural Death-Messenger

I

Any attempt to categorise supernatural beings is fraught with difficulties and uncertainties. Something which by its very nature is mystical, dim and vague cannot readily be fitted into a logical system. Nevertheless, the majority of supernatural beings can be accurately, if not precisely, classified under one of a number of headings, which, though coined by scholars, have a basis in the folk philosophy. One large group — exemplified for instance by fairies and mermaids — has been termed 'nature-beings'; they are imagined to live in, and sometimes to rule over, parts of the physical landscape and they can be sub-divided into beings of the woods, of the mountains, of the sea and so on.[1] While the assumption of their existence explains a number of strange phenomena attached to these localities, little, as a rule, is told of the origin of these beings. Such explanations as are given mostly take the form of legends which may not necessarily have been strongly believed in. Other supernatural beings are in some way or another more strongly connected with man than nature. One category — which has only a marginal connection with the death-messenger complex — consists of beings, often in zoomorphic form, which may be termed free-souls or *alter egos* of living humans. Such *alter egos* may be induced by the human being to leave his body — as when a sorcerer appears as a werewolf[2] or a witch as a hare[3] — or it may leave unknown to him, for example in his sleep.[4] In either case the reasons for the appearance of the *alter ego* are mostly stated or implied to be the fulfilment of specific needs and wishes of its human owner. The basic function of some *alter egos*, though, like the Scottish fetches, which have their counterpart in Ireland, and the Norse *fylgja*, is simply to announce the arrival of their owners.[5]

41

Yet another category of supernatural beings may be termed 'spirits of the dead' — if the term 'spirit' is taken to include any manifestation from the most immaterial souls to the most substantial 'walking corpses'. In spite of all variation it is clear such supernatural beings are imagined to 'be' a specific person. The reasons for the reappearance of such ghosts are very varied but many of them are connected with obligations to them which have not been fulfilled, or obligations they themselves have not fulfilled in life.[6] There are, however, other supernatural beings which can only with difficulty, if at all, be fitted into any of the above categories. The good and evil forces of Christian mythology, angels and guardian spirits, devils and demons, offer special problems. A guardian angel, for instance, may to some extent be considered a person's *alter ego*, but may also be regarded as a dead relative sent back from paradise to protect his kin, or as an independent being. In a similar fashion an 'evil spirit' may be imagined as 'an independent devil' or as the ghost of an evil person.[7] Christian influence has also led to a certain amount of demonisation of nature spirits, so that they, too, are sometimes considered to be devils or akin to the devil. To assess the traditions about the origin of the death-messenger and her kin one must take into account all these possibilities.

II

In the archival material there are 71 examples of what may be regarded as popular explanations of origin; 12 of these stem from the Main Manuscripts, 31 from the Schools' Manuscripts, 2 from letters and 26 from answers to the Banshee Questionnaire (Appendix 1, pp. 247-54). Of the explanations found in the last-mentioned source category, 7 occur in answers to question 1 (dealing with names) and 19 are answers to a direct inquiry about origins, phrased as follows:

> What stories, if any, are there about the origin of the banshee (or other women appearing in connection with deaths)? Give any such story in full. Was it ever said that a particular human woman became a banshee after death? Will such a woman remain a banshee forever or is she condemned to such an existence for a limited period of time?

These questions might have been better formulated. The fact that only 'stories' were inquired about might have deterred some informants who had information on the matter exclusively in the form of short belief statements from answering the questions. The relative scarcity of information in other types of source material, as well as the fact that only one-fifth of the questionnaire correspondents gave positive information can hardly be without significance, however. It must also be taken into account that direct questions of this type may in certain cases entice correspondents to provide answers based on information given in the questionnaire itself, or on their own speculations, rather than on living folk tradition in their respective localities. To this should be added the fact that a great number of correspondents from all parts of Ireland explicitly state they are unaware of any traditions of this type. Typical examples of this are: 'Origin is not referred to' (Kerry 27), 'There was no precise explanation of who she was except that she was not of this world' (Wexford 22) and 'I never heard them try to explain how she came into existence' (Antrim 4). In view of all this it would appear fairly safe to say that, although the question of how the death-messenger came to be has occasionally been raised by the people, it has not been very prominent in their minds. Some of the answers provided may also be occasional borrowings from traditions belonging to other supernatural beings or even individual inventions.

III

One would imagine the very term *bean sí* should invite people to classify her as a kind of fairy. The sources show such an identification has only very rarely been attached to her in genuine folk tradition. Only in one of the Main Manuscripts (Cavan 1.16 (p. 431)), sixteen Schools' Manuscripts (Cavan 33, 42; Clare 34, 36; Galway 23, 39, 50; Kilkenny 11; Limerick 12, 13, 34, 35; Longford 17; Louth 12; Offaly 11; Tipperary 8) and six of the questionnaire replies (Cavan 26; Laois 20; Limerick 2; Louth 4; Mayo 29; Roscommon 1) is a link between the death-messenger and the fairies stated or implied. The relatively high figure in the Schools' Manuscripts should, no doubt, be seen as being influenced by two factors: fairies would be beings with a special appeal to children and a statement from a child that a banshee *is* a fairy may mean nothing more than that the word banshee *means* 'fairy woman'. Likewise the six question-naire replies which imply a connection between the death-messenger and the fairies do so in the context of question 1 which deals with the names of the being in tradition. Here, too, statements such as 'the banshee or fairy woman' or the like, probably mean nothing more than that the word banshee means 'fairy woman'. The common opinion about the death-messenger is rather the one that she was not a fairy, a view which is explicitly stated for instance in the following questionnaire reply: 'Only fairies carried off children and she was not considered a fairy . . .' (Mayo 29), or in one of the letters, where it was stated '[she was not], despite her name, of the fairy folk' (Tipperary 41).

In two records, Cavan 1.8 (p. 429) from the Main Maunscripts and the questionnaire reply Roscommon 21, the death-messenger is linked with the mystical race, the Tuatha Dé Danann. This could be taken to indicate she is of the fairy folk, since the more common learned idea is that the fairies originated from the Tuatha Dé Danann. This idea here, however, is an offshoot of such a literary learned tradition, which has only marginally influenced the fairy faith. It is obvious it is a very occasional intruder into the death-messenger complex.

A further idea which may indicate the death-messenger was one of the fairies is expressed in a questionnaire reply from Mayo:

> When I was about nine or ten years old I could hear the old women of the neighbourhood saying that the banshee was one of the fallen angels which God cast out of heaven (Mayo 30).

This origin legend is commonly told to explain how the fairies came into existence but it frequently adds that some of the angels who fell into the water became mermaids and sea-spirits while still others stayed in the air and inhabit that element ever since.[8] It is easy to understand how such a legend could occa-sionally be extended and used to explain any supernatural being whose origin was not clear. Here, again, one is dealing with an occasional intrusion into the death-messenger complex.

Another connection between the death-messenger and the fairy world is implied in the idea that the death-messenger is a human woman who has been abducted by the fairies but who is allowed to return to cry whenever any of her people die. Such a woman should not, of course, be regarded as a fairy; neither must one consider her to be dead. In fact, only through extension of the term may one refer to her as 'supernatural'. The associations with the fairy world would, nonetheless, have made her strange and eerie. This 'abduction explanation' is not very common but it is found in source material of different kinds and in many parts of Ireland. It is met with in the form of legends in the archival material, in Waterford 46 (M), 47 (Q), Kerry 16 (M), 17 (S), Limerick 18 (S), Louth 11 (S), as well as in the printed sources, Donegal 30 and Waterford 34. Belief statements to the same effect occur in Donegal 10 (S) and Waterford 44 (M). The belief that fairies abduct young women is extremely common in Ireland and has given rise to innumerable legends.[9] The particular motif that an abducted woman could perform the role of death-messenger or the like has no doubt been grafted on to such a legend. It is difficult to say whether this happened once or several times, the strangeness of the motif would favour the first assumption, the scattered and thin distribution the latter. Whatever the correct solution, it is clear the explanation never met with wide or more general acceptance. Yet it is of interest that the 'abduction theory' offers an explanation of the connection between the death-messenger and particular families.

Finally, an isolated attempt to attach the death-messenger to the fairy world is found in a literary account (Louth 10), where the death-messenger, following the Bellew family of Castletownbellew, Co. Louth, is said to be a semi-supernatural being – the daughter of Sir Patrick Bellew and the fairy queen Áine. This contrived story has obviously no real roots in folk tradition.

Something similar would also seem true of the only attempt to explain the death-messenger as a descendant of a mermaid, in a Schools' Manuscript (Kerry 42). According to this legend a man of the Walsh family of Cordal, Co. Kerry, married a mermaid who bore him a daughter but who left him after having retrieved her wand which the man had taken away and hidden. Sounds of revelry were later heard in a room in the house. When the daughter peeped through the keyhole she was blinded and soon afterwards died. Since then, however, she has acted as the death-messenger of the Walsh family.

This story is basically a variant of the migratory *Seal Woman*

Legend (ML 4080)[10] which has been embroidered with the motif about the forbidden chamber[11] and the final tag that the child became a death-messenger after death. It is very doubtful that the story was ever told orally in the form in which it appears in the manuscript. It is noteworthy that the legend is found attached to the Walsh family in another form in which nothing is said about the room or the death-messenger but in which the mermaid bestows the gift of knowledge on the family at her departure.[12]

The basis for considering the banshee a fairy or any other nature-being is very scanty indeed. While some tradition-bearers have very occasionally regarded her to be akin to the fairies, it is obvious her origin, in as far as it can be established, must be sought elsewhere.

IV

If one turns to the explanations based upon the concept that the death-messenger is a demonical being or an angel, the material becomes even scarcer.

Apart from the explanation that the death-messenger is a fallen angel, there is only one source which directly associates the death-messenger with Lucifer's kin:

> I heard it said that the banshee was the devil and he'd come and cry when a person was dying because he was going to be at a loss (Cavan 1.13, pp. 441-2).

What is implied here is that the devil cries or howls because the soul of the dying person is saved and will escape him. The idea of crying and howling devils is, of course, a commonplace which can be traced back to the bible, for example, 1 Peter v.8. The association of these howls with the death-messenger's wails is natural and one can only wonder why this appears to be the only example.

In another source the death-messenger is an evil spirit (Wexford 57 (M)) but this need not necessarily imply she is an 'independent devil'. She may equally well have been assumed to be the ghost of some person who had committed a crime.[13]

Direct links between the devil and the supernatural death-messenger are thus practically non-existent.

Equally isolated is the idea that the death-messenger is a guardian angel, found only the following questionnaire reply:

I was told some years ago that the banshee was in fact a dying person's guardian angel giving a warning of the death by wailing close to the house of the departing soul (Donegal 27).

The connections between the death-messenger and Christian mythology are thus minimal. Although certain Christian ideas and concepts enter into the death-messenger complex, it is in the main surprisingly a-Christian.

V

A survey of the material in which the death-messenger is considered to be the spirit or ghost of a human being is much more rewarding and some specific and interesting reasons as to why the being could not find rest are encountered. These reasons may be divided into two main categories — either the unrest is a result of rights denied to the woman who then becomes a death-messenger or it is the result of her own unjust or improper actions or negligence when she was alive. In the latter case, of course, her state as a ghost will often be considered in Christian terms as a punishment for sins.

In a few instances it is not quite clear which of the above-mentioned alternatives is intended, as in Cavan 1.19 (p. 442):

They'd say that the banshee was a member of the family that died and wasn't happy.

Clearly belonging to the former group are three records — Laois 17 (M), 19 (M) and Galway 64 (S) — stating that the death-messenger is a child who has died unbaptised. Obviously, it is because the rite which would include them in Christian society has been denied them that these beings cannot find rest.[14] The idea that these particular placeless dead should become death-messengers may seem far-fetched but the link — as in the case of the devil above — has probably been crying. One can expect a lonely and deprived child to cry and there are some stories of how pitiful weeping has been heard from the *cillíneach* — the unbaptised children's graveyard.[15] One can understand that these sounds could be confused with the death-messenger's wail. Again it is surprising that this has not happened more often and that the motif has not entered the collective tradition in any area.

Another related motif is that the death-messenger is the ghost of a woman who suffered violence from the progenitor of the family she follows. This motif is conspicuously absent from the archival sources and occurs only in a few literary ones.[16]

It is understandable that such a dramatic motif as the seduction and murder of a maiden should appeal to certain romantic and sensational writers but it must be regarded as uncertain whether it was ever found in this context in genuine folk tradition. If it was, it was never prominent.

Examples of the 'human woman turned into death-messenger after death because of misdeeds or negligence in this life' are somewhat more prominent. In addition to more general statements, such as:

> The old people would say that the banshee was a soul that was doing its purgatory on this earth . . . (Cavan 1.3 (pp. 431-2)),

some specific reasons for the punishment are adduced.

The sin of pride is referred to in particular in Wexford 6 (S), 42 (M) and Tipperary 26 (S). All these records contain the specific motif that the woman was too proud of her beautiful hair. This would hardly seem a grave sin, and perhaps because that was realised the two Wexford examples add she was too bad for heaven but too good for hell and hence was punished by being made to stay on earth — a motif found elsewhere, for example, in the traditions about the origin of Will O' the Wisp.[17] The tradition of a human woman turned into the death-messenger because of the pride she takes in her hair no doubt arose from the combination of the general idea that the death-messenger is a dead woman who is being punished for her sins in this life and the idea that she has long hair which she constantly combs. This latter motif is especially prevalent in east-Munster and in Leinster of which Tipperary and Wexford respectively form part. There can be no doubt there is a generic relation between the two Wexford legends, probably also between them and the Tipperary one. There is no indication the 'pride explanation' has ever been widespread or frequent.

Since some of the names used for the supernatural death-messenger imply she is a keening woman, and that keening and wailing are among her most prominent traits, it is hardly surprising the idea should have arisen that she was a human keening woman who must continue her activity after death, perhaps because of some neglect or defect in her fulfilment of her duties in this life. Twelve examples of such explanations are found in the archival material, one in the Main Manuscripts (Westmeath 3), five in the Schools' Manuscripts (Laois 4; Tipperary 17, 26; Waterford 50; Wexford 7) and six in the answers to the Banshee Questionnaire (Kildare 2; Laois 7; Tipperary 2, 42, 44 and Roscommon 2). The fact that five of the examples stem from Tipperary, where the term *bean chaointe* is found, is likely to be more than a coincidence.

It is not clear from the Westmeath record why a human keening woman might become a death-messenger. The meaning could possibly even be that all keeners were thought to become such beings:

> She (the banshee) was one of th'oul criers. She didn't say who she was, but it was always given down by people then that the banshee belonged to the criers . . . (Westmeath 3).

The informant adds the colourful detail that his own mother who had been a crier feared she would be turned into a death-messenger:

> And God help me, she says, if I'm turned into a banshee when I die (Westmeath 3).

The same lack of clarity as to why keening women had to continue their activity after death is found in Tipperary 17, 26, 42; Roscommon 2 and Wexford 7. From these it appears plainly, however, that the women in question were professional keeners who were rewarded for their services. Thus, it is stated in Roscommon 2:

> In ancient times every Irish family, that is when someone would die in the house, would ask the local keener or crier. They were old women who were recognised for their art and were glad to be asked. The more they cried the more drink they got . . . It is said when these women died their spirits came back to cry for the descendants of the families

they cried for when on earth. A lot of the Irish families
had their own keeners and it is said that they will come
back as a banshee to cry for the name until the end of time.
If the name dies out the banshee for that family will be
heard of no more.

It is perhaps not accidental that payment in alcoholic drink is
mentioned. This practice led to rowdy and undignified behaviour
which, apart from the insincere and excessive grief displayed,
turned the clergy against the institution of keening.[18] To be a
professional keener might thus *per se* make a woman deserving
of punishment after death. The insincerity of the keener is in
fact explicitly given as the explanation of her fate after death in
Laois 7 and Tipperary 2.

The idea that it was essential for a dead person's honour to
be professionally keened (whether sincerely or not) also under-
lies some explanations of the death-messenger's origin. If a
keening woman did not turn up for a funeral — sometimes even
because she herself had died and could not fulfil her promise —
the folk imagination would make her suffer for it in afterlife.
Explanations along these lines are found in Kildare 2; Laois 4;
Tipperary 44; Waterford 50.

Finally a reference from Kilkenny explains the death-messenger
as the spirit of a woman who was perpetually mourning while
alive because of a personal loss:

> It was told that she was the spirit of a woman who had lost
> her family tragically and forever mourned them (Kilkenny
> 15 (Q).

Possibly the underlying assumption is that, while it is right and
proper to mourn the dead, excessive and long-lasting sorrow is
wrong or even sinful.[19]

A curious reference in a Main Manuscript from Waterford to
Rachel being the death-messenger in olden times (Waterford 45)[20]
may also refer to the dangers of such excessive sorrow. The
woman referred to here is the biblical Rachel about whom it is
stated in Matthew 2:18:

> A voice was heard in Ramadh
> Sobbing and loudly lamenting:
> It was Rachel weeping for her children,
> Refusing to be comforted
> Because they were no more.

VI

The idea that the death-messenger is the ghost of a human woman is thus found in several distinct forms. Only one of these ideas, that she was a keener in this life, is of any prominence, but not even that is particularly common or widespread. An additional concept, found in the tradition that the woman is a ghost of a human woman as well as in the abduction and some other explanations, is that there is a particular connection between the death-messenger and the family in which she announced approaching death. In ten references – four from the Main Manuscripts (Cavan 1.14 (p. 431), 1.19 (p. 442), 1.21 (p. 440); Longford 1), two from the Schools' Manuscripts (Cavan 41; Westmeath 8); three from the Banshee Questionnaire (Kerry 27, 45; Mayo 29), and one letter (Laois 1) – apart from those already quoted, such a relationship between the death-messenger, who was thought to have been a human woman originally, and the families she visits, is stated or implied.[21]

Some typical examples are:

One gets the impression that she was one of your own kin and was coming back to forewarn you (Kerry 45).

A lot of people would tell you that she was someone belonging to you that died and was lamenting about some member of your family that was going to die . . . (Cavan 1.21 (p. 440)).

The *bean chaointe* was, I think, regarded as one of the members of a particular family who came to cry as a warning of a death in the particular family (Mayo 29).

They say that the banshee is some friend, a relation that comes to cry their own before they die (Westmeath 8).

The idea that the death-messenger is a dead member of the family in question is found also in some literary sources. When Lady Gregory[22] asked Old Simon, 'what is the banshee?', he said, 'It is of the nature of the Hyneses'. And from Seaghan, Co. Armagh we hear:

Ay, it cried for many on oul family here an' some say it's one that has gone before (Armagh 1).[23]

An idea closely related to this — and sometimes indistinguishable from it — is that the female supernatural death-messenger is 'the spirit of the family', expressed in the following statements:

> The banshee is the spirit of the family that she now comes to warn of approaching death (Cavan 1.14 (p. 431)).

> ... the *bóhaíonta*, a woman ... the old people said she was the spirit of ancient Irish families of that name (Kilkenny 10).

In such connections between the banshee and her kin and a family or certain families — however they are to be understood in detail — one of the most central ideas in the traditions about the being emerges.

VII

The folk-views of the origin of the death-messenger and her relation to other supernatural beings, may be summed up as follows. There is very little foundation for the idea that the death-messenger is one of the fairies and she is very rarely imagined to be related to other nature-beings. Her association with beings of the Christian mythology — devils and angels — is equally negligible. The few examples of such associations as are found in the material investigated are either from sources which must for various reasons be considered spurious or suspect or are inventions of individual informants which have never taken firm roots in the collective tradition in any area. Some are borrowings from other tradition complexes attached to the death-messenger on the grounds of some superficial similarity. The idea that the death-messenger is the ghost of a human woman — though not very common — is still current in many forms in many parts of Ireland. Finally the idea of some sort of connection between the death-messenger and the families she visits has begun to emerge.

3

The Death-Messenger's Connection
with Families

I

The idea that the death-messenger is in some way or another
linked to families – or rather to certain families – is frequently
expressed in the traditional sources. An attachment of this
kind is often mentioned or implied in memorates and belief
statements. It is only rarely met with in legends.[1] In most cases
the connection is expressed by means of a verb or verbal phrase.
The various terms used are listed in Appendix 2.

The term 'follow' is incomparably the most common in
English language sources. Statements of the type 'Here the *bean
chaointe* was supposed to follow the O'Regans and MacDonnells'
(Mayo 29), 'The banshee followed certain families, (Limerick
15), and 'The banshee is supposed to follow a family called Peter
Reillys of Knocknahattina' (Cavan 13) occur no less than 130
times in the archival material. The preponderance of the term
may to some extent be due to its inclusion in the Banshee
Questionnaire – 58 of the examples occur in questionnaire
answers. On the other hand, the fact that well over half of the
examples are found in manuscripts of earlier decades in material
spontaneously communicated and the occurrence of the term in
all counties would seem sufficient to allow one to say 'follow'
belongs to the collective tradition wherever English is spoken in
Ireland. The wide distribution of the term also makes it likely
it is of considerable age. One can hardly doubt it is centuries
older than its earliest occurrence in a printed source which is as
late as 1888.[2]

Since all the names for the supernatural death-messenger are
in the Irish language, and since one may take it as certain the
belief in all its essentials was developed before English started
to be widely spoken in Ireland, one might consider the possibility
that 'follow' may be a translation of an Irish expression. The
term *leanúint*, 'following' is in fact attested from Donegal, Kerry

53

and Waterford (six examples in all). Thus an informant by the name of Ó Curnáin states:

> Do leanadh sí mórán de na daoine atá ina gcónaí anseo timpeall. Lean sí ár dtreibh féin [She used to follow many of the people who live around here. She followed our own family] (Kerry 29).

The idea of 'coming after' or 'following' is also present in the phrase *bheith i ndiaidh* (or the like) met with three times in Waterford and once in Kerry. Once, in a Waterford record, one also meets with *gabháil le*, 'going with', 'accompanying', 'following': *Deirtear go mbíonn an bhadhb ag gabháil le clanna áirithe* ('It is said that the *badhb* goes with certain families') (Waterford 18).

Another verb fairly often used in expressions indicating the link between the death-messenger and particular families is 'cry'; for example, 'It is related by old men that the banshee cries for certain families when a member is about to die' (Cavan 8), 'She cries our people' (Roscommon 25), 'She cried the Mulligans of Moyleroe, Delvin' (Westmeath 6). There are 30 records in which 'cry' is used in contexts of this kind. In 10 the verb is used transitively as in the examples from Cavan, Roscommon and Westmeath.[3] The fact that 'wail' (Westmeath 21) and 'lament' (Meath 24) is also used is one of the indications that 'cry' refers to 'weeping', in particular to a death-lament, rather than to 'shouting'. This is also indicated by the Irish *caoineadh* used in Mayo 11: *Tá treibh daoine ann a gcaoineann sí dófa roimh a mbás* ('There are families for which she laments before their deaths'). In view of the strangeness of the construction 'to cry somebody' one might perhaps again suspect an Irish substratum. It might possibly be a rendering of *caoineadh* (cf., for example, *na mairbh a chaoineadh* – to keen or lament the dead).

Other expressions used to indicate the being's connections with families are so rarely found in the source material that it is difficult to say whether they were ever widely used. The phrase 'run in' is met with in Cavan 27 and the comparable Irish expression *'rith le'* in Mayo 7. These terms would seem to indicate that the death-messenger follows the families from generation to generation. Other English terms met with in the archival sources once, or at most thrice, are 'come to', 'go for', 'belong to' and 'be attached to'. From nineteenth- and early twentieth-century literary sources may be added, for example, 'affected to', 'wait upon', 'attend' and 'haunt' (Appendix 2.3, p. 258). It is probably more accurate to ascribe these to individual usage of the respective authors than to suppose they are survivals of traditional expressions.

It appears, consequently, that the death-messenger is in some way or another attached to families and this is frequently expressed by saying she 'follows' them. For a variety of reasons, such as the subtle shades of difference between various meanings of 'follow' (and of corresponding Irish terms) and the extreme paucity of older source material, it may not be possible to establish with certainty how the 'following' was originally imagined. There is nothing in the material to support the view that the death-messenger 'followed' anybody in the sense 'to come after or behind'. Though the being may sometimes have been feared there is not much in favour of the meaning 'pursue' either. The temporal sense — as in 'follow from one generation to another' — is a more likely interpretation, and this may have been how some informants understood the term, in as far as they have paid attention to it. One may ask whether more than that may have been involved originally. It is tempting to see a connection between the banshee and her kin and a being met with in Old Norse tradition, the *fylgja*, whose very name according to many scholars means 'a follower'. One form of the *fylgja* is a female spirit who is connected with families and who sometimes appears at deaths but who also has a wider function as a guardian spirit and carrier of the luck of the family, in particular of its head.[4] Such a family-connected guardian spirit could be said to 'follow' a family in the sense of 'accompanying' and 'attending' to it. Is it not then possible that the Irish death-messenger belief is a result of a process of narrowing and specialisation? In other words, was the spirit involved at an older stage a guardian spirit very much on a par with the Old Norse female *fylgja*? If that is so, 'follow' and its Irish equivalents might be regarded as vestiges of this older stage of the belief.

II

If the death-messenger was believed to restrict her attention to certain families, which families are these and what, if anything, have they in common?

A list containing surnames associated with the death-messenger is also given in Appendix 2. It is not quite clear what meaning a statement of the type, 'The banshee follows the O'Sullivans', is intended to convey. Obviously, the individual informants reported what was said and believed in their respective areas; their statements are primarily based on manifestations reported regularly to occur on occasions of deaths in families of certain names in their neighbourhood. Nevertheless, the idea that all families sharing these surnames, wherever they reside, are visited is likely to have been held by most informants.[5] Since rules governing folk beliefs are not without exceptions, it is no surprise to find some informants thought only certain families among those who share particular surnames are followed. The idea that the death-messenger may restrict her attentions even within families of the same surname in one and the same parish is illustrated by the following statement from the octogenarian Hugh Curtis:

> She [the banshee] follows up the family of Barney Curtis . . .
> but strange to say she never touches ours (Cavan 1.22).

For such reasons families with the same surname but from different areas are entered separately in the list in the Appendix and the townland and parish where they reside are given. The list contains no less than 180 different names (Appendix 2.4 (a), pp. 261-80). A considerable number of families with other surnames have undoubtedly been connected with the death-messenger, though there are no records of this in the source material. Nevertheless, one can feel assured that the list is representative of the traditional beliefs at the time of collecting.

The statements most commonly met with about families in general are of the following type:

> There is a general belief that she follows families with O or Mac in their names (Antrim 4).

> Families who have O or Mac (O'Malley, MacBride) have banshees (Mayo 28).

> She follows families, anyone with Mac or O in their names (Laois 17).

She is said to follow some families such as O'Keeffes, O'Briens, also those with Mac before their names such as MacSweeney (Cork 11).

This belief (which is met with 84 times in the material) belongs to the collective tradition having been recorded from twenty-seven counties.[6] The reason it has gained popularity in this particular form is no doubt the succinct way in which it has been embedded in a saying: 'the O and the Mac' or 'the Mac and the O'. One is reminded of the Latin distich:

Per Mac atque O, tu veros cognoscis Hibernos:
His duobus demptis, nullus Hibernus adest,

or as it goes in English:

By Mac and O, you'll always know
True Irishmen, they say;
But if they lack
Both O and Mac
No Irishmen are they.[7]

Those versed in genealogy and onomastics may object that this statement is not completely true, since some families who have Mac or O in their names, and whose names are completely Irish, are not of Irish descent. The Ó Dubhghaill, for instance, are of Norse extraction.[8] In other instances the Mac or O might have been added to non-Irish, particularly Anglo-Norman surnames, for example, Mac Óda.[9] Such niceties would not bother the tradition-bearers. In many cases they may not even have been aware of them. Saying that the death-messenger follows 'the O and the Mac' is a concrete way of expressing the idea that she is attached to families regarded as truly Irish. Once a saying of this type has developed it is only natural some informants should take it literally, while others would realise the wider idea it was supposed to express. It is not surprising to find statements like the following:

The banshee is supposed to cry after the Macs and the Os, but she is also supposed to cry after old Irish families such as Dillons, Brownes, Walshes, Dawsons and other families (Westmeath 1).

The list of families in Appendix 2 which the death messenger is purported to follow shows the preponderance of the Mac and O names. The impact of this would have been even more over-whelming if it had not been for the fact that the Mac and O elements have sometimes been dropped in fairly recent times by people who were under pressure to adopt English ways or who wished to do so.[10] Although a family was known as Sullivan only, they themselves and everybody else knew they were originally O'Sullivan or *Ó Súilleabháin*. The dropping of the 'Mac' or 'O' did not, as an informant puts it, 'appear to change the attitude of the banshee' (Roscommon 1). There is an indication here that the attachment to the Mac and O families pre-dates the time when these prefixes began to be dropped. A breakdown of family names (p. 281) given in Appendix 2.4 (b) reveals that no less than 81 per cent of the surnames indicate the 'genuine Irishness' of the bearers and nearly all the remain-ing names belong to families who had become thoroughly hibernicised by virtue of having lived in Ireland before, or at least since, the Middle Ages — for example, families of Norse and Anglo-Norman extraction. Family names of English origin, introduced from the seventeenth century onwards, especially Cromwellian and Williamite names, are almost totally absent from the list.[11]

Only, then, families considered Irish and having old roots in the country were reputed to be followed. Social standing by virtue of such old roots is stressed even by those informants who maintain not all Mac and O families are followed. Thus, a Laois informant by the name of (O) Moore states:

> The banshee followed certain old families, not all old families — my family is a very old family. We have been here in the townland of Morette since 1690 . . . and to my knowledge the banshee was never heard at a death in the family (Laois 20).

The important point here is not so much that the banshee was not thought to follow the Moores in this area as that it causes surprise she does not.

A family that has lived in the same area for many centuries would naturally enough often be regarded as having a special, superior social standing there. It appears that the death-messenger's manifestation was sometimes thought to indicate the person about to die had a certain social standing. Thus according to a legend from Waterford the *badhb*, who would ordinarily cry when any of the Finnucanes died since the Finnucanes 'were old stock', only appeared saying a verse expressing her refusal to cry, when a certain twenty-year-old man of that name died. The reason was that his mother had not been married when he was born, though he had been given the name of Finnucane.[12] More important than this apparently isolated example of the death-messenger's refusal to cry for anybody who was not of legitimate birth is the attitude reflected in the poem by Piaras Feiritéir quoted earlier. The poet says 'the hoarding merchants' of Dingle need not fear the banshee has cried for them; the cry was for one of the noble Fitzgeralds, (Mac Gearailt), a thoroughly hibernicised family who even claimed to be descended from the territorial goddess Áine.[13]

In a similar vein, a story taken down in Kilmalkedar, Co. Kerry in 1936-7 tells that the merchants in John Street in Dingle could be assured the cry was not intended for them; it was for a member of the important Hussey family:

Bhí dream dos na Husaig sa Daingean fadó agus níl aon uair a cailltí duine acu ná go gcloistí an bhean sí ag gol agus ag gabháilt tríd an nDaingean. Bhí duine acu ag fáilt bháis an babhta so, agus lár na hoíche do brathadh an bhean sí ag gol. Bhí Sráid Eoin san am san lán do thithe beaga, is nuair a chualadar í do bhuail an t-eagla iad. Bhíodar scannraithe. Níl aon tigh acu ná go rabhadar ag caint is ag cur uatha – go raibh duine éigint acu chun bás a d'fháilt; agus bhí a fhios ag an mbean sí conas a bhí acu. Do stad an gol sí agus do labhair sí leo:

Éistig, éistig, a cheannaithe an chnósaig!
Ní baol díbhse, ach is eaglach dóibh siúd.
Níor chaoin bean sí riabh 'úr sórtsa.

Thosnaigh an gol sí aríst agus ar maidin lá arna mhárach do chualadar go raibh duine uasal dos na Husaig caillte.

[There was a tribe of the Husseys in Dingle long ago and every time one of them died the banshee was heard crying and going through Dingle. On this occasion one of them was dying and in the middle of the night the banshee was heard crying. At that time John Street was full of small houses, and when they heard her, they became frightened. In every house there was talking and discoursing – that some one of them was going to die; and the banshee knew what they were at. The supernatural crying stopped and she spoke to them:

> Listen, listen, you hoarding traders,
> You are not in danger, but they have need to fear,
> A banshee never keened your kind.

The supernatural crying began again and on the following morning they heard that a gentleman of the Husseys was dead.][14]

The lines in verse in the story are part of Piaras Feiritéir's poem, though here the banshee herself is purported to speak them.

Piaras Feiritéir's poem, written on the occasion of a death that took place c. 1642, offers the oldest evidence of the death-messenger's connection with a particular family and of the hereditary nature of her attentions. It is impossible to say how much older the belief may be. The idea that the being follows the Mac and O families would seem to presuppose the use of these prefixes in family names (as opposed to in their original meaning 'son' and 'grandson'). This development of surnames had begun before the tenth century.[15] The idea that the death-messenger does not deign to cry for foreigners and intruders but confines her cry to the truly Irish could hardly have originated – or at least not have become very strong – before Gaelic society was seriously threatened. It is not unlikely the sentiments expressed in Piaras Feiritéir's poem where the prosperous but ignoble Saxons are contrasted with the noble 'Irish' Fitzgerald family are innovations in the death-messenger tradition, introduced in the seventeenth century when symbols to mark the superiority of the Gaels and the inferiority of foreign intruders were needed. Under the influence of the pressures on Gaelic Ireland in the seventeenth and following centuries the idea that the death-messenger honoured all the Mac and O families might have developed. This does not mean the belief that the death-messenger appeared on occasions of deaths in certain important and noble families might not have existed for centuries before then.

III

If it could be shown that the death-messenger belief known from the nineteenth- and twentieth-century sources contains traces of the idea that the being restricts her attention to the more important members of families, or perhaps exclusively to the heads of them, the hypothesis that the concepts of nobility and prominence played a greater part in an older stratum of the tradition would become more likely. A question concerning these aspects was asked in the Banshee Questionnaire:

> Is it said that she would appear at the death of all members of such families or only at the death of the head of the family? Would she be believed to appear at the death of men, women and children alike? Are there any differences in this regard?

The return to this question was disappointing. Only 36 correspondents (less than one-third) gave answers to the question and only two replies dealt with all its aspects.

Although the majority of the questionnaire replies (22)[16] say the being may appear at the death of any member of the families followed (and often state this includes children), four of them (Cork 38; Kerry 4, 45; Kildare 8) categorically deny she was heard at the deaths of children. If we turn from the statements in the questionnaire replies to the rest of the archival material we find only two records, Leitrim 1 from the Schools' Manuscripts and Cork 29 from the Main Manuscripts, that associated the death-messenger with the deaths of children. This indicates the death-messenger was only very rarely thought to follow children. These – especially infants – were not regarded as full members of the family. The infant mortality rate of former times might have meant that too much notice would not normally be paid to the death of a young child.[17]

The position of women is more ambivalent. Here again many questionnaire correspondents state the death-messenger follows women as well as men. A Kerry correspondent, however, says he has no recollection of the banshee having been heard at the death of a woman. In the corpus of memorates relating to death-messenger manifestations the dying person is a man in 172 instances and a woman in 84, i.e., men figure twice as often as women. So great a difference can hardly be coincidental. One may ask, perhaps, whether it might not reflect the method of collecting rather than the actual emphasis of folk tradition. The fact that the overwhelming majority of Irish folklore collectors have been men and that a greater portion of the material has been collected from men than from women could hardly be of much significance, however. Why should men not equally often tell about manifestations at the deaths of their female relatives as of their male relatives and neighbours if the phenomena were equally distributed between the sexes? It would seem the strong emphasis on the death-messenger's attention to men reflects the outlook that a family is first and foremost represented in a community by its male members. In a few instances, informants more directly state that only the male line of a family is followed; thus in Kildare 1 it is stated that 'the banshee follows families of the name Dunn, men only', and a woman in Laois whose maiden name was also Dunn said the banshee followed only male members of her family (Laois 17). The patrilineal preference of the banshee is also indicated by statements to the effect that the death-messenger which cries for a married woman is the one following her own family rather than her husband's (Mayo 9).

The idea that the death-messenger concentrates her attentions on the most important family members, in particular on the oldest male member or head of a family, is also found in the material. Fifteen questionnaire replies from all the provinces give statements to that effect. For example:

Her (the banshee's) appearance applied mostly to the head of the house . . . (Galway 56).

. . . only for heads of families (Kilkenny 15).

. . . head of family or senior male member (Kerry 45).

Consequently, it appears that there is a male as well as an aristocratic orientation in the death-messenger traditions, likely to have been stronger in earlier times.

IV

The idea that the supernatural death-messenger is linked to families forms part of the collective tradition in Ireland. Equally firmly established and widely spread is the opinion that she follows the Mac and O families, limiting her attention to families of old Irish stock. Less prominent, but nevertheless clearly discernible, is the belief that only certain Irish families are visited by her. Why the being is supposed to attach herself to one family rather than another is seldom directly stated. The families given special mention, however, would in most instances seem to have been regarded as old and important in their respective areas.[18] In other words, the death-messenger seems to bestow a certain amount of status on the family for which she cries. Status factors reflecting the outlook of the tradition-bearers are also distinguishable in the frequency with which the death-messenger appears at the deaths of different categories of members of the families she follows. Although belief statements about this aspect are few and contradictory, the memorates dealing with manifestations of the being show she only very occasionally appears at the deaths of children and that males are visited twice as often as females. Furthermore, there are some clear statements to the effect that the being directs her attention particularly towards prominent male members in the families she follows or even mainly or exclusively towards the oldest male member, who would have been regarded as the head of the family.

While social and cultural pressures may have produced a death-messenger relatively democratic in her activities, behind – and to a certain extend beside – this being an older 'aristocratic' being is vaguely discernible, a being attached primarily to important and illustrious families and in particular to their most prominent members – their chieftains or heads. If this is so, there would appear to be certain points of similarity between this older stratum of the Irish belief and the German and Swedish traditions for example about *'weisse Frauen'*, *'vita fruar'* (or the like) appearing on occasions of death in aristocratic families.[19] The Old Norse *fylgja* would also appear to have been an aristocratic being. She was attached to prominent families, especially their heads, and she is not known to have ever followed a woman. It would not seem impossible that the Irish death-messenger as met in later folk tradition has developed out of a more general family or guardian spirit of the *fylgja* type into a being more exclusively foreboding death. However way it developed, the belief in the banshee and her kin relates not only to the dying and the dead, but also to families who have been bereft, and their interests and standing in their community.

4

Aural Manifestations

I

Our examination of the names attributed to the supernatural death-messenger shows a being clearly thought to be feminine and the terms *bean chaointe, bo (bó) chaointe* and *bo chaointeacháin* describe her role behaviour – her keening. Since the death-messenger is so often imagined to *be* a keening woman, it is not surprising to encounter such origin explanations as that she *used to be* a keening woman before she died and turned into a supernatural being. Though the names, as well as the origin explanations, are secondary to the beliefs about the death-messenger's appearance and behaviour, they are likely to have influenced and strengthened them. Here and in the following chapters we look at the death-messenger's ways of appearing or making her presence known and her behaviour on these occasions.

II

The choice of 'supernatural death-messenger' as a generic term for *bean sí*/banshee, *badhb*, etc. must not be taken to mean that the being is always connected with death, only that this is her most prominent trait. Her connection with death is expressly stated in 545 (59 per cent) of the examined records from all over Ireland and implied in one way or another in many more of them (Appendix 3.4.1, p. 303). From these records it is clear that the collective belief in the whole of Ireland is that the banshee (*badhb* etc.) is noticed mainly when somebody is about to die or has just died. The main exceptions to this occur in certain legends and these will be given special attention later.

The manifestations in connection with deaths are either exclusively aural (the being is heard only) or they may be visual as well as aural (the being is seen as well as heard on the same occasion). There are, interestingly enough, no examples of the being only having been seen in connection with death. In a number of legends, however, especially those dealing with the offended banshee or *badhb*, the being manifests herself through being seen only.

Manifestations at deaths take exclusively aural form in 420 (77 per cent) of the 545 records mentioned. These records consist of belief statements (213), memorates (196) and legends (11) (Appendix 3.3.1 (a), pp. 283-5). The idea that the death-messenger is both seen and heard on the occasion of the same death is far less frequently encountered. The 125 records (23 per cent) of this stem from 27 counties. These records consist of belief statements (37), memorates (82) and legends (6) (Appendix 3.3.1 (b.), pp. 286-7). Visual manifestation on occasions other than death are mentioned in only 133 records (15 per cent of the total material) out of which only a few are belief statements (9) or memorates (21); the others may be described as migratory legends or local legends (Appendix 3.3.1 (c), pp. 288-9).

III

Two geographical areas can be distinguished within the tradition. In the first, comprising Cork and Kerry, the death-messenger is heard only. The being is imagined to be female, since it is referred to as 'she' and since the voice is never said to be male, but no descriptions of female shape or dress occur in genuine material from this area. The following are typical memorates from the area:

> Do chuala-sa an bhean sí trí huaire. Do bhíos ag teacht abhaile, oíche, ó thigh m'uncailí agus do bhí deirfiúr dom in éineacht liom. Do chuala ag olagón í (an bhean sí)[1] agus má sea, níor éirigh sé leis an ndeirfiúr. Do thug sí *brain fever* as agus do cailleadh í . . . . [I heard the *bean sí* three times. I was coming home one night from my uncles' house and my sister was with me. I heard her lamenting (the *bean sí*), and faith, the sister did no good. She got brain fever from it and she died . . . . (Kerry 32)].

I heard the *bean sí* three times and every time someone died a bit after. The first time, 'twas about the month of August. We were binding over at home. Yerra, 'tis thirty years ago now. We were coming home after binding in the 'forty field'. There was Jim and Tom and a couple of more of us there and as plain as you are listening to me now we heard the cry down in Riordan's glen. We thought 'twas a dog first, but faith when we heard it the second time we knew 'twas no dog. 'Twas a long lonesome cry. I never heard anything so lonesome before. We only heard it twice but 'twas enough. We knew then that someone was for the road. That very night again we heard the latch of the room rattling. One of us got up. I don't know which of us 'twas now, an' there was no one there. 'Twas about twelve o'clock at the time too. Then the news came from America — 'twas Lizzie Carey was after dying and they found out 'twas the same time the same evening an' all that we heard the cry (Cork 8).

Only two Cork accounts (Cork 26, 30) state that the death-messenger was seen. Both are literary compositions, however, and no importance can be attached to them. They are clearly out of keeping with genuine folk tradition in the county. Of little or no consequence also is an isolated questionnaire reply from Ballybunion (Kerry 28) which states:

The banshee was usually seen sitting on a rock with her face to the sea combing her long hair down her back.

It would appear that the informant is confusing the banshee and the mermaid. The geographical area in which the supernatural death-messenger manifests herself through sounds only is thus unusually clear-cut.

In the second area, consisting of the whole of Ireland with the exception of Cork and Kerry, the death-messenger can either be heard only or be both heard and seen on one and the same occasion. Peadar Barry of Corneys, Burren, Co. Down, for instance, stated to Michael J. Murphy, full-time collector, that 'the banshee was just the sound of a wailing voice' and also that 'she was a small woman dressed all in white and lamenting' (Down 9).

The following two memorates are also typical of the form the belief takes in this second area:

I heard the banshee when my grandmother died. She was heard on Rathlin too by the people, but I never heard her there. I'd be telling a lie if I did. We were saying the rosary when this cry started and when she stopped and ceased we could hear the long sigh. They said she was a wee woman all in white though I never seen her. We went up to my grandmother's and they were on their knees at the rosary waiting for her to die. That's quite true (Antrim 2).

But I remember clearly my late grandfather (whose name was James Cloney and who died on 23 July 1940, aged 84 years) tell us of seeing the banshee on a few occasions. He saw her once sitting on the window-sill of Richard Barry's house in Nemestown . . . She was combing her hair and every now and again she would utter a scream and end in a kind of *caoine*. The time was around twelve o'clock and I remember the date – it was 16 February 1910 for he said the same Richard Barry died two days after he had seen her (Wexford 19(a)).

All of the 133 records in which the being is only seen on occasions other than deaths stem from the second area. As already indicated, these records consist of legends based on the belief that it is wrong to interfere with or insult the being, and they will be treated in detail in later chapters.

IV

Aural manifestations of the death-messenger are far more common then than the visual ones and an aural manifestation is a *sine qua non* when the being appears in a death situation. The sound of the death-messenger is consequently a basic ingredient in the tradition and deserves special attention.

The sound is described by a variety of terms in English and Irish. The following terms occur in the records investigated:

cry, gol, wail, lament, olagón, ochón, lóg, lógóireacht caoineadh, keen, moan, roar, scream, shriek, screech, scréach, béic, call, glaoch, liú.

Detailed information about the distribution and frequency of these terms is given in Appendix 3.2.1 (a), pp. 290–5, but certain points may be mentioned here. Some of the terms are found all over Ireland, others are confined to a limited area, and still others have been recorded once only and may possibly have no foundation in collective tradition.

By far the most common term is *cry*. There are 266 examples in the records from all over Ireland. The term seems to have been especially common in Leinster (110 examples). The synonymous Irish term *gol* 'crying', 'weeping', has been recorded 12 times. It is found in Waterford and Cork and is most common in Kerry.

The next most common term is *wail* (55 records from 24 counties).[2] This term is more prominent in Munster and Leinster than in Connaught and Ulster.

The term *lament* has been recorded 14 times in all, from 11 counties. There are no examples of it from Connaught. In Munster (Cork 36; Kerry 13, 30, 32) the synonymous Irish term *olagón* is found. This also occurs in a Donegal record (Donegal 21), but it is possible that the informant has been influenced by the Irish version of the Banshee Questionnaire which he has used (Appendix 1, p. 252, question 7). In Waterford the term *ochón* has been recorded once. Like *olagón* this is associated with the performance of keening women at wakes and funerals.

Still another Irish term with the meaning 'cry', 'wail' or 'lament', namely *lóg*, is found in Waterford (4 records), and the form *lógóireacht* 'crying', 'wailing', has been recorded in Galway (Galway 45).

The term *caoineadh* has been recorded 32 times in all from all of the four provinces. It does seem to be most popular in Munster (Cork, Kerry, Tipperary and Waterford).[3] There are also 18 additional examples of the anglicised form *keen*.

There are 6 records of *moan*; Leinster (3), Munster (1) and Ulster (2). In Leinster and Munster (Tipperary, Waterford) *roar* is found (8 examples). The seven recorded examples of the term *scream* stem from the Leinster counties of Kilkenny, Laois and Wexford and from Waterford in Munster. The sound of the death-messenger is referred to as *shriek* in four records (from Meath in Leinster and from Limerick and Tipperary in Munster) and as *screech* in Kildare (1 record). The Irish term *scréach*, 'screech', 'scream', has also been recorded once (in Waterford). Other Irish terms from Waterford with the meaning 'shout', 'yell', 'loud cry' are *béic* (3 records, all from the same informant) and *liú* (3 records).

Finally, the term *call* is recorded three times (from Carlow, Kerry and Waterford); the synonymous Irish term *glaoch* is also found in Waterford.

It is thus apparent that there is a great variety of terms used to describe the sound by which the death-messenger makes her presence known. No single county has less than two terms. The greatest variety is found in what we have called the *badhbh*-area, that is to say the south-eastern counties. Thus there are 6 different terms in Carlow, 7 in Wexford, 8 in Tipperary, and no less than 13 in Waterford (Appendix 3.2.1 (b), pp. 295-6).

From the point of view of their meaning the terms fall into two main groups, though the dividing lines cannot be drawn with absolute precision. Sorrow and grief are the key elements in many of the terms found over the greater part of Ireland. The terms *wail, lament, olagón, lóg, caoineadh, keen* are clear-cut examples of such terms. That the term *cry* in the majority of the instances has the meaning 'weeping' rather than 'shouting' is evident from the contexts and the frequency with which it corresponds to *gol* in areas where Irish survives. Many of these terms express sorrow in general and more particularly refer to the mourning or the mourning sounds made by keening women at wakes and funerals, and there is little doubt, as already indicated, that the banshee and her ilk should, to some extent, be considered the supernatural counterparts of such professional mourners. The terms in this first group also indicate that the supernatural being is sympathetic towards the person on the occasion of whose death she makes her presence known and that she shares the grief of relatives and friends. Her behaviour, in other words, is non-violent and human.

The second group of terms expresses a more fierce and frightening side to the death-messenger. In this group is included terms such as *roar, scream, shriek, screech, scréach, béic* and *liú*, connoting loud, sharp, shrill or piercing qualities. Such sounds would not have been lacking in the performances of professional keeners. They are indeed referred to by observers of real keening performances – especially by those opposed to the custom.[4] Nevertheless, the terms are also suggestive of the non-human sphere. They can be used to denote the sound of wild animals or dangerous and hostile supernatural beings. It is noteworthy that the terms are mainly found in the *badhbh*-area. The image of an aggressive and threatening being would seem to be stronger there than elsewhere in Ireland.

V

The *caoineadh* performed by female mourners often included improvised verses in which the deceased was praised and the sorrow of the survivors expressed. Can this trait, too, be found in the folk traditions about the supernatural death-messenger? To assess this, the following question (Appendix 1, p. 248, question 7) was included in the Banshee Questionnaire:

> Did she use words in her lament? Can versions of these or the notes of her lament be obtained locally?

The answers to this question indicate that the parallelism between the *real* keening and the keening of the supernatural death-messenger does not go this far. It is significant that 99 correspondents refrained from answering this particular question. Most of the other answers state categorically that no words were used. This is a typical example:

> It was a cry or a lament . . . It was just a cry. No words were used (Tipperary 18).

A few answers mention wailing exclamatory phrases such as *och, ochón* (Cavan 1.4 (p. 469), 1.21 (p. 469), 1.32 (p. 470); Down 6; Longford 4; Waterford 53) and *wirra, wirra*[5] (Cavan 44, Westmeath 8).

Meaningful words are referred to in one answer only:

> Yes, the hearer was supposed to imagine some form of words in the cry . . . They were usually the Christian name of the person who was called away (Galway 56 (Q)).

The particular motif that the death-messenger calls out the name of the person about to die is not found explicitly stated in other archival sources. The possibility that the idea is related to the term *call* which is met with in Carlow, Kerry and Waterford cannot be excluded.[6] In one literary source from Cork,[7] the same motif is found as in the Galway reply. It is possible that the questionnaire reply is influenced by a literary source. It certainly seems that the idea that the death-messenger calls out the name of the dying person lacks deeper roots in genuine folk belief and does not form part of the collective tradition in any area. Yet the idea that hearing one's name inexplicably called out is a death omen is not infrequently met with[8] – though not in combination with the banshee, *badhb* etc.

The melody of the death-messenger's lament – no more than her words – cannot be provided from genuinely traditional sources. In a number of printed sources from the last century – Hall, Yeats, McAnally and *The Dublin Penny Journal*[9] – are found musical notations of what is purported to be the death-messenger's wail (Appendix 3.2.2, pp. 296-8). All of these appear to be ordinary airs casually ascribed to the death-messenger perhaps by informants keen to please a curious and unsuspecting inquirer or indeed by the authors themselves for some unknown reason.

VI

Traditional records give some idea of the character of the sound emitted by the death-messenger through the terms they employ to define it and also through many direct and detailed descriptions of its particular qualities. Many of these motifs are what scholars term *criterion motifs*: their function is to prove that the experience encountered could not possibly have a natural explanation.

The records often describe a sound having special connotations of sorrow and bereavement. A detailed list of such descriptions is given in Appendix 3.2.3, p. 299, but here are some typical examples. The death-messenger's cry was 'lonesome' (Cork 8) and 'the lonesomest cry ever you heard' (Cavan 23). In some sixty records the sound is described in such general terms, the terms 'mournful', 'lonesome', and 'sad' being the most frequently used. Occasionally one also meets with additional details to indicate that the sound was of supernatural origin:

Bhí a cuid caointe ní ba uagnaí ná caoineadh saolta [her lamenting was more lonesome than human lamenting] (Galway 54).

Another method of indicating that the experience was of a supernatural kind is the comparison of the sound with something which used to exist but no longer does. Of special interest here are the comparisons with the keening women of former times, of which there are nine examples (Armagh 3 (P); Galway 16, 65 ((P), p. 178), 69 (pp. 126-7); Kerry 28; Limerick 15; Mayo 6 (p. 63), Roscommon 2 , 16). Typical examples are:

> The crying [of the banshee was] loud and mournful something like the keening of long ago . . . (Limerick 15 (S)).
> And she cries like any good crier . . . it was as mournful as the oldest of the women could make it, that was best at crying the dead (Lady Gregory, 1970, p. 178).

> . . . and lamenting in a keen like the old keeners at wakes (Murphy, 1975, p. 76).

Such comparisons are mainly found in the western counties where the practice of keening survived until the turn of the century.[10] The stress on the mournful and sad aspects of the death-messenger's cry is also much stronger in the west, and especially in Munster, than in the east.

Besides comparisons with professional keeners, there are comparisons with ordinary women in sorrow or distress (Cavan 1.39 (p. 469), 1.21 (p. 469); Donegal 11, 27; Galway 45; Laois 17; Longford 9; Roscommon 1; Westmeath 12). Some of these examples should be seen against the background of the origin explanation that the death-messenger used to be a member of the particular family for which she cries, though it is seldom clear whether the informants have made up their minds fully about this. One informant states that the death-messenger sounds like:

> Any woman or child would be crying after the death of a member of her family (Roscommon 1 (Q)).

The opinion that the death-messenger sounds like a crying child is fairly widespread. There are eighteen records stemming from the four provinces (Cavan 1.34 (p. 470), 1.40 (p. 469); Donegal 24; Down 6; Fermanagh 5; Kerry 18; Kildare 2, 8; Laois 11; Longford 33; Meath 4; Monaghan 9; Roscommon 1; Tipperary 44, Tyrone 5; Westmeath 13; Wexford 16; Wicklow 8).

In one record the rise and fall in the cry is also included in the comparison:

it would cry like a little child. It would rise to a high pitch and then fall down again and rise again (Cavan 1.40 (p. 469)).

Again, there is possibly an affinity between the idea that the death-messenger *sounds like* a child and that she *originated from* a particular prematurely deceased child of the family for which she 'cries'. As noted earlier, the death-messenger complex is bordering on, and has been influenced by, the beliefs about children who have died without baptism. In Irish tradition, as elsewhere, such children who have not had the benefit of the appropriate rites to incorporate them into the community are thought to be restless and to express their distress through crying and wailing.[11]

Another big group of comparisons are drawn from the sounds of animals and birds especially those with nocturnal habits. The cry of cats is the most frequently mentioned (Antrim 17 (P); Cavan 1.18 (p. 469), 1.32 (p. 470), 9, 16, 19, 25, 26; Clare 7; Dublin 8; Kildare 2; Leitrim 1; Longford 21; Tipperary 20). More specifically, the comparison probably springs from the similarity between wailing and mourning and the nocturnal cry of mating cats. Though similar to the cat sounds, the death-messenger's cry was nevertheless distinguished from it in some records:

It was a mournful sound. It would put ye in mind of them old yard cats on the wall, but it wasn't cats. I know it myself (Antrim 17).

It would put you in mind at first of a couple of cats squealing, and then it would let an unearthly roar; you would soon know it wasn't cats (Cavan 1.32 (p. 470)).

A similar statement is found in Dublin 8, and in Waterford it is expressed in a proverbial saying *Ní bhíonn aon lóg cathach age 'n chat mar a bhíonn age 'n bhaidhb* (The cat has no sorrowful cry like the *badhb* has).[12]

The howling of dogs, especially at night, is commonly considered to be a death-omen in Irish tradition as well as in many other countries. The tradition that dogs are associated with the O'Keeffe family (*gaidhríní Uí Chaoimh*) is particularly well known.[13] In view of this, it is not surprising that the death-messenger's cry should be compared to a dog's howl. What is noteworthy is rather that this trait is comparatively scarce.

There are only eight instances in the records examined: Cork 1, 8; Limerick 4, 6; Meath 15; Tipperary 18; Westmeath 11; Wexford 10). That the death-messenger's wail, though similar to the howl of a dog, was clearly distinguishable from it, is stated in the following memorate:

> We thought 'twas a dog first but when we heard it the second time we knew 'twas no dog (Cork 8).

The death-messenger's cry is compared to the cry of the fox (Kilkenny 15) and, indeed, more specifically, to that of the vixen, in four other records from Leinster (Kildare 6; Kilkenny 15; Wexford 9, 19). One of them states:

> They (the cries) were a wail, ye know, some kind of a wail, the same — d'y'ever hear a fox wailin' in the night, barkin' in the night? A vixen fox. Well, it's something like that (Wexford 9).

But once again we find that a tradition bearer who is familiar with this simile underlines the differences between the vixen's cry and that of the death-messenger:

> Some people will tell you that it is the cry of a vixen. But to me it is not. I have often heard the cry of the vixen. The way she cries is far different. She cries, then stops to see will any dog bark. But the cry or *caoine* of the banshee don't stop. It goes on and on and on and lasts for a good little while (Wexford 19).

An isolated record states that the death-messenger's cry:

> . . . starts like the kid of a goat maa-ing (Cavan 1.21 (p. 469)).

The comparison with the scream of a hare caught in a trap, a very piercing and pitiful sound,[14] surprisingly, is found only once (Derry 1 (Q)).

Comparisons with bird sounds are much rarer than comparisons with animal sounds. In spite of its nocturnal habits and its ominous character the owl[15] has invited comparison with the death-messenger only once (Donegal 6). There it is said that the banshee sounded like the *scréachán reilige*, literally 'the grave-yard screecher', the screech owl/barn owl.[16] The sound of the *gabhairín reo*, 'the jack snipe',[17] is said to be similar to the cry of the death-messenger in three Kerry records (Kerry 4, 7, 45). This bird, which frequents solitary localities like bogs and marshes, makes an eerie drumming sound with its wings when descending.[18] Thus it appears that comparisons between the death-messenger's cry and bird sounds are not part of the collective tradition, except possibly in Kerry, and then only with the jack snipe. It is most noteworthy that such comparisons are totally absent in the *badhbh*-area.

In certain printed sources[19] the death-messenger's cry is likened to the sound of the wind or the storm. Only once is anything comparable found in the archival material:

> Do bhí an ghaoth anoir-aduaidh ag séideadh . . . agus ag feadaíl go huaigneach tríd na crannaibh ar nós uaillbhrón na mná sí. [The north-easterly wind was blowing and whistling lonesomely through the trees like the sorrowful wail of the banshee] (Kerry 20 (M)).

The wind is here compared with the banshee, rather than viceversa. The style of this is also contrived and atypical of oral rending. The wind simile is undoubtedly a literary device without footing in genuine folk tradition.

Comparisons between the death-messenger's cry and the sound of musical instruments also stand isolated and seem to be inventions of individual informants rather than part of the collective tradition. In Offaly 1 it is said that the banshee sounded like a squeaky violin. In Kerry 27 what was heard:

> . . . sounded like a single note on the *uillin* pipes, then the sound died away across the fields like wren boys leaving the house on St. Stephen's Day.

In Waterford 47 the sound is compared to a fire siren.

In summary the comparisons used to describe the death-messenger's cry, like the terms used for it, express both its mournful nature and its eerie and frightening qualities. These qualities are further emphasised in such comparisons by the fact that they frequently pertain not only to the sound, but also to the type of people or animals emitting it. Details are often added to indicate that sadness and horror are present to such a degree in the cry, believed to be coming from the supernatural death-messenger, as to make it impossible that the sound actually emanated from the person, animal or object to which it is compared. Criteria as to the supernatural origin of the sound can also be fulfilled by mentioning additional qualities of a kind totally alien to the sound of humans, animals or objects used in the comparison. Though we have caught glimpses of some of these criterion motifs already, they deserve more detailed treatment.

VII

The extreme volume[20] of the sound is stressed in a number of records (for example, Cavan 1.28 (p. 451); Down 11; Kildare 8; Kilkenny 20; Longford 19; Mayo 6; Waterford 4, 24, 37, 38, 47; Westmeath 4, 5; Wexford 10; Tyrone 5). According to Wexford 10, it 'filled the whole vault of the heavens'. It is therefore not surprising to find that it could be heard a long distance away (Cavan 1.28 (p. 451); Kilkenny 20; Mayo 6; Waterford 24), that it permeates buildings (Westmeath 5, pp. 42, 44), that the ground in the vicinity shakes, and that even the deaf could hear it:

> Dúirt duine acu liom go raibh an talamh ag crith leis an lóg mór fada uaigneach. [One of them told me that the ground was shaking with the great long lonesome wail] (Waterford 47).

> I heard the banshee; I heard her right here in this town-land one night and the ground was shaking under me with the cries of her; she was making the valley echo. Another woman heard her, Ellen Burns and Ellen was deaf, as deaf as a beetle . . . (Down 11).

The extraordinary duration of the cry is also stressed in records from east-Munster, Leinster and south-Ulster (Cavan 1.18 (p. 450); Down 11; Dublin 8, 15; Longford 29; Tipperary 20; Wexford 19, 38). This quality also serves to prove the sound could not have a natural cause:

> It could not have been an animal as no animal I know could give such a long wail without taking a breath (Dublin 8).

A more firmly established tradition, according to the archival material, is that the cry was heard a specified number of times. In Longford 5 there were 'seven, eight or ten cries' and in Roscommon 2 there were 'three or four wails'.[21] The tradition most commonly met with is that the cry is heard three times. As appears from Map 4 this motif is especially common in Waterford in Munster where there are twelve examples, ten of which are in the Irish language (Waterford 15, 16, 17, 22, 30, 33, 37, 38, 41, 46), and two (Waterford 1, 24) in English. It also occurs in Leinster (Kilkenny 7; Longford 4; Louth 11; Meath 10; Westmeath 17; Wexford 4, 8, 9; Wicklow 4, 5, 8). Outside these areas only three isolated examples of this motif have been found (Donegal 16; Galway 56; Tyrone 5). All these examples come from questionnaire replies and it is possible that the enquiry about the number of wails in question 7 of the Banshee Questionnaire (Appendix 1, p. 248) prompted answers which were not really traditional in their respective areas.[22] Repetition in three is commonly met with in connection with magic and the supernatural, but the south-easterly concentration of the motif in relation to the death-messenger's wail is hardly incidental. Rather, the distribution pattern gives the impression that the trait was originally attached to the *badhb* in Waterford and spread from there eastwards and northwards. It is again noteworthy that the three cries are frequently met with in memorates from Waterford and that they are there used to test the reality of the experience at its very occurrence, as shown in the following example:

> Thuit seo amach i mí Lúnasa 1913. Bhíos im'thigh féin i mBaile an Ghambóna agus an t-am idir an dá sholas sa tráthnóna. D'airíos an bhéic is uaigní do bhuail riamh ar mo chluasa. Mheasas go raibh an glór sin tuairim is dhá chéad slat thíos an bhóthair ón dtigh. Bhíos ag brath go dtiocfadh ceann eile agus, gan mórán moille, tháinig, agus timpeall an fhad céanna ar an dtaobh eile den tigh. Bhíos, agus mo chluasa ar tinneall agam ag feitheamh leis an tríú béic. Nuair a tháinig, chuir sí crith millteach im' bhalla uile. Ba shin an méid, ach ar maidin bhí comharsa béaldorais ar an gclár dá thórramh. Colbárd a b'ainm den duine seo, agus nuair a d'inis mé mo scéal bhí sé i mbéal gach duine go mbíodh an bhadhbh riamh agus i gcónaí i ndiaidh na treibhe sin — Colbárd. [This occurred in August

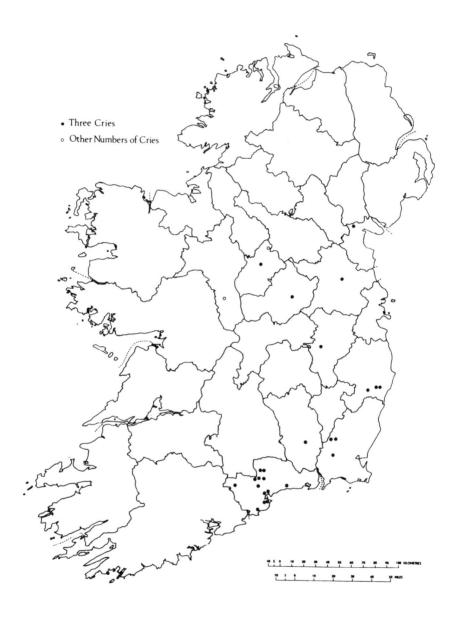

4. Number of cries

1913. I was in my own house in *Baile an Ghambóna* at twilight. I heard the most lonesome screech that ever hit my ears. I judged that the sound was about two hundred yards down the road from the house. I was expecting that another one would come, and it did come without much delay, and it was about the same distance at the other side of the house. I had my ears cocked waiting for the third shout. When it came it made every member of my body shake terribly. That was all, but in the morning a next-door neighbour was being waked. His name was Colbert. When I told my story everybody said that the *badhb* ever and always used to follow that family — Colbert] (Waterford 38).

Another interesting trait is that her cry will stop at command. The following are clear examples from the archival material:

When one would hear her, one would say 'cuss, cuss'[23] and the banshee would stop (Longford 14 (S)).

... if you speak when you hear her crying, if you say 'whist'[24] — like you know, there would be another talking and you would say to them 'whist!' — well she'd stop then and you would hear no more (Mayo 9 (M)).

She can be heard by a group of people. If one of these says, 'stop! do you hear the banshee?', then she will stop crying. That's the only way the old people knew it was the banshee and not some live person (Roscommon 2 (Q)).

One night a man heard the banshee crying in the old cemetry and he said 'shi!', then she stopped crying (Sligo 7 (S)).

... if you say 'stop!' and listen you won't hear no more; 'stop!' and you won't hear another sound (Westmeath 11 (M)).

The same belief is also likely to underlie the following statement:

People who heard her say that no-one should speak while she is crying or she will cease immediately (Longford 17 (S)).

As noted, these examples stem from Mayo, Sligo and Roscommon in Connaught and from the adjacent Leinster counties of Longford and Westmeath.

The only printed source referring to the belief — from Iorrus Aithneach, Co. Galway, in *Loinnir Mac Leabhair*,[25] contains a curious variation, that the death-messenger will do the opposite of what one tells her.

> Éist, éist![26] i.e. bí i do thost. Deirtear nach cóir 'éist!' a rá nuair a cloistear an bhean sidhe, ach má abruighthear 'éist!' leanfaidh sí do'n chaoineachán. [Stop! stop! i.e. be silent! It is said that it is not right to say 'be silent' when the banshee is heard for if it is said she will continue crying].

It is difficult to say whether this particular form of the motif is traditional or just an individual invention. The idea that things are inverse in the supernatural sphere is a common one. Also, the refusal of the death-messenger to obey the command of a mortal gives her the image of a proud and mighty being. At the same time humans can find comfort in the thought that she can be outwitted. Whatever the solution one proposes for this particular problem it is obvious that the silencing motif in both forms can fulfil the role of a criterion motif.

A further indication that the sound is of a supernatural kind is that it was clearly heard by some people but inaudible to others.[27] This is mentioned in six records from the northern part of the country (Cavan 1.25 (pp. 460-1); Down 8; Longford 21; Mayo 28, 30; Meath 4). Sometimes only one person in a particular gathering will hear the sound, as in Mayo 30, and in the following two extracts from memorates told by the same informant:

> . . . about two nights before the sister died my brother and myself went out to put in the dogs and I heard shocking wailing and crying near the place where this old girl was sick. I drew my brother's attention to it and he listened but couldn't hear it (Cavan 1.25 (p. 460)).

> The time that old Mrs. Connolly of Tanderagee was sick I heard the cry going in the direction of where the woman was sick. I was listening to it for about half an hour but Farrelly couldn't hear it at all . . . (Cavan 1.25 (p. 461)).

A great variety of criterion motifs are connected with the directions from which the sound is heard and how it moves. A few records (Cork 1; Tipperary 44) state that the sound can be heard from all directions at once. More frequently one meets with the idea that the sound is elusive. It is impossible to pin down the direction from which it comes or it comes from different directions at extremely short intervals (Armagh 6; Clare 13, 23; Cork 21; Galway 47; Kerry 13, 27; Laois 10, 16; Monaghan 9; Tipperary 8; Waterford 47; Westmeath 13; Wexford 13). One informant states the following:

> Ní thugann sí aon dá lóg san áit chéanna [She never cries twice in the same place] (Waterford 47).

Alternatively it is said that the sound keeps moving away as one tries to approach it:

> ... and when they went to where they thought she was, there was no trace of her there. After a while they heard her crying at the back of Shannon's mountain and when they went there she was below at Peter Kelleher's Cross (Clare 13).

> When you think you are getting close to her she starts to cry further away than ever (Monaghan 9).

The extraordinary speed at which the sound is imagined to travel is illustrated by the following statements:

> At one time the cry would be near and in about a second it would seem to be miles away (Clare 23).

> Ní túisce an bhean sí ag an teach ná raibh sí deich míle uaidh. [No sooner was the banshee at the house than she was ten miles away] (Galway 47).

People claiming to have heard the death-messenger have frequently and in a colourful way described this particular quality of the sound to me during fieldwork, obviously regarding it as one of its main characteristics.

Another indication that the sound emanates from a banshee, *badhb*, or such like, is that it is heading for, encircling, or leaving the house of a sick or dying person. The death-messenger most commonly makes her presence known at or near the house of the person who is about to die. Twenty records expressly state that the cry was heard heading for the house of a person who was known to be ill or dying (Cavan 1.25 (p. 461), 3; Clare 35; Cork 7, 8, 42; Galway 45; Kerry 2, 4, 7; Limerick 25; Leitrim 10, 16;

Longford 1; Meath 4; Roscommon 18; Tipperary 46; Tyrone 5; Wexford 13, 19, 55). The following are examples:

'Diabhal pioc ar bith,' dúirt sé, 'ar fhad an tsléibhe anoir ach an caoineachán agus an lógóireacht mar bheadh bean éigin dá crá.'

'Gaibh a chodladh buachaill,' dúirt sí, 'agus ná bac leis an gcaoineachán.'

D'oscail muide an doras agus nár airigh muid an caoineachán ar fad ag g'óil anoir go dtáinig sé chomh fada leis an abhainn amuigh agus leanadh don chaoineachán taobh amuigh dhon tigh tamall maith dhon oíche.

D'fhan mise insa tigh aici an oíche sin. Bhí iomarca faitíos orm corraí as an áit.

'Á, tá Seán bocht caillte,' dúirt sí, 'tá Seán bocht caillte agus is maith athá fhios agam é.'

An lá 'nár gceann tháinig scéala aniar ó ospidéal na Gaillimhe á rá gur cailleadh Seán i dtús na hoíche chéanna. ['Devil a bit,' said he, 'the whole length of the mountain over but the wailing and lamenting as if some woman was in torment.'

'Go to bed, lad,' said she, 'and never mind the wailing.'

We opened the door and didn't we hear all the wailing coming east until it came as far as the river outside and the wailing continued outside the house for a good part of the night. I stayed with her in the house that night. I was too frightened to move from the place.

'Ah, poor Seán is dead,' said she. 'Poor Seán is dead, and it's well I know it.'

The following day news came from Galway hospital that Seán had died early that same night] (Galway 45).

The other time I heard it was when Mrs. Barrett above here died . . . It came up along our boreen and on up through the fields making straight for Barretts (Cork 8).

No doubt one is to imagine that the sound gets gradually louder as it approaches. Indeed this is directly stated (Kerry 4; Limerick 25 and Wexford 55) and it is also said that the sound faded away once it had passed the house of the dying person. Sometimes we are told that the sound started high up in the air and gradually descended upon the house for which it was heading

(Clare 35). Twice we hear that the sound disappeared upwards into the sky (Roscommon 1, 2).

Thirteen records from Connaught, Leinster, Munster and Ulster (Cavan 1.21 (pp. 443-4); Clare 34; Donegal 16; Fermanagh 1; Galway 45; Kerry 2, 45; Limerick 33; Longford 24, 26, 30; Mayo 25; Tipperary 11) state that the cry followed the course of a stream or a river. The explanation for this may be that sounds, in the stillness of the night, carry along or across water. In one solitary record (Kerry 45 (Q)) it is mentioned that the cry always travels against the stream. This — like the idea that the death-messenger continues to cry if told to stop — seems to be based on the idea that things happen in a reverse sequence in the supernatural sphere.

Twelve archival records (Cavan 13, 22; Clare 35; Cork 42; Kerry 7, 19, 27; Limerick 25; Leitrim 1; Offaly 15; Waterford 16, 41) say that the sound encircled the house. In the following example, which also contains the trait that the sound starts high up in the air, the encircling is said to have occurred three times:

> They heard the wailing and crying coming towards the house ... First it seemed high up in the air, and then it came lower, and finally it went around the house three times and went away in the air wailing (Clare 35).

The encircling is mentioned in only a single printed source (*Ireland's Own*, 28 Sept., 1946, p. 16). This again shows that literary sources must be regarded with suspicion, not only because they may contain motifs which are not rooted in oral tradition, but also because they may frequently lack many traits which are quite prominent in genuine oral tradition. Contrary to what one might expect, it is nowhere indicated in any source, archival or printed, whether the encircling was withershins or sunwise, *tuathal* or *deiseal*.

In a few scattered records from different parts of Ireland (Cavan 1.8 (pp. 450-1); Cork 27; Leitrim 1) a sound is identified as emanating from the death-messenger because it headed for the house of a dying person and also because it went on from there to the graveyard:

> ... She was heard crying first around the house where he

was lying sick and then she travelled on and continued her *caoin* to the graveyard where he was to be buried (Leitrim 1).

This trait does not seem to have been firmly established in the collective tradition of any particular area.

VIII

The effects of the sound on those who hear it comprise another set of criterion motifs. Apart from the abundant general statements indicating that the cry was firghtening (Appendix 3.2.3, p. 299) there are some sources which tell of tangible physical effects upon humans who heard it. The following memorate exemplifies this:

> You know she would get on your nerves crying; its terrible.
> It would bring the cold sweat out on you listening to her.
> This is mostly how you know that it was not something
> from here like (Laois 19).

An expression commonly used in connection with the fear experienced when the death-messenger was heard is 'it would put the hair standing on your head' (Cork 20 (S), 38 (Q); Dublin 16 (P); Kildare 8 (Q); Kilkenny 15 (Q); Louth 2 (Q); Roscommon 2 (Q), 20 (P); Wexford 8 (M), 60 (M)). It is likely that most informants have taken this phrase quite literally.

The fright occasioned to animals by the cry tends also to prove the genuineness of the phenomenon, particularly in the case of animals commonly believed to possess occult hearing and the ability to distinguish between the natural and the supernatural.

Dogs are frequently credited with the ability of seeing and hearing ghosts,[28] are often found in or near houses, and indeed are sometimes especially attached to the person about to die. They are mentioned in eight records (Cavan 1.21 (p. 470); Cork 1; Laois 17, 19; Limerick 10, 25; Tipperary 40; Waterford 33). The following examples are typical:.

> Oh! the dogs kick up an awful racket and if there are any
> dogs on the street when she is around . . . they are barking
> and she is wailing (Laois 17).

There wouldn't be a dog in the side of the country but would start barking when they would hear it. They wouldn't stay near it; they would keep a good bit away from it (Cavan 1.21 (p. 470)).

Dogs would even ensure that humans were made aware of the death-messenger's cry by waking their masters if they were asleep:

Bhí an madra ag scríobadh agus ag déanamh poll sa talamh ag a cheann . . . Dhúisigh sé, agus rith sé leis go raibh sé timpeall lár na hoíche, nuair a dh'airigh sé liú mór ag déanamh anuas scathamh beag anonn uaidh insan sliabh . . . [The dog was scraping and making a hole in the ground at his head . . . He awoke and it occurred to him that it was about midnight, when he heard a great shout coming down the mountain a short distance away from him . . .] (Waterford 33).

Fright or panic in horses is only met with twice in the records although horses are thought to be just as skilled in identifying supernatural beings as dogs (Limerick 10; Wexford 4).[29] The reason they are seldom mentioned in connection with the death-messenger may be that they are less easily observed by people in or near the house.

There is one isolated account (Tipperary 1 (S)) of sheep refusing to pass a spot where the death-messenger was reported to have been heard.

IX

Having surveyed the main aural manifestations one may summarise accordingly. Aural manifestations are exceedingly prominent in the tradition and one whole area, namely Cork and Kerry, in which the being manifests herself through sounds exclusively has been identified.

The great variety of terms for the banshee's sound fall into two main groups — those which denote a mournful and plaintive sound and those which denote a frightening and animal voice. The latter group is most prominent in south-eastern Ireland, in the *badhbh*-area, and reflects the special character of the belief there.

The banshee's cry in genuine folk tradition is imagined to consist exclusively of inarticulate sounds or isolated interjections. Statements about distinguishable sequences of words are nowhere found and specific melodies in her wail are mentioned in spurious literary sources only.

Descriptions of the death-messenger's cry make comparisons with the voices of humans, that is professional keeners, ordinary women in sorrow and weeping children. The sound is also compared with cat cries, the howling of dogs and the noises of some other animals and birds. Comparisons with the sounds of certain musical instruments seem to be purely individual inventions with no firm footing in the collective tradition. Only in a few sources, literary or coloured by literature, are there comparisons with the wind. A variety of criterion motifs are employed to prove that the sounds were genuine and did not emanate from the beings or objects to which the sounds were compared.

Other qualities of the sound which are stressed in the records in evidence of supernatural origin are loudness, duration and repetition (most frequently three times). The idea that the sound will stop at the command of a human being is confined to Mayo, Roscommon and Sligo in Connaught and the adjacent counties of Longford and Westmeath in north-Leinster. Yet another criterion motif with a northerly distribution describes the sound as inaudible to some people and clearly audible to others. There are also statements that the sound is heard from all directions, that it travels at an extraordinary speed, that it follows the course of a stream or river, that it increases in volume as it approaches the house of the dying person, that it encircles it and so on.

The sound is said to have physical effects on humans and animals who hear it and there are reasons why certain animals rather than others are thought to take note of it.

Most of these traits are part of the collective tradition in large areas of Ireland.

The common denominator of many of the most frequent traits is a death situation.

5

Visual Manifestations

I

The inventiveness of our imagination seems to be without boundary as far as supernatural beings are concerned. Some are imagined as living in organised communities, perhaps ruled over by a king or a queen. These are the so-called social beings. Others, such as the *leipreachán*, are imagined as living on their own, so-called solitary beings. There are species of beings of which all are of one sex only, and species with members of both sexes. Many supernatural beings are man-shaped and others are animal-shaped and there are those who combine human and animal shape. Still others are shapeshifters and may appear in various human and animal forms. Beings may be imagined as small or tall, beautiful or ugly. Some are confined to certain elements, the sea, the air, woods, mountains, while others have many habitats.

The borderlines between different types of supernatural beings are seldom clear-cut. In areas where traditions about a particular type of being are strong the tradition dominant[1] will heavily influence the image of other beings. Special geographical, historical and social conditions in a country or region will be reflected in the image of its supernatural beings. Above all, supernatural beings, even if one regards them purely as figments of the imagination, fulfil vital functions in the lives of the people who believe in them and these functions have a bearing on the appearance of the beings.

II

One of the most distinct traits in the traditions about the death-messenger is that she is a solitary being. The names ascribed to her all include the definite article — *an bhean sí*, the banshee, *an bhadhb*, etc. Occasionally people imagined that there was

87

only one single banshee. This is how a questionnaire correspondent puts it:

> People seem to have thought that there was just one banshee in the same way as children think there is only one Santa Claus (Donegal 16).

This is not the common view. The consensus is that certain families have their own death-messenger. Several of them exist, but they are never imagined to live in communities or even to associate with each other. As Pádraic Colum[2] puts it, 'It is wrong to speak of . . . a company of Banshees'. We are entitled to say that the supernatural death-messenger is a solitary being *par préférence*.

Just two of the archival records mention more than one death-messenger as being present at the same time. One of them (Westmeath 5) mentions 'a hundred little banshees' crossing a road in front of a woman out late at night searching for her son. This item probably reflects traditions about the activities of the fairies or the dead. There are no other similar narratives in which a banshee or comparable being is mentioned. It is in every aspect atypical of the death-messenger tradition and can be safely ignored. The other item in which many death-messengers figure (Galway 11 (M) is an aetiological legend explaining the origin of the placename *Áth na gCeann* (Headford).[3] This has a literary flavour and is equally atypical of genuine death-messenger tradition. In a literary source it is stated that more than one banshee may appear at the death of certain people:

> The honour of being warned by more than one Banshee is, however, very great and comes only to the purest of the pure (McAnally, 1888, p. 114, see also pp. 112-3).

A similar statement — indeed so similar that McAnally is almost certainly its source — is found in Yeats:[4]

> When more than one banshee is present and they wail and sing in chorus, it is for the death of someone holy or a great one.

This statement of Yeats is in turn the source of the following sentence in Katharine Briggs's *Dictionary of Fairies*:[5]

> When several keen together it foretells the death of someone very great or holy.

It is regrettable to encounter such literary speculation, totally without foundation in genuine folk tradition, elevated to the status of fact in a handbook on folklore. Unfortunately, examples of this are legion.

III

Almost as firmly established in folk tradition as her solitary character is the concept that the death-messenger — in so far as she can be seen at all — is an anthropomorphic being, more particularly a woman. Once that has been established, and we shall later look at possible exceptions, the question as to what she looks like arises. As one would expect, there are a variety of answers to this. Supernatural beings may be depicted differently in different areas or in different genres. The death-messenger met with in belief statements and memorates may be different in legends, especially since certain legends, such as those about the insulted banshee, reflect activities peripheral to her ordinary role as an announcer of death. The variations in the descriptions of the death-messenger's appearance are, nevertheless, surprisingly great, even in one and the same area, or even in statements from one and the same informant.

The following extract from a collection entitled 'Description of the banshee from local sources' compiled by P.J. Gaynor, a part-time collector in the area of Bailieborough, Co. Cavan in July 1950, illustrates this point:

John Cullen said that some people described her as 'a woman dressed in grey'. He heard other people saying she was a 'little woman like a young child'. He heard it said by some people that she wore a white dress. Mrs. Soden said that old people about Mullagh described her as being like a little child. James Soden said that in Upper Lavey it was said she was like a woman. People there did not say how she was dressed or whether she was tall or small. Peter Clerkin said that she was a small white woman. Charles King said that in Virginia district the people said she was a small white woman. James Argue said that the old people said she was a little woman dressed in white. John Coyle said, she is generally like an old woman. She would be small. The old people said she was wearing an ordinary old

woman's dress. Sometimes she'd be dressed in white and
other times she'd have a dress of some other colour. Peter
Clarke, Urcher, said he always heard she was a small wee
woman. Thomas Tinnelly, Urcher, said he actually saw a
banshee and she was a little woman of about a foot high.
She was about the size of a year old child, and she wore a
red dress. Thomas Connolly said she wore a white dress
and a white cap. Mrs. Annie Clark, Drumore, said 'I heard
of a man that was beside one of them. She was a small
wee woman and was wearing a long grey cloak that was
touching the ground. Her head of hair was touching her
waist and it was the same colour as the cloak'. Mrs. Ward,
Tanderagee, said that the late Phil Smith, shoemaker,
Bailieborough, told her he saw a banshee. She was sitting
on Maggie McEntee's window-sill and her combing her
hair. She had a red cloak on her. He described her as a
little red woman. Charlie Lynch, aged 81, Bailieborough,
(a native of Upper Laragh) said he heard her described by
old people as 'a small grey woman'. She would be about
the size of a four year old child. Michael Moore said he
always heard she was a wee white woman. John Gibney,
Mullagh, said the banshee was always described as a very
small woman and she would always be dressed in white
(Cavan M 1209: 461-6).

Faced with such variation in one small area, one may despair
of presenting a meaningful picture of the death-messenger's
physical characteristics. Few other Irish supernatural beings have
been investigated in detail and variation in their appearance may
be greater than would appear from a cursory examination of the
records. Yet it cannot be doubted that the death-messenger's
appearance is more varied than that of most other beings. For
example, the variations stand out as very great indeed in comparison with the relatively staple appearance of the *leipreachán*,
a being who, like the banshee, would be considered typically
Irish.[6]

It is also noticeable from the extract that the variations tend
to flock in binary oppositions — the being may be beautiful or
ugly, old or young, small or tall, appear in dark or bright colours
and so on. To establish the frequency of the respective traits
and the reasons for the variations, one must examine the records
closely.

IV

Although the death-messenger belongs to the 'fair sex', only eighteen records describe her as beautiful. Thirteen of these stem from the archival material (Clare 19 (Q); Kilkenny 7 (Q); Mayo 17 (S); Meath 7 (S), 17 (S); Tipperary 3 (S), 44 (Q); Waterford 36 (S), 42 (M), 46 (M), 47 (Q); Westmeath 4 (Q); Wicklow 5 (S)). The remaining five are from literary sources (Keegan (1839, p. 368), Hall (1843, p. 105), Lageniensis (1870, p. 64), McAnally (1888, p. 114) and Wilde (1890, p. 83)).

It is mentioned, or implied, in these records that the beauty is especially due to the long yellow or golden hair, or to the fine clothes, or to a combination of these traits:

She was a beautiful lady with a white cloak and long golden flowing hair (Mayo 17).

It is possible that some of the informants who state that the being had long or flowing hair, without stating that it was beautiful, have imagined it to be so. Long blonde hair is in Ireland a stereotype to denote female beauty. But other stereotypes found in Irish literature expressing the beauty of women, such as snow-white hands, cheeks red as the mountain foxglove, pearl-like teeth or eyes hyacinth blue,[7] are conspicuously absent from the records. This is in keeping with the absence of amorous and erotic elements in the death-messenger tradition. One does not hear that a banshee or a *badhb* fell in love with a mortal man, or that a mortal man was attracted by such a being or made advances to her.[8]

One of the reasons for the apparent absence of erotic traits in the traditions is that the occasion on which the being appears – that of death – is the furthest possible removed from the romantic or sexual sphere. It is also noteworthy that most of the records describing the being as beautiful stem from the Schools' Manuscripts. Children more easily confuse banshees and fairies and children are especially attracted to bright and glimmering colours.

The records from the *badhb*-area (Waterford 36, 42, 46, 47), all from adult informants,[9] do need to be especially noted, particularly because records depicting the *badhb* as ugly are scarce in the Waterford tradition and descriptions of the being often include such traits as tallness, long golden hair and white clothes, indicating the beauty of the being and reminiscent of the beautiful women of the Otherworld.

The idea that the death-messenger is beautiful when she is well-disposed towards a family, but a horrible hag when she is ill-disposed towards it, is found in McAnally,[10] yet another of this author's artificial distinctions.[11] We may say then that the image of the death-messenger as a beautiful woman is quite rare, though occasionally encountered, especially in the *badhb*-area and in the children's traditions. One might have expected this. It is more surprising that sources in which she is explicitly described as ugly are even more rare. There are seven archival records. In five of these (Kildare 6 (Q); Roscommon 2 (Q), 16 (Q); Tipperary 15 (Q); Wexford 5 (M)) the general ugliness of her face is stressed. In the sixth (Carlow 1 (Q)) her teeth are missing and her nose is crooked. The seventh (Galway 64 (S)) describes her face as 'all full of holes like a riddle'.[12] Sensational details, not typical of genuine folk tradition, are added in some literary sources. Thus, Maria Edgeworth[13] describes her as 'hideous' and McAnally[14] states that she is 'a horrible hag' and that 'maledictions are written in every line of her wrinkled face'. Grotesque ugliness, such as is found in descriptions of witches and giants in the folklore of many countries, is thus seldom met with in genuine folk tradition about the death-messenger.

From the viewpoint of offering criteria to prove that the being encountered was no ordinary human being, statements about her beauty and her ugliness may be employed: it would be known that nobody with such long hair or such fine clothes or, indeed, with 'a face full of holes like a riddle' lived in the area, so it *must* have been a supernatural woman. Beauty-ugliness, however, is not a central opposition in the death-messenger complex.

V

The question of what the death-messenger's age is, or appears to be, is very closely related to the question of her beauty or ugliness. There is a strong correlation between youth and beauty in Ireland as in many other western cultures. The idea that the being is young may therefore be implied in the sources describing her as beautiful. It may also be taken that the origin legends

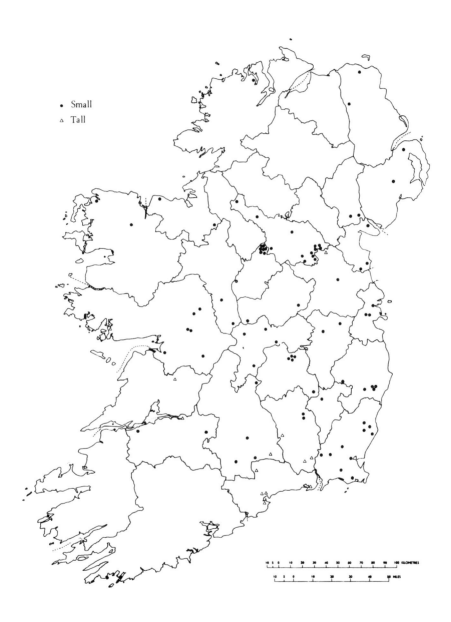

5. Stature of the death-messenger

and statements in which the death-messenger is said to have been a prematurely deceased child, convey the idea that she is young in her after-life role as well. Direct statements that the being is young occur very rarely, even in literary sources where there appears to be only a few such references.[15] The idea that she is an old woman, on the other hand, is firmly established in folk tradition (35 records; see Appendix 3.3 (a), p. 300). In addition to these direct statements the frequent mention of her white or grey hair and certain aspects of her stature and clothes, indicate that she is generally imagined as being old. There is also a correlation between old age and the idea that the being is an ancestor of the family for which she cries. The association between death and old age seems to have been a decisive factor in creating the dominant image in folk tradition of the banshee, *badhb* etc., as an old woman.

VI

The image of the death-messenger's stature follows a pattern similar to the concept of age. The being is described as a tall woman in only twelve archival records (Clare 34 (S); Galway 56 (Q); Kilkenny 1 (S), 15 (Q), 17 (S); Limerick 2 (Q); Meath 6 (M); Tipperary 16 (Q); Waterford 12 (M), 32 (S), 42 (M), 46(M)). Although there are scattered examples from Clare, Galway, Limerick and Meath, the tallness of the being is not firmly established in the collective tradition except in the *badhbh*-area, the trait being especially prominent in Waterford. Direct statements to the effect that the death-messenger is a small woman, on the other hand, are found over most of the country (Appendix 3.3 (b), p. 300 and Map 5). There are 79 archival records in which the smallness of the death-messenger is expressly stated and these are supported by a number of printed sources, including some nineteenth-century ones, for example.[16] To these may be added a number of sources in which the small stature is implied in one way or another. The more exact size is seldom specified — one foot (Cavan 1.41 (p. 463)) and four feet (Kildare 8: Wexford 13). Three further accounts (Cavan 1.21 (p. 461), 1.24 (p. 465), 1.41, p. 463) indicate that she was the size of a young child. No doubt the being's smallness functions as a criterion of her supernatural character. It would also appear that her tallness in the *badhbh*-area fulfils the same function. There is also a marked correlation between the image of the death-messenger as small and the idea that she is old. In this respect Keegan's statement (1839, p. 368) well reflects the collective tradition in most parts of Ireland:

> her general appearance is in the likeness of a very old woman, of small stature, and bending and decrepit form . . .

VII

Descriptions of special facial features of the death-messenger are rarely encountered: a few have been mentioned in relation to her possible beauty or ugliness. The only significant feature of the death-messenger's appearance upon which folk tradition has focused its attention is her hair.

The hair is expressly stated to be long in 83 archival records from the four provinces (Appendix 3.3 (c), p. 301 and Map 6). The trait is very prominent in Leinster (45 examples) and also in Tipperary (11 examples) and Waterford (9 examples) in Munster. Sometimes specific details are added to indicate its great, or even unnatural, length: 'long hair tipping the ground' (Wexford 33); 'long hair down to her feet' (Wexford 48); 'very long hair down to her toes' (Wicklow 7); *gruaig fhada . . . síos go sála*' (long hair . . . down to her soles) (Waterford 36). In other records (Cavan 1.14 (p. 464), Donegal 6, Longford 29, Tipperary 2, Wexford 22) the hair is said to be waist-length.

Older literary sources in English make mention of the being's long hair too. Illustrations in works of nineteenth-century writers such as Croker, Hall and McNally,[17] contain this detail which is also referred to in these texts and in a number of other works from the nineteenth and early twentieth centuries.[18] While in general keeping with genuine folk tradition, some of these literary sources blur and distort it through exaggerations. The following is an example of this from Todhunter (1885, p. 153):

> The first thing I tuk notice to, Misther Harry, was her hair, that was streelin' down over her showldhers, an' a good yard on the ground on aich side of her. O, be the hoky farmer, but that was the hair! The likes of it I never seen on mortial woman, young or ould, before nor sense.

6. Long hair

In view of the fact that the being's long hair is so prominently recorded in folk tradition it seems strange that no reference is made to it in folklore handbooks such as Ó Súilleabháin's *Handbook of Irish Folklore* and Funk and Wagnalls *Standard Dictionary of Folklore, Mythology and Legend*.

Since the long hair is to the fore in the death-messenger tradition it is natural that the being should ordinarily be imagined to be bareheaded. This is at variance with what would be normal practice among older Irish country women who would wear their hair covered. In one specific situation, however, namely when keening and mourning, older women would wear their hair loose.[19] This offers one explanation of why long free-flowing hair is such a common trait in the death-messenger's appearance. It is also possible that her long hair is a survival from a similar characteristic of supernatural or Otherworld women such as Fedelm, Clíona, Étaín[20] and the *badhbh*-figures.

The hair is described as golden in six records from the four provinces (Cavan 137 (p. 458) (M); Clare 36 (S); Laois 6 (M); Mayo 17 (S); Meath 17 (S); Tipperary 44 (Q)). In five records (Offaly 12 (M); Wexford 22 (Q); Wicklow 2 (S), 3 (S), 6 (S)) it is said to be yellow, and four further records refer to it as fair (Cavan 16 (S), Clare 19 (Q); Kilkenny 7 (Q); Wicklow 4 (S)). An isolated source (Tipperary 3 (S)) mentions auburn hair. Most of these 'fair' beings are also said to have had long hair. The tradition of a fair or golden-haired death-messenger is not as firmly established as might appear from the number of examples. A high proportion of the examples are derived from Schools' Manuscripts and it is likely that they reflect the children's preference for shining, glittering and 'friendly' colours.

One must also take account of the influence of 'fairies' as depicted in children's books and of the mermaid tradition in which long, golden hair is firmly established. The auburn colour borders on red and red is mentioned in reference to the being's hair in three records (Armagh 2 (Q); Roscommon 23 (Q); Westmeath 4 (Q)). The absence of this colour in the south of Ireland is noteworthy and one might also mention that there are two records of the death-messenger being *dressed* in red from Westmeath. Some other examples of the red dress stem from counties bordering on those where her hair is said to be red. Red is a colour generally associated with fairies — not those common in children's books but those from genuine folk tradition

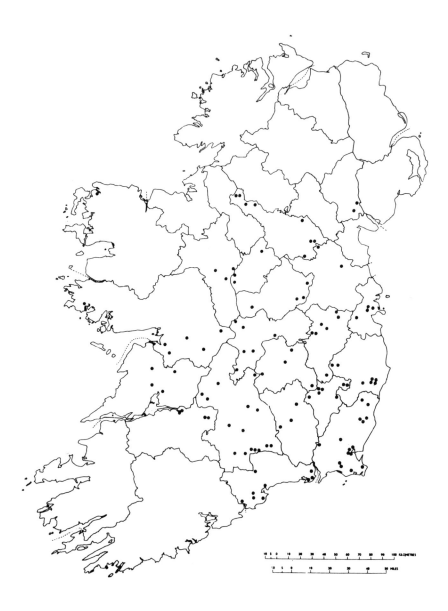

7. Combing her hair
References to her combing her hair in legends *not* included

— as well as with magic and the supernatural.

Brown and black hair are referred to in only one record each (Waterford 1 (L); Wexford 19 (Q)). These colours may have been avoided because they would not be visible in the dark, the time when the death-messenger was commonly believed to appear. They are atypical. More prominent is the colour grey. There are nine records from east-Munster, Leinster and south-Ulster (Armagh 8; Cavan 1.14 (p. 463-4), 23; Laois 11, 18; Tipperary 15, 20, 44; Westmeath 2). The tradition that the death-messenger is white-haired is much more firmly established. There are 17 records in all (Carlow 1; Cavan 31; Dublin 9; Kildare 8; Kilkenny 1, 26; Laois 9, 21; Longford 29; Offaly 1; Tipperary 17; Waterford 18, 28, 32, 35; Wexford 54; Wicklow 14). This tradition has a wide distribution and is especially prominent in Leinster. The grey and white colours are in keeping with the image of an old woman, and they have associations with the realm of death. Also human keeners would mainly be elderly women, with grey or white hair.

In view of the popularity of the traditions about the death-messenger's hair it is appropriate that the being should be thought to be engaged in combing it. The Comb Legend, a migratory legend to be treated later, is connected with this activity. The combing is also encountered in belief statements and memorates. In the orally-collected sources there are 113 references to combing (Appendix 3.3 (d) p. 301) in addition to those found in versions of The Comb Legend.[21] Only two additional examples have been noted in nineteenth-century literature [22] — yet another illustration of how important aspects of folk tradition have been overlooked by writers of fiction and how lack of literary reference cannot be taken as evidence that a tradition was less prominent before organised folklore collecting began. The combing belief can be numbered among those beliefs which are firmly rooted in folk tradition. The belief has a marked regional distribution (Map 7). The combing is more prominent in Leinster (62 examples) and parts of Munster (31 examples, most of which stem from Tipperary and Waterford) than in Connaught and Ulster (10 examples each). The tradition is limited to the area in which the being is believed to be seen as well as heard but does not cover the whole of this area. There is a marked correlation between the distribution of the combing belief and the belief that the death-messenger's hair is long.

The significance of the combing has not loomed large in popular imagination. In the Schools' Manuscripts there is an isolated statement to the effect that the banshee's wail was the noise of the comb when she drew it through her hair (Limerick 24). This is also stated in a questionnaire reply from Wexford (Wexford 38). In spite of the fact that the Banshee Questionnaire contained a direct question as to the reason for the being's combing,[23] only two more pieces of information relevant to the subject came to light. One correspondent states that the combing symbolises 'a joyful passing or a happy death' (Longford 29); another maintains that the activity announces 'the combing of the hair of the corpse' (Galway 56). While there is some kind of connection between the two sources which link the sound of the combing with the banshee's wail, these explanations appear to lack foundation in collective traditional beliefs. Neither can one attach importance to the explanation appearing in Pádraic Colum's *A Treasury of Irish Folklore:*[24]

> . . . those who have looked upon her (the banshee) describe her as drawing a comb through her hair; she is probably tearing her hair out in the manner of the ancient mourners.

Traditions about human keening women have influenced the beliefs about the supernatural death-messenger, but none of the many genuine sources about combing give the least indication that the hair was believed to be torn out. If Colum's statement is based on oral information it is likely to be the outcome of an individual explanation. More probably the interpretation is his own. While there is a possible similarity of function between the combing of her hair by the death-messenger and the tearing of their hair by the human mourners, it is likely that the combing motif has wider and more ancient connotations.

While there is little profit in seeking for traditional explanations of the death-messenger's combing, one might look at the motif in the wider perspective of beliefs and legends attached to the combing activities of other supernatural beings. A few references to Otherworld women visibly engaged in combing their hair are met with in early Irish literary sources and these will be treated later. For later discussion also are the folk tradition sources in which the combing activity is — apart from the banshee and her kin — attached in particular to the mermaid. The firm, and apparently old, connection between the mermaid and combing may account for the absence of the combing motif, as attached to the death-messenger, in coastal areas where the mermaid was the tradition dominant.

A being depicted as combing her hair is assumed to be doing so with a comb of one kind or another. The comb is in fact the object most commonly associated with the supernatural death-messenger, though one feels that this object is even more firmly attached to the mermaid. Descriptions of the death-messenger's comb are found not only in The Comb Legend where the comb is essential to the action, but also in some belief statements and memorates. It has been variously described as golden (Dublin 15); silver (Wexford 19 (b)), iron or steel (Roscommon 8; Wicklow 4, 5, 6, bone (Laois 17) and wooden (Tipperary 18). It is also described as glittering (Wexford 33), red (Meath 24) and blue (Laois 24). Further details characterise it as very small (Westmeath 2) and broken-toothed (Westmeath 2; Wexford 32).

In most instances the motifs are introduced to prove that the comb was unusual and strange, so that it could not have belonged to an ordinary human being. The colour and size of the comb also correspond to the ideas people themselves have about the colour preferences of the death-messenger and about her stature. While The Comb Legend – in which combs of gold,[25] silver,[26], iron or steel[27] and bone[28] as well as a very small comb[29] also figure – is founded on the general belief in the death-messenger in her combing role, it is also possible that descriptions of the comb in the legends have secondarily exercised an influence on belief statements and memorates.

VIII

As already indicated, the perception of the death-messenger's clothes relates to the idea that she is beautiful or ugly, young or old. Archival records assign the colours white, grey, red and black/brown to the death-messenger's clothes (Map 8). These colours appear in most older sources as well – in so far as colours are mentioned. It is clear that colours such as green, blue and yellow are alien to the death-messenger tradition. Todhunter's assertion,[30] repeated by Yeats[31] and Briggs,[32] that she wore a green gown stands isolated as a literary invention.

The dominant colour in the death-messenger tradition (67 ar-

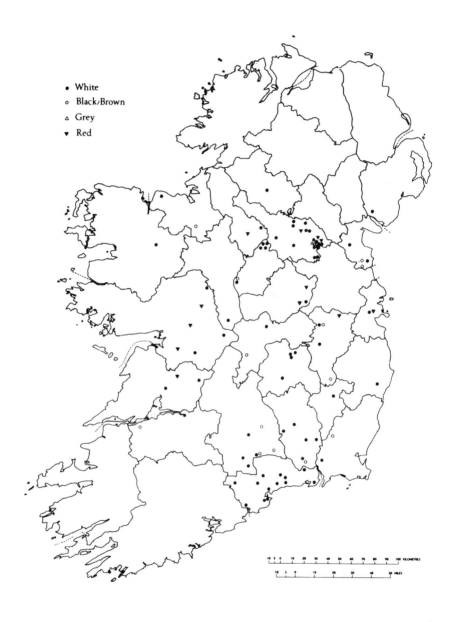

- • White
- ○ Black/Brown
- △ Grey
- ▼ Red

8. Colour of her clothes

chival records, see Appendix 3.3 (e), p. 302) and the colour found over practically the whole area where the being is said to be visible, is white. This colour is practically without competition in the *badhbh*-area and the only one attested in Waterford, where we also find it in a proverbial saying – *Thá gach éinne 'n a bhaidhb bóthair inniubh* – of girls in white dresses.[33] Additional examples of white are found in certain literary sources such as Croker, Keegan, Hall, Murphy and Dease.[34] There are two archival examples of grey (Cavan 1.14 (p. 463), 1.21 (p. 461)). Examples of black/brown (13 archival records) are unevenly scattered over parts of Leinster, Connaught and Munster and are slightly more common in Leinster than elsewhere (Kildare 2, 8; Kilkenny 16; Limerick 32; Longford 29; Louth 4, 5; Offaly 1; Sligo 1; Tipperary 16, 20, 44; Wexford 19). Black is also referred to by Westropp.[35] There are twelve examples of red, unevenly scattered and notably absent in the *badhbh*-area (Cavan 1.18 (p. 463), 1.41 (p. 463), 1.43 (p. 465); Clare 34; Dublin 5; Galway 6, 52, 63; Kildare 7; Leitrim 7; Westmeath 4, 12).

The colour red in association with the death-messenger is somewhat surprising but it does appear to be traditional, though not very common. The main reason for its occurrence is probably that red is thought to have associations with magic and the supernatural.[36] Because of its associations with blood, red may have been thought appropriate when the death-messenger appeared in the context of violent deaths. The dark colours black/brown and grey – apart from being mysterious and ominous – would convey associations with death and mourning. They are also in keeping with the image of the death-messenger as an old woman, since old country women seldom, if ever, wore bright-coloured clothes. Since black/brown and grey seem so well suited to the being, why is white so dominant? A number of reasons for this may be adduced. Like black, white would be especially associated with death; ghosts and revenants are believed to appear in white; a corpse would turn whitish pale and the winding-sheet would be white. Also, the being was, for a variety of reasons, believed to be seen mainly at night-time. In order to prove that something had been seen in the dark, an element of brightness would be necessary, and since gay colours would be unsuitable in the death context, it is not surprising that white should have come to hold the dominant position which it occupies.

The records have less to say about the kind of clothes than about their colour. Headgear — more specifically a white cap — is mentioned only twice in the records (Cavan 1.18 (p. 463); Leitrim 1). Such caps were commonly worn by married women in the nineteenth century,[37] but it is not surprising that they should be rare in the death-messenger tradition. The trait would be at variance with, or detract from, the firmly established tradition of the being's long free-flowing hair which she would keep combing. The cap-wearing death-messenger appears to be a regional innovation, which has not established itself outside Cavan-Leitrim.[38]

More common is the tradition that the death-messenger wears a cloak. There are nineteen records of this in all (Cavan 1.14 (p. 464), 1.43 (p. 465); Clare 34; Dublin 8; Galway 63; Kildare 2, 8; Kilkenny 15; Laois 18; Limerick 32; Louth 4; Mayo 17; Meath 5, 25; Tipperary 16; Westmeath 4; Wexford 19, Croker and Todhunter, repeated by Yeats and by Briggs.[39] There are also occasional references to her cape (Dublin 5), jacket (Cavan 23) and shawl (Antrim 6; Donegal 16; Offaly 5; Roscommon 1; Sligo 1). Since the being is almost exclusively imagined to appear in the open air and after sunset, when the weather would have turned cold, the occurrence of outdoor garments is not surprising. Neither is it surprising that the style of clothing is conservative and old-fashioned. The mantle or cloak was a common garment of men and women[40] and was worn by old country women up to our time.[41] Because the being was so often imagined as wearing a long outer garment, other articles of clothing are rarely mentioned. A dress is mentioned in six archival records (Cavan 1.18, 1.19, 1.41 (p. 463); Dublin 4; Kildare 2; Longford 29) and a dress is also referred to by Todhunter (1885, p. 153). One single record (Longford 29) mentions an apron — obviously an individual invention.

The old-fashioned Irish cloak reached down to the feet. Because of this there is scant reference to the death-messenger's footwear. The Schools' Manuscripts mention 'red shoes' once (Meath 24) and one questionnaire reply refers to 'lovely golden slippers' (Tipperary 44). It is more interesting that four records (Kildare 2; Kilkenny 13; Limerick 2; Wexford 19 (a)) state that the being is barefoot. This is in keeping with the old-fashioned lifestyle of the death-messenger and it also reflects a characteristic of the keening women. It is not so long ago since shoes were seldom worn by Irish country women, except on special occasions.[42]

IX

The main traits in the appearance of the female supernatural death-messenger have now emerged. In summary she is generally imagined to be old and small, even though she may appear as a vigorous tall woman in certain parts of the country, notably in the *badhbh*-area, especially in Waterford tradition. Her hair is generally said to be long, and white is the predominant colour. In an area in Leinster and Munster (especially in Tipperary and Waterford) and in some parts of Connaught and Ulster, she is believed to comb her hair. She also appears commonly in white garments, though dark and red ones are also mentioned. These colours are suited to her role as a supernatural being specially associated with old age, sorrow and death. The types of clothes she wears are in keeping with her appearances in the open air and they reflect the styles predominant among country women of previous centuries and of the oldest generations in isolated areas until fairly recent times. Although the general picture is one of considerable variation in the death-messenger's appearance, it has been possible to sort out certain traits of special frequency and with a large distribution, constituting the core of the collective Irish tradition. This core has been more clearly visible when the husk of unreliable literary records has been winnowed away. One final and especially complicated problem remains. To what extent, if at all, is the death-messenger imagined to have appeared in bird or animal shape?

X

In a number of references to the death-messenger in dictionaries and handbooks, it is stated that she assumes the shape of a bird, more particularly a crow. Thus in Dinneen's dictionary *badhbh* is glossed as follows:

> a female fairy or phantom, said to be attached to certain families, appearing as a scald-crow or royston-crow.

Similarly in Katharine Briggs's *Dictionary of Fairies*[43] *sub* Badb or Badhbh (bibe) is found the following:

> The Celtic goddess of war, who, according to Evans Wentz in *The Fairy-Faith in Celtic Countries* (pp. 302-5), incorporated the three goddesses, NEMAN, MACHA and MORRIGU in a single form, that of a Royston or hoodie crow. The mythology has declined into folklore, and a crow perching on a house is often the form taken by the BANSHEE or 'fairy woman'.

To help assess the frequency of such a belief, question 3 in the Banshee Questionnaire was phrased in the following way:

> Is there a belief that the banshee (*badhbh* etc.) could appear in the shape of a bird or animal? Is any particular bird in your locality referred to as the banshee or the like?

In view of the fact that Badb, a goddess of war, appears in the shape of a crow in many early Irish literary texts[44] one might expect that the death-messenger would appear in that form, especially in the area where the term *badhb* (and similar forms) has been preserved, namely in what is referred to as the *badhbh*-area. The answers to the questionnaire coupled with an investigation of the other sources, archival and printed, referring to folk tradition in this century and the last, appear not to provide any solid evidence that the *badhb, bean sí* — or the death-messenger under any of her other appellations — ever appeared in the shape of a royston or scald-crow or any bird of the crow family. A questionnaire correspondent from Waterford summarises the findings very succinctly as follows:

> Tá ceangal idir an bhean sí agus an fheannóg i gcuntais na leabhar, ar ndóigh, ach bíodh gur tuar bháis an feannóg uaireanta ní luaitear mar bhadhb í. [There is a connection made between the banshee and the scald-crow in the literary accounts, indeed; but, although the scald crow is sometimes an omen of death, it is not referred to as a *badhb*] (Waterford 47).

From this one must conclude that the belief about the death-messenger in crow-shape has not existed within living memory and probably died out long before that. Dinneen's statement is likely to be derived from early Irish sources and Briggs's assertion that the banshee is 'commonly' believed to appear as a crow in modern Irish folk tradition is inaccurate.

XI

Was the death-messenger believed to appear in the shape of any other bird? Fifty questionnaire correspondents answered this question in the negative, and the fact that seventy-one additional correspondents left the question unanswered indicates that they were unaware of such a belief. Seventeen replies (Antrim 4; Cavan 1.19, (p. 462), 24, 29, 31; Clare 14; Donegal 14, 23; Down 14; Fermanagh 1; Laois 20; Longford 21; Roscommon 2, 17, 18, Wexford 23; Tyrone 6) were, or — to phrase it more carefully — appear to be positive and deserve close consideration.

Assuming that these records reflect, in all instances, a genuine belief, their distribution raises some scepticism. There is only one example from the *badhbh*-area and the belief is totally absent from Waterford. Consequently, there is no special connection between the death-messenger name *badhb* (and similar forms) and any bird. Also, the very scattered distribution pattern indicates that the idea of the death-messenger in bird-shape was never part of the collective tradition in any particular area.

There are special reasons, however, for probing further into the seventeen records and for analysing what they say and how they came to exist. The following is what we find in one of them (Cavan 29):

> I got one instance of the banshee appearing in the shape of a bird and sat on the window-sill of the room in which the person lay ill. She came regularly for about a week before the person died.

It is obvious that this correspondent, in a laudable effort to assist the Department of Irish Folklore in its work, tried very hard to find a banshee in bird shape, a matter especially enquired about in the questionnaire. It is doubtful if the informant would have associated this particular ominous bird with the banshee had he not been confronted with a direct question. Similarly the robin appearing as an omen of death (Down 14)[45] would not have been called a banshee had the term not been invited by the questionnaire. The statement given in another record (Roscommon 17) is unclear and ambiguous:

> Sometimes people would say they heard a bird crying in
> the mountain referring to the banshee.

The informant may have meant merely that the banshee's cry
might be compared to a bird call.

The remaining fifteen replies to the questionnaire similarly
do not stand up to the kind of source analysis applied above.
One further example, which is particularly illustrative of the
way in which the erroneous notion might have arisen occurs in
an interview which took place in May 1976 between Michael J.
Murphy (MJM), full-time collector, and his informant, the
excellent tradition-bearer Michael Rooney (MR) of Blacklion,
Co. Cavan:

MJM	'Well, this is about the Banshee, Michael, you know? The old people, they'd use the word "banshee", wouldn't they?'
MR	'Yes.'
MJM	'And would they say it was a woman now?'
MR	'They said it was a bird, a bird.'
MJM	'Yeh?'
MR	'A bird.'
MJM	'Did anyone ever see her?'
MR	'No, no.'
MJM	'How did they know it was a bird?'
MR	'Well, the flutter of the wing, the wing. Like you heard a snipe, a rattle snipe, a snipe, she'd be flying up and she'd make ... its with her wings that she ... that she puts that sound out. And they say it's a bird, not a woman, a bird.'
MJM	'I see. Well, just when you're talking, was there ever any word of them calling a certain bird "a banshee"?
MR	'No.'
MJM	'Nothing like that?'
MR	'I never heard it. No.'
MJM	'And they never seen a wee old woman going round, just a bird?'
MR	'Just a bird.'

Murphy then questions Rooney on the route the death-messenger takes to the house.

MR   'Aw, just if you were going up to your house this thing would rise in front of you, maybe two hundred yards and let a wail.'

MJM   'And they said it was a bird?'

MR   'They said it was a bird. Aye, the banshee was supposed to be a bird. Well, of course it *must*[46] have been a bird when you'd see nothing and she went away in the distance...'

MJM   'They used to say in some parts she was a wee woman, you know and she was always combing her hair, do you know? Did you ever hear that?'

MR   'No, I never heard that... She was a bird, you'd hear the flutter of the wings, well, the wee woman, she couldn't fly, she had no wings. You'd have a chance of seeing her sometime, or somebody'd see her; but nobody living ever saw a banshee if people would tell the truth. They never did.' (Cavan 24).

From this one can discern how an experienced collector, through tactful and unobtrusive questioning, can establish that the idea that the banshee would appear in bird-shape is not part of a general belief in the area but rather an individual interpretation by the informant. Certainly there is no clear indication that the death-messenger was ever firmly believed to appear as a bird in any specific area and even in the unlikely event that further and more clear-cut examples would come to light, one may be sure that the trait was nowhere part of the collective tradition.[47]

In regard to the appearance of the death-messenger as an animal the questionnaire replies elicited only one positive answer:

There was a belief that there was a connection between the banshee and the hare; consequently people hesitated to shoot the hare (Roscommon 16).

All over Ireland a variety of superstitions were connected with the hare. It was commonly thought that hags transformed themselves into hare-shape to suck milk from their neighbour's cows. Legends about the shooting of such hag-hares are often encountered.[48] It is nowhere else mentioned, however, that such hares had any connection with the banshee or her kin. This trait is clearly an isolated intrusion into the death-messenger complex. Something similar holds true about a statement in a Schools' Manuscript (Wexford 27) that the *bow* was seen in the shape of a rabbit with a human face. The being is supposed to have appeared in a lane, known as The Black Cow, in Wexford town. From other accounts it appears that this lane was thought to be a favourite haunt for the *bow*,[49] but neither in these, nor in any other source, do we hear that she took the particular form referred to in Wexford 27 nor indeed any form other than the usual female one. It is tempting to believe that the school-child who wrote the account actually saw a rabbit, perhaps acting in a strange way, in the lane and referred to it as a *bow* because of the reputation of the place. Be that as it may, what is clearly involved here is an individual concept without footing in genuine folk tradition.

A Schools' Manuscript from Kerry (Kerry 37) states that the banshee appeared in pig-shape and a literary source, Maxwell, [50] refers to her as 'a black bitch'. Here again one is obviously dealing with isolated confusions between the death-messenger and other demoniac spirits believed to appear at night.[51]

The reference to the death-messenger in fox form, made by Alice Dease,[52] is of a somewhat different character:

> There are families in which the spirit appears in the form
> of a fox which howls with mournful lament before the
> death of the head of the house.

Foxes differ from the other animals so far dealt with in as far as they, like the supernatural female death-messenger, are sometimes believed to follow certain specified families. The most notable example is probably the Preston family of Gormanstown Castle, Co. Meath.[53] In no other instance except in Dease's book is a fox — or foxes, since many of them were sometimes thought to appear on the occasion of one and the same death — called banshee, or *badhb*, or referred to by any other name used to denote the female supernatural death-messenger. It is therefore inaccurate to refer to the death-announcing foxes by any of these terms and there is no indication that foxes have been regarded as such beings in animal guise. They may, however, because of their special 'family connections', be regarded as functional variants of the female death-messenger.

There is one record in which the banshee is stated to have appeared in the form of an insect. This is from a questionnaire correspondent in Fermanagh:

> Martin Gallagher from Tyrone told me his mother said it was like a butterfly. It cried in the room at the wake. Someone let it out the window. It was a butterfly banshee (Fermanagh 5).

There is a wide-spread belief that the soul can be seen leaving the body in the form of a butterfly when a person is asleep[54] or, especially, at the moment of death.[55] Obviously the banshee has been accidentally grafted on to this tradition in the above example. The informant would probably not have done this had he not been confronted with the questions about bird or animal shapes in the Banshee Questionnaire.

The evidence then indicates that within memory — and probably for centuries — there has been no established tradition that the banshee, *badhb* etc., appeared in the shape of a bird, animal or insect. In so far as the supernatural death-messenger is seen at all, she traditionally appears only in the shape of a woman, the most prominent features of whose appearance, summarised above, are decidedly anthropomorphic.

6

The Manifestation Situations – Time and Place

The most prominent trait in the image of the supernatural death-messenger is that she is, in one way or another, connected with death. Direct statements in support of this are found in almost 60 per cent of the total material examined (see Appendix 3.4.1, p. 303) and many more or less clear indications to the same effect can be added to this figure. One might argue for the generic term 'death-foreboder' in preference to 'death-messenger' for the being because in 80 per cent of the sources connecting her directly with death she is imagined to have appeared *before somebody's death* (Appendix 3.4.2 (a), p. 303-4 and Map 9). However, since the rule is not without exceptions, the wider term 'death-messenger' has been adopted.

There are 84 sources or 15 per cent of the relevant material (Appendix 3.4.2 (d), p. 305) in which the time of the manifestation in relation to death is not specified. Apart from these there are some records in which the supernatural being is stated to have appeared *at the precise moment of somebody's death* or *after it*. The former statement is found in four records only or less than 1 per cent of the relevant material (Antrim 3 (L); Cork 8 (M); Donegal 22 (Q) and Down 11 (M)). This is therefore a rare trait and is not firmly established in the collective tradition of any particular area (Map 9). A noteworthy common factor in the four records is that they all deal with the manifestation of the being in Ireland on the occasion of death abroad. It is apt that relatives and friends should be informed of the exact hour of a death concerning them, while foreknowledge would have been of little or no avail to them. Before the introduction of the telegraph and telephone it might have taken days or weeks before they could establish contact with the place where the dying person dwelt and then they would find that the person was dead anyhow. There is also a possible connection between the death-messenger's appearance at the exact moment when somebody expires and various other supernatural phenomena believed to take place at that very moment, phenomena such as pictures falling down or clocks stopping of their own accord. The importance which mourners attached to recording the precise time of a death is also apparent from the widespread custom of stopping clocks when somebody has expired.[1]

Manifestations of the death-messenger after deaths are also rare, amounting to 24 references or 4 per cent of the relevant material (Appendix 3.4.3 (b), p. 304 and Map 9). The thinly scattered distribution of this trait — most counties are represented by only one or two records — indicates that the idea was nowhere uppermost in the popular mind. Most of the examples are also found in somewhat unreliable sources in which the existing traditions may not have been accurately reported. This may hold true of some, or even all, of the seventeen records from the Schools' Manuscripts (Clare 29, 35; Cork 9; Galway 47; Kilkenny 18; Laois 21; Limerick 13, 25, 37; Longford 20; Mayo 20; Meath 24; Tipperary 17, 23; Waterford 32; Wexford 33; Wicklow 3). It is noteworthy that most of these do not say how soon after a death the manifestations occurred. For more reliable material it appears that such manifestations would either be noticed immediately after a death (Cavan 21; Laois 17) or at some stage during the wake (Cavan 19; Dublin 12; Kildare 6; Roscommon 2; Waterford 48). It is not difficult to understand that anything unusual seen or heard at such a time should be interpreted as a banshee or *badhb*. What calls for an explanation is the rarity of the trait, but this will be dealt with later.

II

The collective tradition all over Ireland favours the view that the death-messenger manifests herself *before* deaths. How closely before the deaths is she generally supposed to appear? The records are not clear-cut on this. It is evident, however, that the manifestations are normally imagined to occur within minutes or hours or, at most, a day or two before a person expires. This can be deduced with safety from at least 263 records or 48 per cent of the relevant material (Appendix 3.4.3 (a, b), pp. 305-6). In more than half of these records we also meet with the idea that

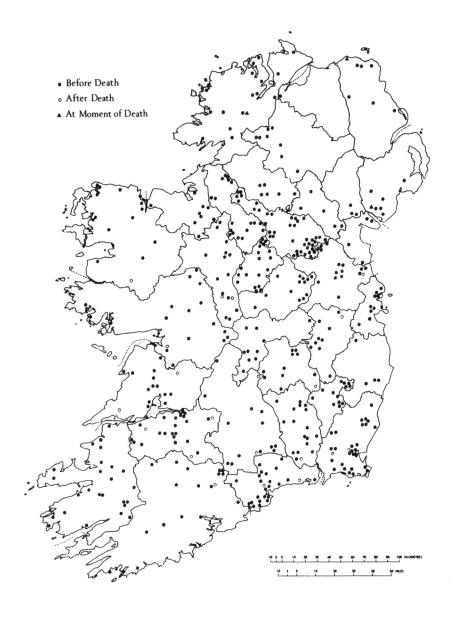

- Before Death
- After Death
- At Moment of Death

9. The occasions of manifestation

people would know that a death was impending, with no recovery possible, before the manifestation (Appendix 3.4.3 (a), pp. 305-6). The following is a typical example:

> In any story I ever heard the banshee is represented as coming when it is fairly obvious the sick person had little hope of recovery (Wexford 45).

This is not very different from saying that no recovery was possible once the death-messenger had been heard or seen, as stated in the following example:

> One thing was certain according to their belief, that there was no chance of recovery for the sick person [for] whom it was heard crying near their house (Cavan 41):

There is also the belief that a sick person, or one who belonged to a family for which the death-messenger was wont to cry, *could not* die until she had manifested herself:

> The relatives of the sick person will not believe that the sick person will die until the banshee is heard (Mayo 28).

Such situations as those described above are aptly exemplified in the words of a Donegal questionnaire correspondent:

> When especially an elderly person in the locality was known to be nearing death, the atmosphere and attitudes of the people became very apparent — expectancy would be the word . . . (Donegal 20).

Since anticipation and expectancy form such essential parts of the *Sitz im Leben* of the death-messenger belief, it is no surprise to find that some tradition-bearers maintain that the being manifests herself exclusively before the deaths of old and ill persons and never before deaths due to accidents. There are two typical examples:

> She never cries before an accident; it is always for the sick person that is going to die (Roscommon 2).

> The banshee appeared to healthy people forewarning them of a sick person's death, but not of accidental death (Antrim 6).

Though such statements express the common traditional belief there are certain exceptions.

III

Manifestations of the death-messenger in connection with sudden and unexpected deaths,[2] are referred to in 19 records. In twelve of these (Carlow 19; Cavan 3, 4, 20, 25; Clare 25; Galway 14, 37; Kerry 40; Leitrim 10; Waterford 46; Wexford 13) the death-messenger is not seen or heard by the person who is destined to die. The following examples may be regarded as typical:

> Michael McMahon of Fountain, Ennis, heard great crying in the middle of the day. It went from the back of his house to where John Keane, a neighbour of his, lived. In half an hour's time he heard that John Keane was dead. The banshee always followed the Keane family (Clare 25).

> . . . the cry went along the valley under Aughermon, and next day Anastasia Doyle of the same place died suddenly. I remember that quite well. She was putting on her hat when she dropped (Wexford 13).

Such memorates are in accordance with the general belief that the dying person does not himself see or hear the death-messenger. In another group of traditions the supernatural being appears to a healthy person who cannot imagine that his own death is foreboded and wrongly believes that the death-messenger is crying for somebody else. Here one is not dealing with memorates but with a legend containing a fully-developed plot and a surprise element, in other words a *fabulate*. The following two versions may be regarded as typical:

> Bhí fear thiar in Clais Mhór, Joe Condon a bhí air agus bhí mé féin agus é féin ag baint prátaí i bhfochair a chéile agus an lá so nuair a tháinig sé go dtí mé bhí deallradh cráite air. D'fhiafraigh mé de cad a bhí ag déanamh caithimh dó agus dúirt sé liom gur dh'airigh sé an bhadhb agus go raibh duine éigin a bhain leis chun bás d'fháil. 'Óise, nár leige Dia a leithéid', arsa mise. Ar maidin do bhíos ag obair agus dúirt muintir an tí liom nuair a tháinig mé isteach go raibh Joe tar éis bháis ó aréir. [There was a man beyond in Clashmore, Joe Condon was his name, and he and I were digging potatoes together. This day when he arrived he had a tormented appearance. I asked him what was troubling him and he told me that he heard the *badhb* and that some-

10. Legend: Who is going to die?

one belonging to him was going to die, 'Oh, may God forbid,' said I. In the morning I was working and the people of the house told me when I came in that Joe was dead since last night] (Waterford 13).

One day when Mr. Duggan was a young boy, himself and another man were coming up the banks. They heard a *bean sí*. The man with him said that somebody was going to die. The next morning the man went to the wood for sticks. Another man was cutting a tree. He told him to keep out of the way. Just as he was nearly clear of the tree it fell on top of him and killed him. So the *bean sí* had cried for himself (Sligo 4).

This legend has never appeared in print, nor is it referred to in any scholarly or popular treatment of the banshee. Five further versions (Cavan 5 (S); Cork 27 (S); Limerick 21 (S); Meath 18 (S); Offaly 6 (S)) have, however, come to light in the archival sources. The reason why the versions appear in Schools' Manuscripts may be that the grim humour has had a particular appeal for school children. The curiously scattered distribution of the legend (Map 10) could be interpreted as indicating a spread from the south, perhaps from Waterford, northwards. It is also quite likely that the legend is of fairly recent origin. It may not be as rare as the figure given above would suggest. It should be noted that no mention is made of it in the Banshee Questionnaire. – indeed its very existence had not been observed when the questionnaire was drafted.

IV

There are then few exceptions to the rule that the supernatural manifestations occur before somebody expires and that they normally take place before the passing away of people who were known to be at death's door. In a few records, however, it is stated that the appearance of the being was thought to forebode somebody's death though it was not heard later that somebody in particular had expired. No doubt such instances were more common than the available source material shows: a story to this effect is lacking in dramatic interest and an experiencer might not even tell it to others or, if he did, few would report it further. Only instances lending themselves to substantiation of the general belief would be given wider circulation. In view of this it is easy to understand that even manifestations which were not followed by a death in the family or in the immediate neighbourhood would not seriously shake the belief. It could be said that the death-messenger had been on her way to cry for somebody in a distant place.

> I remember my parents going out to the yard to listen to her . . . Always my father used to say 'I wonder who it is tonight? The talk of the shop next morning was, 'did you hear her last night?, she was going the hills; she was so far away it must be someone in Tullagher' (Kilkenny 15).

Similar explanations of apparently 'meaningless' manifestations are given in two other records (Cavan 1.9; Kerry 33). Again one may assume that these were more common than the available source material indicates. Even manifestations then which at first glance would appear to have no function are thus neatly slotted into the general tradition category – the being has appeared before somebody's death.

V

Since deaths constitute the main manifestation occasions, and since people die all year round, it is natural that traditions concerning especially frequent appearances at Christmas, New Year, May Day, Hallowe'en and other red letter occasions, which are dominant in the beliefs and stories attached to many other supernatural beings, are conspicuously absent from the death-messenger complex. Moreover it has not been possible to establish any correlation between the frequency of the manifestations and any particular season of the year. One might have expected that the old folk-belief – that most people, particularly old people, die in the winter or early spring – should be reflected in the material, especially as this belief is rational.[3] Many of the records do not state clearly at what time of the year the manifestations are supposed to have occurred. It is thus not out of the question that the kind of correlation indicated could be spotted if the corpus of material were larger and more detailed.

Likewise people die at all times of the day and night and one

would have thought it impossible to discern any fixed pattern
as to the time of the manifestations during the twenty-four
hours. This is not so. Certain specified times stand out prominently in the material. True enough, as much as 50 per cent
of the records do not give any indication as to when the supernatural phenomena occurred, but it is no coincidence that in as
little as 2 per cent of the material is it stated that they occurred
during day-time.[4] A night setting occurs in 41 per cent of the
sources,[5] late evening or dusk is referred to in 5 per cent of
them,[6] and early morning (when it is likely to have been dark
or beginning to dawn) in 2 per cent.[7] There is thus a clear
preponderance of the dark and grey hours. There are reasons,
rather than one single reason, for this. The idea is probably
rational that illnesses are aggravated at night[8] and that deaths
occur more frequently at night and in the early morning than at
other times. This is probably part of the explanation, but hardly
more than a small part. Surely of more significance is the idea
that night and darkness belong to supernatural beings, especially
those associated with death. One may cite the many stories
about people out late at night who have been confronted by a
ghost or fairy admonishing them with *Bíodh an lá agatsa agus
an oíche againne* ('You have the day and let us have the night'),
or some such saying.[9] It is in keeping with this that the solemn
midnight hour, *am mharbh na hoíche*, so favoured also by
ghosts, is specified as the exact time for the death-messenger's
appearance in 4 per cent of the relevant material (Appendix 3.5,
(b), p. 307). The following is an example:

> She (the banshee) would be heard at twelve o'clock, the
> night before the person would die (Meath 8).

The records which state that manifestations took place at
dusk, twilight or *clapsholas* are typified by the following
example:

> Thuit seo amach i mí Lúnasa 1913 . . . agus an t-am idir
> an dá sholas sa tráthnóna [This happened in August 1913
> . . . and the time was between the two lights in the evening]
> (Waterford 38).

These together with those stating or indicating that they took
place at dawn conform with a popular belief that these hours
belonged to the supernatural since they were border-hours,

neither day nor night. When something unusual was seen or heard or both at such a time it would be a strong indication that it could not have a natural explanation and if somebody was actually known to be ill the death-messenger would immediately spring to people's minds.

One must also take into account that strange sounds and peculiar shapes lending themselves to supernatural interpretations would be experienced more frequently during the dark and grey hours than in clear daylight. And we see that the predominant idea that the death-messenger appeared late in the evening, at night, or in the early morning would not preclude her foreboding deaths occurring during daytime. Since she is generally believed to manifest herself before deaths, the tradition has an in-built flexibility. Many days or weeks could not be allowed to elapse between the foreboding manifestations and the ensuing deaths, this would cast doubt upon the reality of the phenomena and hold the belief up to ridicule. That something happening the following day should be foreboded the previous evening or night would be, on the other hand, fully in keeping with the code of the supernatural.

VI

Through the very terms themselves — banshee, *badhb*, and similar — by which she is known, the death-messenger advertises herself as an Irish being. It is no wonder then that the overwhelming majority of manifestations occur in Ireland. The exceptions to this rule, though not many, are of special interest. Manifestations abroad fall into two groups — those which occur on the occasion of local deaths and those which occur on the occasion of deaths in Ireland, in the old homeland.

All emigrants carry with them some of their old traditions. A number of these traditions may live on for a long time; others quickly disintegrate or disappear due to changed conditions of life and the acceptance of new traditions prevalent among other and larger population groups in the new country. As a rule, supernatural traditions do not fare well in new surroundings. Yet it is not surprising that traces of the death-messenger belief are found in countries such as the USA and Canada where there are large Irish communities. One can say little about these traces because not only are they faint but collecting them has been on a very modest scale. A story about a manifestation abroad related to a death there would stand only a faint chance of being reported to Ireland. Such material must be collected mainly where the manifestations occurred. Some efforts have been made to assemble sources abroad,[10] especially in the USA (Appendix 5.2, p. 362) but it has not been possible to cover this aspect as well as the Irish scene.

Four American sources (USA 1, 3, 4, 6) deal with a manifestation there on the occasion of a local death. Two records from Ireland (Kerry 29; Laois 7) are also considered in this context because they refer to manifestations in North America on the occasion of deaths there. Unless these particular traditons were invented in Ireland, which seems unlikely, they would have been carried back home over the Atlantic. It is worthy of note that four of the six records (USA 1, 3, 6; Laois 7) state that the whole family of the person whose death was foreboded had moved to the USA. Such a mass emigration would have provided a good growing ground for the belief and good conditions for transmission when a story had taken shape. It also signifies that the need to employ the death-messenger as a vehicle for communication with Ireland would not have been felt. It may also be mentioned that the experiencer in a further record (Kerry 29), which deals with a manifestation and a death in Canada, is said to have been from the same parish in Ireland as the man whose death was foreboded.

One might suppose that traditions of the death-messenger proclaiming deaths occurring in Ireland to relatives and friends in other countries would also mainly be found abroad, in countries with large Irish communities. So far no such records collected abroad have come to light. There are four sources from Ireland, though, dealing with such manifestations, three from the archival records (Galway 56 (Q); Longford 29 (Q); Tyrone 4 (M), and one literary source, Yeats, 1892, p. 232). In all these a death in Ireland is proclaimed in the Americas. Here it seems likely that a phenomenon interpreted as the death-messenger (in retrospect once news from Ireland was received) was reported back to relatives in Ireland rather than that a story about a manifestation overseas was invented in Ireland. All manifestations of the death-messenger in the source material, with the few exceptions above, are supposed to have occurred in Ireland.

VII

Though probably more common than the available material indicates, traditions of manifestations abroad do not belong to the core of the banshee corpus. A richer material is at hand to support the view that the death-messenger is believed to appear in Ireland if an Irish person, at least one whose family she is wont to follow, dies abroad. Such manifestations, which are commonly said to take place in the old home parish or sometimes, more specifically, at the old family home, are referred to in thirty-six records from twenty-three counties (Appendix 3.6 (f and cf. d), pp. 310, 309). No doubt there would have been many more examples had collecting been more intensive half a century ago, or earlier, while a higher percentage of first generation Irish dwelt abroad. The high number of available records is also remarkable in view of the fact that no direct question about this aspect of the tradition was included in the Banshee Questionnaire.[11]

As might have been expected in view of the scope and significance of Irish emigration to the USA, most of the examples, 24 records in all, refer to manifestations in Ireland on the occasion of deaths there.[12] There is one record (Wexford 9) of a death in Canada, supernaturally announced in Ireland. There was also mass emigration to Britain[13] and many seasonal migrants from Connaught and Ulster worked in England and Scotland.[14] Two records (Down 11 and Tyrone 2), both of which refer to manifestations in Ireland on the occasion of deaths in Britain, should perhaps be viewed against this background. A death in Australia is announced at home (Cavan 1.1 and 24) and in one record (Westmeath 5) the death-messenger even carried her tidings from the West Indies to Ireland. It is not clear what brought these particular Irishmen to such exotic places but it is evident that service in the army and navy of the British Empire carried many Irishmen to distant countries in earlier times[15] and that their deaths abroad would provide a fertile ground for this type of tradition. The following was written by McAnally:

> From North America, the West Indies, Africa, Australia, India, China; from every point to which Irish regiments have followed the roll of the British drums, news of the

prospective shedding of Irish blood has been brought home, and the slaughter preceded by a Banshee wail outside the ancestral windows.[16]

Though exaggerated, this statement provides an essentially correct picture of the traditions as they were in the nineteenth century. Stories about manifestations so long ago have now almost faded away from folk memory. But the motif is certainly fairly old. In her *Memoirs of the Life and Writings of Mrs. Frances Sheridan*,[17] Alicia Lefanu refers to the banshee being heard at the Sheridan residence at Quilca, Co. Cavan on the occasion of the death abroad of Mrs. Frances Sheridan. The motif can indeed be traced back to the seventeenth century. In his elegy on the death in Flanders c. 1642 of Muiris Mac Gearailt mac Ridire Chiarraí, Piaras Feiritéir states that the death was proclaimed by Áine Chnoic Áine, whom we must consider as a kind of banshee (*Do bhí Áine Chnuic Áine dot fhógradh* . . . Áine of Knockainey was proclaiming you . . . (your death)).[18]

The traditions dealt with here show the supernatural being carrying her sinister message a long distance in a short time. This characteristic is also found in some, though not many, of the manifestations in Ireland on the occasion of deaths there. The belief is expressed in the following two records:

> Strange as it may seem if a person left the village and lived miles away . . . and let nothing be left but the track of the house, and when that person was dying, the banshee would come and cry where that person was born (Roscommon 2 (Q)).

> It is also said that whether the person would die near the place or not the cry would be heard near the old home (Galway 23 (S)).

Seven further records (Kerry 2, 26; Leitrim 5, 10, 15; Longford 33; Monaghan 8) deal with manifestations in the home parish on occasions of deaths in far away parts of Ireland. In three of these sources (Leitrim 5, 10, 15) the being appears before the death takes place; in the others, however, it is not clear whether the manifestation takes place before death or at the moment of death.

VIII

The great majority of the manifestations, amounting to 62 per cent, have two factors in common: they occur where the dying man is and he is in his own home parish.[19] One of the main reasons for the preponderance of this type of manifestation is that most Irishmen — in spite of emigration and seasonal work outside their parish boundaries — actually died at home. Another reason, already touched upon, is that manifestations in other parts of Ireland or abroad on occasions of deaths there may not have been properly recorded. There are other aspects to these manifestations which cannot be fully understood solely from the point of view of where the dying man is. Before dealing with these, which necessitate taking into account the totality of the experiencers and their situation, one must consider a number of specialised locations favoured by the death-messenger.

Nature is a powerful moulder of the ideas people have of the appearance and behaviour of supernatural beings. Certain beings are associated with specific habitats, such as woods, lakes, rivers or the air. More specifically, many an unusual nature formation, for example a hollow tree or a cave, is imagined to be the favourite haunt or the dwelling-place of a supernatural being or supernatural beings of one kind or another.[20] Prominent and strangely-shaped rocks and hills can stir people's imagination. It is often believed that they are frequented by fairies or other such beings. Since a cry or call emanating from such a place would be heard far away these locations are occasionally associated with the supernatural death-messenger.

Such rocks are *Creagán na gCat* in Clare and 'Hilly Holly' in Wexford town:

Tá cnoc i gCúil Mín ar a dtugtar 'Creagán na gCat'. Seo mar do ainmníodh é. Bhí bhean sí riamh ag muintir Uí Loinsigh sa chuid seo den Chlár agus nuair a bhíodh duine acu marbh do dheineadh sí a dreas caointe i gcónaí ar an gcnoc seo. Do dheineadh sí an caoineadh díreach mar a bheadh cait ag gol is ag béicigh. Uime sin tugadh 'Creagán na gCat' ar an gcnoc. [There is a hill in Coolmeen called *Creagán na gCat*. This is how it was named. The Lynches in this part of Clare always had a banshee and when one of them was dead she always keened on this hill. She keened just like cats would be crying. Because of that the hill was called *Creagán na gCat* ¦ (Clare 7).

The manifestation known in most Irish areas as the 'Banshee' is known in Wexford town and rural hinterland as 'The Bow'. (To rhyme with *bough*, of a tree). In my lifetime it has been associated with the southern portion of the town limits i.e. Bride Street parish and has been heard, and only heard, specifically emanating from the townlands of Whiterock, Whitemill and Mulgannon. To be more specific, its sound has been associated with an area in Mulgannon known alternatively as 'The Rocks' — and/or Hilly Holly at the back of Cromwell's Fort . . . I specifically want to draw attention to the location of the manifestations. The Horse River, the Trespan Rock, and Bernadette Place are all in close proximity to the Bow infested location I have mentioned (Wexford 38).[21]

In some instances such rocks are chair-shaped[22] and this invites the idea that the supernatural beings are wont to sit on them. Rocks of this kind, associated with the death-messenger, are *Carraig na Baidhbe* in Ballynaguilkee and 'The Banshee's Chair' in Modeligo, Waterford, 'The Banshee's Chair', Corby Rock Mill in Monaghan and 'The Bow Stone' in Patrickswell, Carlow:

> I gceantar Bhaile na Giolcaí Iochtarach, ar bhóthar na habhann idir Sráid an Mhuilinn agus Muileann an Choirce agus ag cor an bhóthair, tá dhá charraig mhóra de chloch aoil, ceann acu ina suí ar an gceann eile agus iad i bhfoirm cathaoireach. Tá an suíomh ar ard ós cionn an bhóthair. Deirtí go bhfeictí an bhadhbh i bhfoirm mná bhreá dhathúil, gruaig fhada de dhath an óir síos go sála uirthi, í ina suí ar an gcathaoir seo agus í ag cíoradh a cinn. Sin é scéal sean-dhreama na háite atá anois ar an tsíoraíocht leis na cianta. D'airínn m'athair is mo mháthair ag caint ar seo go minic. [In the townland of Ballynaguilkee Lower, on the river road between *Sráid an Mhuilinn* and *Muileann an Choirce*, at the turn of the road, there are two large limestone rocks, one of them sitting on top of the other, and in the shape of a chair. The situation is on a height above the road. It is said that the *badhbh* used to be seen in the form of a fine handsome woman, with long golden hair

down to the soles of her feet, and she sitting on this chair and she combing her hair. That was the story of the old stock of the place who are long since in eternity. I used to hear my mother and father often talking about this] (Waterford 36).

In the parish of Modeligo, and townland of Mountain Castle, in the County of Waterford, so late as the beginning of the present century, a Badhbh, Bo Chaointe, or Bean Sighe, was in the habit of appearing just before the death of any member of the old Milesian families resident in the parish. Her chair, which was made of rough stone, was placed on an elevation over the river Finnisk on the lands of a small farmer named Brown, and opposite the lands of Mr. Edmund O'Daly, of Farnane, on the other side of the river — and, unless it has been removed very lately, the Bean Sighe's chair is still to be seen there. There are hundreds of people still living who have heard her mournful wails ... (O'Kearney, 1855, pp. 109-10 (= Waterford 34).

In a rock at the Corby Rock Mill there is a square seat carved in the rock and before anyone dies in the neighbourhood a banshee sits on the stone and cries. This stone is called 'The Banshee's Chair' (Monaghan 7).

In the adjoining field about 100 yards from the well, there is a similar wedge-shaped stone, which is called the 'Bow Stone'. The local name for the 'Banshee' is the 'Bow', (*Ir. Badhbh*) and Mr. Timmin often heard the old people say that the 'Banshee', or 'Bow', always sat and cried on this stone when any member of the family which lived in Patrickswell House in ancient times was about to die (Carlow 15).

Apart from rocks, the death-messenger is also associated with a lane, known as The Black Cow, in Wexford Town:

The tradition of the Bow is not confined to rural areas. I clearly remember the tradition in Wexford town that the bow used to be seen and heard in an old lane or cul-de-sac ... in Bride Street Parish ... known as 'The Black Cow' (Wexford 38).

Finally, an area in Co. Clare is associated with the banshee:

11. Associated with water
(References to association of the death-messenger with
water in legends not included.)

The banshee . . . appears sitting on a rock in an area called the 'Bottles' (Clare 19).[23]

No specific questions were asked in the Banshee Questionnaire about the death-messenger manifestations at rocks or similar nature formations or at any particular locations. It may then be that such manifestations were more common than the material to hand indicates. But one can be quite sure that specific associations with localities of this kind have never been prominent in the tradition.

Though the death-messenger is never thought of as a water being, she is more commonly imagined to appear close to water, at lakes, rivers or wells. The corpus examined contains 70 belief statements and memorates in which the death-messenger is associated with water[24] (Map 11). Of these, 22[25] stem from replies to question 15 in the Banshee Questionnaire,[26] in which it was asked whether the banshee was 'associated with particular streams, lakes, ponds . . . or the like'. Perhaps the word 'particular' ought not to have been included in the question. Some correspondents, familiar with traditions generally connecting the death-messenger and water, may not have answered the question simply because they had not heard of any specific body of water at which the being was wont to appear. Notwithstanding this a number of water formations at which manifestations are said to have occurred are mentioned in the questionnaire replies and in the earlier English sources. Lakes include Lough Allen (Leitrim, 8, 10),[27] Caherglassaun Lake (Galway 40),[28] Cloggagh Lough (Cavan 11),[29] Lough Derg (Tipperary 31),[30] Lough Gowna (Longford 7),[31] Lough Hackett (Galway 22),[32] Lough Macnean Upper (Fermanagh 1),[33] and Teevurcher Lough (Cavan 15).[34] The named rivers are the Barrow (Kilkenny 15),[35] the Boyne (Meath 24),[36] the Daelagh (Clare 15),[37] the Horse (Wexford 38)[38] the Millburn (Antrim 13),[39] the Multeen (Tipperary 11)[40] and the Shannon (Tipperary 31).[41] Two wells — St. Patrick's Well (Carlow 15) and *Tobar na Baidhbe* (Waterford 9) — are also among the named manifestation places.

References to manifestations close to water are found in all the provinces but they are more numerous in Leinster (25 records) and in Connaught (19 records, 9 of which stem from Galway). In Munster the trait is prominent in Clare and in the east of the province, in Tipperary and Waterford, only; there are no record of it in Cork, Limerick has only one example and Kerry two. Eighteen records stem from the *badhbh*-area. It is noteworthy that all references to manifestations at wells come from this area (Carlow 15; Waterford 5, 6, 9; Wexford 13), and the place-name *Tobar na Baidhbe* indicates that the connection between the *badhb* and wells is of some age in these parts of the country.[42]

As a rule, the rivers, lakes and wells figuring in the material are said to be near the home of the person whose death is announced. No doubt the manifestations have often been localised at these water formations simply because they were prominent landmarks in the locality. Rivers and lakes often formed borders between parishes, townlands and farms. In some records (Antrim 13; Galway 8, 45; Kerry 2) it is specifically stated that the rivers and streams referred to were such boundaries. Liminal areas play an important role in folk tradition where they are regarded as the special property and the favourite haunts of supernatural beings.[43] In the description of aural manifestations the belief that the death-messenger's cry follows the course of streams and rivers has been noted. To some extent this belief is based on the fact that sound carries well over or along water. Once a sound heard in this fashion has been given a supernatural interpretation it is easy to conclude that the being from whom it emanates is positioned near to the water.

The appearance of the death-messenger at the side of a lake or a river must also be considered in connection with a special activity sometimes attributed to her — namely her washing. The washing activity in early Irish sources is ascribed to the goddess of war — Badb or Morrígan. In folk tradition the motif is apparently first noted in Matthew Archdeacon's *Legends of Connaught* (1839):

> Sometimes she (the banshee) be's seen at the sthrame beetlin' the windin' sheet . . .[44]

Further references to the death-messenger's washing are found in the folklore manuscripts throughout this century, from the nineteen thirties to the early nineteen seventies. These sources also refer mainly to Connaught, in particular to Galway. Question 15 in the Banshee Questionnaire also enquired about the washing. The nine replies received (Clare 37; Galway 56; Kilkenny 15; Longford 29; Louth 6; Roscommon 1, 16; Tipperary 44; Westmeath 4) contained little that was new but

• The Banshee
o Other Washerwomen

12. Supernatural washerwomen at streams, rivers and lakes

they signified that the motif was more widely distributed than the sources previously available had indicated. A further pointer to this was obtained through field work in Kildare (Kildare 13) in 1978. All in all, 19 belief statements and memorates relating to the death-messenger's washing have now come to light.[45] The motif is also found in certain legends, especially in The Shirt Legend[46] which will be treated later. While the direct connection between the banshee and foreboded death is absent or unclear in the legends, it is generally implied or expressed in the belief statements and memorates (see for example, Longford 29 and Louth 6). The exact nature of the connection between the washing and the foreboded death remains obscure in the majority of sources. There are three exceptions (Galway 56; Louth 6; Westmeath 4) in which it is indicated that a shroud or a winding sheet is being washed.

The present distribution of the beliefs in the washing death-messenger (Map 12) shows some interesting features. Galway and border regions of adjacent counties form the core area, but the belief is also occasionally attested as far east as Westmeath, Kildare, Kilkenny and Louth. One gets the general impression, however, that the belief is not only more common but also more concretely expressed in the core area. Legends in which the being occurs in the role of a washerwoman are also confined to the core area. The Shirt Legend, in which this role is found in all the versions, is exclusive to parts of Galway. It is possible that the legends, and The Shirt Legend in particular, have been instrumental in conserving and reinforcing the beliefs in the core area. It is also noteworthy that supernatural washerwomen of another type – not referred to as banshees and not particularly connected with death – are frequently met with in the folk tradition of Galway and Mayo (Map 12).[47] Traditions about such supernatural washerwomen also extend not only into Clare, but also into Kerry and Cork,[48] areas where traditions about a washing death-messenger are apparently absent. Since a belief in a death-messenger in the shape of a washerwoman could hardly be held unless it was reinforced by an association with water and by visual manifestations, it is not surprising that the being does not figure in that capacity in Cork and Kerry where she is, as noted earlier, never seen but only heard, and also where an association of the being with water is virtually non-existent. It is very difficult to understand why the washing motif is so poorly represented in the *badhbh*-area in the south-east, where there is one doubtful record only (Kilkenny 15), and where one might have expected to find more evidence of it because of the strong connections between the death-messenger and water there, and also because of the washerwoman role of the *Badb* in early Irish literature.

It is likely that the belief in the death-messenger appearing as a washerwoman was more prominent and more widespread in earlier times than it now is. It is reasonable to suppose that there is a close generic relationship between the washing death-messenger in Ireland and the Scottish-Gaelic supernatural washerwoman, the *bean-nighe*, who is also a foreboder of death.[49] Direct contacts between Galway and Scotland could possibly account for these similarities but it is more likely that the connections date from a time when a tradition channel extended from the east to the west. It is just possible to vaguely trace such a channel from the scattered easterly references on our distribution map.[50] The assumption that the Irish and Scottish-Gaelic washerwoman traditions are generically related would also involve the likelihood of venerable age for these traditions.

IX

The manifestations of the death-messenger as a washing woman, like the being's manifestations close to water in general, usually take place in the vicinity of a house, most often that of the person whose death is foreboded. The house is the manifestation *locus par préférence* in the death-messenger tradition.

Out of the 388 records[51] in which manifestations on occasions of death are localised, no less than 277 or 71 per cent are so situated (Appendix 3.6 (a-e), p. 308-9 and Map 13). Not surprisingly the majority of these 'house manifestations', 214 records,[52] take place at the house of the dying person. In the past the great majority of people, particularly old people, died at home rather than in hospitals or institutions for the aged.

The dying person's place of residence is the focusing point to such an extent that the death-messenger is sometimes directly stated to have manifested herself there, even though the death foreboded or proclaimed took place in a local hospital (Cork 1; Fermanagh 5; Galway 45; Laois 14, 17; Wexford 4; Tyrone 5,

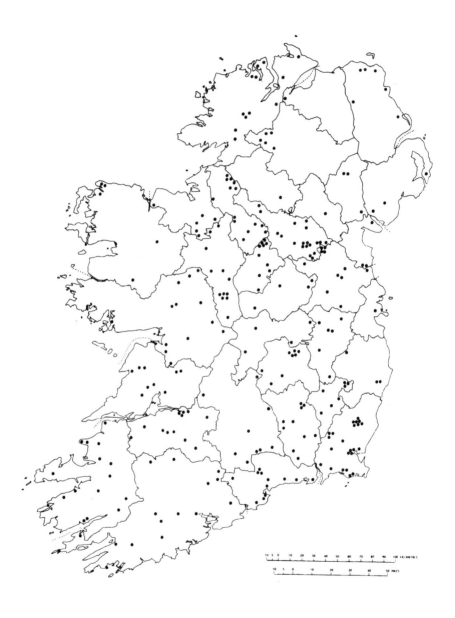

13. Manifestations at house

6). Manifestations at hospitals are referred to in only a few records
(e.g., Armagh 6; Limerick 16; Waterford 30; Wexford 21; Tyrone 6).

X

Many records not only state in general terms that the manifestations took place at a house, or in its vicinity, but also furnish
more specific details.

In discussing the death-messenger's dress it has been noted
that she is an outdoor being. In this respect she differs radically
from 'white ladies', *'weisse Frauen'* and other ghostly appearances
foreboding death in Britain, Scandinavia and on the continent.[53]
These are often seen *in* castles, manor-houses, etc. Only one
solitary — and certainly atypical — literary source, McClintock,[54]
refers to a banshee inside a house; in genuine folk tradition the
death-messenger's cry is never heard emanating from the inside
of a building, nor is she seen indoors.

Specific manifestation *loci* outside the house occasionally
referred to in the material are 'the garden' (Cavan 9; Tipperary
2, 18), 'the orchard' (Meath 7), 'at the turf stack' (Cavan 23)
'at a stile' (Clare 24), 'at the end of a bohereen' (Waterford
32). Some of these places are prominent and likely to attract
attention at night; some are high places from which sound
would carry well. Many have the characteristic that vision would
be blocked or hampered to some extent so that anything
appearing and disappearing from them would invite interpretation along supernatural lines.

More commonly mentioned than the garden or parts of it,
are the openings or entrances to the house. Somewhat surprisingly
the chimney is referred to only twice in the material (Cavan 1.22
(p. 452); Cork 8). The door is mentioned five times (Cavan
1.41 (pp. 470, 472), 26; Galway 56; Tyrone 6). The window is
specified as the place of the manifestation on no less than 57
occasions in the archival records (21 per cent of the 'house
manifestations'). 'Window manifestations' are particularly prominent in Leinster (28 records, out of which 7 stem from
Wexford) and in Ulster (15 records out of which 7 stem from
Cavan (Appendix 3.6 (g), p. 310 and Map 14). The window also
figures frequently in The Comb Legend. In literary sources
manifestations at the window are seldom referred to, apart from,

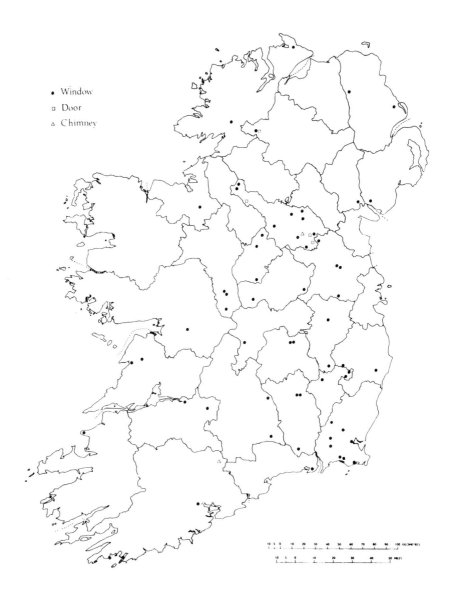

14. Manifestations at openings and entrances of the house

for example, works by Edgeworth, Croker, Keegan and McAnally.[55]

A special feature of some of the 'window manifestations' is that the being is said to sit on or under the window-sill — *leac na fuinneoige*. The appearance *on* the window-sill is referred to in 8 records (Antrim 6; Cavan 1.43 (p. 465), 9, 16, 19: Westmeath 11; Wexford 19, 33), while manifestations *under* it are referred to only twice (Longford 31; Wexford 6). The trait is rather thinly and unevenly distributed in Leinster and Ulster and it may be an innovation. The type of window-sills the informants had in mind are probably those consisting of large stone slabs. These would offer good seats and it would also be possible to hide under them.

Doubtless there are a number of reasons why the window came to occupy a prominent place as a manifestation *locus*. Sounds localised outside the house could be investigated through the window and, if no natural agent from whom it might have emanated could be seen, a supernatural interpretation was close to hand. If something was seen the overwrought and often tired attendants of the dying person would readily attribute the traditional shape and behaviour to whatever might have been suddenly appearing and disappearing. The following example well illustrates one way in which such interpretations were made:

> One night the *bean sí* went to a house in Sleevemeel (Slievemweel in the *Townland Index*) where there was an old woman sick. The night before the woman died the *bean sí* cried outside the window and when the people looked out they saw her combing her hair . . . (Carlow 13).

Here something was heard and even at that stage the cry was identified as that of a banshee; then attention was drawn to-wards the window and something was seen which was not only given the shape of the being but also endowed with a behaviour typical of it.

XI

Several factors clearly emerge then, from consideration of the time and place of the manifestations.

The death-messenger is, in the whole area of the tradition and in the vast majority of the sources, believed to manifest herself before a death takes place. Manifestations simultaneous with, or subsequent to, deaths are exceptional, the former all relate to appearances in places far away from the locality in which the announced death takes place.

The time period between the manifestations and the deaths foreboded varies but is almost always between a few minutes or hours and two or three days. A longer interval would after all cast doubts on the genuineness of the connection between the 'foreboding' and the foreboded.

It is not possible to identify in the archival material any special preference on the part of the death-messenger for particular days or seasons.

There is a marked correlation, however, between the manifestations and the dark or grey hours. Midnight, dusk and dawn are especially favoured. These hours are regarded as the special property of Otherworld beings; light and sound conditions at these times also favour supernatural interpretations of phenomena to which a natural explanation would have been attributed if they occurred in the day-time.

Though we occasionally hear of manifestations in foreign countries on the occasion of deaths of Irish people there or in the old country, and also of manifestations in Ireland on the occasion of deaths of Irish people abroad, the overwhelming majority of the records deal with manifestations in Ireland relating to deaths there. It is also clearly evident that all but a very few manifestations occur in the home parish of those destined to die.

The vast majority of the manifestations take place in the vicinity of a house, ordinarily the house where the dying person dwells. In genuine records there is no exception to the rule that the manifestations occur outdoors. The garden, or some prominent feature in it, is mentioned but the place especially favoured is 'outside the window'. Sometimes it is stated in particular that the being sits on, or under the window-sill.

Certain specific locations such as prominent and strangely-shaped rocks and hills are sometimes favoured by the death-messenger. More commonly, she appears at the side of a river, lake or well. In an area consisting mainly of Galway and border regions of adjoining counties the being appears as a washer-woman. This appears to be an old trait and very likely it is connected with the Scottish-Gaelic traditions of the *bean-nighe*.

The common features of many of the manifestation places are that they are high and prominent and that sound would carry well from them. Often they are situated in such a way that whatever may be noticed there might quickly and easily disappear under or behind something.

Clearly a fuller understanding of the manifestations at the above-mentioned times and places requires a careful analysis of the most important factor in the drama of manifestation, namely the human experiencers involved. Such an analysis must be the next stage of enquiry into the death-messenger tradition.

7

The Experiencers

I

The belief in death forebodings and death omens may be regarded as an attempt to compensate for a deeply-felt limitation in human knowledge – the hour of death, our own and that of those with whom we are concerned, is uncertain. Supernatural agents serve to inform people that they themselves will soon be called away or they prepare people for the imminent departure of those whose deaths will in some way or another affect them. One and the same omen or foreboding may fulfil both these purposes. Sometimes a supernatural phenomenon is experienced simultaneously by the person whose death is foreboded and by people around him. Though a person may have had a supernatural foreboding of his own death and kept the matter secret he is more likely to communicate his experience to others. Unless he tells at least one person there will be no tradition to pass on. A person may be told (or in other ways understand) that others have had forebodings about his death, though he himself has not experienced anything out of the ordinary, or he may have experienced something strange but not understood that it foreboded death until the interpretation was provided by somebody present. Not only then must one take into account the experiencers of the death forebodings but also those who are able to react to, and act upon, the foreknowledge obtained by being informed about the experience.

The emphasis on which different groups of people experience, or are informed, of the supernatural forebodings may vary in different countries and cultures. Such differing emphasis arises from the prominent social and religious values and attitudes towards death in the respective cultures. Where it is considered especially important to be prepared for one's own death more of the death omens are likely to be experienced by the dying themselves. The survivors will more often be the experiencers in surroundings where much stress is placed upon the proper attention to the dying and the dead. These important and complicated aspects of supernatural experiences cannot be studied without a wide comparative background. Such an investigation falls outside the scope of this work although the material presented here may hopefully prove of value to research in this field. Also the different categories of experiencers appear to reflect different types and characters of the omens and forebodings. Death omens involving malfunctions of the body such as itching, sneezing etc., are among those which are almost exclusively experienced by the dying themselves.[1] Here, too, detailed investigations are necessary before much can be said by way of generalisations. The present task is limited to the modest objective of determining, on the basis of the available source material, whether the banshee and other Irish supernatural death-messengers of her kind appear primarily for the benefit of the dying or of the survivors.

One must begin with a survey of the tradition in which the death-messenger is said to have manifested herself to those who are about to depart.

II

Reference has been made earlier to the legend about a man who saw or heard the death-messenger and drew the conclusion that somebody in the neighbourhood would die. It soon turned out it was his own death that was foreboded. Though the man who is going to die is himself the experiencer of the foreboding here the whole point of the legend is that the message was misunderstood. In this instance no message on which anybody could act before the death has taken place has been communicated. The legend, as already pointed out, is fairly rare: it has a limited distribution and perhaps a rather late origin and it does not reflect a common belief. One need say no more about it at present.

III

Traditions to the effect that the person destined to die receives and correctly interprets a message from the banshee or *badhb* are rare. From the older source material in English there appears to be one instance only, namely Thornbury[2] where one encounters the following statement:

> Well a banshee was heard the night my mother died . . .
> when my poor mother and she in her death-struggles
> heard the terrible wail that she knew was not human and
> she down in her fever, and she says to my father, says she
> 'Denis, I must go', and sure enough she died that week.

The provenance of this tradition is probably Connemara, Co. Galway. Eight further examples are found in the folklore manuscripts.[3] Their distribution is illustrated on Map 15. All these examples follow a similar pattern. They occur in memorates and it is stated or implied that the dying man communicates his experience to someone present or nearby, in most cases a near relation. The following example may be regarded as typical:

> There was a fellow called Con Kelly living in Virginia
> and the banshee cried for the whole family. Con got sick
> and he was lying in a room at the back of the house. One
> night it cried out on the window-sill. He heard it and called
> his sister and he told her that he was going to die. He died
> between five and six o'clock in the morning. (Cavan 1.4
> (pp. 421-2)).

In one instance (Leitrim 7) it is clearly stated that bystanders as well as the dying person heard the cry, but that it was the latter who identified it as the death-messenger's call:

> One night there was a woman dying in a house below
> Dromahaire. At two o'clock a pitiful cry was heard outside.
> Some of the people who were staying in the house did not
> know what it was, but the dying woman heard it too. She
> told them not to be alarmed, that it was the banshee.

Statements to the effect that the death-messenger cannot be seen or heard by those destined to die are more numerous and derived from all over Ireland. The following are examples:

> The person who is going to die never hears the *bean sí*
> (Galway 39).

> It is in my head that the person dying cannot hear it
> (Cork 1).

15. Dying person experiences death-messenger

> I never heard of the banshee appearing or crying to the person who was dying; it was always someone else who heard her (Longford 21).

> She was heard by relatives of people about to die rather than by the individuals themselves (Armagh 8).[4]

A statement of this fairly prominent feature in pre-twentieth-century sources is noted in McAnally,[5] but it is widely implied in nineteenth-century literary accounts in English, which serves to indicate that it is not a late trait.

As well as in belief statements, the idea that the dying person cannot see or hear the death-messenger is expressed in memorates and also in legends such as the following:

> There was a family living in Killeeney (Killeeny in the *Townland Index*) called Caseys and the *bean sí* was said to cry after every person of that family. One evening they were all weeding in a bog near a big hole called the 'Poll Rua' and the *bean sí* began to cry and walk around the bog and they all heard her but one of the girls, and they wondered why she could not hear her. But that evening she was washing her hands at the 'Poll Rua' when she fell in and was drowned. It is said that the person that the *bean sí* is crying for can never hear her (Longford 25).

The idea that hearing the death-messenger guarantees your own safety is also found in belief statements:

> If you hear the banshee then you are not the person who is going to die; if you were, you would not hear her (Wexford 53).

These widely distributed direct statements that the death-messenger is not seen or heard by those about to pass away are supported by negative evidence; only rarely, and in exceptional cases, is there anything to the contrary. The evidence then supports the hypothesis that death-messenger traditions are directed towards the survivors rather than the dying. The limitation of the motif 'I am going to die' to two relatively small areas — Waterford/south-Kilkenny and Cavan/Leitrim/Roscommon — as well as its scarcity in the large corpus covered show that it has never been especially prominent and that it does not form part of the collective tradition.

IV

The relative prominence of the trait that the dying do not themselves experience the death-messenger's manifestations may be partly due to the human expectancy about super-natural phenomena. The death-messenger is firmly believed to appear before deaths – especially in certain families. Family members and members of the community are not only sub-consciously inclined, but consciously determined, to hear or see something which may be interpreted as an apparition, when-ever somebody is known to be seriously ill or dying. A dying man may of course share these beliefs, but could be too ill to notice anything or to communicate his experience to others. Also the dying person is a single individual, those who know of his condition are, as a rule, many. It is no surprise then that many more experiencers should be found among the survivors than among the dying.

The idea that the dying do not see or hear the death-messenger may be based on the assumption that foreknowledge is useless or even harmful, especially if his state is such that he cannot act upon the foreknowledge.

V

Most death-messenger manifestations occur when it is known that a person is ill or dying (Appendix 3.4.3 (a), p. 305-6). The experiencers therefore fall mainly into two categories, relations of the dying person (often resident or staying in the house in which death is about to occur) and neighbours and friends (often present at the deathbed or at least living nearby). Given the strong family connections of the death-messenger one might expect that the former group would be the larger. This is not the case. Only in 93 records, or 17 per cent of the relevant material, is it clearly indicated that the experiencers, or some of them, were relatives of the person whose death was fore-boded (Appendix 3.7 (a), p. 311). The following is one of the statements substantiating this belief:

Bíonn an bhean chaointe ag rith le treibheanna agus dá mhothaíodh duine den treibh sin í ag caoineadh, bhíodh

siad cinnte go mbíodh an bás i ndán do dhuine den treibh
sin gan mhoill. [The *bean chaointe* runs with certain
families and if any member of that family heard her keening they were certain that death was in store for some
member of the family without delay] (Mayo 7).

Direct statements expressing the belief that *only* members of
the dying person's family can hear the death-messenger are
rare and atypical (Cork 17 (S); Donegal 27 (Q)). Statements to
the opposite effect are also rare. The following is an example:

The people in the house in which the death was to occur
might not hear her but other people would; the neighbours
would hear her (Cavan 1.21, p. 444).[6]

Very occasionally also it is said that both neighbours and
relatives might hear the death-messenger, but that the nearest
relatives, or at least those present at the death-bed, are excluded:

The lonely cry is not heard by the members of the household but by neighbours and relatives (Laois 5).[7]

The common opinion in most parts of Ireland has undoubtedly
been that both relatives and neighbours of the dying man may
experience the death-messenger but the latter everywhere figure
more prominently than the former.[8]

VI

There may be many reasons why the death-messenger is more
commonly experienced by neighbours and friends of the dying
person than by his closest relatives. To discover what some of
these may be one must discover what functions the death-
messenger's appearance fulfills. A death situation is always
fraught with fears and anxieties: people's conscious and sub-
conscious wishes are likely to create conflict and stress. Logical
reasoning and logical behaviour are not what one would expect.
Feelings and desires conflict and all of this has an influence on
the traditions about the supernatural death-messenger.

The question whether or not recovery is possible would be
uppermost in the minds of those present where someone is
lying severely ill. In traditional Irish society those present would

be mainly the closest relatives. Since they held the belief that the death-messenger manifestation meant death was inevitable they could not but watch out for such signs. Though they might expect them they would often fear them and be reluctant to accept or verbalise the experiences which they might imagine themselves to have had. People not so close to the ailing person if present might then very naturally be the experiencers of the manifestations. Thus the family members at the death-bed would not suffer direct exposure to the supernatural death-message. The fact that non-relatives experience the death-messenger directly more frequently than relatives[9] may in this way be regarded as a kind of concern on the part of the tradition for the feelings of those most closely involved.

Yet even in the not infrequent instances where the relatives are the direct experiencers the shock following upon the super-natural message may often bring relief, especially if the sufferings of the ailing person have been difficult and prolonged. Intolerable uncertainty has been replaced by certainty. It is accepted that death will occur. Nothing more can be done for the dying. The strenuous efforts to keep him alive will cease, thoughts of guilt caused by things neglected, or imagined so, will vanish. Responsi-bility for the dying and his death is removed from the bystanders. Their concern will now be for his wake, his burial and his memory. This acceptance for a period before the death takes place will enable those present to face the actual passing away in a calmer frame of mind. Once death has occurred they will be less likely to be panic-stricken and left in a state of inactivity. Thanks to the foreboding the survivors are better prepared to fulfil the obligations and perform the duties required by the new situation. A death-foreboding conveyed by a banshee or *badhb* can thus be of great psychological benefit to those who attend a death-bed.

Yet foreknowledge is often not as marked a need for those present at a death-bed as for those who are not there. The former would see death as imminent without the need of any-thing miraculous. Sayings such as *Ní bheidh sé i bhfad eile ann anois* ('he won't live long more now') — so common in such situations – will to some extent fulfil the same function of psychological preparation for the inevitable as a supernatural foreboding.

The need for information is greater for neighbours and absent relatives. Even having heard that somebody they know and care for is ill they cannot judge the seriousness of the situation. Thanks to manifestations of the death-messenger they may be induced to go and see the dying person and give much-needed help and assistance to families in distress. Thus a record from Kerry tells that neighbours gathered from all over the townland and even from other parts of the parish to ensure that the hay was saved before a person whose death had been foreboded by a banshee had passed away (Kerry 13). Even old disagreements which had pestered neighbourly relations were set aside thanks to the forewarning of the death-messenger, as the following account declares:

> A woman who was not on friendly terms with a sick man heard the banshee on her way to town. On her way home she went into the man's home and told the people that he was going to die because she had heard the banshee. She had not been on friendly terms with the man, but she went in and made friends with him. He died later (Cavan 28).

The most important reason, however, for neighbours knowing about an impending death was not that they should be given time to visit the dying before death but rather that they should arrive at his home as soon as possible after he had passed away. The death-messenger belief mirrors the prevailing attitude towards death in Irish traditional society: death is not as much a private as a communal affair. The presence of many people at wakes and funerals reflected high honour upon the dead and his family, and the sooner the neighbours were informed the greater the chances that crowds would gather to pay their respects. The core of the death-messenger traditions can be seen as part of the large body of folk traditions which reflects man's wish to achieve the impossible. In a critical situation, such as on the occasion of a death, there was need of a messenger who could spread the news speedily and folk imagination serviced the need by creating a being who could communicate the message even before the event had taken place.

The underlying reason for the period of waiting between the manifestation of the death-messenger and the death itself does appear to be a wish to attract people to the wake and funeral. This is reinforced by the fact that manifestations experienced by relatives and friends abroad, or at home in Ireland on the occurrence of a death abroad, or in far away parts of Ireland — relatives and friends who would be unable to attend the wake and funeral — often lack such a period between manifestations and deaths.

Yet another reason why neighbours are more numerous than relatives as experiencers of the death-messenger may have to do with the idea that the being follows old Irish families. The appearance of the banshee or *badhb* at a death would be a matter of pride for the family. Since self-praise is frowned upon it may have been more important to the status and fame of the dead that the community at large rather than the family should have been made directly aware of the death-messenger's presence.[10] This may sometimes have facilitated the passing on of traditions about neighbours more frequently experiencing manifestations than about family members experiencing them, even within the family of the deceased. Knowledge of the channels through which the traditions have passed is not such that this theory can be put to the test.

Very likely the manifestation of a death-messenger contributed to making a death memorable and topical. Thanks to such supernatural intervention the relatives and the community at large would have opportunities of directing conversation to the deceased while the experience was fresh at the wake and funeral, and for a considerable period following. No doubt praise of the dead person which increased his own and his family's honour and reputation would have been considered appropriate on such occasions.[11]

VII

In summary an analysis of the various experiencers of the death-messenger manifestations has shown that the tradition is primarily centered upon those who survive and their concerns and needs. Only to a lesser extent, and mainly in legends and belief statements of limited distribution, are the death forebodings experienced by those destined to depart.

The majority of the manifestations are experienced in the vicinity of the person destined to die either by relations, who would frequently be present at the death bed, or by neighbours. The latter group figures more prominently in tradition than the former.

Very likely the preponderance of neighbours as experiencers is due to the emphasis on death as a communal concern in Irish society. It was regarded as obligatory to inform the neighbours as soon as possible after a death had occurred and their presence in large numbers at the wake and funeral conveyed status upon the dead and the bereaved family. The supernatural death-messenger would ensure that the news was spread with the utmost speed even before a death had occurred.

Foreknowledge could benefit relations of the dying person whether their experience of the supernatural manifestation was direct or indirect. Thanks to the knowledge that a foreboding had been noticed the shock when death actually occurred would be likely to be lessened and the survivors would be better equipped for the practical tasks required in the new situation.

Finally the supernatural manifestation would give rise to opportunities to talk about the dead. This would very likely lead to praise of his good qualities and expressions of sympathy with the bereaved. All this would contribute to restoring equilibrium and normality after the disturbance and upheaval which death always causes, especially in close-knit societies where practically everybody knew and was dependent upon each other.

The death-messenger tradition — in addition to its family-centred aspects — is strongly oriented towards the interests of the whole community. It is to a great extent a social tradition, fulfilling important needs for those who share the belief.

8

The Folk Beliefs about the Insulted Death-Messenger

I

The perception that supernatural beings should not be annoyed or interfered with is deeply rooted in the popular belief of all countries. A being whose main function is to forebode death is likely to be taken even more seriously than other types of supernatural being. People faced with the major crisis of death are less inclined towards mockery or horseplay. Yet occasionally some people might fail to observe decorum even on such solemn occasions and yet again the death-messenger might be encountered when not attending to her accustomed business. In many of the belief statements presented here it is not clear in what precise situation the being has been accosted but it is obvious it was considered very dangerous to be aggressive or discourteous towards her.

Belief statements regarding interference with the death-messenger cannot be traced far back in time. What appears to be the earliest example is found in the nineteenth-century source — John Keegan's *Legends and Tales of the Queen's County Peasantry:*

'Better for you shoot your own mother than fire at the Banshee any-how ... Let her alone while she lets you alone, for an hour's luck never shone on anyone that ever molested the banshee.'[1]

As is already evident the character of the older source material is such that very few conclusions, if any, can be drawn from its silence. In all likelihood the belief in the disastrous consequences of interfering with the death-messenger was firmly established long before it can be traced in the preserved records.

In the folklore manuscripts from the nineteen thirties onwards, there are several examples of the belief that annoying or teasing the being might have very serious consequences — a sprained foot (Longford 15), a crooked mouth (Wexford 44), **blindness** (temporary) (Cavan 1.8 (pp. 411-2)), or even death (e. g., Cavan 1.8 (pp. 410-11); Limerick 14; Roscommon 3).[2]

There were reasons to believe that this particular aspect of the tradition might be more prominent than the earlier material indicated and so question 13 was framed in the Banshee Questionnaire in 1976 (Appendix 1, p. 249).

Are there any stories about people who insulted the banshee (threw stones at her, fired at her or the like) and the consequences of their actions?

In view of the unfortunate phrasing of the questions, inducing correspondents to regard only 'stories' and not simple statements as of interest to the enquirers, only 18 answers were received.[3] These emanate from Antrim in the north-east to Kerry in the south-west and they confirm and expand our previous knowledge. The serious view which many up to this very day take of anything which might be interpreted as mockery of the death-messenger is colourfully illustrated by a questionnaire reply from the journalist Nicholas Furlong. Referring to a humorous column which he contributes to the *Wexford People* under the pen-name 'Pat O'Leary' he has this to say:

I have always reported and commented on bow hearings and their locations in my weekly Pat O'Leary column . . . However, in the case of the bow, I must confess that it was with the purpose of fun creation. Nevertheless, I have been frequently and solemnly taken to task by women following such utterances in print to the effect that it was no matter for jokes and that I could well find the laugh put on the other side of my face (Wexford 38).

In the course of collecting from an experiencer in Laois in 1976 it emerged that it was considered unlucky even to take the being's name in vain. In answer to a question whether people would ever scare children with the banshee the informant made the following statement:

No never! She wouldn't be meddled with in that line; they would be afraid they would bring her wrath on them (Laois 17).

The belief then that it was dangerous and wrong to interfere with the being was clearly strong and widespread. The safest thing to do was to avoid her altogether:

> ... agus creideadh nár cheart baint di ar dhóigh ar bith nó thiocfadh léi dochar a dhéanamh don té a bhainfeadh di [... and it was believed that it was not right to interfere with her in any way because she could do harm to the person who would interfere with her] (Donegal 6 (Q)).

II

The general belief that it might be dangerous and indeed disastrous to meddle with the death-messenger is the nucleus around which a number of legends have developed. Referred to here as 'Interference Legends' they deal with physical confrontations between the supernatural being and humans; they therefore presuppose that the being is seen and this explains their absence in Cork and Kerry, the areas where the being is heard only. Three of the interference legends have fairly well-developed and close-knit plots. As a result they entertain as well as serving to warn against wrong and indecorous behaviour towards the death-messenger. They illustrate well the belief under discussion here. Indeed they may very well have served to strengthen this belief. They have been neglected or unnoticed in previous scholarship and are worthy of a certain detailed treatment here.

9

Interference Legends 1 – The Comb Legend

The most widespread and most frequently recorded of the
interference legends is The Comb Legend, so called because
the vast majority of its versions involve the comb which, according
to the traditional belief in parts of Ireland, is the death-
messenger's most cherished possession. This object figures
prominently of course in the area where the death-messenger
is depicted as combing her hair. In some of the records where
the comb is mentioned it is said that the being may throw it
at those who mock or molest her.[1] The consequences for the
victims are often said to be serious, even fatal. The Comb
Legend as defined here, however, is a more fully developed
story, a fabulate or migratory legend, consisting of two incidents
– how the object was lost or stolen and how it was retrieved.
The following version contains most of the traits ordinarily
met with in the legend.

A Banshee Story

One night at about 12 o'clock as a man was crossing home
from Ardfinnan he heard something moaning but he could
not see anything. He walked on for some distance and then
he was in another field when he saw something in the
corner of the field wearing a long white dress. He walked
over towards it and it kept standing still. It was a woman
combing her hair. He ran after her and she dropped the
comb and he took it up. That night when he was in bed
he heard knocks at the window and he also heard moaning.
He slept for a while and then he awoke and he saw something at the window. He got up and he put the comb into
a tongs and he gave it out the window to her and when she
was taking it she took half of the tongs with her (Tipperary
9).

154

II

Apart from a passing mention in Seán Ó Súilleabháin's *A Handbook of Irish Folklore*, the legend has been given no attention in scholarly literature. It has not been included in any of the better known collections of Irish tales and legends and it has only rarely been committed to print in other connections. Nevertheless, it has been rather popular in certain parts of Ireland and versions of it can still be collected in many places. The corpus forming the basis of the following investigation consists of 81 versions, the earliest a printed one from 1891 and the latest a tape recording made in 1979.

A break-down of the corpus according to the different types of source material shows that there are 7 versions from printed sources, 9 from the Main Manuscripts prior to 1976, 44 from the Schools' Manuscripts compiled between 1937 and 1938, 12 in answer to the Banshee Questionnaire 1976, 4 from letters following a radio talk in 1976 and 5 tape-recorded versions between 1976 and 1979.

In order to establish the reliability of the source material, it is necessary to analyse the sources critically and in particular to test the possibility that printed variants may have exercised influence on the orally collected versions.

The earliest version of the legend — to my knowledge — is a rather summary item in Patrick Barden's *The Dead-Watchers, And Other Folk-Lore Tales of Westmeath* (1891, p. 82).[2] This lacks many traits common in orally-collected versions, and it is virtually concealed as a note in the appendix of the book. It is, thus, unlikely to have influenced oral tradition.

An atypical version in the 1909 issue of the *Journal of the County Kildare Archaeological Society and Surrounding Districts*[3] is also unlikely to have attracted much attention among a wider public.

Three versions included in the popular weekly journal *Ireland's Own*, would be much more likely to re-enter the oral mainstream. One of these versions in the issue of 15 December 1934 stems from Tipperary. The provenance of the other two, both in the issue of 27 November 1954, is unknown. The three conform closely to orally-collected versions. Yet no orally-collected version encountered contains any verbal echoes or any specific details to force a conclusion that it derives directly from any of the versions in *Ireland's Own*.

The two remaining printed versions are included in Nicholas Furlong's column in the *Enniscorthy Guardian* on 14 October 1967 and in the *Wexford People* on 16 July 1976, respectively. The following is the 1976 version:

> Mr. James Hess submits that a drunkard took the comb out of the Bow's hand in the Black Cow in November and was then put supernaturally up on the window-sill where he remained with the comb glued to his hand for 48 hours. It was then taken out of his hand at 12 midnight, two nights later and restored to the Bow by means of an iron tongs. Only then was he restored to the ground and to the bosom of his family. When the fire brigade tried to get him down before the Bow gave her permission they found an invisible wall there to contend with (Wexford 37).

Certain motifs here, such as the hand stuck to the comb and the invisible wall which is also in the 1967 version (Wexford 35), are absent in all orally-collected versions. It is likely that they, as well as certain other mock-humorous details and phrases, are the columnist's embroideries. Other than these there is little doubt that the essence of what Furlong reports is a genuine Wexford version of the legend.

Newspapers and other ephemeral publications may contain versions which have escaped notice but one can say with a degree of assurance that printed versions have been of little or no importance in the transmission of The Comb Legend. In fact the printed versions seem mostly to reflect genuine local tradition and they may be used with due caution in comparative analysis.

The 9 Main Manuscripts versions, the 4 from letters and the 5 tape-recorded versions are in most instances full and detailed. Since the legend is mentioned in Ó Súilleabháin's *Handbook*, it may seem surprising that the versions in the Main Manuscripts are so few. No doubt an important part of the explanation for this is that the legend was most popular in Leinster where there has been only very occasional collecting activity by full-time or part-time collectors.

A number of the 44 Schools' Manuscripts versions are short and threadbare and some of them are probably to be regarded as summaries rather than faithful renderings of versions actually told. However, a significant number of them are quite fully and vividly told and give a good picture of the versions children relate. The 12 versions obtained through answers to the questionnaire are sometimes also mere summaries but many of them are of high quality. The fact that all Leinster schools took part in the collecting scheme of 1937-8 and that a good many Leinster correspondents answered the 1976 Questionnaire is part of the explanation for a high number of versions in these source categories. The predominance of the Schools' Manuscripts versions reflects The Comb Legend's popularity among children.

The material then is of varying character and not entirely flawless. Nevertheless, the corpus is of such quantity and quality that it is possible to arrive at certain definite conclusions regarding the distribution of the legend and its variations.

III

The vast majority of the versions of The Comb Legend have been collected in Leinster – 50 of the 79 versions of known provenance. Munster is represented by 17 versions, Connaught by 11 and only one single version has emerged in Ulster (Appendix 4.1 (a), p. 313). Only three versions — all from Connaught (Galway 24, 55; Mayo 18) – are in the Irish language. Map 16 shows that the distribution area extends like a corridor across Ireland from the south-east towards the north-west. Within this corridor the distribution has been ripple-like except at its north-western extremity where the examples are fewer and farther apart indicating a distribution by leaps and bounds. That the main thrust of the dissemination has been towards the west is also demonstrated by the somewhat anomalous nature of the most westerly versions. In the two versions in Irish from Galway the object removed from the death-messenger is thus not a comb but a beetle, a bat-like object used for washing clothes. A beetle, but this time in addition to the comb, also figures in Galway 41. In one of the Mayo versions (Mayo 27) the stolen object is a sheet. The beetle and the shirt properly belong to another legend which will be treated later and which is indigenous to these areas. The mark of her five fingers which the being leaves on the

16. The Comb Legend

shovel (Galway 24) is a further intrusion of a motif from another legend into The Comb Legend. Such instability is to be expected at the periphery.

Returning to the heartland of The Comb Legend one notes that Westmeath, Kildare and Dublin all show versions but there are none from Meath and Louth. A single version from a Schools' Manuscript is found in east-Cavan. The scarcity of the legend there is confirmed by its absence in the huge collection of folklore from the area compiled by the part-time collector P.J. Gaynor (Cavan 1). In spite of extensive collecting the full-time collector Michael J. Murphy has also failed to unearth variants from other parts of Cavan, or from Louth, Monaghan or Armagh. The legend was obviously rare or indeed unknown in this part of north-Leinster and Ulster.

The absence of the legend from wide areas of the south-west, north-west and north invites comment. Its absence in Cork and Kerry is easily accounted for. As already stated, the death-messenger is believed to be invisible in these counties. She is heard only, never seen. There is thus no basis for a legend involving a violent physical encounter with her. One is still left with other areas in the south-west such as Clare and Limerick as well as almost everywhere in the north and north-west.

The Comb Legend obviously derives from the general belief that the banshee is often engaged in combing her long hair. If one glances at Map 7 showing the 'combing area' and compares it with Map 16 illustrating the distribution of The Comb Legend one notes that the distribution patterns virtually overlap. The scattered examples of a combing belief in Clare and Limerick hardly provide grounds for the legend there and north-Leinster, Ulster and the Mayo area of Connaught show that the belief and therefore the legend are virtually absent.

There is a further explanation as to why the combing motif is lacking in the south-west and north-west especially. Long hair and combing in these areas was attached to another supernatural being which figured prominently in the tradition there – the mermaid. Some of the informants and tradition-bearers in the areas have themselves suspected this. The enquiry in the questionnaire[4] whether the banshee was believed to be seen combing her hair prompted several answers of the following type:

There are no stories of a comb or combing hair. Such stories are told about mermaids (Mayo 29).

No traditions. The mermaid was always seen combing her hair, not the *bean sí* (Donegal 11).

Ní scéalta faoin mbean sí iad san ach scéalta faoin mhaighdean mhara [These are not stories about the banshee but about the mermaid] (Donegal 22).[5]

It is worth noting that several of the statements refer to the mermaid's comb in stories rather than in general belief. No doubt what the informants had particularly in mind was a mermaid legend of great popularity in the west of Ireland, a fabulate entitled The Seal Woman in Reidar Th. Christiansen's *The Migratory Legends*.[6] Since the supernatural actor in Irish tradition is almost always a mermaid, not an enchanted seal, this legend is here called Man Marries Mermaid (Map 17).[7] The gist of the legend is as follows:

A man steals an object — usually a cloak, hood or the like — from a mermaid who does not notice him when he creeps up on her. It is said that she does not observe him because she is engaged in combing her long beautiful hair. Having been deprived of the specified object the mermaid is unable to take to the water. The man brings her home and marries her. At some stage she retrieves the stolen object, runs away and disappears into the sea.

The distribution of Man Marries Mermaid coincides remarkably with the areas from which The Comb Legend is absent (Map 18). Its distribution is westerly and of course coastal. Two legends so similar can be expected to give rise to hybrids and so there are versions of Man Marries Mermaid in which the object stolen and retrieved is a comb rather than a cloak or the like.[8] Examples of the intrusion of motifs from Man Marries Mermaid into The Comb Legend are also found in Roscommon where the two traditions confronted each other.[9] Such hybrids are exceptions. More often the two legends seem to have been regarded as too alike to be told in the same area. Most tradition-bearers who already knew Man Marries Mermaid might have reasoned like the questionnaire correspondents from the area where this legend is known — a legend about a supernatural being with a

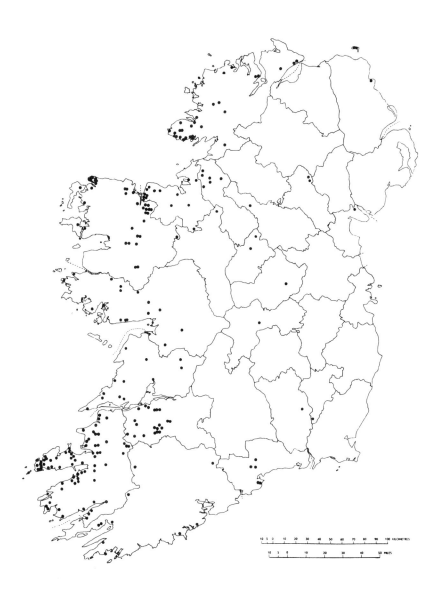

17. Man Marries Mermaid Legend

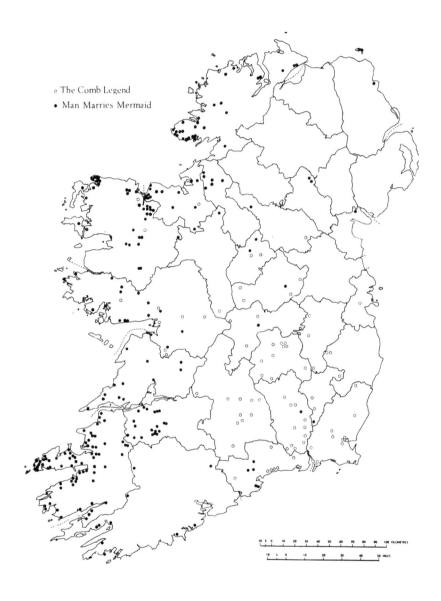

o The Comb Legend
• Man Marries Mermaid

18. The Comb Legend and Man Marries Mermaid Legend

comb is not about the banshee but about the mermaid. Man Marries Mermaid might thus have presented a barrier in the west inside which The Comb Legend could only very occasionally penetrate. If this is so it follows that The Comb Legend was created later than Man Marries Mermaid, an assumption that seems reasonable on other grounds as well — Man Marries Mermaid is also found outside Ireland and in much earlier sources, for example.

Having discussed the distribution of The Comb Legend one must analyse the main variations in the different versions and discover why these exist.

IV

In any study of a large number of versions of a particular tale one is invariably amazed at the extraordinary way in which folk-narrative varies and is susceptible to adaptation to the requirements of the telling occasions and the tastes of the tellers and their audience. One might imagine that a legend like The Comb Legend, which never contains more than two main episodes and two main actors, would leave little scope for significant variation. The contrary is in fact the case. If one takes length as a criterion there are versions so short that they can be told in less than half a minute, such as one recorded in 1976 from Mrs. Bridie Dunn, Mountmellick:

Well, she — my grandmother — was telling me that she was going home from town one day. She picked up a lovely comb and brought it home with her. And that night there was an awful noise at the door and the old man said he would get up and see what it was. So she told him not to. And he suddenly saw the comb and he put the comb on the tongs, you know, and sure he put the tongs out the door with the comb and the tongs was broken in his hands (Laois 15).

At the other extreme there are long elaborate versions well suited to form part of a storytelling session. The Galway version collected by Seán Ó Flannagáin in 1937 from the farmer

Séamus Ó Cealla exemplifies this:

> I used to hear my father saying (the bed of heaven to his
> soul) that there was an old man of the Regans who lived
> here in Killeen a good many years ago. There were no
> candles or lamps going in them times, but 'twas how every-
> one used to go to the bog and root up a good thick block
> of bog deal timber and bring it home with him. He'd get
> his hatchet then and split that block up into *sliseógs*,[10] nice
> thin long *sliseógs*. Them *sliseógs* then used to be dipped
> into tallow that they'd get out of the cattle or sheep they'd
> kill, and then whenever they'd want a light they used one
> of them and someone would hold them in his hand, or
> maybe they'd put it standing in the middle of a heap of
> potatoes while they'd be eating them for supper. Them
> *sliseógs* that they used to burn that way were called
> *caisnes* or *caisníns*.[11] They usen't have the *caisníns* burning
> all the night like the lamps are burning now. Devil a long
> they'd hould if they'd be wasting them like that. They'd
> use them only while they'd be putting down a pot or taking
> up a pot or if they were looking for something around
> the house. For the rest of the time they'd be sitting around
> the fire and 'tis how they'd be telling stories to one another
> and putting down on the ould times. The light of the turf
> fire was enough for them and there was some of the old
> people and they could hould telling stories forever. Well, this
> ould man of the Regans — he'd be Pateen Regan's great
> grandfather, so that'll tell you that it must be a good long
> while ago — he had a big stump of bog deal like that
> beyant in Carrachán Bog, just at the foot of the mountain
> or in the mountain as you might say. He had the stump
> rooted up and all, had it thrown up on the bank ready
> to bring home and as soon as night had fallen he made
> over across towards Carrachán. There is a stream running
> down this side of Carrachán and didn't he hear the beetling
> (Plate 1) going on, on the top of the big flag that you'd
> pass going over. He was a kind of harum-scarum of a
> young man then and the devil one if he'd care for
> either *deamhan* or *deabhal,* he had that cutting in
> him. He made over across to where he heard

Plate 3. Women beetling clothes at a stream
(Mr. and Mrs. S. C. Hall, *Ireland: It's Scenery, Character, &c.,*
I, 1841, p. 130)

the beetling going on and sure enough he saw her there and
she having the beetle in one hand and a lovely rack (comb) in
the other. He stepped lightly in behind her, snapped the rack
out of her hand and made one leap for the other bank and
away with him home, and look here, the March wind before
him couldn't keep before him and the March wind behind
him couldn't keep up with him, he was that quick on his foot.

Away with the *bean sí* hither after him and every scream
out of her worse than one another. She caught the beetle
that was in her hand and flung it after him and I suppose
that 'twas God that saved him or that he didn't give her
the power to hit him, but anyways the beetle went whistling out by his poll and if he got it in the poll he was a
dead man. Regan was a great runner and maybe 'twas
how that Almighty God didn't give her the footing that
he'd gave to Regan, but anyways, he was always able to
keep before her. When she came up to the beetle she caught
it the second time and Regan could hear it whistling out
by his ear and I suppose it was promised to him, but anyways, it missed him the second time. The banshee came
up with the beetle the third time and as soon as she caught
it Regan was just turned in home at his own gable-end and
didn't the banshee fire the beetle for the third time. Regan
was just landed inside his own door when the beetle struck
the gable-end and shook the house from head to bottom.
He bolted the door and secured it from the inside with the
maide éamainn[12] that they used to have in them times to
secure the door in the time of a storm. They were all
sitting down within at home and wasn't the heart put
across them when they heard the scream outside the
door. She told them in Irish to put out the rack to her
or that she'd knock the house. Regan rose and he took the
spade and he left the rack on the top of the spade and
caught the spade by the *feac* (handle) and pushed the rack
out under the door to her. Half the iron of the spade was
outside the door and the other half was inside. She caught
the rack and half of the iron that was outside and brought
the rack and half the spade with her. When they pulled in
the spade again wasn't half of it gone! Next morning when
they got up and went outside didn't they find the gable-

end of the house split in two even halves from thatch to ground and any day that you go over to see Regan's ould *cabhail* (ruin) you'll see the gable-end split in two even halves and that's how it happened. (Galway 41).

The unusual length of this version has been achieved by a variety of devices. Certain motifs and episodes, such as the beetle and the dramatic pursuit, have been borrowed from another legend current in the area. Runs, formulas and other stylistic ornaments more commonly found in folktales rather than in legends have been used, for example, *You'd think the March wind before him couldn't keep before him*. Explanations and discourses only marginally relating to the plot are lavishly supplied. The description of the different uses of bog deal is typical.

V

The amount of variation and the myriad reasons for it makes it entirely impracticable to survey the entire corpus of the legend but the most important features can be identified here (see Appendix 4.1, pp. 313-5).

Two main forms of The Comb Legend may be discerned. These may be termed the A-redaction and the B-redaction.

The A-redaction contains an initial encounter between a human and the supernatural being. The supernatural being is always referred to as a banshee or *badhb*. She is depicted as a washerwoman in variants which are influenced by The Shirt Legend (Galway 24 and 41 – see Chapter 11). The A-redaction is the more common of the two, represented as it is by 60 versions or 75 per cent of the Comb Legend corpus (Appendix 4.1 (b), p. 313). In 44 versions (Appendix 4.1 (c), p. 314) the meeting implies tangible violence towards the supernatural being. The human actor 'snaps', 'snatches' or 'wrenches' the comb from her. More rarely, in 16 versions (Appendix 4.1(d), p. 314) it is said that the being is merely startled or frightened so that she leaves her comb behind her when she runs away.

The B-redaction, represented by 21 versions or 25 per cent of the legend corpus lacks such an initial encounter (Appendix 4.1 (e), p. 314). Instead it is stated that the comb is accidentally found in some place frequented by the being.

One may incline to the view that the A-redaction is older and more original and that the B-redaction is a truncated form of it. There is some support for this in that the geographical distribution of the A-redaction is wider than that of the B-redaction (Map 19). Whatever the case it would not be correct to maintain that the latter redaction is inferior to the former. The story stands up and makes perfectly good sense in the shorter B-redaction form. Moreover one ought not to attach undue importance to the distribution pattern of the two redactions. The preference for one form over the other appears to depend upon the sex and age of the main actor in the legend and in all likelihood also upon the sex and age of those telling the legend and of their audience. Significantly, the main human actor is a grown-up male in all but 5[13] of the A versions while a woman takes this part in 6[14] and a child in 2[15] of the B versions. The violent actions against the supernatural being in the A versions have obviously been thought improper or inappropriate behaviour for a woman or child.

The name of the human actor or details sufficient to identify him or her are given in 35 of the variants (Appendix 4.1 (f), p. 314). One has the impression that the absence of such detail is often due to shortcomings in the written records rather than to their absence from oral tradition. It is noteworthy that 22 of the 46 records which are lacking such traits are written by school children (Appendix 4.1 (g), p. 314).

Additional information in most variants touches upon the main human actor's activities at the time of, or immediately before, the encounter with the supernatural being. Not unexpectedly many common country activities are referred to and some are worthy of note. It is often implied, especially in the A versions, that the person has done something which is not entirely approved of such as staying out too late rambling or card-playing, or at a dance, or the like.[16] It is also said that the encounter took place when the person was on his way home after sitting up with a dying person[17] or attending a wake.[18] Such information offers an explanation as to why the death-messenger is roaming around.

The time and place of the initial encounter or the finding of the comb is linked to the occupation or activity of the human

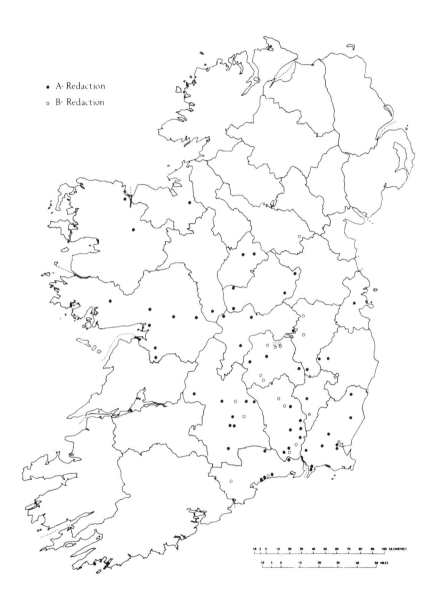

19. The Comb Legend: Redactions

actor. The dark, or grey hours dominate[19] and the encounter *locus* is sometimes the vicinity of a house,[20] usually that of the human actor, but sometimes a rock,[21] a stile,[22] a stack of turf,[23] or the like; the proximity to water is stressed especially in Galway tradition.[24] These times and places are in agreement with the general beliefs about the death-messenger. They bear witness to the correctness of von Sydow's characterisation of legends as crystallised folk beliefs.[25]

The object, the loss of which initiates the further action in the story, is a comb in all but five variants (Map 20). Certainly the comb figured in the legend from the very beginning. In two variants (Galway 24, 55) the object is a beetle and in two other versions (Mayo 27; Tipperary 32) it is a sheet. As already indicated these objects have been introduced through the process of hybridisation. The occurrence of a shawl in the fifth variant (Westmeath 16) is atypical and incidental.

The comb, or other object, seized or found is almost always brought into the house of the person who seized or found it. In two variants (Wexford 35, 37) the action takes place outside the house and in another (Longford 4), which was told by a traveller, the house has been replaced by 'a camp-fire'. This latter variant is, in other ways also, skilfully adapted to the conditions imposed by nomadic life. The occasional instances in which the comb is brought to a wake house (Carlow 13; Kilkenny 18; Laois 11; Wexford 30) — and not to the house of the main human actor — are undoubtedly due to general associations between the banshee, *badhb*, etc. and death. In a Galway variant where the object appropriated is a beetle, this is atypically thrown back to the supernatural being by the human actor before reaching his house (Galway 55). This, and the dramatic pursuit of the human actor by the supernatural being in the same variant and in another (Galway 41), are further results of the process of hybridisation.

The next episode, the supernatural being's retrieval of her comb, is usually somewhat delayed and her arrival at the house is announced by cries and wails (Appendix 4.1 (h), p. 314) heard in particular at the window or door.[26] The being's behaviour is once again in accordance with general folk belief about her.

The arrival of the death-messenger at the house leads to the most dramatic point in the legend, the returning of the object.

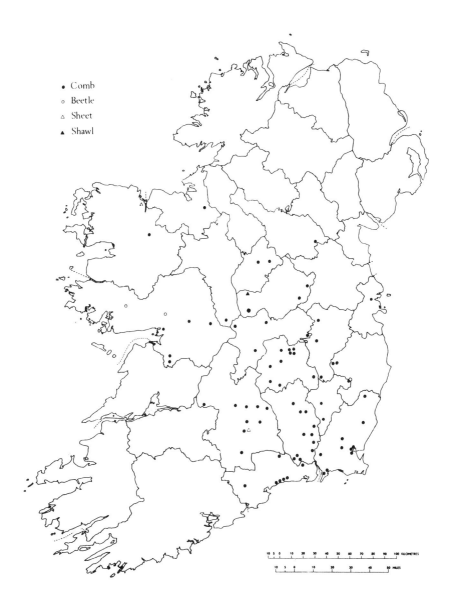

20. The Comb Legend: object taken from the death-messenger

This is where The Comb Legend differs most radically from Man Marries Mermaid with which it otherwise has so many affinities. The stolen object in the latter legend is accidentally found by the supernatural being and its retrieval involves no danger of physical harm to the human actor. In The Comb Legend the behaviour of the supernatural being is quite the contrary, demanding and threatening, and great caution must be exercised in dealing with her.[27] Usually the offender understands the reason for the being's arrival and himself devises the necessary means for handing back her property without exposing himself to risk. In one variant, a printed source (Kildare 9), the being herself delivers instructions as to how the comb is to be returned to her. In speaking, instead of merely crying or wailing, the death-messenger is here violating her customary behaviour, and very likely this trait is an individual invention without foundation in oral tradition. More worthy of note are the 13 variants in which a supporting human character is introduced at this point in the role of adviser. In three of these variants (Galway 24; Laois 20; Tipperary 2) the adviser is a family member, but in the other instances (Carlow 11; Kilkenny 18, 19; Longford 6; Waterford 40, Wexford 14, 51; Wicklow 12, 13) he is a priest. Apart from illustrating the general belief in the power and wisdom of the priest,[28] this also indicates the absence of a feeling that the clergy took objection to belief in the being.

Whether advised by somebody else or not, the main human actor invariably exercised the utmost caution when handing back the object to the supernatural being. The common tradition is that the object is given back through a small aperture (Map 21) and a strong sturdy implement of one kind or another is used in the procedure.

There are 21 variants in The Comb Legend corpus which do not mention any aperture through which the object taken from the death-messenger is restored to her for the following reasons: the object is not taken into the house in the first instance; it is not returned to the being at all; it is left outside on the window-sill for her; no details are given.[29]

The door is the aperture involved in ten variants. In two of these (Carlow 11, Waterford 19) the door was opened 'a few inches'. A better way to prevent the angered being from enter-

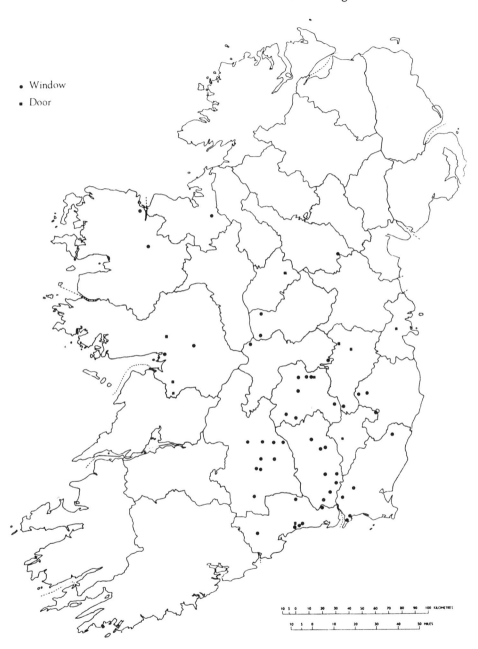

21. Apertures through which the comb is returned to the death-messenger

ing by pushing the comb out under the door is employed in five variants (Dublin 6; Laois 15, Longford 6, Galway 41, 46). In a further two variants (Galway 24; Kildare 13) it is not clear whether the door was opened and the object handed out. In an atypical variant contributed by a schoolboy (Kildare 2) the comb is said to have been handed out through the keyhole. To make this method credible he adds that it was 'the smallest comb in the world'.

The window is much more frequently mentioned than the door. It occurs in no less than 50 variants (Appendix 4.1 (i), p. 315). Since it is also found over the whole distribution area of the legend one may take it that it occurred in the original form or *Urform*. The reasons for its popularity are easily seen. In the first place it caters well for the needs of the plot: it provided a suitable aperture for handing out the comb or other object without risk of anything entering. Secondly the window, according to the general traditional belief, is a favourite manifestation place for the death-messenger.

Further protective measures were taken when restoring the object to the death-messenger. In the majority of the variants, 55 in all, the comb or other object is returned by the use of some sturdy implement.

There are 26 records in which the use of an implement for this purpose is not mentioned for the following reasons: the object is thrown to the pursuing death-messenger out-of-doors; it is not returned; it is thrown out; it is left outside on the window-sill; the human actor hands it to her; she puts her hand through the window and seizes it herself; there is a lack of sufficient detail in the sources.[30]

Five implements figure in the corpus — ploughshare (*soc*), poker, fork, spade, shovel and tongs (Map 22). The ploughshare is mentioned only once:

> The only way they could hand it back was to get the *soc* of a plough and redden it in the fire (Galway 37).

The ploughshare would seem to be most unsuitable for handing out a comb or other object through a window and this may be the reason why it is not otherwise met with in connection with the supernatural death-messenger despite the firm belief that it offered protection against magic and the

- • Tongs
- ○ Poker
- ■ Shovel
- □ Spade
- ▲ Ploughshare

22. Implements used to give back object to death-messenger

supernatural. It was used, for instance, for detecting butter stealing hags[31] and for banishing changelings.[32] The statement, however, may refer to the iron *soc* found on some old wooden ploughs which was not unlike a spade-blade[33] (Plate 2) and thus quite suitable for handing out the comb.

The poker also occurs in one instance only (Tipperary 42). Such an iron implement associated with fire would be believed to offer protection against supernatural forces but its unsuitability for the purpose of handing out a comb would have prevented it from becoming established in The Comb Legend. The same holds true for the fork (Mayo 27). In the context in which it occurs it fulfills its function since the object handed out there is a sheet.

More commonly found are shovels (Galway 24; Kilkenny 3; Laois 1; Waterford 19, 26) and spades (Galway 41; Kilkenny 18). These tools are well suited to the purpose of reaching objects out through a window while preventing intrusion. They are also iron in substance and associated with protection against supernatural beings as exemplified by their use in changeling traditions.[34]

The most common implement in The Comb Legend corpus, 45 variants in all (Appendix 4.1 (j), p. 315), is the fire tongs (Plate 3). Such an implement, ready to hand in every house, was ideal for grasping an object. Tongs forged by local blacksmiths and found in Irish country houses were also large and strong. Their apotropaic propensities were obvious to all in the traditional society. For this reason and because of their wide distribution in The Comb Legend, one may assume that they belong to the *Urform*.

Four variants stand apart in that there is no reference to an implement being used for handing over the comb or to any other safety precautions. In one of these (Kilkenny 15) the human actor's hand is said to have shrivelled away when the supernatural being touched it. In all other variants the human actor escapes without physical blemish, but it is stated in 51 variants (Appendix 4.1 (k), p. 315) that the implement suffered badly. In a few atypical variants (Kilkenny 5, 19) from the Schools' Manuscripts the supernatural being simply wrenches it out of the hands of the holder. Far more commonly we hear that she violently marks or damages it. Three Galway variants

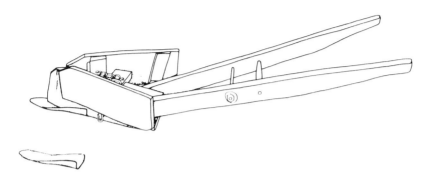

Plate 4. Wooden moulding plough from the Cliffs of Moher area, Co. Clare;
note resemblance of share to spade blade
(The Elizabeth Talbot Memorial Museum, Bunratty Folk Park, Co. Clare)

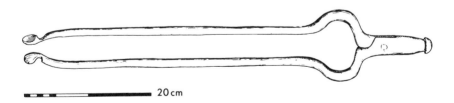

20 cm

Plate 5. Smith-forged iron tongs from Lackagh, Co. Kildare

(Galway 24, 37, 38) and a Mayo variant (Mayo 27) say that the being leaves the imprint of her five fingers on the object. This is undoubtedly due to hybridisation with another legend, The Imprint of the Banshee's Five Fingers.

The dominant motif, then, is that the supernatural strength of the being is illustrated in the way she warps and twists the solid iron object. The following variant is typical:

> He couldn't get the tongs back in. It was bent up into a lump — twisted the same as if you were after getting a lump of twine and knotting it (Laois 17).

One can well imagine, without being told, what would have happened to the human actor's hand if no precaution had been taken. Nevertheless, some variants (Longford 4; Tipperary 2; Waterford 26; Wexford 4, 14, 40, 43; Wicklow 12) expand on the subject:

> If he had taken it in his hand to give it to her, she would have taken his hand from him (Longford 4).

The motif of extraordinary strength expressed through deformation of iron objects[35] is also found in the migratory legend entitled The Visit to the Old Troll. The Handshake,[36] where it is frequently included in a longer tale, The Dream Visit.[37] It is possible that the twisting of the iron in The Comb Legend is a borrowing from The Dream Visit. There are similarities even in detail. The implement in The Dream Visit is often a pair of fire tongs and the ploughshare is also found in some variants. The ways in which the respective implements are twisted and warped is often described in similar terms in the two narratives. Whether these similarities are direct borrowings or not, it is evident that The Dream Visit has influenced some variants of The Comb Legend, namely those in which the supernatural being herself makes a statement to the human actor such as 'It is well for you that you did not put out your hand!' (Carlow 11, 13; Galway 32; Kilkenny 7, 16; Laois 20; Sligo 9; Tipperary 43; Westmeath 9, 16; Waterford 19). Such a statement occurring in most variants of The Dream Visit is out of place in The Comb Legend because in genuine sources the supernatural death-messenger is not believed to make statements containing intelligible words.[38]

One cannot reconstruct the *Urform* of a story in minute

detail but it can be said on the basis of the frequency and geographical distribution of the respective traits that The Comb Legend originally contained certain clear elements. These are that the being is bereft of her comb which the culprit brings to his house and from there it is returned to her by means of a pair of fire tongs which is reached out through the window. These elements are also those most current in twentieth-century tradition.

VI

It remains to consider the functions of the legend. The Comb Legend, like so many other belief legends, warns about and teaches proper behaviour in dealing with supernatural beings. It does so by implying that the being should have been avoided in the first place and by prescribing the right methods of dealing with her when an encounter is unavoidable. For believers who think that they might meet the being such knowledge is valuable since it alleviates their fears.

The legend also teaches good behaviour in general and it warns against a number of actions and activities considered asocial and improper. People should not steal or interfere with the property of others. One should not accost another, least of all a defenceless woman. If it should transpire that the woman is a banshee or *badhb* and is well able to defend herself such aggressors will be properly punished. Many of the variants stress that the encounter with the being and the improper actions towards her are the result of a dissipated life – being out late at night carousing and card-playing or the like.[39] Refraining from such activities would ensure that one avoided the disapproval of one's neighbours and did not run the risk of meeting the death-messenger either. There is no sure way of measuring to what extent people acted upon the advice but the message inherent in the legend, like the death-messenger belief in general, had a positive effect on people's morals. Significantly certain variants stress that the culprit was reformed as a result of his experience. Thus the drunk who took the comb is said subsequently to have taken a pledge to abstain from alcoholic drink (Waterford 40) and the gambler 'got such a fright that wild horses wouldn't bring him out of the house late at night after that' (Tipperary 3).

Moral lessons of this kind are mainly to be drawn from the A versions in which the human actor drastically misbehaves by directly accosting the being. The B versions teach their own lesson warning people, especially young children, not to pick up combs they might accidentally find. There are versions in which this lesson is very direct and these include some of the most recent ones which have come to light. Thus a version collected in 1976 (Laois 19) states 'They (people) would say "Don't pick up that comb, it belongs to the banshee, you know!" ' and a version collected in 1979 is unequivocal:

> I remember one day we were out cutting corn, we were out binding up . . . and I found this blue comb . . . And I said to my father: 'Look at the comb I'm after finding here in the ditch.' 'Oh,' says he, 'that's the banshee's comb, leave that down!' So I said no more about it and when I came in . . . my aunt now . . . when I came in I was telling her about it and she said 'I hope you didn't bring it into the house.' I didn't – sure I dropped it the very minute he said . . . And I remember to this day it was a blue comb (Laois 12).

In this way the legend was actualised and such lessons were not only long remembered but they actually deterred many a child from picking up combs which might contain infectious matter. The Comb Legend thus fulfilled a variety of functions and exercised a significant influence on people's behaviour.

VII

In summary one may say that in spite of its rarity in printed sources The Comb Legend was quite common in the English language in Leinster and Connaught and it is still part of the living tradition there.

The main direction of the dissemination appears to have been from east to west. The Cork and Kerry belief that the death-messenger cannot be seen, but only heard, has formed a barrier which has prevented The Comb Legend from spreading to the south-west and its similarity to the Man Marries Mermaid Legend explains its rejection in the western and north-western coastal areas where the latter is popular.

The legend may be told in passing in a few short sentences or it may be spun out at considerable length to suit a more formal storytelling occasion, yet always retains its basic structural unity.

Two main redactions, A and B, have been discerned. In the former, which appears to be the older, the comb or other object is taken by force from the supernatural being, while it is accidentally found in the latter.

Variation within the redactions is the result of hybridisation with other legends, the influences of different local beliefs, customs and other conditions of life. Yet The Comb Legend may be said to have crystalised around a core of beliefs attached to the supernatural death-messenger. Apart from serving the general function of presciding avoidance of supernatural beings and caution when meetings with them are inevitable, the legend also teaches the value of good behaviour in stressing that those who are violent, discourteous towards women or given to drunkenness and late hours may run great risks. The lesson not to pick up combs and such-like objects accidentally found is also spelled out, especially to children, in the B versions.

10

Interference Legends 2 – The Imprint of the Banshee's Five Fingers

I

Some versions of The Comb Legend contain the trait that the supernatural death-messenger left the imprint of her hand or fingers on the implement used for passing the comb out to her. The motif of the imprint of the five fingers forms the core of another legend in which the imprint is left not upon an object but on the head or face of the person who has accosted the supernatural being. The following, which is the fullest version yet encountered, was told in 1937 by Séamas Ó Cealla from Killeen, Beagh, Galway — the same man who told the longest version of The Comb Legend:

The Banshee

Thomas Harte's uncle was coming home late from his *cuaird* this night and it was a bright night and the moon was high in the sky. Outside his house was a green flag, and the flag is there to this day. When he was coming in near his home didn't he see the woman on the green flag. He thought that it was some neighbouring woman that was there and that it was how she was trying to knock a start out of him. Over he goes and he claps his hand on her shoulder. The very minute he did, — God bless us and save us all and may everyone be well where it is told — she raised her hand and caught him by the crown of the head and lifted him clear up off the road. And she hit him down against the ground again but she did not kill him. He got a terrible fright. And may God bless and save us all, when he got up in the morning the print of her five fingers was on the top of his head and his hair had turned as white as the snow from the dent of the fright (Galway 42).

182

Though the banshee is not mentioned in this version, except in the title, it is likely that it was the storyteller and not the collector who concluded that she was the supernatural being involved. The legend is found attached to the banshee in three other versions. Two of these (Galway 15, 52), from Annagh-down and Ardrahan respectively, are contained in the Schools' Manuscripts while the third (Kildare 6) was contributed by a questionnaire correspondent. The Galway versions were told in Irish, the other two in English (Appendix 4.2, p. 316). Regarding the Kildare reply it should be mentioned that no specific question about The Imprint of the Banshee's Five Fingers was asked in the Banshee Questionnaire for the simple reason that the very existence of the legend as attached to the banshee had not been discerned in 1976 when the document was sent out.

II

The frequency, dissemination and place of origin of this legend cannot be fully determined until an extensive and systematic enquiry is carried out. It does seem from present knowledge though that its heartland is a limited area of Galway (Map 23). This is indicated by the fact that three of the four recorded versions are from Galway and by the fact that the versions of The Comb Legend which mention the imprint of the death-messenger's five fingers on the implement on which the comb is reached out are from there and from a bordering area in Mayo. Because it is rare and of limited geographical distribution the motif of the imprint left by the banshee as found in The Comb Legend appears to be borrowed from The Imprint of the Banshee's Five Fingers legend. The isolated version from Kildare is problematic. It may be a stray version introduced by somebody who moved there from Galway but this is not known. Perhaps the Galway versions and the Kildare version are independent offshoots of a more widespread tradition that ghosts and revenants leave the mark of their hands or fingers on people or objects. One is dealing here with the motif 'Ghost touches man's neck, leaves impression of hand on neck'.[1] This happens in the case of an unspecified ghost who figures in the Cork

23. The Imprint of the Banshee's Five Fingers Legend

legend about the washerwoman of Inis Céin[2] and in a recent recording from Roscommon a man is said to have got a slap on the face from his dead fiancée, so that 'the mark of the five fingers was burned into his face'.[3] General traditions attached to the dead have often been ascribed to the death-messenger and it is possible that general traditions about imprints left by the dead or by unspecified supernatural beings are the basis of the legend as it is told about the banshee in Galway and Kildare. Because of this, it is conceivable that the motif of the imprint of the five fingers has been attached to the banshee independently in Galway and Kildare. It also seems likely that The Imprint of the Banshee's Five Fingers never had a much wider distribution than it has at present. A local legend like this could have existed for centuries without being noticed by outsiders but it is more likely to be a relatively recent creation. The only fixed point in its nebulous chronology is the *terminus ante quem* provided in the version quoted (Galway 42) which the storyteller learnt c. 1917 from his father who was then seventy years of age.

III

Since the versions of The Imprint of the Banshee's Five Fingers are few and from a small area, they are quite uniform. What little variation there is concerns details which have little significance except perhaps that the supernatural being is depicted as a washerwoman in one of the versions (Galway 15). What they have in common is noteworthy. The human actor is always a man and he is invariably out late at night. All versions state that he first mistook the banshee for an ordinary woman whom he accosted and the punishment he suffered was the mark of the banshee's five fingers on his face. Thus many of the traits in the legend accord with general folk beliefs about the death-messenger and the basic plot is quite similar to The Comb Legend. One could then regard The Imprint of the Banshee's Five Fingers as a three-way amalgamation involving the motif 'Ghost touches man's neck, leaves impression of hand on neck', the general beliefs attached to the death-messenger and the Comb Legend.

IV

Like the Comb Legend, the Imprint of the Banshee's Five Fingers teaches the necessity for caution in dealing with supernatural beings and warns against being out late hours and indecorous behaviour towards women. The latter lesson is perhaps more firmly impressed by The Imprint Legend than by The Comb Legend. Young men who accost women at night ought to beware — what is there may not be a human woman but a banshee!

11

Interference Legends 3 – The Shirt Legend

I

Like The Comb Legend, the Shirt Legend arises from a special activity of the death-messenger's, her washing. The legend, referred to here as The Shirt[1] Legend, like The Comb Legend and The Imprint of the Banshee's Five Fingers, illustrates the dangers involved in accosting or mocking the supernatural death-messenger. The following version was recorded by Ciarán Bairéad from Seán Glionnáin, Waterdale (Eochaill), Claregalway, Co. Galway in 1954:

Fear a bhí ag dul isteach ar an Móinteach oíche ag tórramh nó isteach ag damhsa. D'airigh sé an bhean sí ag níochán, ag sliseáil léi le slis. Bhí slis ag gach uile bhean an uair sin – ní raibh morán gallúnach amuigh mar 'Lux', ach neart a gcnámha agus an slis a oibriú ar na héadaigh ansin.

D'fhiafraigh sé di an nífeadh sí a léine dó – diabhal mé nó sílim gur ar tórramh a bhí sé ag dul! Ach shuigh sé síos in aice leis an doras dúnta ag an tórramh. Chuir sí a lámh isteach an doras dúnta agus thug sí an brollach amach as a léine. D'ardaigh sí léi é agus bhuail sí suas san éadan air é, faoi bheith ag magadh fúithi. Le magadh a d'iarr sé uirthi an nífeadh sí a léine, sea, gan dabht. Dá scaoilfeadh sé thairis í gan bacadh léi, ní bhacfadh sí leis, deamhan bacadh, muis! [A man who was going into Montiagh one night, for a wake or a dance. He heard the banshee washing, beetling away with a beetle. Every woman that time had a beetle – there was not much soap like Lux about but the strength of the limbs and to work the beetle on the clothes then.

He asked her if she would wash his shirt for him – the devil, but I think it was to a wake he was going! But he sat down near the closed door at the wake-house. She put her hand in the closed door and she took the front out of his shirt. She went off with it and she came back when it was washed and she threw it into his face because he was making fun of her. It was in mockery that he asked her if she would wash his shirt, yes, without a doubt. If he had let her pass without bothering with her, she would not have bothered with him, the devil she would, *muis*!] (Galway 17).

II

The source situation for The Shirt Legend is similar to that for The Imprint of the Banshee's Five Fingers. Only seven versions, all in the Irish language have come to light (Galway 16, 17 — both from Waterdale in the parish of Claregalway; Galway 19, 20, 21 — from Montiagh in the same parish; Galway 28 — from Baunmore in the parish of Annaghdown; Galway 57 — from Tiernakill in the parish of Ross) (Appendix 4.3, pp. 317-20). There appears to be no reference to the legend in printed sources; all the above versions stem from folklore manuscripts, four from Main Manuscripts compiled prior to 1954 (Galway 17, 20 21, 28)[2] and the other three versions from Schools' Manuscripts compiled in 1937-38. Like The Imprint of the Banshee's Five Fingers, The Shirt Legend had not yet been noticed at the time of the Banshee Questionnaire: no questions were asked about the legend and no answers referring to it were received.

III

The distribution area of The Shirt Legend as now known from the available sources is even smaller than that of The Imprint of the Banshee's Five Fingers. Six of the seven versions stem from two parishes on the south-east shore of Lough Corrib (Map 24). A complete search of the manuscripts from Ross parish on the north-west side of Lough Corrib has been carried out. Folklore collecting has been extensive here over the years yet no further variants have been found. It is therefore likely that the Ross version (Galway 57) is a stray introduction there.

It was probably carried to Ross from the south-east by the numerous individuals who plied Lough Corrib in boats and steamers.[3] The distribution area in the south-east may, of course, have been larger than it is now but we may assume that the legend has always been local and confined mainly to the south-east of Lough Corrib.

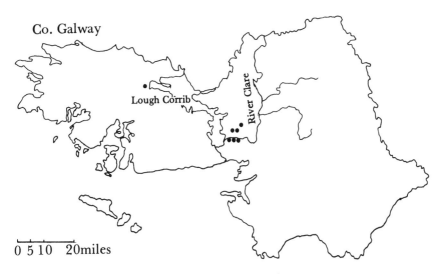

24. The Shirt Legend

IV

There is little significant variation in The Shirt Legend. The common traits within the versions are more interesting than the differences. Four of the seven versions (Galway 16, 17, 28, 57) contain all the following traits: a man out late at night on his way to a wake sees the banshee washing at a lake or riverside; he mockingly asks her to wash his shirt; later, when he sits down in the wake-house near the door, the banshee comes and tears the shirt off his body. The remaining three versions (Galway 19, 20, 21) are similar but lack the trait of the banshee coming and tearing off the offender's shirt. Instead she grabs a fistful of his hair. The setting late at night and the appearance of the being in connection with a visit to a wake are ingredients of the general death-messenger belief. Traditions about the death-messenger in the role of a washerwoman are of a more limited distribution but they are fairly prominent in Galway. The Shirt Legend appears to have arisen from the combination of such beliefs and motifs and the perception that it was dangerous to mock or tease the being. As in the case of The Imprint of the Banshee's Five Fingers, little can be said with certainty about the age of the legend except that it must have been current in the nineteenth century: it was taken down in the 1930s from old people who had heard it from people of a previous generation. The limited distribution, however, indicates that it is not especially old.

V

The main functions of The Shirt Legend are the same as those of The Comb Legend and The Imprint of the Banshee's Five Fingers. The being should not be interfered with — since *Níor thaithn leis an mbean sí caidéis ar bith a chur uirthi* ('The banshee did not like to be accosted at all'). It is also implied that one should not be out alone late at night and that one ought to be polite and courteous towards women. Warnings against the use of glib language are more prominent in The Shirt Legend than in the other interference legends. In one version the man involved deserved what he got because he spoke so inadvisedly — *bhí an tubaist ar a bhéal* ('misfortune was on his mouth') (Galway 28) and in another it is said that the man had *an iomarca fad ar a theanga* ('his tongue was too long') — he spoke too freely and too sarcastically (Galway 57). The legend teaches that those who refrain from such talk will fare well, while those who indulge in it have to answer for the consequences.

12

Origin of the Supernatural Death-Messenger Belief and Other Related Questions

I

The main traits in the folk traditions about the supernatural death-messenger in Ireland have now emerged. There is great variation in the traditions about the being but the core of the belief concerns a solitary, crying female supernatural being who is perceived as an ancestress of the family she attends.[1] One discerns in the traditions about her an older 'aristocratic' being of the *fylgja* type who stands in a special guardian-type position to noble and illustrious personages and families, specifically in the context of death. Alongside the predominately benign and sympathetic aspect of the death-messenger in the traditional material one also detects a frightening and aggressive aspect to her behaviour especially in the *badhbh*-area. There are also traces of a washing activity connected with her in areas mainly outside the *badhbh*-area.

It is with these attributes and characteristics of the death-messenger in mind that attention can be focused on the pre-nineteenth-century literary texts. In treating the names of the being it became evident that the beliefs, whatever their origin, were fully developed in Gaelic Ireland. Thus one is led to an examination of texts in Irish to determine whether or not the female beings foreboding death mentioned in them are related to the *bean sí, badhbh*, etc. If they are indeed so related one must assess what they tell about the nature and origin of the supernatural death-messenger of Irish folk tradition. And in the origin of the death-messenger may lie the solutions to certain other questions about the belief complex which have so far remained unanswered – the exact nature of her connection with families and the significance of her association with water and her hair-combing activity.

The literary texts consist of prose narratives from the Old to the Early Modern Irish periods and, in the case of

191

bean sí alone, poetry texts from the seventeenth and eighteenth centuries. The use of literary sources of this kind presents many problems of a source critical nature. Some of these problems have been touched upon in the treatment of the names of the death-messenger and others will arise here.

Because of the cultural unity which existed between Ireland and Gaelic Scotland from about the fifth to the seventeenth centuries and because of the conservatism of the Scottish Gaelic tradition generally, one must take account of the traditions of the supernatural washerwoman foreboding death in Gaelic Scotland in order to properly assess the Irish supernatural death-messenger belief.

Etymological examination of the names of the death-messenger, particularly of *bean sí*/banshee and *badhbh*, seemed to point to two main earlier strata of the death-messenger belief in Ireland termed here the *sí*-woman-stratum and the *badhbh*-stratum. It will be shown that these two strata represent the duality of aspects within the person of a single deity and that they are to be understood in terms of the 'fundamental nexus' of sovereignty as outlined by Mac Cana.[2]

One must divide the texts into two groups — *sí*-woman-texts and *badhbh*-texts. The *sí*-woman-texts will consist of those in which a female being, or beings, connected with deaths are known (or could be known, or became known in subsequent tradition) as *bean sí*. The *badhbh*-texts are those in which a female *badhbh*-figure forebodes death by washing. It will become clear that the female beings connected with deaths depicted in the two groups of texts — most particularly in the Medieval *badhbh*-texts — differ substantially from each other not only in general appearance and behaviour but also in their attitudes to the person or persons who are about to die. It will emerge however that the two strata were coming closer together as the centuries went by and that it is likely that it was from their interaction in the course of time that many of the attributes of the death-messenger of folk tradition have come. It will be demonstrated that it was the *sí*-woman-stratum which ultimately became and remained predominant even in the *badhbh*-area and yet a particular characteristic of the Badb (modern Irish *badhbh*), her washing foreboding death, is largely to be found in areas where the name *bean sí*/banshee is applied to the death-messenger.

II

THE *SÍ*-WOMAN-TEXTS

The first text, *Táin Bó Fraích*, The Cattle Raid of Froech, is a *remscél* or foretale prefatory to *Táin Bó Cuailnge*. Like the Táin it is set at the court of Medb and Ailill at Cruachain in Connaught and it has been dated as early eighth century by Carney.[3] In it are found weeping *mná síde* connected with death. The relevant episode in the story may be summarised as follows: Froech mac Idaith, son of Bé Find from the Otherworld, comes to Cruachain to woo Findabair, the daughter of Medb and Ailill. Through their treachery, he is wounded by a water monster. (In the later folktale and ballad versions of the story he dies from his wounds.)[4] On the orders of Medb and Ailill he is brought to the fort of Cruachain. While his wounds are being attended to there the sound of weeping is heard over Cruachain *(Co cúalatar ní, a ngolgair for Crúachnaibh)* and one hundred and fifty beautifully clad women are seen. Messengers go to them to learn what they keened *(Tíogair chuccu do fhis scél dús cid ro chaínset)*. One of the women replies that it is for Froech mac Idaith that they cry. Froech hears their lamenting and says 'This is the crying of my mother and of the women of Boand' *(Gol mo mátharsa inso 7 bantrochta Bóinni)*. He is brought forward to the women and they carry him away into the Otherworld mound of Cruachain *(Dothíagat na mná immi 7 berdait úadib i ssíd Crúachan)*. In order to comply with the cattle-raid theme of the story Froech comes back from the Otherworld accompanied by fifty women who had the apparel of Otherworld women about them *(co n-écosc ban síde impu)*.[5]

One can discern a relationship between the weeping women in this text and the death-messenger of the archival records. First of all, the lamenting women are *mná síde* (plural of *ben síde*) and they are crying for Froech who is to die — they carry him into the subterranean abode of the dead, *Síd Crúachan*. It seems therefore, that *ben síde* in the meaning 'supernatural death-messenger' can be dated to the eighth century.

Two of the terms, *gol* 'to cry' and *caín* 'to weep', in the text referring to the sounds of the *mná síde* correspond to terms used to describe the aural manifestation of the death-messenger in the traditional accounts. Thus it seems the crying or lamenting element of the traditional death-messenger manifestation can also be dated to the eighth century at least. Furthermore, Froech is an illustrious youth and he stands in a special relationship to the divine women who keen him, the women of the Boyne and particularly his mother, the divine Bé Find, sister of Boann, the tutelary deity of the river Boyne.[6]

The main divergence between the Froech tale and the traditional record is the apparent absence of the solitary manifestation which is central to the traditional aspect. But this may indeed be only apparent in that the emphasis in the Froech tale is more on the crying of Bé Find, the mother of Froech, and the reference to thrice fifty beautifully clad women may be due to the nature of the text. It can be regarded as a stylistic device to stress the nobility of Froech and the magnitude of his loss. The loud lamentation raised by the thrice fifty women of Eamhain Macha previous to the death of Cúchulainn may be similarly interpreted.[7] Alternatively the reference to such a large number of women and the descriptions of their beauty may reflect a concept of the Otherworld as 'The Land of Women' (see p. 32). While bearing these factors in mind, one may consider the divine beings, the *mná síde* of the Froech tale, as functional equivalents of the death-messenger of folk tradition.

III

The next texts concern the traditions surrounding the Battle of Clontarf in 1014 and Aoibheall of Craig Liath in Clare. In two accounts of the battle – the twelfth century[8] *Cogadh Gaedhel re Gallaibh*, 'The War of the Gaedhil with the Gaill'[9] and the thirteenth-century[10] *Annals of Lough Cé*[11] – it is said that on the eve of the battle Aoibheall (Oebhinn as she is called in the *Annals of Loch Cé*) came to Brian Boru and told him that he would be killed in battle the following day.[12] This incident is not recorded in the other annalistic accounts of the battle and clearly has been taken from the popular traditions which grew up around the heroic figure of Brian and his part in the battle. It is therefore older than its first appearance in literature in the twelfth century. Aoibheall's prognosticating role in the texts seems to be connected with her function as territorial goddess of the land of Thomond and later tutelary spirit of the royal house of the O'Briens. As such she would be concerned with the fortunes of the royal house and of Brian the High King, which had an intimate bearing on the economic and political well-being of the region, and, to some extent, the country as a whole. In the *Cogadh* she decides which of Brian's sons should gain the sovereignty of Ireland after Brian's death.

It is through the concept of sovereignty that some of the fundamental questions relating to the death-messenger belief may best be understood. There are many similarities between Aoibheall as depicted in those texts and the death-messenger of folk tradition. As a tutelary being she had a special relationship, as guardian, with the noble house of the O'Briens. She manifested herself alone and in connection with death. Also in the later literary and oral traditions she became known as a *bean sí*. She differs from the death-messenger in that the foreboding of death is experienced by the person doomed to die, a situation also obtaining in the *badhbh*-texts and very likely arising from the martial nature of the narratives. The knowledge that his death was inevitable also adds to the heroic stature of Brian. Despite the differences one may say that Aoibheall as depicted in these twelfth- and thirteenth-century texts is a precursor of the death-messenger of folk tradition.

IV

From Aoibheall one moves forward in time to the middle of the seventeenth century where Áine is found functioning as a death-messenger on the death of Maurice Fitzgerald (c. 1642). Aspects of Piaras Feiritéir's elegy for Fitzgerald have already been dealt with in the course of examining the archival material. Reference to it again here is helpful in that it shows very clearly part of the lineage of the death-messenger of folk tradition. The attributes of the death-messenger perceived in Aoibheall are more clearly discernible in the *persona* of Áine. She has a special relationship with the noble Fitzgerald family as former territorial goddess and ancestress of the family according to literary tradition.[13] She is a solitary being and is now also depicted as a weeping *bean sí*.

This latter characteristic is evident again in a reference to Clíona functioning as a foreboder of death in an eighteenth-century poem.[14] In the poem there is mention of Clíona's long hair which she allows to hang loose in her sorrow – this is a typical feature of the supernatural woman in Aisling poetry. The association of the death-messenger with a former land goddess who is now a *bean sí* is again evident in Clíona, territorial goddess of south-Munster, and as such intimately connected with important families and individuals in the area.

V

In all the pre-nineteenth-century *sí*-woman-texts the beings are foreboders of death[15] and they are, or can be understood to be, *mná síde*. These beings are generic predecessors of the death-messenger (except in regard to the washing activity and aggressive behaviour in the *badhbh*-area) and they thus give insights into the original nature of the supernatural death-messenger of folk tradition. They were originally divine beings and had a particular connection with aristocratic and politically important individuals and families. An ancestral relationship is very clear in the Froech tale and it is also inherent in the original territorial goddess roles of Aoibheall, Áine and Clíona. With the exception of the Froech tale and perhaps also the reference to Clíona in the eighteenth-century poetry text, the association with the individuals or families can be understood to be politically based. The beings' forebodings are about people whose actions and deaths will have a decisive bearing on the future political and economic well-being of the region. They are in essence beings representing the sovereignty of regions of Ireland and, in the case of Aoibheall, perhaps also the country as a whole.

There is one other aspect of the *sí*-woman-texts that needs examination. The foreboding women are very beautiful, unlike the 'ugly more so than beautiful' visage of the folk death-messenger. The portrayal of these beings as beautiful women can be explained in terms of their original divine nature and the aristocratic milieu in which they function. While these characteristics of the Otherworld women above may still be reflected in the Waterford material in particular, which describes the death-messenger as a tall beautiful woman with long golden hair, the death-messenger of the traditional accounts no longer functions in an aristocratic and heroic society. Her visage has been determined by the tradition bearers' perceptions of her as a family ancestress, by her connection with deaths and through analogy with the appearance and behaviour of the human keening women.

VI

THE *BADHBH*-TEXTS

The connection of the Badb, a war-goddess, with battle, strife and death is well attested in early Irish literary texts and these have been dealt with by Hennessy.[16] In Chapter 1 the treatment of the *badhbh*-appellations of the death-messenger outlined the characteristics of the Badb in ancient Irish literature in relation to the *badhb/babha*, etc. of oral tradition. The conclusion was drawn that the latter being is to some extent a descendant of the ancient Badb.

In Chapter 6 it was demonstrated that the central motif in the image of the Badb prefiguring death — her washing — was almost completely lacking in the south-east (in east-Munster and south-Leinster) in what is termed the *badhbh*-area but that it is to be found outside that area where the being is known as *bean-sí*/banshee.

The following analysis deals with three texts[17] ranging from the Medieval to the Early Modern Irish periods in which an encounter with a 'Washer at the Ford' is a foreboding of violent death for those who meet her: the 'Washer at the Ford' is the dread female seen before a battle washing the mangled limbs, clothes and armour of those who are doomed to die. The texts offer further insight into the nature and origin of the death-messenger of folk tradition. They also provide possible explanations for the lack of the washing motif and other enigmas in the death-messenger traditions of the *badhbh*-area.

VII

In *Aided Con Chulainn*, 'The Death of Cú Chulainn'[19] the *Badb* is depicted as washing Cú Chulainn's spoils. The washing motif occurs in the Early Modern Irish version of the tale[20] but it is likely to have been found in earlier versions also. Pokorny has dated the oldest nucleus of the tale before the middle of the eighth century[21] and the motif may well date from the Old Irish period. In the tale *Badb*, who has appeared to Cú Chulainn in many shapes such as a crow, and a hag roasting dog-meat on a spit, also appears as a young beautiful woman washing his spoils at a ford as he sets out for his final fateful battle. Despite the pleas of Deittine his mother, Emer his wife, and Cathfad the druid, he leaves Eamhain Macha accompanied in the end by Cathfad, and

> ní cian rángatar ón dúnad, an tan tarrla dóib ingen cháem chorpgeal chubhaidh ar bél Átha na Foraire ar Mag na hEamna, 7 sí ac torrsi 7 ac truaghnemélai, 7 faidhbh corcra cirtha créchtnaigthi aca fásgadh 7 aga fuarnighi a heoch-arimlibh in átha aici.[22] [they had not gone far from the fortress, when they encountered a beautiful, white-bodied, well-proportioned maiden in front of *Áth na Foraire* on the Plain of Emain, who was moaning and complaining and squeezing and washing purple, hacked, wounded spoils on the bank of the ford].

Cathfad interprets the omen and tells Cú Chulainn that the girl is '*ingin Baidhbhi*,' 'Badb's daughter', and that she is foreboding his death (*ac innisin do thuitme-si*) by her washing and wailing. Cú Chulainn replies that he will not go back 'though Badb be washing my spoils' (*gé atá in Badbh ac nighi m'faidhbhe-si*).[23]

The description of the Badb in this text as a young beautiful woman is unusual in the context of the other two texts to be considered here in which she also appears as a washer-woman; but one may compare it to a somewhat similar reference to Morrígan (Badb)[24] as she appeared to Cú Chulainn in *Táin Bó Cúailnge*.[25] There is also a resemblance to the descriptions of the death-messenger in the *badhbh*-area, in Waterford. The descriptions are possibly related to each other not just in terms of genre parallelism but thematically as well.

VIII

A foreboding washerwoman is also encountered in *Reicne Fothaid Canainne* dated by Meyer to the end of the ninth century or the beginning of the tenth.[26] There one finds the following reference to the Morrígan whose washing is connected with violent and fatal conflict — 'horrible are the huge entrails which the Morrígan washes ... many are the spoils she washes'. There is also a reference to her hair — 'she has flung her mane (*mong*) over her back'. The use of the word '*mong*' shows that her hair was envisioned as long and flowing.[27]

IX

In *Togail Bruidne Da Choca*, 'The Destruction of Da Choca's Hostel', which according to Mac Cana[28] predates the year 1000, Cormac Conloingeas, son of Conchubhair Mac Nessa, King of Ulster, is on his way from Connaught to Ulster to assume the kingship after his father's death. Like Cú Chulainn he is forced, in the course of his journey, to break his taboos. When he and his followers reach the river Shannon they see

a red woman on the edge of the ford washing her chariot and its cushions and harness. When she lowered her hand, the bed of the river became red with gore and with blood. But when she raised her hand over the river's edge, not a drop therein but was lifted on high; so that they went dryfoot over the bed of the river.[29]

The text identifies the woman as '*in Badb*', 'the Badb', and when Cormac questions her about her activity she adopts the stance of a sorceress, standing on one foot with one eye closed[30] and she chants in reply that it is his own harness and that of his trusted followers that she washes. Like Cú Chulainn, Cormac understands the grim prophecy, and she has also compelled him to break yet another taboo — to cross the Shannon dry-foot.[31]

When Cormac and his followers are lodged in Da Choca's hostel the Badb approaches in another guise. A description of her personal appearance includes a reference to her hair,

> Swarthy she was of hue and a dusky mantle covered her;
> her mouth was big and grey hair fell over her shoulders . . . [32]

Implicit in this description of her hair is that it is long.

X

In *Caithréim Thoirdhealbhaigh*, 'The Triumphs of Turlough',
written it seems about the middle of the fourteenth century[33]
the army of Donnchadh O'Brien, on its way to the Battle of
Corcomroe Abbey in north Clare on 15 August 1317, is said
to have encountered a hideous loathsome hag called a *badb*
washing mangled heads and limbs on the shore of Lough Riasc
(near the village of Ballyvaughan, Clare). Donnchadh asks her
who she is and who the maltreated dead are. She replies that she
is brónach of Burren (*brónach Bóirne mo buanainmsi*) and that
the slaughter heap is his army's heads and that his own head is
in the middle. Donnchadh tells his army to heed her not and says
she is the friendly *badb* of his opponent Clan Turlough. The
army then hurries on to the ridge of Corcomroe Abbey where
Donnchadh and most of his kindred are slain before evening.[34]
  Caithréim Thoirdhealbhaigh also deals with the battle of
Dysert O'Dea, May 1318.[35] It was an important battle because
it put an end to any hopes which the Normans held of supre-
macy in Clare. The relevant episodes may be summarised as
follows. Richard de Clare, the leader of the Normans, was
marching to what he thought would be an easy victory over
the O'Deas of Dysert. As he and his army were about to cross
the river Fergus they saw at the ford an horrific *badb* (*go
bfacatar ar in áth ar a gcionn badb ghér ghoblom. . .*) washing
armour and rich robes till the red blood squirted and fell from
them dyeing the river. De Clare called an Irish ally to ask the
badb whose gear and armour she washed. She replied that it
was the 'armour, raiment and other strippings' of De Clare,
his sons and the rest of his royal entourage, most of whom
would soon be dead. She identified herself as *in dobarbrónach*,
'the Water-Dismal One'. De Clare instructed his army to ignore

her, saying that it is for the benefit of Clan Turlough that she came to frustrate the expedition on them (*óir aithnigmid gurab ar maithe le cloinn Toirdelbaig táinic sí do tairmiosc na tosca so orainn*).[36]

The two *badhbh*-figures, *brónach Bóirne* — brónach of Ceann Bóirne or the Hag of Black Head (a peninsula in north-west Clare), and *in dobarbrónach* may be regarded as identical both in nature and function. Their washing connects them with the Badb, a goddess of war. Their identification with the land and clan of Turlough O'Brien and their support for Turlough in the political conflict shows that they represent the sovereignty of the territory. The equation of Badb and guardian spirit of the clan in this text represents a shift of emphasis from the earlier *badhbh*-texts. The *Caithréim* is a late and highly stylised text and while it was doubtlessly written by John Magrath[37] the hereditary historian of the O'Briens in order to extol the O'Brien clan, nevertheless it indicates a changing perception of the role of the Badb in its connection of the *badhbh*-figures with particular families in the sense familiar from the traditional material. The *badhbh*-figures in the *Caithréim* texts are both horrible creatures and the description of the hair of '*brónach Bóirne*' is as follows: *folt fraechda fathmandgarb flescláidir fraechgarbruadliath femnachda fuirre* . . . .'[38] 'she was thatched with elf-locks foxy-grey and rough as heather, long as sea-wrack, inextricably tangled . . .'[39]

<h2 style="text-align:center">XI</h2>

The literary texts in which a foreboding *badhbh*-figure appears as a 'Washer at the Ford' range then from the Medieval to the Early Modern Irish periods. Thereafter, the motif seems to have largely lost its generative force in the literary tradition and persisted mainly in modern manuscript copies of the story of Cú Chulainn's death.[40] It remained, however, in the oral traditions of the *bean sí*,[41] and, apart from twentieth-century folk tradition from Co. Galway which retained recollections of the 'Washer at the Ford' in her ancient context — beetling in a stream before the Battle of Aughrim 1691[42] — the washing motif, in relation to the death-messenger, is connected with non-conflict situations. It was in Gaelic Scotland that the washing motif flourished in the traditions of the *bean-nighe*.[43]

The 'Washer at the Ford' who forebodes death in the Irish texts is connected with the Badb, an ancient goddess of war. This colours the occasions on which she is manifested, her function, her behaviour and her image. She is a solitary female being of frightening and threatening visage with long, loose and sometimes tangled hair and — particularly in the earlier texts — she is connected with the death in battle of heroic personages. As the references to the manifestation of Aoibheall at the battle of Clontarf (p. 195) show, the foreboding of death in the context of a conflict situation is, in these *badhbh*-texts, experienced by the doomed person or persons. This type of manifestation is very rare in the Irish folk traditions of the death-messenger,[44] though it seems to have survived more strongly in Scottish Gaelic traditions of the *bean-nighe*. In the *badhbh*-texts there is also a dialogue between the *badhbh*-figure and the doomed individual in which the prophecy implied in her washing is further expounded. Virtually unknown in the folk tradition of the death-messenger in Ireland, this trait, too, has remained part of the *bean-nighe* belief in Gaelic Scotland. One can also perceive an element of hostility in these texts towards the person or persons who are destined to die, and this is still vaguely discernible in the more aggressive nature of the death-messenger of folk tradition in the *badhbh*-area.[45]

Implicit in the Badb's washing activity, which we have been discussing, is her connection with water, a connection that must be considered in more detail later.

XII

On the basis of the *sí*-woman-stratum-texts discussed so far in this chapter, the indications are that a form of the death-messenger belief existed in Ireland in the eighth century. The beings depicted in both sets of texts and their methods of foreboding death are diametrically opposed; the *badhbh*-texts show a being who is aggressive and sinister, while the *sí*-woman texts depict a beautiful and prosperous being (or beings). But, subsequent sections of this chapter will show the two strata are largely in harmony by the eighteenth century, and by that time – and indeed in the previous century as is seen in the reference to the death-messenger manifestation in Piaras Feiritéir's elegy on Maurice Fitzgerald c. 1642 (cf. section 4) – the image of the death-messenger of folk tradition is fully developed.

There is another foreboding female figure who seems to embody the attributes of the beings of both strata. This figure is Fedelm *banfháidh* who is encountered at the outset of *Táin Bó Cuailnge*. Just as Medb is about to depart from Cruachain for Ulster at the head of her royal army she sees a very beautiful maiden coming towards her. The maiden is in a chariot drawn by two black horses in the oldest recension of *Táin Bó Cuailnge* in *Leabhar na hUidhre*, compiled in the twelfth century but probably derived from two written sources of the ninth century.[46] Very beautiful, she is richly dressed. She has yellow hair woven into three plaits. Two of these are wound around her head and the other hangs down her back touching her calves behind. In her hand she has a weaver's beam of white bronze. Medb asks her what her name is and the maiden replies *Fedelm banfili do Chonnachtaib mo anim-sea* (I am Fedelm the poetess of Connaught). She then asks her if she has the power of prophecy called *imbass forosna*.[47] When Fedelm replies she has, Medb asks her to look for her and tell her how her hosting will fare. Each time Fedelm looks she replies '*Atchíu forderg, atchíu ruad* 'I see it bloody, I see it red' and then she chants a poem in which she prophesies the heroic deeds of Cú Chulainn during the Táin and the destruction he would wreak on Medb's army.[48]

From the knowledge of the *badhbh*-figures gleaned from the survey of them in the foregoing sections, Fedelm can also clearly be considered such a being. She is a seer and her connection with the colour red shows her to be akin to the Badb in *Togail Bruidne Da Choca* (above p. 199) who is there a 'red woman' and a seer. Her identification as the Badb may be further inferred from her riding alone in a chariot – there is a similar description of the Badb in *Táin Bó Regamna*.[49] Her appearance as a beautiful woman also recalls the description of Badb in *Aided Con Culainn* (p. 198). The lack of the motif of mangled heads, arms, limbs, armour, etc. which prefigures death in battle, may merely be apparent. While the actual washing of these items is missing, the motif is present in another form. Fedelm is a weaving prophetess — she has a weaver's beam in her hand in this text and in *Táin Bó Cuailnge* from the Book of Leinster she is actually weaving a fringe.[50] A.J. Goedheer's consideration of the weaving of Fedelm in *Irish and Norse Traditions about the Battle of Clontarf* has been noted by O'Rahilly.[51] Goedheer discusses a passage from the Song of Dörruðr in *Njal's Saga* which describes some women weaving in a weaving house: 'Heads of men were the weights, but men's bowels the warp and weft, a sword was the sley and arrows were the reels'.[52] The weaving women sing a song describing the gory woof which is set up to announce a murderous battle. Goedheer refers to Fedelm *banfháidh*, the 'weaving prophetess'[53] in the Book of Leinster version of the Táin[54] and compares her weaving and prophecy of battle with the incident in the late thirteenth-century *Njal's Saga.*[55] He notes that her weaving, though less gory, is not merely 'an incidental ornament' but is 'connected with her original character as a sorceress, for weaving includes a magical power in primitive belief'.[56]

In the later Book of Leinster (twelfth century) and the Stowe versions (thirteenth-fourteenth century)[57] of the Táin, while all the Badb-like attributes of Fedelm which have been mentioned are still apparent, nevertheless, what one may call her *sí*-woman attributes are being developed. When Medb sees the girl approaching her, in these versions, she asks her what she is doing there. The girl replies she is promoting Medb's interest and prosperity, gathering and mustering the four great provinces of Ireland with her to go into Ulster for Táin Bó Cuailnge. When Medb asks her why she does that she replies, 'I have good reason to do so . . . I am a bondmaid of your people.' Medb then asks her who she is and the girl replies *Feidelm banfáid a Síd Chrúachna atamchomnaic-se* 'I am Feidelm the prophetess from Síd Chrúachna'.[58] The battle divination of Fedelm then follows.

These attributes of Fedelm — her solitary female manifestation, the aristocratic milieu in which she appears as a beautiful woman connected with death, and the special relationship which exists between Medb and Fedelm who is 'promoting' Medb's 'interest' and 'prosperity', recall the *sí*-women of the *sí*-woman-stratum who are tutelary beings. Furthermore, Fedelm is *a Síd Chrúachna* 'from the Síd of Cruachain'. Therefore, although she is not expressly called a *ben síde* in the text it may be assumed that the compiler of the Book of Leinster version in the twelfth century understood her to be such a being.

Thus Fedelm — a predecessor of the death-messenger of folk tradition — exemplifies the fundamental nexus in which the seemingly contradictory characters of the beings in the *badhbh* and the *sí*-woman-strata come together. In her are equated war-goddess and land-goddess, death, aggressiveness, ugliness, old age, youth, beauty, abundance and benignity. Professor Mac Cana who has traced a sovereignty goddess theme in many areas of Irish literature sees in it a solution to the duality of aspects of the goddess in Irish literature such as is seen in the *persona* of Fedelm. He states:

> All the seemingly contradictory characteristics of the deity — maternal, seasonal, warlike, young, aged, beautiful or monstrous — may be referred to this fundamental nexus, and it is significant that, in general, each individual goddess reveals several or all of these characters, and even though one of them may predominate, the others are rarely absent (Mac Cana, 1973, p. 94).

Fedelm, then, may be considered the personification of sovereignty. Similarly, the death-messenger of folk tradition, who embodies characteristics of both the *sí*-woman- and *badhbh*-strata, may, by analogy with Fedelm, also be considered to be in origin a sovereignty goddess. This function of the being may still be discerned in the traditions which associate her with families.

XIII

The identification of the foreboding beings in the literary texts as goddesses of sovereignty has become more and more obvious. The sovereignty goddess symbolised not merely the soil and substance of the territory, but also the spiritual and legal dominion which the rightful king, her spouse, exercised over it. In most of the *bean sí*-texts and in the latter *badhbh*-

texts such as the *Caithréim*, the foreboding female being symbolised the land of the family or clan to which she belonged and she symbolised also their rightful title to it as opposed to the claims of usurping foreigners. It would appear, then, that the connection with families in these texts can be understood in terms of the ancient concept of sacral kingship – the rightful king was accepted as her legitimate spouse by the sovereignty of the territory over which he ruled.[59]

The underlying tradition envisaged the goddess 'espoused to the rightful king'. It also regarded her as 'the mother of such a king and the ancestress of a royal line'.[60]

Thus, for example, Brian Boru is the rightful spouse of his kingdom as personified by Aoibheall and, as noted, she is depicted as deciding which of his sons shall succeed to the kingship of Ireland after his death (p. 195). Likewise, the association of the Anglo-Norman Fitzgeralds with the goddess Áine – regarded in literary tradition as the ancestress of the Fitzgeralds – is a device to legitimise their ownership of lands originally confiscated from Irish chiefs. The concept of rightful kingship remained firmly embedded in the literary tradition, and even in the eighteenth century the poets saw deliverance from English oppression in terms of the restoration of the native kingship. With the native Irish nobility either dead or exiled, they turned to the Scottish Stuarts for a symbol of their deliverance. In thus making Ireland's salvation conditional upon the accession of a rightful and acceptable king they were, as Mac Cana has pointed out,[61] 'acting as the faithful transmitters of an age-old and uninterrupted belief'.

Does this belief find expression in the traditions of the people in the *persona* of the *bean sí*/banshee, *badhb* and their like? If it is accepted that the death-messenger originally symbolised the sovereignty of the land, then her ancestress-type connection with families can be more readily understood on the basis of the concept of sacral kingship. The acknowledgement that the *bean sí*/banshee, *badhb*, etc. followed a family can then be interpreted as indicating the family in question had an ancestral claim to the land, they being the rightful spouses of their lands. On the other hand the denial of the death-messenger to foreigners who settled in lands obtained particularly as a result of the Cromwellian or Williamite confiscations and forfeitures of the seventeenth and eighteenth centuries,[62] can be understood in political and ethnocentric terms as indicating that they were intruders and not the rightful spouses of the lands they possessed and that they were also of dubious ancestry.

This would appear to be the original nature of the connection of the death-messenger with families and it confers venerable age on this aspect of the death-messenger belief. According to Mac Cana,[63] 'The notion of a mystical or symbolic union between the king and his kingdom is older than Indo-European society.'

We will move on to consider the process of harmonisation of the *badhbh-* and *sí*-woman-strata apparently already in progress in the fourteenth-century *Caithréim* text discussed in section 10. While the process involved changes in both, it seems to have been the *badhbh-*stratum which underwent most modification.

XIV

References to beings similar to the supernatural death-messenger in Irish folk tradition seem to be non-existent in Irish literature between most of the fourteenth century and the middle of the seventeenth century. This dearth of reference is no doubt due, in some measure, to the character of the literature which prevailed during most of the period — the learned literature of the bardic order.[64] Even in the seventeenth- and eighteenth-century texts, the references to the death-messenger belief are not very common but they are, nevertheless, sufficient to show that not only did the belief continue to exist during the previous centuries but also that it underwent changes in that period. In the absence of references to the death-messenger in the post-fourteenth- and pre-seventeenth-century texts, only suggestions as to the underlying reasons for the changes can be offered.

XV

The three hundred years between the fourteenth and seventeenth centuries were times of political, social and cultural change in Ireland, particularly in the province of Leinster, and also in east-Munster. These changes contributed in no small way to the shaping of Irish folk traditions.[65]

The *sí*-woman-stratum seems to have been best able to adapt and remain relevant in the changing times. While the main lines of the stratum remained the same, there were also some changes and these must have been followed by a period of consolidation. By the seventeenth century the divine nature of the being is no longer dominant and she is known simply as *bean sí*.[66] Her association with families in the sense familiar from the traditional records, and her connection with 'ordinary deaths' is fully developed.[67] In the eighteenth century and, no doubt, long before that, the term *bean sí* is fully established in the *badhbh*-area.[68] Although the earliest reference to her washing activity connected with death dates only from the beginning of the nineteenth century, it was undoubtedly during the preceding century, or centuries, that the *bean sí*/banshee acquired this attribute (see section 17). The washing motif does not occur in the *sí*-woman-stratum-texts and in attempting to find out how it became attached to the *bean sí*/banshee it is necessary to take into account what was happening in the *badhbh*-stratum.

XVI

Though the word *badhbh* in the meaning 'scold', 'curser', 'quarrelsome woman' and 'bogey' has remained widespread in Ireland,[69] one cannot be sure how extensively the motif of the washerwoman foreboding death was initially distributed. From the traces of this belief which have remained in the folk tradition, it would appear to have been fairly widely disseminated (pp. 130-133 and Map 12). Although these traditional records date mainly from the twentieth century it is not unlikely they represent the distribution of the motif as it may have been some centuries earlier. It is improbable it ever existed in Cork and Kerry and this is not only because of the dominant position which the *sí-bhean* has held in the oral and literary traditions there and in Munster as a whole, but also because of the lack of visual manifestations of the death-messenger and the virtual absence of an association of the being with water in that region.[70] But it is the very poor representation of the washing motif in the south-east of the country (Map 12) where there is a fairly strong connection between the death-messenger and water (see section 18) and particularly in those parts of east-Munster and south-Leinster where the name *badhbh* in its various dialect forms has persisted that is most puzzling.

The early literary texts in which the Badb was a foreboder of war, belonged to a period of strong Gaelic culture when the belief seemed to relate equally to both sides of the conflict. In other words, reference to the appearance of the Badb foreboding violent death in battle presupposed a certain cultural unity between the warring sides such as existed, for example, in wars between Irish families, or between Irish and Anglo-Norman families or in the inter-clan warfare of Gaelic Scotland. As times became more peaceful in Leinster and with the extra-strong Anglo-Norman-Gaelic fusion in the south of the province, internal political conflict was much reduced.[71] It is likely that it was in the climate of relative peace which prevailed in the wake of the Anglo-Norman settlement of much of Leinster by the thirteenth century that elements of the *badhbh*-stratum began to be fundamentally modified. The decline then in consistent deadly warfare in the province between Anglo-Norman and Gael meant the belief in a foreboding female being connected primarily with violent death in battle was no longer relevant and neither was her most outstanding characteristic in the pre-battle context – her washing. It was possibly at the same time and for the same reason that the bird form, which was also part of the battle field image of the ancient Badb – if it ever existed in this area – also went into decline.[72] That these two characteristics of the *badhbh*-figure – the washing and the bird form (if it existed) – had declined considerably by the second half of the eighteenth century can be deduced from the lack of any mention of them in two literary references to the *badhbh* from that period (see pp. 35, 40). A faint trace of the washing motif still remains in the *badhbh*-area (Kilkenny 15) but it is connected with the *bean sí*/banshee (cf. pp. 132-3), while there is no reference whatsoever to the bird form.

In the centuries after the Anglo-Norman conquests in Leinster and Munster, the wars and conflicts which erupted there were struggles for power which, generally speaking, concerned

English power in the area rather than being exclusively internal struggles. Coupled with this was a rapid decline in Gaelic culture in the province.[73] A weak and only partly Gaelic culture could hardly sustain such a striking and developed figure, dependent on ancient cultural survival, as the *badhbh* seems to have been. Rather, the more simple contrast and the cultural diversity between native and foreigner could be more aptly accommodated in the *sí*-woman stratum. Thus, as the *badhbh*-stratum was becoming more and more modified the way was clear for the more relevant and appropriate *sí*-woman stratum to become established in the *badhbh*-area. There can be little doubt that it was the ultimate fusion of the dominant *sí*-woman stratum with what had survived of the characteristics of the ancient Badb (especially her name, her aggressive appearance and behaviour, her connection with water and to some extent, also, her washing activity) which produced the image of the death-messenger found in the traditional records from the *badhbh*-area. Although the name *bean sí* gained a firm hold in the area — in O'Brien's dictionary (1768) it is used synonymously with *badhb* — it has not succeeded so far in ousting the more deeply-rooted *badhbh* names (unlike the *bean chaointe* term in Limerick).[74]

It is not possible to say in the absence of literary evidence when the *sí*-woman stratum first gained a firm footing in the *badhbh*-area. The main thrust of this stratum probably came from Munster which appears to have been largely an area where the *bean sí*/banshee did not wash while foreboding death (Map 12) and where the *sí-bhean* has been prominent in the oral and literary traditions of the people. It is likely that the *sí*-woman-stratum was for centuries exerting influence on the periphery of the *badhbh*-area and it must have been firmly established within the area well before the eighteenth century. That the fusion of the two strata was already complete in the area in the eighteenth century is evident from the entry in O'Brien's Dictionary (1768) in which *badhb* is glossed *Bean-Síghe* and the connection of the being with noble Irish families is stressed. Furthermore, in an Irish elegy composed in Wexford in 1781 the death-messenger is called *badhbh* but her characteristics resemble those of the *sí*-woman-stratum figures (section 19 and note 96 below).

XVII

In areas (apart from Cork and Kerry where the death-messenger is never seen) where a stronger Gaelic culture survived, like north-Leinster, south-Ulster, north-Munster (Clare) and Connaught, the motif of the washerwoman foreboding death survived to a somewhat greater extent, though in modified form (see section 18). The being was no longer known as Badb but rather as *bean sí* and she was connected with 'non-violent deaths'.

In the late (fourteenth century) and highly stylised *Caithréim Thoirdhealbhaigh* (see section 10), *badb* is used synonymously with *cailleagh* and *aimid*,[75] in its general derogatory sense denoting the horrible, evil, witch-like and aggressive appearance and behaviour of the being rather than to identify her as Badb, goddess of war. By the fourteenth century the identification of the washing foreboding *badb* as a war fury was probably becoming vague and blurred. As the perception of the washerwoman foreboding death as a goddess of war was declining it is likely the force of the word *badb* to denote her was also diminishing. It is possible she then began to be perceived simply as a *sí*-woman, a *bean sí*. She was associated with water as were the *sí*-woman-stratum beings[76] mentioned above, and it is well established in Irish tradition that a woman seen near water is thought to be a *sí*-woman.[77] All of this facilitated the change of name from *badb* to *bean sí*, as did the tendency in the early literature to associate the Badb and Morrígan with the *Síd*.[78]

After this stage had been reached it is possible that the washerwoman foreboding death came more and more under the influence of the *sí*-woman-stratum and one can be fairly sure it was the connection of the washing motif with the vibrant *sí*-woman-stratum which enabled it to survive in the death-messenger tradition into the twentieth century. As this happened the connection of the being with heroic individuals in a battle context in the early texts developed to include non-violent deaths in particular families.[79] Consequent on this development, the traces of hostility towards the doomed person discernible in the old texts would have tended to fade away (but not completely as we have seen) and the dialogue between the washing figure and the person destined to die would also have eventually faded away.

The pre-nineteenth-century literary texts in Irish and English do not furnish any evidence to support these suggestions as to why and how the changes in the scope and function of the washing motif came about. Consequently, they are of no assistance in trying to date the changes as they occurred. Nevertheless, on the basis of the nineteenth-century and later-traditional material, one can speculate with some confidence that the evolution was largely along the lines suggested. In Matthew Archdeacon's *Legends of Connaught*[80] the banshee is depicted as washing the winding-sheet as a sign of imminent death and she is also said to follow particular families. Likewise, early twentieth-century folk tradition from Clare[81] would also seem to corroborate these suggestions because in it the identification of the washing *badb* of the fourteenth-century *Caithréim* with Aoibheall, the territorial goddess and tutelary spirit of the O'Briens is evident. Furthermore, there are records in the traditional material from within the *badhbh*-area (Kilkenny 15) and from certain areas outside, or on the periphery of the *badhbh*-area (Map 13), in which the *bean sí*/banshee washes as a sign of death in the family she follows. The apparent lack of any definite connection between the supernatural washerwoman foreboding death in Scottish Gaelic tradition, the *bean-nighe*, and specific families, would also seem to confirm that this element became more developed in the traditions of the foreboding washerwoman in Irish tradition under the influence of the more dominant *sí*-woman-stratum.

The washerwoman motif presupposes the being in question is associated with water. Although she is not thought to be a water being, the trait is common in the oral traditions of the death-messenger in Ireland and in the supernatural washerwoman traditions in Gaelic Scotland. What is the nature and significance of the connection with water in relation to the *bean sí*/banshee, *badhb* etc.?

XVIII

In Chapter 6^{82} the manifestation locations of the death-messenger were treated on the basis of archival records. It was noted that the appearances of the being occur commonly close to water, at lakes, rivers and wells.[83] The connection with water is not confined to the *badhbh*-area but it is more common there in belief statements and memorates and in Leinster as a whole than in the other provinces.[84] The examination of the early Irish literary texts in this chapter has shown that the connection with water is intrinsic in the *badhbh* narratives,[85] and it has been seen that the washing activity of the death-messenger connected with death is generically related to the similar activity of the ancient Badb, a goddess of war, in these texts.[86] The connection with water, therefore, in the archival records which depict the death-messenger as a washerwoman, is self-explanatory. It is not certain how widely dispersed the washing motif was formerly,[87] but it is likely the distribution of the being's association with water gleaned from the traditional records essentially represents the areas where the washing motif was originally to be found. With the passage of time and a changing society such as we have described in the previous section, it is reasonable to infer that, while the actual washing motif faded away in many areas, the association with water remained. The fact that the *badhb* continued to be so strongly connected with death in the *badhbh*-area, even though the washing motif had practically disappeared from the belief there, would seem to indicate that this was in fact happened. A factor which may have helped to preserve the connection with death is, that in some early Irish literary sources, water — as well as other landscape features such as mounds and hills — has been perceived as providing a link with, or entry to the otherworld, the land of the dead.[88]

We must also bear in mind the inherent association of the beings of the *sí*-woman-stratum with water (p. 211).

The connection of the supernatural death-messenger with water is then a survival of a similar characteristic, especially of the ancient Badb and also of the *sí*-woman-stratum beings, and it is thus illustrative of the supernatural or otherworld nature of the being and also her connection with death.

The association of the death-messenger with water can also be seen in terms of the warlike and benevolent attributes of the beings in the *badhbh-* and *sí-*woman-strata, respectively (above, p. 205). As such it can best be understood in terms of the sovereignty goddess theme in which Mac Cana[89] sees a solution to the contradictory characters of the deity in Irish literature. It may be added that the depiction of the sovereignty of Ireland as a woman (Étaín) sitting by a well is attested in Irish literature as early as the ninth century.[90]

XIX

Another activity attributed to the death-messenger of folk tradition is the combing of her hair. The scope and distribution of this characteristic is dealt with in Chapter 5 and The Comb Legend is treated in Chapter 9. It has been seen that there is a noticeable correspondence between the distribution of the combing motif and the belief that the death-messenger has long hair. The latter motif has been noticed mainly in east-Munster (Tipperary and Waterford) and Leinster, and we may suppose that it spread from the *badhbh-*area in the south-east, north-wards and westwards into the areas where the being is visually manifested.

The traditional records offer only four explanations of the hair-combing activity of the death-messenger and it has been shown that none of these belongs to the collective tradition. Furthermore, no parallel activity seems to be associated with the female beings connected with death in the *badhbh-* and *sí-*woman-strata already discussed in this chapter. How, then is the combing activity of the death-messenger to be explained?

The combing of her hair is an activity which is not exclusive to the supernatural death-messenger. It is also connected with other female supernatural beings associated with water and not ostensibly appearing in a prognosticating role, in literary and oral tradition. It is found as a literary motif as early as the ninth century in the story of Étaín and it also appears to be associated with Boann.[91] In Irish folk tradition it is connected with Áine of Lough Gur, Co. Limerick and the motif also survives in the folk tradition of other female supernatural beings in Ireland and elsewhere.[92] It seems, therefore, that the combing of her hair is also an attribute of the Otherworld woman, an understandable characteristic in view of a depiction of the Otherworld as a land of beautiful women with long flowing hair.[93] Thus, the combing activity of the supernatural death-messenger is, along with her connection with water, another indication of her Otherworld origin. The Otherworld in Irish tradition is, however, also the land of the dead and since the comb is also connected with death,[94] one of the roles of the Otherworld woman — in this context the woman associated with water and combing her hair — can be that of death-messenger. Thus, the combing activity of the supernatural death-messenger can be regarded as an integral part of her message of death, a point which seems borne out by those records[95] which state that she combs as she cries and, thus, link her combing with what is essentially her death message, her crying. The combing has remained part of the death-messenger belief and it is most prominently associated with the being in the *badhbh*-area, an association mentioned in an eighteenth-century Wexford manuscript[96] but is undoubtedly older than that. This association is understandable in view of the descent of the death-messenger in that area, to some extent at least, from the ancient Badb, a goddess of war, herself so intimately associated with water and death.

Undoubtedly, the combing of her hair by the *bean sí, badhb* etc., also reflects to some extent the tearing of the hair by mourning women in Ireland[97] and this association has also helped to keep the combing motif very much alive in the death-messenger belief.

In view of the connection of the combing activity with Étaín, Boann and Áine — sovereignty goddesses all three — it seems that, as with the connection with water in the previous section, the hair-combing activity of the supernatural death-messenger represents the duality of aspects or contradictory characteristics of the sovereignty woman — youth/beauty and old age, life and death, for example. This enigma is most obvious, perhaps, in the descriptions of the *badhb*, the supernatural death-messenger in Co. Waterford tradition, as a tall, beautiful young woman, combing her hair, a depiction reminiscent in some respects of the description of the Badb, a goddess of war in the story of the death of Cú Chulainn (cf. p. 198).

XX

One cannot be sure when using such old sources whether they reflect a belief which existed at the time of composition, or one known, perhaps, several centuries before but since gone into decline. The developed state of the *sí*-woman motifs in the eighth century, and the washerwoman motifs from the Medieval period, is an indication that they are older still. However, on the basis of the traditions which still exist about the supernatural washerwoman foreboding death (both in the Scottish Gaelic and Irish traditions), and the elements of the *sí*-woman belief still in the *bean sí*/banshee belief in Ireland (outside the *badhbh*-area and excluding the washing motif), one can be reasonably sure the texts represent beliefs held at the time of composition and also that their portrayal of the beliefs is accurate. It has been possible, therefore, to offer suggestions about the origin of the belief and also to establish a *terminus ante quem* for the existence of the death-messenger belief itself and for many of its main components. It has also been possible to discern, and to suggest explanations for the changes in the two strata down the centuries.

XXI

The death-messenger of the traditional records is derived from two main strata of the belief: the *sí*-woman stratum can be dated to about the eighth century (pp. 193-4), and while the *badhbh*-stratum is expressly manifested in the Medieval period (pp. 198-200) it probably had earlier roots.

   The beings depicted in these strata in the eighth century are similar in some respects but diametrically opposed in others. They are solitary female beings and they are first and foremost *foreboders* of death. The group of female beings mentioned in *Táin Bó Fraích* has been shown to be a stock literary motif. The washerwoman of the *badhbh*-stratum, the 'red woman', is concerned primarily with violent bloody death in battle and is an aggressive and horrible figure. The *sí*-woman figure, on the other hand has a more benign, ancestral role. She is a type of guardian. Both sets of beings function in an heroic and aristocratic milieu and are associated with heroic and illustrious individuals and families. They are weeping figures and the term *bean sí* has the meaning 'supernatural foreboder of death'.

The dual aspect discernible in the *badhbh-* and *sí*-woman – strata is crystallised in the pivotal figure, Fedelm *banfháidh*, who embodies all the attributes of the beings in the two strata. She appears to represent a pre-eighth-century stage of the belief.[98] On the basis of research by Mac Cana into the sovereignty-goddess theme in Irish literature Fedelm may be the personification of sovereignty. The death-messenger of folk tradition also incorporates these contradictory attributes and the analogies with Fedelm indicate her origin as a sovereignty goddess.

Since the sovereignty of the land was perceived as a woman who espoused the rightful king and, thus, conferred on him dominion over it, the connection of the death-messenger with families in modern folk tradition (stimulated, no doubt, by the land confiscation in the seventeenth century (cf. pp. 60, 206-7, 209-10)), can be explained in terms of survivals of the concept of sacral kinship into modern times.

The main changes in the *badhbh-* and *sí*-woman-strata appear to date from the fourteenth century onward. Because of the source situation prior to the middle of the seventeenth century, the changes cannot be dated accurately. Even though the earliest record of the *badhbh* being glossed *bean sí* is in the eighteenth century, we can safely assume the major changes in the two strata had taken place by the seventeenth century. The period from the fourteenth to seventeenth centuries, one of great political, social and cultural change – particularly in Leinster – brought euhemerisation and popularisation of the belief. The *sí*-woman stratum remained relatively stable and it was the *badhbh*-stratum that underwent most modification during the period. The washing activity attributed to the being went into decline in many areas, including the *badhbh*-area of south-Leinster and east-Munster, as apparently did the word *badhbh* to denote a supernatural washerwoman foreboding death, in favour of the term *bean sí*/banshee. The connection of the *badhbh* with clans or families would also have developed to include 'ordinary death' during this period, presumably under the influence of the *sí*-woman stratum. As the term *bean sí*/banshee became established in the *badhbh*-area, it was, presumably, from the interaction of the two strata, representing the dual aspects of the patron goddess, that the special characteristics of the death-messenger in the *badhbh*-area emerged.

In Cork and Kerry, the apparent lack of the washing characteristic of the death-messenger there, is probably due to the virtual lack of visual manifestations of the being and of an association with water in that tradition area. Outside that region, and in areas where the washerwoman attribute is not recorded, it is likely that the connection with water is a survival of the former washing activity of the *badhbh* and also of the inherent association of the *sí*-woman beings with water. As such it is an indication of the Otherworld origin of the supernatural death-messenger and her connection with death.

The combing activity of the death-messenger in the traditional records is not paralleled in the *badhbh*- and *sí*-woman-texts examined. Such combing is, however, associated with other female supernatural beings not necessarily in a prognosticating role, and is another attribute of the Otherworld woman which has survived in the supernatural death-messenger belief in Ireland. The Otherworld woman can also be considered a messenger of death and as such her combing activity is also connected with death. It is not so surprising, then, in view of the intimate connection between the ancient Badb and death that the combing motif has remained so prominent in the supernatural death-messenger belief, particularly in the *badhbh*-area.

While the age of the many and varied elements which constitute the death-messenger belief differs, it is evident it is very old. The belief and its many components have been moulded by generations of people in Ireland — native and later arrivals. By adapting to the changing social climates, it has survived as an integral part of Irish belief systems, even into the twentieth century. But will the death-messenger belief continue, or will it become irrelevant and fade away for ever in this age of technology?

13

Continuity and Change in the Death-Messenger Tradition in the Twentieth Century

I

A sizeable amount of material referring to death-messenger manifestations of the nineteen sixties and nineteen seventies has been adduced throughout this work. From this material it is evident that the core of the contents of the tradition has remained unchanged up to the present time. Nothing has come to light to indicate that any basically new components have been added to the corpus of the beliefs or legends in the last few decades. It may be possible, however, to observe some minor adaptations of belief motifs and legends to modern social and environmental conditions. The main changes are likely to relate to the intensity and frequency with which the beliefs were held in the beginning and at the end of the period under investigation. The problem concerning the fluctuations in the number of holders of the belief and the intensity of their belief is beset by imponderables, however.

The year in which individual items were collected is known in the vast majority of cases, and sometimes the manifestations described took place shortly before the collecting dates. Not infrequently, however, there has been a time-lag of very many years between the experiences and the collecting dates, and in still other instances, no precise information enables the time lapse to be assessed. It is in any event clear that some of the sources reflect conditions as they were a generation or so ago rather than the present state of general belief in their respective areas.

It is often very difficult to decide how deeply the tradition-bearers actually believed in what they reported. The folklore texts as written down by the collectors are usually all that is available. Only occasionally are the collectors' comments on their impressions of the narrator's seriousness from the tone of voice, gestures and general behaviour given. Records of the latter kind refer mainly to the most recent decades when the collectors' awareness of the importance of such material has increased.

219

It is obvious, too, that many people for a variety of reasons, are reluctant to admit to a belief in the supernatural.[1] On the other hand, tradition-bearers are also often extremely obliging and they may sometimes have told collectors what they thought they wanted to hear.

Above all, belief is a quality which defies exact measurement. Apart from firm believers and total disbelievers there were, in the period of the investigation — and no doubt always — those who wavered or whose attitude was ambivalent. Moreover, belief is not always of constant strength or weakness in any individual tradition-bearer. In this century as well as in previous periods, there have been conversions to the death-messenger faith as well as apostasies from it. It goes without saying the most favourable conditions for the belief are the occurrence of something inexplicable — at a time when a person's mind is occupied with death. He will tend to become a firm believer if the supposed omen is drastically 'confirmed'.

The processes of conversion and apostasy can be illustrated by a number of concrete examples. This, for instance, is how Con Egan of Ballydaly, Wheery, Co. Offaly came to be convinced of the existence of the banshee:

> To tell the truth . . . I did not believe in the banshee until it came home to me that there is such a thing as the banshee. I proved it. I was putting in the cows one evening. We had three cows and I put in a mash for one of the cows. When I was coming down with the cows I heard a terrible cry, and didn't I run down. I thought someone was after meeting with an accident. But there was nothing wrong with any beast or human.
>
> Now, when we seen that nothing happened, it kind of left our heads what occurred. But that same evening I heard the cry, Mary Anne (narrator's sister) had a letter in her pocket. She took out the letter which was from a brother of ours who was in North America. Martin was his name. And Martin said in the letter that another brother of ours had gone to hospital, he wasn't so well. About three weeks after that we got word that he was dead. So it would appear that at the time we heard the terrible cry our brother, Mike, was after dying. But I wouldn't believe in such a thing unless it came home to me. And that's not such a terrible long time ago (Offaly 13).

If one is to believe a record from Donegal, a personal experience in a death-situation would even be enough to convert a clergyman to belief in the banshee:

> In Rylands, Newtowncunningham, there once lived a family named Dunn, and, queer as it may seem to most of us, the wail of the *bean sí* was always heard before the death of a member.
>
> A clergyman thought that this was all nonsense until he was called to the bedside of a dying Miss Dunn. Her friends sat around. He joined the company, and after a prayer was very much surprised to hear in the distance the wail of someone in distress. The others heard it too and shortly afterwards the patient passed away. From that time onwards the reverend gentleman often told the above story, remarking that, 'there are more things in heaven and earth than are dreamt of in your philosophy' (Donegal 25).

The frequent re-telling of the episode referred to in the above record would have tended to confirm the experiencer's belief.

Another example of belief retained over a long period in spite of a life-style one might have supposed to be very unfavourable to such beliefs, is given by a Mayo correspondent. Speaking about a keening sound he and others heard prior to a boating tragedy in which a number of men were drowned he says:

> Forty-five years or more have passed since then, and for twenty of these years I have been absent from my native county, and as a result I have, I dare say, become more materialistic and sophisticated. But I am just as much, and more if possible, convinced today that the crying I heard was not that of a human being but was rather that of a person who was not mortal (Mayo 6).

On the other hand, there are also tradition-bearers who begin to waver in a faith they held for most of their lifetime:

> Looking back now and bowing to this age of disbelief and cynicism, I feel it could have been a bird or some small animal and the boy's death coincidental. I spoke to my sister about this recently and she agrees and says that birds often do make very queer sounds in the late evening (Roscommon 17).

The material tends to support Lauri Honko's assertion that tradition-bearers adopted a much more critical attitude towards supernatural experiences than they are usually credited with.[2] They were often quite reluctant to accept anything except what they themselves or people they knew and trusted had experienced. The example just cited shows they were not lacking in self-criticism either. On the other hand, it is important to realise the reluctance or total refusal to accept a particular death-messenger manifestation as genuine does not necessarily mean the belief as a whole is abandoned or even weakened, any more than doubts about individual miracles will turn devout Catholics into non-believers. Only when death-messenger manisfestations are becoming very scarce, and when those that occur and those of the past are generally ascribed to misunderstandings of natural causes, are we in the position to talk of significant decline in the beliefs. Admittedly, there are indications of a vanishing belief in the records we have quoted above. One of the informants who retained his belief finds it surprising he should have done so in view of the general sophistication and materialism which he considers to be a result of being out of touch with the old and traditional way of life; another informant ascribes his recent doubts to influence from what he terms 'this age of disbelief and cynicism'. Direct statements from the tradition-bearers themselves about their outlook on the death-messenger beliefs now and earlier in life are not so many, however, that they *per se* are sufficient to prove a considerable weakening of the belief has taken place, and, as already indicated, doubts, disbelief and apostasies must not be considered to be exclusively recent phenomena.

Other records of rational explanations of occurrences first thought by some to be manifestations of the supernatural death-messenger may, perhaps, favour the argument that there has been a recent decline in the belief. Those sources in which the death-messenger's cry is explained as the sound of a bird or animal (as in the Roscommon record above), and manifestations which turned out to be the result of impersonations or imitations of the death-messenger, undertaken for various purposes by human beings are examples of this.

II

In the treatment of the aural manifestations of the death-messenger, it appeared the being's cry was frequently compared to that of a bird or an animal, for example, an owl, a jack-snipe, a dog or a fox.[3] The possibility that the sound could actually have emanated from such a source is refuted in these records, usually for some specific reason: the sound, though similar to what it is compared to, is at the same time markedly different, or the sound seems to rise from a place where it is unlikely or impossible birds or animals could be. One would not, of course, be entirely wrong to take the view that many of the examples cited to prove the supernatural origin of the phenomena are mere figments of fertile imagination, and the fact such details are so often mentioned in the sources may, to some extent, prove the strength of the will to believe.

It is equally possible, however – and equally justifiable – to stress that these sources also reflect the suspicious and critical attitude of the tradition-bearers. It would be entirely wrong to suppose the vast majority of Irish country people of past generations, living in such close contact with nature, naïvely thought all nature sounds were voices of supernatural beings. The unusual quality of what was heard may, of course, frequently have been exaggerated due to the conflicts and stresses of a death situation, but one may with some confidence take it that many of the phenomena interpreted as the death-messenger's cry were, in reality, of an unusual kind. This is not to deny that sounds emanating from birds and animals stimulated many of the death-messenger manifestations. On the contrary one may be sure the correct explanation is often to be sought along those lines. On the other hand it would be rash to resort to this interpretation as a blanket explanation for all the phenomena and for the ultimate origin of the belief. Folklorists have endeavoured all too often to reduce supernatural phenomena to nothing but unusual or erratic animal behaviour, in extreme cases even settling upon a particular species, for example, the explanation that the Wild Huntsman is in reality nothing but migratory geese.[4] As far as the death-messenger manifestations go it must be realised that not only is it likely they have been prompted by birds and animals of many different kinds, but also that these zoological stimuli form only part of the explanation complex.

If one supposes a considerable number of death-messenger manifestations were prompted by unusual animal sounds, and if account is taken of the way the tradition-bearers themselves investigate and weigh the evidence before they accept anything as supernatural, one need not be surprised to find a number of manifestations have been given rational explanations along the zoological line either by the experiencers themselves or by other tradition-bearers around them.

The material relating to this aspect contains some interesting records which confirm the opinion that people familiar with a locality and its nature, did not easily mistake an animal sound for a supernatural call. These sources also indicate a tendency to regard outsiders' experiences with suspicion. Thus a wail in the Wicklow mountains attributed to the banshee by visitors was explained by a local sheepman as emanating from rutting deer (Wicklow 11) and according to a questionnaire reply from Donegal (Donegal 16) the sounds which frightened a newcomer to the area — the wife of a Presbyterian minister from Belfast — were in reality the roars of seals.

The idea that women — who would not normally be so familiar with wild nature and animal and bird sounds since they stayed more in the domestic area — would be more easily deceived than men, also seems to underlie some of the records. This is a first-hand memorate of an Antrim man:

> One night here Séamas Leech's wife went wild because I was leaving when the banshee was crying around the house: 'Leaving me and the youngsters and her around!' It was only an old fox crying and I knew it was (Antrim 10).

While it is clear from this account that Séamas Leech's wife was a firm believer, it is difficult to assess whether the man who told the story had his doubts about the banshee in general or whether he only realised there was a natural explanation for this particular phenomenon.

Independent of what the informant himself believes, the records often indicate the person to whom a rational explanation is offered either rejects it totally or accepts it only after intense persuasion, as in the following example from Wicklow:

> I was coming home one night and Pat Keogh was with me

and we heard the terrible *caoin* below in the knock[5] . . . Pat stopped up all of a sudden. I knew well on the minute that it was a fox. 'Be cripes,' says Pat, 'that's the bow.' 'Not at all', says I, 'that's a fox.' 'Yearra, go on with your fox now,' says he. I could not convince him that it was a fox. 'Sure that's the bow.' But then I think he heard them then again a few times after that and then he believed me (Wexford 5).

Here again it was the informant's familiarity with the area that caused him to deny the genuineness of what his companion took to be the death-messenger's cry. The informant previously told us he often before heard foxes 'over there on the knock' when he was coming home. He also called attention to the foxes' habit of 'calling one another', and one may conjecture that such calls in turn from different quarters underlie the belief that the death-messenger can be heard from all directions simultaneously, or that her cries keep coming from many places at very short intervals.[6] In any event the source illustrates Pat Keogh's belief was firmly held, and however determinedly the man who told the story may have opposed him and other people who thought they heard the death-messenger in that particular locality, it is not impossible he himself might have believed in other circumstances. That is a possible interpretation of the words with which he introduces his story: 'Did you ever hear a fox caoining in the night? Well, it is the same as the banshee.'

It would, however, also be possible to take the informant's statement to mean all supposed banshee wails are nothing but foxes' cries. There is little doubt that such, or similar views are, and were, held not only among so-called educated people but also, to some extent, among some people who were part and parcel of the old traditional society. The rarity of such considered opinions, amounting to a total abnegation of the existence of the death-messenger in the archival sources and among informants the author collected from, can hardly be the exclusive result of the folklorists' greater interest in documenting beliefs rather than disbelief. It would appear to be more likely the confirmed rationalists were, until quite recently, in the minority among those who were in close contact with the traditions. The best example of what would appear to be a non-believer on principle of the type here under discussion, is a correspondent from Donegal — the same man who contributed the information about the wife of the Presbyterian minister. In connection with this incident, he also makes a general statement that he thinks seals are to a large extent the explanation for the banshee belief in his area, and he goes on to say the following about foxes:

> Foxes, too, make an eerie noise when they are mating; it is a wailing noise very much like a human cry. I well remember one night more than ten years ago when I stood by the roadside for perhaps fifteen or twenty minutes studying a fox's wailing. As I approached home a few minutes later I met a lady in her seventies and she was very frightened indeed. Although I explained to her that it was merely a fox crying I still think that she just did not believe me (Donegal 16).

It is interesting that the man here is one who had repeated direct experiences of groundless fears aroused in people he considered to be ignorant and credulous, by phenomena he well knew to be derived from natural causes. That such observations could lead to a more or less general and categorical denial of the reality of any death-messenger is understandable. It is also worthy of note that the believer we are confronted with in this record is again a woman and that she is also said to have been old. This might indicate the informant was of the opinion the belief was on the wane and now held mainly, or exclusively, by certain categories of people and age-groups, clinging to the old ways. Though there may be much to say for this opinion, it is nevertheless clear that the death-messenger belief may remain basically unchanged in frequency as well as in depth, even though it is brought home to some people that there are natural explanations for some of the supposed manifestations. Neither can there be any doubt that natural explanations of the type now discussed were given even at the time when the belief was at its peak.

III

The opinion that it was both wrong and dangerous to mock, ridicule or imitate any kind of supernatural being was firmly held in folk tradition in Ireland as elsewhere. When a being was considered to be as sinister, strong and ferocious as the death-messenger there were even more weighty reasons to avoid such behaviour. Nevertheless, a number of records indicate there were people who impersonated the being or imitated her cry. The question to what extent – if any – these actions can be taken to prove the belief in the being was on the wane must be asked.

One reason for impersonation or imitation of the death-messenger – the exploitation of the belief as a cover for theft – is represented by one twentieth-century record only, in a Schools' Manuscript (Mayo 21). The same idea occurs in an older source, namely Croker.[7] The circumstances there are so different from those in Mayo 21 that it may be taken for granted the latter source is independent of the former. The use, or misuse, of people's beliefs in the supernatural for criminal ends is an interesting field which is as vast as it is unexplored. No specific questions about the subject in relation to the death-messenger belief were asked either in the *Handbook* or in the Banshee Questionnaire. It may be, therefore, that occurrences of this kind were more common than the scant material to hand indicates. While it is understandable, in view of the general source situation, that there is only one reference in nineteenth-century works, it is difficult – in spite of the omissions in the *Handbook* and the Questionnaire – to explain the absence (with the exception of Mayo 21) of other twentieth-century records unless activities of the kind actually were scarce then. Be that as it may, it would hardly be possible in any case to base any definite conclusions about the intensity of the belief on the frequency of occurrences of this type. Those who indulged in them need not necessarily have been non-believers; greed and hope of gain may have counterbalanced fears of the super-natural being's revenge. On the other hand, it is obvious it would have been counter-productive and hazardous to engage in death-messenger impersonations unless it was certain the victims were firm believers. If it can be proven on other grounds that there has been a marked decline in the general belief in later years, it should consequently cause no surprise that recent examples are lacking.

There are also records of death-messenger impersonations, or – since most of these sources deal with reproductions of the being's cry only – death-messenger imitations of another type — those in which the motive for the activity was simply to play pranks on people to frighten and ridicule them. These records pose a number of problems. Some are similar to those already met but others are of a somewhat different character. The material contains six records of this category, five of which were acquired in response to part of question 21 in the Banshee Questionnaire: 'Have you heard people being ridiculed because they believed in the banshee? Have you heard any stories about people impersonating a banshee in order to play a prank or frighten others?' The records of such pranks, though few in absolute numbers, are thus more numerous than the references to impersonation for criminal purposes. Furthermore, several of them state, or imply, the activity was common.

Perhaps the most surprising piece of information contained in the descriptions of pranks is that some people even constructed special contraptions in order to imitate the being:

> There were people that would imitate the banshee. They'd get a tin can or cannister and tie the hide of a rabbit or some other animal around the mouth of it. They would remove the hair from the hide before they'd put it on the vessel. And they'd make a little hole in the skin and insert a well-resined bullrush into it. And they'd get at the back of a ditch at night and keep drawing the bullrush back and forth through the hole and it would make weird sounds that resembled the cries of a banshee. Plenty of people were frightened that way and they would go home and say that such and such a person was going to die because they had heard the banshee (Cavan 1.8 pp. 466-7).

Although this Main Manuscripts record is the only description of the type, its factual and concrete nature vouches for its authenticity and it can safely be assumed that this, and other similar contrivances, were used for the same purpose, not only in the area in Cavan to which the record refers, but also in other parts of Ireland. It would seem, however, that the imitation was more commonly achieved through the human voice only as in the following example:

> Sure, there were lads'd jook down, maybe they'd find (hear) a couple of women coming or something that they'd know would be afraid and they'd do their best to cry like

the banshee and you'd hear the chat stopping like hell; there wouldn't be another word, and the cracks of their heels — the speed of it'd be a holy terror (as they fled) — (Cavan 23).

In this record the perpetrators of the pranks were 'lads' — adolescent boys or young men — and this was probably generally the case. It is also implied that the victims favoured were female. Part of the reason for this might simply be that it would give boys and young men more enjoyment to frighten someone of the opposite sex. It is quite possible, however, that women were picked out because they were considered, possibly correctly, to be more 'superstitious'. The use of the word 'women' rather than 'girls' by the informant would indicate he had grown-ups and, perhaps, elderly women in mind.[8]

That the victims of the pranks were selected with some care is also evident from the following statement:

I have heard people ridiculed because they believed in the banshee and often pranks were played specially on such people by someone impersonating the banshee (Donegal 16).

It is not possible to say with certainty what exact views perpetrators of such pranks held on the existence of the death-messenger. Adolescent boys and young men would wish to be brave and anxious to prove they were so. They could, therefore, very well engage in imitations of the death-messenger even though they believed in her to some extent and thought they ran the risk of raising her displeasure and being struck by her revenge. Although there are no records of such pranks from the nineteenth or earlier centuries, it seems likely they were played even then. That they were not confined to the last few decades of this century is indeed indicated by a Roscommon correspondent who states: 'There are many stories in olden times of people impersonating the banshee.' From the continuation of his statement it also appears, however, that these old traditions often tended to confirm rather than shake the belief in the death-messenger. Those who imitated the banshee, he says

. . . usually got a far greater fright themselves than that which they intended to give. While they would be waiting for a person they intended to frighten something would appear to them, sometimes with terrible results (Roscommon 1).

Although the lads might have gone out to play their tricks more or less convinced only elderly women took the death-messenger seriously, they might have returned as firm believers. It also goes without saying that there would be no point in playing pranks of this type if the belief in the being was not held by a fairly sizeable section of the community. One might therefore be tempted to say, that the traditions about the death-messenger imitations for the purpose of simply frightening people – like the imitations for criminal purposes – on the whole prove the belief was strong rather than weak. On the other hand, it may be more than a coincidence that the only record in which we hear of catastrophic consequences for the perpetrators of the activity, due to the death-messenger's objections to such mockery, refers to the old times. The custom was perhaps most common during a transition period when a generation gap between an older generation of firm believers and a younger generation of sceptics or non-believers had arisen. Part of the explanation for the absence of records about death-messenger imitations in so many areas at the present time or in the very recent past, may also be that the belief had become so weak there, that it would be hard to find anybody to ridicule. Other explanations are possible, however. It must, for instance, be taken into account that adolescent boys and young men of today have such a variety of outlets for exhibiting dare-devilry and worse that they may well frown upon such old methods as outmoded and childish. Since the sources referring to death-messenger imitations are so few and their interpretation fraught with so many difficulties, one must look elsewhere to discover whether there has been a significant decline in the death-messenger belief in recent decades.

IV

People always seem to have been under the impression that belief in supernatural beings is on the wane. For this reason we should not be surprised, perhaps, to find a number of nineteenth- and early-twentieth-century writers, such as Maria Edgeworth,[9]

T. Crofton Croker,[10], Mr and Mrs Hall,[11] McAnally[12] and Wood-Martin[13] talk of belief in the banshee or *badhb* as a by-gone or rapidly waning 'superstition'. There are a variety of reasons why one must regard such statements with great suspicion, apart from their character of commonplaces thoughtlessly borrowed by one writer from another. Some of the authors might have misled deliberately. Irishmen writing about their country, especially if they addressed themselves to a foreign readership, would sometimes be loath to admit their compatriots were less sophisticated and modern than people in other countries. In so far as they mention folk beliefs at all, they are therefore apt to ascribe such 'superstitions' to the past. Certain writers with scholarly ambitions may also depict the customs and beliefs they have met with as old and rare to give added importance to their own findings. Still other authors may not be guilty of direct dishonest intentions, and their statements reflect their own ignorance rather than the true state of affairs. It is not uncommon, for instance, that conditions as they were, or might have been, in a particular area are generalized, so that we are led to believe they hold true for the whole country. Furthermore, some of these writers were foreign visitors who did not stay long enough in the country to gain any intimate knowledge of the customs and beliefs there; sometimes they would also have been deliberately misled by people who found them inquisitive and troublesome. Last, but not least, the majority of these early writers were gentlefolk far removed from the ordinary people and unable to converse with them and understand their way of thinking.

In the light of the massive body of firm and solid belief in the death-messenger from the first decades of this century met with throughout this work, the statements about a vanished or vanishing belief in the nineteenth century appear not only dubious but even ludicrous. If one were to maintain the death-messenger beliefs were moribund by the nineteenth century, one would have to resort to the entirely unsupported and highly unlikely hypothesis that there was a drastic revival in the belief at the turn of the last century. One may take it, therefore, that conditions around 1900 were very much the same as around 1800. Even with the proviso touched upon above that some of the sources from the nineteen twenties and nineteen thirties refer to manifestations which took place and beliefs that were held two or three decades before the collecting date, it is for a variety of reasons, (for example, from sources written in the nineteen fifties, sixties and seventies referring to the conditions some twenty or thirty years ago) obvious, the belief in the supernatural death-messenger was commonly held practically everywhere in Ireland (Map 2) and probably embraced by the great majority in most areas at least as late as the nineteen twenties and thirties. This conclusion becomes even more inevitable if one takes into account that the collected records, rich though they are, are likely to represent only a small proportion of the traditions actually in existence.

In the course of fieldwork in the 1970s the author also met elderly informants who suggested that the death-messenger belief was accepted as something natural in the early years of their lives, some thirty or forty years previously. Thus Hannah Fitzsimons, formerly of Delvin, Co. Westmeath, said:

> I would like to impress upon you how much part of life the belief was. It was accepted as being something completely natural.

Similar statements can be adduced from the archival material. A questionnaire correspondent, also from Westmeath, writing in 1976, is one of the many who remembers the same state of affairs a few decades previously:

> The banshee crying was accepted quite casually locally. 'John so-and-so died last night', a neighbour might say and get the reply 'Is that so? I heard the banshee a few nights back' (Westmeath 2).

Far from being extraordinary and sensational — as certain authors indicate — the death-messenger belief was, therefore, at the beginning of this century, and definitely at least as late as the nineteen thirties, still taken for granted as normal, a fact of life which did not call for much comment. In a society where the belief enabled people to cope more efficiently with death, the final human crisis, it is not so much the belief which has to be accounted for and explained as the disbelief which also existed, though on a minor scale.

V

In the beginning of the previous section the dangers involved in relying uncritically on various people's impressions of the intensity and frequency with which a belief is held, even when several statements may be unanimous were outlined. When a sizeable volume of concordant information is to hand from persons one has reason to trust, the causes for doubt will naturally be fewer. Such a body of impressions and opinions relating to the death-messenger belief as it now is, and as it was some decades ago, is available thanks to the correspondents who answered the part of question 21 in the 1976 Banshee Questionnaire, which goes as follows:

> What attitude do (and did) people in your area take towards the banshee and what was told about her? Would you describe the belief as strong and widespread or weak and vanishing?

In assessing the reliability of the answers to these questions one should take into account that all, or nearly all, of the correspondents possess the very qualities lacking in the nineteenth-century writers who described the death-messenger belief as exclusively, or mainly of the past. The questionnaire correspondents as a rule know the only objective of any enquiry is to establish the truth, and they also know they do not run the risk of their statements being used to expose themselves, their area, or their country to ridicule; with few exceptions they would not be people with literary or scholarly ambitions; their reports refer only to the area in which they live, and this is nearly always the same area where they were born and bred, and which they know intimately; many of them are active tradition-bearers themselves and all can easily establish contacts with knowledgeable informants in their respective communities who would often be their friends and next-door neighbours.

In the questionnaire answers, much is found to substantiate the view that belief in the death-messenger was strong and widespread a few decades previously. Strikingly, the questionnaire correspondents in general do not characterise the belief held in the 1970s as strong, while it is described as weak and vanishing in answers from all over Ireland ('... all interest and knowledge of her have almost disappeared in this generation.' Ker. 45).[14] It is also characterised as a belief now held mainly by elderly people (e.g. Armagh 8; Cork 38; Donegal 11, 21, 22; Galway 56; Leitrim 8; Longford 21; Mayo 3; Roscommon 1, 21; Westmeath 2; Wexford 23), and, indeed, in a number of replies it is even stated that the belief has vanished from the areas to which they refer (e.g. 'The belief in the banshee is completely gone in this part of Kerry now,' [Ker. 4] – which is not, of course, the same as saying that the belief is gone everywhere in these counties).[15] Even if we take into consideration that nobody, no matter how well he or she knows an area, can be familiar with everything that everybody there thinks or believes, and that some of the reports which state that the belief has completely vanished may, therefore, be exaggerated, it is obvious that the replies give evidence of a substantial weakening of the belief in fairly recent decades.

It would thus appear indubitable that a very significant change has taken place – and is still taking place to some extent – resulting in a weakening and vanishing of the belief. It would seem that the change began to be noticeable in most places in the nineteen forties and that there has been continual decline of the belief in the succeeding decades.

VI

Many people blame the disappearance of folk beliefs on education – and no doubt something is to be said for this view. The clergy, who were largely responsible for education were not, on the whole, hostile to folk beliefs; they seem to have either tolerated them or pretended they did not exist. None of the records suggest priests or clergymen condemned the death-messenger beliefs.[16] The absence of such accounts is especially noteworthy in view of the close attention paid to indecorous and indecent behaviour at wakes and funerals. Drinking, games and keening on such occasions were condemned and forbidden in scores of statutes and directives issued by episcopal synods and individual bishops from the seventeenth century onwards, as well as in innumerable sermons.[17] It is remarkable no mention is made of the banshee or *badhb* in such a context.

General primary education in Ireland dates back to the nineteenth century. It is doubtful, however, whether this had any noticeable effect on the pupils' attitudes towards folk beliefs. The teachers were often country people who shared the views commonly held on this subject. A new, and perhaps more powerful element of sophistication might have been brought in with the secondary schools.[18] It is possible a more critical attitude towards irrational beliefs was instilled into the pupils at this stage. It is also conceivable that certain concrete facts they learned, about animal behaviour, for example, might have enabled them to detect or form an opinion about natural causes for supposed death-messenger manifestations.

Of more importance is the fact that increased literacy and greater availability of reading material — books, newspapers and magazines — gradually exposed larger and larger sectors of the population to ideas which would make them question their old values and beliefs. Time spent reading also encroached upon the oral culture which had been part and parcel of life. Storytelling sessions, once the main form of entertainment — at least in the country — became more scarce. The strange appearances and strange noises that were noticed might still frighten people but the experiences would more often stay at the omen-stage, to use Lauri Honko's term — only seldom would the *nomen* banshee or *badhb* be given to them since the collective tradition had begun to be eroded.[19]

The newspapers were only the first among the media that gradually undermined the oral culture which was the growing ground for the death-messenger traditions as well as other folk traditions. They were to be followed by the radio.[20] Broadcasting started in Ireland in 1926[21] and in the nineteen fifties radios would have been found in most homes even among less well-off people and in rural areas.[22] At the same time other types of entertainment, such as the cinema, began to fill a greater part of people's spare time. The heaviest blow to storytelling and conversation was struck by television from 1961 onwards.

Newspapers, radio and television not only meant talking had to stop when people were reading, listening and watching, and gave people new interests and ideas, but they also provided new topics for discussion. The time spent in conversation about local topics, such as the old traditional beliefs, was limited even more. The news media also had the effect that people spent more of their time, especially at night, at home. The old custom of visiting the neighbours at night — the rambling, *bothántaíocht, scoraíocht* etc., — was abandoned. It was exactly in this setting that the talk would so often turn to supernatural experiences and where those who had had them were given opportunities to convince those who were young and weak in their faith.

The connection between the strength of the beliefs in the old days and night rambling has been seen by the questionnaire correspondents. This is what one of them says:

> Amusement was very scarce and there was no radio or wireless, no, nothing, only crowds of . . . we'd gather into a house to *céilí* at night and they chatted on everything and then they started onto ghosts and every one of them told what they seen and what their father before them seen . . . banshees and ghosts and everything that ever was (Cavan 23).

When the night visits stopped, people also had fewer reasons to walk in the dark. Walking, especially at night, was of course also an exercise becoming less common as communications improved. The number of private cars in Ireland increased from 19,848 in 1925 to 711,098 in 1984[23] and the public bus-service was extended even into remote country areas during the same period. The possibilities of experiencing phenomena one might be inclined to ascribe to supernatural causes are many when one is out walking late at night. Most of these things one would not even notice in a car. As telephones became more common many visits which formerly involved being out after nightfall also became unnecessary. People did not even need a death-messenger to inform their neighbours or absent family members or relatives of a death. They could be telephoned.

Another feature of modern technology which is likely to have played an important part in the decline of the death-messenger belief is electrification. The Rural Electrification Scheme was initiated in 1947 and extended practically to the whole of Ireland in the late nineteen fifties and mid-nineteen sixties.[24] It is generally said the ghosts and fairies disappeared when electricity was introduced, and the same seems to a large extent to have happened to the banshee and *badhb*. It is not difficult to understand why. If a house was well lit, wild birds and animals — the releasing stimuli for many a death-messenger manifestation — would not come near it. Lights from the windows of a house would also enable people approaching it to see the 'something' which had attracted their attention was not a death-messenger. Light from lampposts and other outside lights, which have become increasingly common even in small villages and private houses in the country, will no doubt have dispelled many an image, which might otherwise have impressed itself on the observer's mind as a banshee or some supernatural being.

Improvements in the road system, new agricultural methods and many other advancements in technology have also brought about drastic changes in the physical landscape and in the flora and fauna of the country. Thus, some of the animals and birds which formerly provided releasing stimuli for the death-messenger believers are now unlikely to be found, or are extremely rare, in some areas where they were formerly common, and many a place which used to be lonely and eerie now has nothing to distinguish it from any other place.

While the death-messenger belief is not exclusively a rural phenomenon, it had, nevertheless, its stronghold in the country, where the communal tradition was richer and sounds and sightings which could be given a supernatural interpretation were more frequently noticed. There are, thus, good reasons for the characterisation of the belief in some of the questionnaire answers (Cavan 9; Galway 56; Kerry 2; Roscommon 2; Tipperary 18; Westmeath 2; Wexford 17) as rural rather than urban. The massive population movement from the country into the towns and cities is, consequently, also likely to have been instrumental in speeding up the decline of the belief. The importance of the factor will be appreciated from the fact that in 1926 only 32% of the population of Ireland lived in towns and cities while the figure for 1981 was almost 56%.[25]

Though all the factors hitherto discussed are likely to have been important, it is, nevertheless, probable that changes in the way people die and in attitudes towards death, have meant even more. Death was still very much a public affair in Ireland in the nineteen twenties and thirties, and to some extent also in the next two decades. Most people, in the country at least, died at home, surrounded not only by many of their relatives, but also often by friends and neighbours. It was this atmosphere of intimacy with death, with all the cares and worries it involved, that was the main *Sitz im Leben* of the death-messenger belief. In such a situation, death-messenger manifestations were expected, and for that very reason experienced. Now, when dying in hospitals has become the rule rather than the exception, death has also become more private and secretive. Life may nowadays be prolonged in the dying and their pains reduced to such an extent that neither the patient nor his relatives even know he is dying. Seldom would anybody but the closest relatives be present in a death-situation — often the dying person is alone with doctors or nurses. Ireland may not yet be in 'the age of the invisible death',[26] but it is certainly on the verge of it. In such an age, a death-messenger, natural or supernatural, is not an asset but an embarrassment.

VII

In view of the strength and complexity of the forces through which the changes have been brought about, the cause for wonder is not the decline in the death-messenger belief, but rather that so much of it has survived for so long. Many pockets of belief are undoubtedly still to be found, and it is not unknown to hear of manifestations in places where the belief is regarded as extinct. In the course of fieldwork in 1976, the author has been privileged to meet with firm believers, especially Jenny McGlynn of Mountmellick, Co. Laois and Anne Hill, Drimnagh, Dublin. Through their narrative style, tone of voice and general behaviour it was forcefully brought home to me how deep and natural their belief was. Jenny McGlynn was, as she herself said 'born to hear and born to see'. Although the vividness of their narrative style is lost in the transcriptions, these quotations from the material recorded from Jenny McGlynn and Anne Hill illustrate that the beliefs still held by some informants are as strong as any met with in the early years of this century and for centuries before:

Jenny McGlynn (28 June 1976)

Jenny: I heard tell of the banshee. I heard her myself. She follows families. She follows part of my family and we usually get a notice before anyone belonging to us is dead. We hear her crying. Before we get word — they could be dead at the time — but we hear the banshee beforehand and then we get news that someone belonging to us is dead. Last year a cousin of mine died up in Dublin and we heard the banshee the night before we got word that he was dead. Of a Saturday night he died and Sunday at dinner time we got a telegram to say the boy was dead. He died of asthma and he must have been dying at the time we heard the banshee down here. He was originally from Mountmellick(M 1840: pp. 3-5).

(29 June 1976)

Jenny: Well, didn't I tell you yesterday that the banshee was out the night before last and yesterday evening there was a man dead from the street. Me brother-in-law (a gravedigger) is burying him, that's how I know ... It was on Tuesday night. It was over in Chapel Street. The man lives in Chapel Street ... It was about half past one ...

Author: You are quite sure that it was the banshee?

Jenny: Oh! definitely. Sure I'm convinced that it was the banshee (M 1840, pp. 217-21).

The following extracts, from material collected in 1982, testify to the persistence of the death messenger tradition in an apparently uncongenial contemporary urban environment. Anne Hill's account is a remarkably comprehensive summary of the major characteristics of the death-messenger tradition in the east of Ireland. Further, like the material collected from Jenny McGlynn, it indicates how these traits were pre-served — embellished and re-enforced by individual and par-ticular circumstances.

Anne Hill (15 December 1983)

A.H.: Years ago, years ago, me father always told us years ago that the banshee followed his family ...

Author: Was it down in Offaly that he heard the banshee or did he hear it here in Dublin as well?

A.H.: Oh, he heard her here in Dublin when his mother died . . . The first time I heard the banshee it was when his brother died, me father's brother. . . .
So then, the next time I heard her then was last Thursday (8 Dec. 83) I . . . . . heard this ter-rible screaming — it came to the back window. It was just like as if someone was outside the

window. So I ran to the window to look out thinking I was going to see something. And I kept staring. I couldn't see anything and the screaming kept getting louder in the window.

So then it went away then, a bit back, . . . and then it went again and again — about four times I'd say, until it just faded out. Me mother was upstairs and I ran up and I said, 'mother, did you hear anything?' She said 'no'. And I said 'well if you didn't, the banshee was at the window down there' and she said 'don't start! ' So, the next day I was coming home from work, I was coming up the road and I seen me mother running down the road and I said, 'Ah there's something wrong'. So I said, 'oh what', I said, 'where are you going?'. She said, 'oh your Aunt Jane died last night'. That's my father's sister. I said, 'I told you', I said, 'that woman was at the window last night' . . .

So I was telling my cousin about it and he said that . . . it's usually that only one in the family that the banshee comes to, you know. The rest of the family wouldn't hear her. Me mother was there, me sister was there; they never heard nothing. And yet you couldn't but hear it now, it was screaming. I thought first now when I heard it that it was a cat or something, but no . . . 'Well,' I said, 'it must be the banshee then'. It was nothing else, because . . . I couldn't see anything, or hear anything else, cats or anything. And I have two cats there of me own, so I ran in to have a look at them the first minute I heard it, because they'd jump up if it was cats, but they never moved; they were asleep. So I said, 'well it's not cats anyway'.

Author: What was its cry like?

A.H.:   It was . . . loud; when it starts first, like . . . did you ever hear cats screaming? It was just screaming, screaming, like a piercing sort of scream, it just goes on and on and then it gets slower, you know, . . . kind of fades away then, just fades off and off and

off. I heard that's the way the banshee does cry —
that she fades, fades away. You see it's so long
since I heard her before I kind of forget it now.

Author: And was it something like that on Thursday
night of last week when you heard it?

A.H.:. Yea, that's the way it was last week, now when I
heard her. It was just like, now, as if they were
just sitting on the window outside. Well, we used
to hear that she sat on the window. When she was
coming to the house it was on the window-sill
she sat. But you could never see her. That's why I
jumped up to look out the window and I said
'maybe I'll see something'. But I couldn't see
anything and I was shaking. I was running out
and then I said, 'ah', says I 'it's only the banshee . . . it won't do me any harm'.

Author: Have you any descriptions of what the banshee
is supposed to look like?

A.H.: Well, according to what I heard, what they used
to say years ago, you know, cousins and all, they
used to say that she . . . was real small and kind
of long goldish hair, you know, fairish, goldish or
whatever colour, and real small. That's all now I
think I heard about her.

Author: Would you hear that in Dublin or was it down the
country?

A.H.: Ah, no, I heard it in Dublin. They used, . . .
the kids, we all used to say about her, about her
comb and all, if we found a comb and if there was
teeth missing out of it it was the banshee's comb.
So you couldn't pick that up. If you did pick it
up the banshee was supposed to come to you.
You'd drop the comb and run, yea.

Author: Did she comb her hair?

A.H.: Oh, yes, she was always combing her hair. She
was supposed to sit on the window-sill outside
your window when she came to you and she was
always combing her hair.

Author: Would your parents tell you not to pick up a
comb or did all the children know that they
shouldn't pick up combs?

A.H.:   Well all, all the children used to say the same — it
         was always about the banshee, you know, about
         the comb, so I can't now remember ever being
         told not to pick up combs, you know, that way.
Author: Now, would she come back to the house looking
         for her comb?
A.H.:   I never heard, never heard of that now if she did,
         you know, come back to the house looking for
         it; never heard that now.[27]
Author: What was she supposed to wear?
A.H.:   She was supposed to wear a shawl, a shawl around
         her shoulders and a long dress thing — I don't
         know what the dress was supposed to be like;
         they used to say a long dress with a black shawl
         around her.

VIII

What does the future have in store for the death-messenger
belief? One would hardly be mistaken in supposing that the
belief will decline further. In various connections mentioned
above, scattered examples of adaptations in the belief to modern
conditions have been noted. Thus a banshee in America (USA 1,
p. 362) was heard crying for a stillborn child, while the general
opinion, reflecting the high child mortality rate of former times,
is that the being ignores the deaths of young children. In a few
instances the banshee has also been heard crying outside
hospitals.[28] Such examples resemble plants trying to survive in a
changed environment. It is unlikely, however, that the
death-messenger belief will survive indefinitely in new forms
through adaptations of this kind. There is, perhaps, a better
chance that the belief will continue to survive for a longer period
in children's traditions, where other customs and belief have
found refuge. This is likely to be the case in urban as well as
rural areas of Ireland, as knowledge of the banshee tradition
among children has been noted in the major cities in recent
times; indeed there appears to be a widely-held belief in the
banshee among Dublin's schoolchildren.[29]

The degrading fate of being relegated to the obscure field of
folklorismus,[30] which became the lot of so many other

supernatural beings once belief in them died out, has been spared the death-messenger to a surprising extent. There are few examples of exploitation of her in advertisements or for other commercial purposes. A short-lived feminist magazine, the first issue of which appeared in 1975, was called *Banshee*, the title chosen not only because the being is feminine, but also because her appearance and behaviour do not correspond to conventional male ideas about what a woman should look like and be like.[31] A punk rock group formed in the late nineteen seventies called themselves 'Siouxsie and the Banshees'[32] for reasons too obvious to call for any explanation. Likewise, there are no toy or souvenir banshees or *babhbs* to compete with the millions of leprechauns on the market in Ireland and elsewhere.

All the indications are, therefore, that the death-messenger should soon be silenced. On the eve of the third millennium, however, despite continuing social and cultural change, the banshee's cry is still heard in Ireland. Patron goddess and personification of the land, caring for the fortunes of the people in the locality associated with her she may have been in origin, but her continuing significance and relevance today lie rather in the believer's perception of her as a family messenger of death – 'one of your own' coming to announce death, and to accompany you, as it were, across the great divide into the company of your ancestors. Even in the fast-approaching age of invisible death and unbelief, when the banshee's cry might well disappear, the Irish supernatural death-messenger will remain an intrinsic part of our cultural inheritance, reaching back as she does to the Celtic goddess of sovereignty, or even 'endlessly through aeons' to traditions more remote.

List of Abbreviations

Manuscript References

* IFC	Main Manuscript Collection, Department of Irish Folklore, University College Dublin, 1928 ff.
* IFCS	Schools' Manuscript Collection, Department of Irish Folklore, University College Dublin, 1937-1938.
IFC Schools' Copybooks	The original school copybooks in which the school children wrote the traditions that they had collected from their families and others, during the 1937-1938 Schools' Scheme. These copybooks are preserved in the Manuscript Archive of the Department of Irish Folklore.
* IFC L	Letters dealing with death-messenger traditions and related phenomena received in the Department of Irish Folklore in 1976 and later, as a result of radio and press publicity
* IFC Q	Questionnaires forming part of the Main Manuscript Collection
UFTM	Death-messenger material from the Ulster Folk and Transport Museum Archive
R	Death-messenger material taped in the field by the writer and others
P	Death-messenger material in printed works
I	Irish
E	English
Ms (s)	Manuscript (s)

* Referred to as M, S, L. and Q respectively, for brevity

Lexical and Linguistic References

DIL	(*Contributions to a*) *Dictionary of the Irish Language*, RIA, Dublin,1913-76
OE	Old English
ON	Old Norse
Mod. W	Modern Welsh

† *Provenance References*

O.S.	Ordnance Survey Sheet (The Six-Inch Survey 1834-1841) ††
Provinces	C (Connaught); L (Leinster); M (Munster); U (Ulster)

† For the map showing the provinces of Ireland and county names in abbreviated form see frontispiece (xiv).
†† Information from Ordnance Survey, Dublin.

Counties

Ant.	Antrim
Arm.	Armagh
Car.	Carlow
Cav.	Cavan
Cl.	Clare
Cork	Cork
Der.	Derry
Don.	Donegal
Down	Down
Dub.	Dublin
Fer.	Fermanagh
Gal.	Galway
Ker.	Kerry
Kild.	Kildare
Kilk.	Kilkenny
Lao.	Laois
Leit.	Leitrim
Lim.	Limerick
Long.	Longford
Lou.	Louth
Mayo	Mayo
Mea.	Meath
Mon.	Monaghan
Off.	Offaly
Ros.	Roscommon
Sli.	Sligo
Tipp.	Tipperary
Tyr.	Tyrone
Wat.	Waterford
Wmea.	Westmeath
Wex.	Wexford
Wick.	Wicklow

Genre References

bs	belief statement
m	memorate
l	local legend
ml	migratory legend

Appendices

UNIVERSITY COLLEGE DUBLIN
DEPARTMENT OF IRISH FOLKLORE
QUESTIONNAIRE
THE BANSHEE

(a)

The banshee is so closely associated with Ireland that she is almost a national symbol, very much like the shamrock, the shilelagh and the leprechaun. The 'tourist image' of the banshee is a false and superficial one, though, and has little in common with the genuine folk beliefs. While it should be obvious that a study of the banshee traditions would yield much of the greatest interest and deepen the understanding of beliefs and social conditions in our country, what has hitherto been written on the subject is both limited in scope and largely based on insufficient knowledge.

The Department of Irish Folklore intends to fill this gap. A study on the banshee and related phenomena is now in the course of preparation. Though the manuscripts already in our possession contain much untapped material, which has now been brought together and systematised, it is obvious that many geographical areas and many types of traditions are rather poorly represented. Since we have reason to believe that much can still be collected orally we turn to you for assistance.

It should be stressed that any information, however insignificant it may appear in isolation, may turn out to be of the highest value when put in a wider context. Because of this *we hope you will not hesitate to send in your answer even in the event that you are only able to give information on a few of the points enumerated here below.*

Please read the whole questionnaire carefully before you start answering the individual points.

Do not write in the margin of the paper supplied, since the material will eventually be bound.

Try to give all stories and other particulars as fully as possible. The closer you are able to stick to the actual words and expressions used by the people you have heard the information from, the more valuable your material will be to us and to the future generations in whose interest we work.

Since we may want to make further inquiries on points of particular interest (and perhaps try to tape some of the most outstanding material) it would be helpful if you could mention the names of the people who told you the stories, wherever that is possible and let us know whether they are still alive. We assure you that such information will be treated with the utmost discretion and we undertake, if you so wish, not to contact any particular person you may refer to without being in touch with you previously.

We would be especially grateful for answers on the following points, in so far as they are relevant to your district.

1   Is the word banshee used in your area to denote a supernatural woman
    believed to appear in connection with deaths? Is such a woman known
    by any other names (*badhbh* 'bow', *bean chaointe* etc.)? Is anything
    known about how widely these names are used and what they mean?
    Are there any names (Áine, Clíona etc.) referring to one individual
    banshee in your area?

2   What stories, if any, are there about the origin of the banshee (or
    other women appearing in connection with deaths)? Give any such
    story in full. Was it ever said that a particular human woman became a
    banshee after death? Will such a woman remain a banshee forever or
    is she condemned to such an existence for a limited period of time?

3   Is there a belief that the banshee (*badhbh* etc.) could appear in the
    shape of a bird or animal? Is any particular bird in your locality
    referred to as 'the banshee' or the like?

4   Give as full a description as possible of the banshee's appearance,
    behaviour etc. Is anything in particular said about her shape or size? Is
    she thought to be young or old, beautiful or ugly? Any particulars
    about length or colour of hair, dress (cloak, hood and their colour etc.)?
    Is she always believed to appear alone or have several banshees ever
    appeared at the same time? Is anything said about the way she moves?
    Would she appear for any length of time or only for a short while?

5   In many areas little or nothing is said about what the banshee looks
    like. Is your area one where she is heard only? What other details
    would people give in order to confirm that what had appeared was in
    fact a banshee?

6   Give details about lights, sounds (tappings, knocks, rustling noises,
    etc.) believed to be caused by the banshee or accompanying her
    appearance.

7   Was the banshee believed to cry, lament or sing? Write down every-
    thing that is said about her wails and lamenting (the number of wails,
    whether the lament was said to be beautiful or horrible or frightening
    etc.). Did she cry for a particular dead person (or one about to die)?
    Did she use words in her lament? Can versions of these or the notes
    of her lament be obtained locally?

8   On what occasions did the banshee appear? To healthy persons fore-
    warning them of death, perhaps through accidents or the like? To sick
    people shortly before their deaths? At the actual moment of death?
    Some time after death has occurred?

9   Where and to whom did she appear? Outside the house where the
    dying or dead person dwelt (in the garden, under the window etc.)?
    In the room where the dying or dead person was lying? To relatives
    or other persons far away from the dying or dead person? Are there
    any traditions of banshees appearing abroad (in America, for instance)
    on the occasion of deaths abroad?

10 Is the banshee believed to 'follow' only particular families? Is it believed that the banshee 'follows' families with *O* and *Mac* in their names? Give a list of particular families believed to have a banshee. Is it said that she would appear at the death of all members of such families or only at the death of the head of the family? Would she be believed to appear at the death of men, women and children alike? Are there any differences in this respect?

11 Is anything told about the banshee having deserted certain families for one reason or another? Is anything supposed to happen when a family whom the banshee 'follows' moves to other parts?

12 Was the banshee ever seen except in connection with deaths? What were the reasons for her appearance in such cases? Was she believed to take away children or cause harm in other ways? Was it, under any circumstances regarded as lucky to see a banshee?

13 Are there any stories about people who insulted the banshee (threw stones at her, fired at her or the like) and the consequences of their actions? Give any such stories in full.

14 Is the banshee supposed to be seen combing her hair? Are there any particulars about special times or reasons for this? Is anything told about what the comb was made of or what it looked like? Are there any stories in your locality about how the banshee lost and recovered her comb? Write down any such stories in full.

15 Is the banshee associated with particular streams, lakes, ponds, trees or the like? Is she believed to be washing? Is anything said about what she is washing and what the reasons for her washing are?

16 Are there any sayings, proverbs or proverbial phrases about the banshee ('to be wailing like a banshee' or the like)?

17 Do you know of any rhymes, poems or songs about the banshee, or in which the banshee is mentioned?

18 Does the title of any musical composition played in your area contain the word 'banshee', or is any piece of music in one way or another associated with the banshee?

19 Is the crying or pouting child referred to as a banshee (female children only, or both male and female children)? Is 'banshee' used in any other way about human beings to express spite, contempt, or otherwise? What exactly is meant in such cases?

20 Was the banshee (*badhbh* etc.) used as a bogey to frighten children, e.g. through saying 'the banshee will get you' or the like?

21 What attitude do (and did) people in your area take towards the banshee and what was told about her? Would you describe the belief as strong and widespread or weak and vanishing? Are there any differences as to the strength of the belief between different social classes, groups of occupation, age groups, men and women, or in any

other ways? Have you ever witnessed anything that you yourself or others present on the occasion thought to be a banshee? Have you met people who maintain that they have seen or heard a banshee? Have you heard people being ridiculed because they believed in the banshee? Have you heard any stories about people impersonating a banshee in order to play a prank or frighten others? Write down any such stories in full. Have you witnessed any such happenings or do you know anybody who has?

22 Have you come across any descriptions of the banshee or any stories about her in local magazines and newspapers? If you have any cuttings in your possessions we would be most thankful for the loan of them. They will be faithfully returned within a few days.

23 Give any other information that you have come across in your area about the banshee and other female supernatural beings appearing at deaths.

24 What other supernatural appearances were connected with deaths in your area? Give accounts and descriptions of such things as the 'headless coach', the 'death coach', phantom funerals in the sky, etc.

We express our heartfelt thanks to all our old questionnaire correspondents for their generous help and their understanding and appreciation of our efforts to save the folk traditions of Ireland. Many more workers are needed in this field and we extend a hearty welcome to those who are newcomers. Please remember that we are most thankful for suggestions of people you think will be willing and able to answer enquiries of this kind.

1976

AN COLÁISTE OLLSCOILE, BAILE ÁTHA CLIATH
ROINN BHÉALOIDEAS ÉIREANN
CEISTIÚCHÁN
AN BHEAN SÍ

(b)

Tá baint chomh dlúth sin ag an mbean sí le hÉirinn gur beag ná go bhféachtar uirthi mar shiombail náisiúnta, ar aon dul leis an tseamróg, an bata draighin is an leipreachán. Íomhá bhréige gan bunús atá in 'íomhá turasóireachta' an bhean sí, áfach, agus is beag cosúlacht atá ag an íomhá sin leis an mbéaloideas ceart. Is léir go mbeadh toradh fiúntach ar thaighde cheart ar an mbéaloideas faoin mbean sí ó thaobh an bhéaloidis agus an tsaoil shóisialta in Éirinn. Mar sin féin, tá a bhfuil scríofa faoin mbean sí go dtí seo teoranta go mór ó thaobh scóipe agus bunaithe cuid mhaith ar eolas easnamhach.

Tá i gceist ag Roinn Bhéaloideas Éireann an bhearna a líonadh. Tá taighde á cur ar siúl faoi láthair ar an mbean sí agus ar nithe a bhaineann léi. Tá cuid mhaith ábhar nár scrúdaíodh go mion cheana inár gcuid lámhscríbhinní, ach is léir nach bhfuil go leor againn ó chuid mhaith ceantar agus go leor faoi chuid mhaith cineálacha traidisiún. Ós rud é go bhfuil cúiseanna ann le go dtuigfimis gur féidir mórchuid ábhar a bhailiú fós, táimid ag iarraidh cúnta ortsa.

Is féidir go mbeadh tábhacht mhór ag baint le heolas ar bith, cé go mb'fhéidir go gceapfaí nach mbeadh, nuair a chuirtear é i gcomhthéacs níos leithne. Dá bhrí sin, *tá súil againn nach mbeidh leisce ar bith ort freagra a sheoladh chugainn, fiú i gcás nach bhfuil tú in ann ach eolas a thabhairt faoi chuid de na pointí thíos.*

Léigh an ceistiúchán go léir go cúramach, le do thoil, sula dtosaíonn tú ar fhreagra a thabhairt ar na pointí aonair.

Ná scríobh ar imeall an pháipéir, ós rud é go ndéanfar an t-ábhar a cheangal níos déanaí.

Déan iarracht ar gach scéal agus ar gach eolas eile a thabhairt chomh hiomlán agus is féidir. Is úsáidíde dúinne agus do na glúnta atá le teacht a bhfuilimid ag saothrú ar a son, tú a bheith ag cloí chomh dílis agus is féidir leat leis na focail agus na habairtí mar a bhí ag na daoine ar chuala tú an t-eolas uathu.

Ós rud é go mb'fhéidir go mbeidh uainn a thuilleadh fiosraithe a dhéanamh maidir le pointí spéisiúla áirithe (agus, b'fhéidir, cuid den ábhar is fearr a chur ar téip), ba chabhair dúinn é dá bhféadfá ainmneacha na ndaoine ar chuala tú na scéalta uathu a lua, nuair is féidir sin, agus más beo fós dóibh. Deimhnímid go ndéileálfar go fíor-dhiscréideach leis an eolas sin; agus, más maith leat, ní rachaimid i dteagmháil le haon duine faoi leith a ndéanfaidh tú tagairt dó/di gan bheith i dteagmháil leatsa ar dtús.

Bheimis buíoch duit as freagraí ar na pointí seo a leanas, chomh fada agus a bhaineann siad le do cheantarsa.

1 An úsáidtear an focal 'bean sí' i do cheantarsa le haghaidh bhean osnádúrtha a gcreidtear go bhfeictear í i gcás báis? An dtugtar ainm ar bith eile ar an mbean sin (badhbh, *bow*, bean chaointe. etc.)? An bhfuil aon ní ar eolas faoi chomh forleathan is a úsáidtear na

hainmneacha sin agus cén chiall atá leo? An dtugtar aon ainmneacha (Áine, Clíona etc.) ar bhean sí faoi leith i do cheantarsa?

2 An bhfuil scéalta ar bith sa cheantar faoi bhunús an bhean sí (nó faoi bhunús ban eile a bhfuil baint acu leis an mbás)? Tabhair scéal den sórt sin go hiomlán. Ar dhúradh riamh go ndearnadh bean sí de bhean daonna faoi leith tar éis bháis di? An mbeidh bean mar í sin ina bean sí go deo, nó an bhfuil sé i ndán di bheith ina bean sí go ceann achar áirithe aimsire?

3 An gcreidtear go bhfeictear an bhean sí (badhbh etc.) i riocht éin nó ainmhí? An dtugtar 'bean sí' nó a leithéid d'ainm ar éan faoi leith i do cheantarsa?

4 Tabhair cuntas chomh hiomlán agus is féidir ar an gcuma atá ar an mbean sí, agus ar céard a dhéanann sí? An ndeirtear aon ní faoi leith faoina crot nó a méid? An gcreidtear go bhfuil sí óg nó sean, álainn nó gránna? Aon eolas faoi fhad nó dath a cuid gruaige, a cuid éadaí (fallaing, cochall etc.)? An gcreidtear i gcónaí go bhfeictear an bhean sí léi féin nó an bhfacthas riamh scata ban sí ag an am céanna. An ndeirtear aon ní faoin mbealach a bhogann sí ó áit go céile? An mbeadh sí le feiceáil ar feadh méid áirithe ama nó ar feadh achair ghearr?

5 Ní deirtear dada i gcuid mhaith ceantar faoi cén chuma atá ar an mbean sí. An bhfeictear í i do cheantarsa, nó an amhlaidh nach bhfuil sí ach le cloisteáil amháin? Cén bealach eile a bheadh a fhios ag daoine gur bean sí i ndáiríre a bhí feicthe nó cloiste acu?

6 Tabhair cuntas ar shoilse, fuaimeanna (bualadh, cnagadh, fuaimeanna siosarnacha etc.) a gcreidtear gurb í an bhean sí a dhéanann iad, nó a bhfuil baint acu léi.

7 An gcreidtí gur ag olagón nó ag canadh a bhíodh an bhean sí? Scríobh síos gach ní a deirtear faoina cuid olagóin nó caointe (an méid olagón, cé acu an ndeirtí go raibh an t-olagón binn nó gránna nó sceonmhar etc.) An ndéineadh sí caoineadh ar dhuine faoi leith a bhí marbh (nó ar dhuine a bhí le bás d'fháil)? An mbíodh focla aici sa chaoineadh? An bhfuil leaganacha díobh siúd nó ceol an chaointe le fáil sa cheantar?

8 Céard iad na hamanna a bhíodh an bhean sí le feiceáil nó le cloisteáil? Ag daoine ina sláinte ag tabhairt foláireamh báis dóibh, b'fhéidir trí thimpistí nó a leithéidí? Ag daoine a bhí tinn go gairid roimh bhás dóibh? Ag nóiméad an bháis? Tamall tar éis bháis?

9 Cá háit a bhfacthas nó ar cloiseadh í, agus cé a chonaic nó a chuala í? Lasmuigh den teach mar a raibh an duine marbh, nó an duine a bhí ag dul chun báis, ina chónaí ann (sa ghairdín, faoi bhun na fuinneoige etc.)? Sa seomra mar a raibh an duine a bhí marbh, nó a bhí ag dul chun báis, ina luí? An gaolta nó daoine eile i bhfad as an áit a chonaic nó a chuala í? An bhfuil aon traidisiúin ann faoi mhná sí a bheith le feiceáil nó le cloisteáil thar lear (i Meiriceá, mar shampla) nuair a fuair duine bás in Éirinn, nó in Éirinn nuair a fuair duine bás thar lear?

10 An gcreidtear go 'leanann' an bhean sí teaghlaigh áirithe? An gcreidtear go 'leanann' sí daoine le *Ó* agus *Mac* ina sloinnte? Tabhair liosta de theaghlaigh faoi leith a gcreidtear go bhfuil bean sí acu. An ndeirtear go mbeadh sí le feiceáil nó le cloisteáil i gcás duine ar bith de chuid an teaghlaigh sin, nó i gcás cheann an teaghlaigh amháin, a bheith ag fáil bháis? An gcreidfí go mbeadh sí le feiceáil nó le cloisteáil i gcás fear, ban agus páistí araon a bheith ag fáil bháis? An bhfuil difríochtaí ar bith i gceist anseo?

11 An ndeirtear aon ní faoi an bhean sí a bheith ag tréigint teaghlach áirithe ar chúis amháin nó ar chúis eile? An gcreidtear go dtiteann rud ar bith amach do theaghlach a 'leanann' an bhean sí iad, má bhogann siad go háit eile?

12 An bhfacthas nó ar cloiseadh an bhean sí riamh ach amháin i gcás báis? Cén fáth go bhfacthas nó gur cloiseadh í sna cásanna sin? Ar creideadh go bhfuadaíodh sí páistí, nó go ndéineadh sí díobháil ar bhealaí eile? Ar creideadh go raibh ádh ag baint leis an bhean sí a fheiceáil, in aon chás?

13 An bhfuil aon scéalta ann faoi dhaoine a thug masla don bhean sí (clocha a chaitheamh léi, urchar a scaoileadh léi, nó a leithéidí), agus faoinar thit amach dóibh dá bharr? Tabhair na scéalta sin ina n-iomláine, más ann dóibh.

14 An ndeirtear go bhfeictear an bhean sí ag cíoradh a cuid gruaige? An bhfuil eolas ar bith ann faoi amanna faoi leith nó cúiseanna faoi leith a bheith ag baint leis seo? An ndeirtear aon ní faoi céard as a bhí an cíor déanta, nó faoin gcuma a bhí air? An bhfuil aon scéalta i do cheantarsa faoi cén chaoi ar chaill an bhean sí a cíor agus ar tháinig sí air arís? Scríobh síos scéalta ar bith dá leithéid go hiomlán.

15 An bhfuil baint ag an mbean sí le sruthán, lochanna, linnte, crainn, etc., faoi leith? An gcreidtear go mbíonn sí ag déanamh níocháin? An ndeirtear aon ní faoin rud atá á ní aici, nó faoi cén fáth go bhfuil sí ag ní rudaí?

16 An bhfuil seanfhocal nó ráitis ann faoin mbean sí ('ag olagón ar nós bhean sí', nó a leithéid)?

17 An bhfuil rainn, dánta nó amhráin ar eolas agat faoin mbean sí, nó a ndéantar tagairt don bhean sí iontu?

18 An bhfuil an focal 'bean sí' le fáil sa teideal atá ar phort ar bith atá le fáil i do cheantarsa, nó an bhfuil baint ag dreas ceoil ar bith leis an mbean sí ar bhealach ar bith?

19 An dtugtar 'bean sí' ar leanbh a bhíonn ag gol nó ag pusáil (cailíní amháin, nó buachaillí agus cailíní)? An úsáidtear an focal 'bean sí' ar bhealach ar bith eile le cur síos drochmheastúil a dhéanamh ar dhaoine? Céard go díreach a bhíonn i gceist sna cásanna sin?

20 An úsáidtí an bhean sí (badhbh etc.) mar rabhadh le heagla a chur ar pháistí, e.g. trína rá 'gheobhaidh an bhean sí greim ort' nó a leithéid?

21 Céard a cheap pobal do cheantairse den bhean sí, agus céard a deirtí fúithi? An gcreidtear go láidir inti fós, nó an bhfuil an chreidiúnt ag imeacht? An bhfuil an chreidiúint níos láidre i measc aicme faoi leith daoine, grúpaí faoi leith, daoine óga nó seandaoine, fir nó mná, etc? An bhfaca tú féin, nó ar chuala tú féin, rud ar bith ar cheap tú, nó ar cheap daoine eile a bhí ar an láthair, gurbh í an bhean sí a bhí ann? Ar bhuail tú le daoine a chreid go bhfaca siad, nó gur chuala siad, an bhean sí? Ar chuala tú go raibh daoine ina gceap magaidh toisc gur chreid siad sa bhean sí? Ar chuala tú scéalta ar bith faoi dhaoine a lig orthu gurbh iad an bhean sí le bob a bhualadh ar dhaoine eile? Scríobh síos na scéalta sin go hiomlán. An bhfaca tú féin daoine á dhéanamh sin, nó an bhfuil aithne agat ar aon duine a rinne é?

22 Ar tháinig tú ar chur síos ar an mbean sí in irisí áitiúla nó i nuachtáin? Má tá gearrúcháin ar bith i do sheilbh bheimis fíorbhuíoch duit dá dtabharfá ar iasacht dúinn iad. Cuirfimid ar ais chugat iad gan teip tar éis cúpla lá.

23 Tabhair eolas ar bith eile atá i do cheantar faoin mbean sí agus faoi neachanna neamhshaolta baineanna eile a mbíonn baint acu leis an mbás.

24 Céard iad na rudaí eile a bhíodh le feiceáil nó le cloisteáil agus baint acu leis an mbás i do cheantarsa? Tabhair cuntas ar rudaí mar chóistí bodhra, cóistí gan cheann, sochraidí neamhshaolta sa spéir, etc.

Ba mhaith linn ár mbuíochas ó chroí a chur in iúl dár gcomhfhreagróirí uile as a gcabhair fhlaithiúil agus as an tuiscint atá acu do na hiarrachtaí atá ar siúl againn le béaloideas na hÉireann a tharrtháil. Tá gá le lámha cúnta breise sa saothar seo, agus fearaimid fáilte ó chroí roimh ár gcomhfhreagróirí nua. Ná déan dearmad, le do thoil, go mbeimis buíoch as aon mholtaí maidir le daoine ar dóigh leat go mbeadh siad in ann, agus toilteanach, ceisteanna den sórt seo a fhreagairt.

1976

APPENDIX 2

The Connection between the
Supernatural Death-Messenger and Certain Families

2.1 Distribution and frequency of terms in the archival material denoting the connection between the death-messenger and certain families.

a) Terms in English Accounts

follow
Ant. 4(Q), 6(Q), 7(UFTM), 12(Q); Arm. 7(Q), 8(Q); Car. 6(S), 7(S), 12(Q); Cav. 1.22(M), 3(M), 9(Q), 13(M), 16(S), 21(Q), 26(Q), 29(Q), 35(Q); Cl. 24(Q), 25(S), 34(S); Cork 2(S), 11(S), 29(M), 38(Q); Der. 1(Q); Don. 11(Q), 14(Q), 16(Q), 25(S), 28(Q); Down 26 (UFTM); Dub. 4(S), 7(S), 11(Q); Fer. 1(Q); Gal. 49(S), 50(S), 52(S); Ker. 2(Q), 4(Q), 7(Q), 18(L), 19(Q), 27(Q), 28(Q), 45(Q); Kild. 1(S), 4(S), 8(Q), 13(Q); Kilk. 9(Q), 15(Q), 22(S), 26(S), 27(S); Lao. 6(M), 15(Q), 17(Q), 18(M), 19(M), 20(Q); Leit. 6(S), 8(Q); Lim. 1(Q), 2(Q), 3(S), 15(S), 16(S); Long. 27(S), 30(S), Lou. 3(S); Mayo 2(S), 9(M), 29(Q); Mea. 7(S), 16(S), 17(S), 18(S); Mon. 10(S); Off. 1(Q); Ros. 1(Q), 16(Q), 17(Q), 21(Q); Sli. 1(Q), 6(S), 10(M), 11(M), 12(M); Tipp. 2(Q), 7(Q), 15(Q), 16(Q), 18(Q), 19(Q), 20(Q), 44(Q); Tyr. 1(UFTM), 2(Q), 3(M); Wat. 1(L), 4(S), 5(S), 12(M), 21(M); Wmea. 2(Q), 4(Q), 11(M), 21(S); Wex. 2(S), 5(M), 6(S), 12(S), 17(Q), 19(Q), 20(M), 40(Q), 42(M), 43(S), 44(S), 47(S), 58(M), 61(M); Wick. 2(S), 3(S), 4(S), 6(S), 8(S), 14(S).
Total number of counties: 32
Total number of examples: 130 (M = 19; S = 48; Q = 58; L = 2; UFTM = 3)

cry
Cav. 8(S), 22(S); Cl. 36(S); Fer. 5(Q); Gal. 58(S); Leit. 4(S), 9(S), 16(S); Lim. 25(S); Long. 1(M), 5(M), 7(S), 12-15(S), 24(M); Mayo 1(S); Mon. 5(S); Off. 7(S); Ros. 7(M), 25(M); Sli. 5(S), 7(S); Wmea. 1(S), 6(S), 7(S), 10(M); Wex. 7(S); Wick. 2(S).
Total number of counties: 15
Total number of examples: 30 (M = 6; S = 23; Q = 1)

255

Other Terms
wail: Ant. 2(M); Wmea. 21 (S).
lament: Mea. 24(S)
heard after: Cl. 13(S).
come: Cav. 7(S); Kilk. 9(Q); Mayo 8(M).
go: Wex. 50(L).
runs in: Cav. 27(Q).
associated with: Lao. 5(S).
attached to: Ros. 6(S).
belongs to: Cl. 7(S); Mayo 17(S).
troubled by: Kilk. 14(S).

b) Terms in Irish Accounts
i ndiaidh: Ker. 31(M); Wat. 14(M) *[as diaidh]*, 38(S), 49(M) *[as diaidh]*.
lean: Don. 22(Q); Ker. 29(M), 32(M), 33(M); Wat. 32(S), 39(M).
ag gahbáilt le: Wat. 18(S).
ag rith le: Mayo 7(M).
thiocfadh (would come): Wat. 48(M).
caoin: Mayo 11(M).

2.2   The occurrence of the 'archival' terms, 'follow', 'cry', 'attach', 'belong', and 'come' in nineteenth- and twentieth-century literary sources, denoting the connection between the death-messenger and certain families.

follow
E. Brady, 1975, p.23 (Dub. 17); J. Forbes, 1957, p.39 (Don. 19); Miss Greene, 1909, p.174 (Kild. 9); Lady Gregory, 1970, p.179 (Gal. 65); W.B. Yeats, 1888 (and subsequent reprints), p.108.

cry
Lady Gregory, 1920, pp.172, 178 (Gal. 65).

attach
The Shamrock, 1874, pp. 440 (provenance unknown); John Keegan, 1839, p. 368 (Lao. 9); W.H. Maxwell, 1832, p. 294 (Mayo 32).

belong
T.C. Croker, III, 1828, p.10 (provenance unknown); John Keegan, 1839, p.368 (Lao. 9).

come
G.H. Kinahan, 1881, p.121 (provenance unknown).

2.3   Terms found in literary accounts only
                   (provenance unknown in each case).

affected to
J. O'Brien, 1768 *(s.v. Sith-Bhrog).*

attend
A. Dease, 1910, p.75; P.W. Joyce, I, 1903, p.264;
D. R. McAnally, 1888, p.109.

haunt
P. Colum, 1954, p.397.

wait upon
Mr. and Mrs. S.C. Hall, III, 1843, p.106.

2.4   Families reputed to be followed by the
           supernatural death-messenger.

The family names listed below are those found in the archival and printed source material in Appendix 5. The list contains details of (a) the family names mentioned, e.g., O'Brien, Doyle, Power, Deering, etc., (b) the location of these families, e.g. O'Brien, Killaloe, Co. Clare,* and (c) their extraction, e.g. Irish, Anglo-Norman, Anglo-Irish.

According to tradition, the death-messenger follows the O and Mac families. These prefixes are found in native Irish family names, e.g., Ó Súilleabháin and MacMathúna. They also occur in the Gaelicised forms of names of families of Norse, e.g., Mac Síoghair - Sigerson (Woulfe, 1923, pp. 14-17), and Anglo-Norman extraction. The early Norman families particularly in the twelfth and thirteenth centuries (MacLysaght, 1957, p. 285), assumed surnames after the Irish fashion by prefixing *Mac* to the names or other designations of their ancestors (Woulfe, 1923, p.32), e.g., Cody - *Mac Óda* from Odo le Ercedekne, Staunton-*Mac an Mhíleadha* from Milo de Sdondon, Jordan-*Mac Siúrtáin* from Jordan d'Exeter, etc.

In addition, the prefixes are found in the Gaelicised forms of some Anglo-Irish family names, e.g., *Mac Síomóin* - Fitzsimons. Scottish family names found in Ireland retained the prefix *Mac*, e. g., MacCabe, (Mac) Sheehy and (Mac) Sweeney. These were the names of galloglasses† who came to Ireland from Scotland in the thirteenth, fourteenth and fifteenth centuries, respectively.

But other old families of non-Irish origin who were among the earliest settlers or who were settled in Ireland prior to the seventeenth century and whose surnames lack the prefixes O and Mac, are also believed to be followed by the death-messenger. Included in this category are Anglo-Norman families, the Gaelicized form of whose names lack both prefixes. (e.g. *Bairéad, Diolún*, etc.), and those which retained the prefix 'de', (e.g. *de Barra* - Barry, *de Róiste* - Roche, *de Búrca* - Burke, etc.), and 'le' (e.g. *le Curteis*, etc.), and also Anglo-Irish families such as Deering - *Díring*, Blaney - *Bléine*, etc.

The names Cartwright, Potterton and Scott are English surnames which have come to Ireland in recent times. They are exceptions in that almost all the other family names in the list were known in Ireland before or at least by the seventeenth century.

The names are arranged alphabetically. The prefixes O and Mac are

*MacLysaght's *Irish Families*, 1957 includes a map showing the location of the principal Gaelic septs and leading Norman families (1300-1600), cf. also MacLysaght, *More Irish Families*, 1982, pp. 235-238.

†galloglass (Irish: *gallógach*) heavily-armed mercenary soldier, usually of Scottish origin (MacLysaght, 1982, p. 230).

placed in brackets except in cases where they are almost invariably retained in modern usage, e.g., O'Donohue, MacCarthy (Mac Lysaght, 1964, p.16).

The anglicised forms of Irish surnames as they appear in the source material are given first and these are followed by the Irish forms listed by MacLysaght in *Guide to Irish Surnames*, 1964, and *More Irish Families*, 1982, which basically follow the norms of Classical Irish. Where no Irish form appears in MacLysaght, Woulfe's *Sloinnte Gaedheal is Gall* is used. In instances where none of these sources provide a form, a suggested one is given and this and other forms considered doubtful are marked with a question mark.

The anglicized forms of Anglo-Norman surnames as they occur in the source material are given first; these are followed by the French form and then by the Gaelicized form, e.g. Barry (*de Barri, de Barra*).

Other family names are dealt with as follows: The anglicised and Gaelicised forms only of the names of families of Norse extraction are given e.g., Sigerson — *Mac Síoghair* (Woulfe, 1923, p. 406). The Gaelicised forms (where they exist) of Anglo-Irish names are also listed, e.g., Blaney - *Bléine*. Where no Irish form for a name is given this means that it is not found in either MacLysaght or Woulfe, e.g., Dowse.

The townland and parish (or parish only as the case may be) of the family in question are listed. Where the townland and parish names are identical, the name is not repeated.

In order to place some families in their true Irish context and also for the purposes of assessing the correct Irish forms of some family names, the reader is referred for additonal information to Edward MacLysaght's works on Irish Families, especially *Irish Families*, 1957 (*IF*); *Guide to Irish Surnames*, 1964 (*Guide*); *More Irish Families*, 1982 (*MIF*)* and also to Rev. Patrick Woulfe's *Sloinnte Gaedheal is Gall*, 1923 (*Sloinnte*).

The apparent origin of each family as stated in Woulfe or MacLysaght is indicated in the following manner:

AI: Anglo-Irish. These were families of English origin who, in the main, settled in Ireland before the seventeenth century and became assimilated to the Irish nation.

I: Irish. Native Irish families.

N: Norman. Families of Anglo-Norman extraction who came to Ireland from England and Wales mainly in the twelfth and thirteenth centuries.

Norse: Descendants of the Norsemen who settled in Ireland between the eighth and eleventh centuries.

OF: Old French in origin.

SG: Scottish Galloglass. Descendants of Scottish soldiers of fortune in the service of Irish Chiefs.

W: Welsh.

?: Origin uncertain.

*Since this is a revised and enlarged edition of *More Irish Families* (1960), and incorporates *Supplement to Irish Families* (1964), I have mentioned also these earlier works.

a) The Families

(O) AHERN
(*Ó hEachthigheirn*)

Athboy, Co. Meath (I).

BARRETT
(*Baróid in Munster,*
Bairéad in Connaught)

Ballyshane, Lea, Co. Offaly
(N); *Guide* 24; *IF* 51-52.

BARRY
(*de Barri — de Barra*)

Nemestown, Kilmore, Co.
Wexford (N).

(O) BEGLIN
(*Ó Beigléighinn*)

Kilcock, Co. Kildare (I).

BELLEWS
(*Bel Eau — Beilliú*)

Castletown, Co. Louth (N);
Sloinnte 57.

BENNETT
(*Binéid*)

Gallowshill, Delvin, Castletowndelvin, Co. Westmeath (AI); *MIF*
32-33.

BLANEY
(*Bléine*)

Ballykinard, Clondavaddog, Co.
Donegal. (AI, 16th Century);
MIF 35, *Sloinnte* 58, 230.

BODKIN
(*Bóidicín* - an offshoot
of the Fitzgeralds).

Ballymoe, Drumatemple, Co.
Galway (N).

BRADLEY
(*Ó Brollacháin*)

Clonee, Myshall, Co. Carlow
(I or N).

(Mac) BRADY
(*Mac Brádaigh*)

Kilmore, Killenkere, Co. Cavan
(I).

Munterconnaght Parish, Co.
Cavan (I).

(O) BRENNAN
(*Ó Braonáin*)

Ballynamona, Moybolgue, Co.
Cavan (I).

BROWNE
(*de Brún*)

Bealin, Ballyloughloe, Co. Westmeath (?)

BURNS

Bailieborough, Co. Cavan.
(S or I).

BURKE
(*de Burgh – de Búrca*)

America, Moore Parish, Co. Roscommon (N).

(O) BYRNE
(*Ó Broin*)

Mulhuddart area, Co. Dublin (I).

Cushenstown, Carnagh, Co. Wexford (I).

Kinawley Parish, Co. Cavan (I).

Aughrim, Ballykine, Co. Wicklow (I).

(Mac) CAFFREY
(*Mac Cafraidh*)

Mulhuddart area, Co. Dublin (I).

CALFE
(*Veale – de Bhial,
le veel* – the calf)

Ahenny, Newtownlennan, Co. Tipperary (N); *Guide* 37.

(O) CAHILL
(*Ó Cathail*)

Rathdowney, Co. Laois (I).

CALDWELL
(An English name used as
an anglicised form of
Mac Conluain in Co.
Cavan.)

Munnterconnaght Parish, Co. Cavan (I); *Guide* 37.

(O) CAREY
(*Ó Ciaráin?*)

Coolaneague, Macroney, Co. Cork (I); *IF* 73.

(Mac) CARNEY
(*Mac Cearnaigh*)

Kinnegad area, Co. Westmeath (I); *MIF* 50.

(O) CARROLL
(*Ó Cearbhaill*)

Bailieborough, Co. Cavan (I).

Ballynacloona, Kilmurry, Co. Tipperary (I).

CARTWRIGHT

Drumrockady, Killashandra, Co. Cavan (E).

(O) CASEY
(*Ó Cathasaigh*)

Coolavin, Kilcoleman, Co. Sligo (I).

Rathcoffey, Ballraheen, Co. Kildare (I).

(O) *Muintir* CHATHÁIN	An Blascaod Mór, Co. Kerry (I) (Last of the islanders settled on the mainland in 1953).
(O) *Muintir* CHORRÁIN	Paróiste na Dromad, Co. Kerry (I).
(Mac) CLAFFEY (*Mac Laithimh*)	Moate area, Co. Westmeath (I).
CODY (*Mac Óda – Odo le Ercedekne – Archdeacon*)	Crinkell, Birr, Co. Offaly (N).
(Mac) COUGHLAN (*Mac Cochláin*)	Cussane, Aglish, Co. Kilkenny (I); *IF* 82.
(Mac) CLANCY (*Mac Fhlannchaidh*)	Leitrim, Co. Leitrim (I).
(O) CLARKE (*Ó Cléirigh*)	Creaghagibney, Larah, Co. Cavan (I); *Guide* 43.
	Beaghy, Larah, Co. Cavan (I).
(O) CLAVIN (*Ó Claimhín*)	Mosstown, Kildare, Co. Westmeath (I).
COLBARD (*Colbert*)	Cahernaleague, Seskinan, Co. Waterford (AI, 15th Century); *Guide* 46, *MIF* 59, *Sloinnte* 65, 238.
(Mac) COLE (*Mac Giolla Chomhghaill*)	Carnalynch, Killenkere, Co. Cavan (I).
COLEMAN (*Ó Colmáin*)	Mulhuddart area, Co. Dublin (I).
(O) *Muintir* CHONAILL (O'Connell)	Paróiste Chathair Dhomhnaill, Co. Kerry (I).
(O) CONNOLLY (*Ó Coinnghealaigh*)	Old Leighlin, Co. Carlow (I).
	Ticknevin, Kilpatrick, Co. Kildare (I).
	Ballyshane, Lea, Co. Offaly (I).

(O) CONNOLLY
(*Ó Conghalaigh?*)

Aghyaran, Termonamongan, Co.
Tyrone (I); *Guide* 49.

(O) CONROY
(*Ó Conratha?*)

Morette,   Coolbanagher,   Co.
Laois (I).

(O) CONWAY
(*Ó Connmhacháin*)

Srahmore, Burrishole, Co. Mayo
(I).

(O) COONEY
(*Ó Cuana*)

Goldengarden, Kilpatrick, Co.
Tipperary (I).

(O) CORRIGAN
(*Ó Corragáin*)

Lisnaskea, Co. Fermanagh (I).

(Mac) COYLE
(*Mac Giolla Chomhgaill*)

Cam, Co. Roscommon (I).

COX
(*Mac Quilly – Mac an
Choiligh*)

Cloonmorris, Mohill, Co. Leitrim
(I); *Guide* 53.

(Mac) CROSSAN
(*Mac an Chrosáin*)

Bailieborough, Co. Cavan (I).

(O) CULLEN
(*Ó Cuilinn*)

Aughrim, Ballykine, Co. Wicklow (I).

(Mac) CULLETON
(*Mac Codlatáin*)

Nemestown, Kilmore, Co. Wexford (I).

(O) CULLINANE
(*Ó Cuileannáin*)

Ballingarry, Co. Limerick (I).

CURTIS
(*le Curteis – de Cuirtéis*)

Corraweelis,   Enniskeen,   Co.
Cavan (N).

COURTNEY
(*Ó Curnáin*)

Paróiste Chathair Dhomhnaill, Co.
Chiarraí (I); *Guide* 53.

CUSACK
(*de Cussac – de Ciomhsóg*)

Athboy, Co. Meath (N).

(Mac) CUSKLEY
(*Mac Giolla Choiscle*)

Ballinlug,   Rathconrath,   Co.
Westmeath (I).

(O) DALY
(*Ó Dálaigh*)

Tyrrelspass, Clonfad, Co. Westmeath (I).

Ballinclare, Ballycarew, Co. Wexford (I).

DALTON
(*D'Alton — Daltún*)

Colligan, Co. Waterford (N); *Sloinnte* 72, 247.

Curraghboy, Co. Roscommon (N).

DARLEY

Moyleroe, Castletowndelvin, Co. Westmeath (AI, 17th century).

DAWSON
(*Dásan*)

Bealin, Ballyloughloe, Co. Westmeath (A1, 17th century); *Sloinnte* 73.

DEERING
(*Díring*)

Delvin, Castletowndelvin, Co. Westmeath (AI 16th century), *Sloinnte* 73.

(O) DEERY
(*Ó Daighre*)

Lisnaskea, Aghalurcher, Co. Fermanagh (I).

(O) DEMPSEY
(*Ó Díomasaigh*)

Morett, Coolbanagher, Co. Laois (I).

DEVEREAUX
(*D'Evereux — Deabhrús*)

Brownbog, Toem, Co. Tipperary (N).

(O) DERVAN
(*Ó Doirbheáin*)

Abbey, Abbeyknockmoy, Co. Galway (I).

(O) DEVLIN
(*Ó Doibhilin*)

Kells, Co. Meath (I).

DILLON
(*Diolún*)

Kilmore, Co. Cavan (N).

Annagh, Kilkenny West, Co. Westmeath (N).

(O) DOLAN
(*Ó Dubhláin*)

Termonamongen Parish, Co. Tyrone (I).

Blacklion, Killinagh, Co. Cavan (I).

Cam, Fuerty, Co. Roscommon (I).

O'DONOHOE (*Ó Donnchadha*)	Newtown, Ballynakill, Co. Galway (I).
	Kilmihil, Co. Clare (I).
(O) DOOLAN (*Ó Dubhlainn –* *Ó Dúnlaing – Dúllaing?*)	Ballyshane, Lea, Co. Offaly (I); *Guide* 68, 69.
(O) DOOLEY (*Ó Dubhlaoich*)	Crinkell, Birr, Co. Offaly (I).
(O) DORAN (*Ó Deoráin*)	Kinnegad area, Co. Westmeath (I).
O'DOWD (*Ó Dubhda*)	Cross Keys, Denn, Co. Cavan (I).
DOWSE	Tinahely, Kilcommon, Co. Wicklow (OF, 14th century).
(O) DOYLE (*Ó Dubhghaill*)	Aughermon, Taghmon, Co. Wexford (Norse).
	Clologue, Kilbride, Co. Wexford (Norse): *IF* 128.
(O) DUFFY (*Ó Dubhthaigh*)	Cloonish, Gallen, Co. Mayo (I).
(O) DUNN (*Ó Doinn*)	Mountmellick, Co. Laois (I).
	Carbury, Co. Kildare (I).
(O) DWYER (*Ó Duibhír*)	Bregaun, Tullahought, Co. Kilkenny (I).
	Killenaule, Co. Tipperary (I).
ENNIS (*Ó hAonghuis*)	Ticknevin, Kilpatrick, Co. Kildare (I).
	Knockbine, Ambrosetown, Co. Wexford (I).
EUSTACE (*Iústás*)	Castlemore, Fennagh, Co. Carlow (N).

(O) FALLON
(*Ó Fallamhain*)

Cam, Fuerty, Co. Roscommon (I).

Ballymackeogh, Bally, Co. Mayo (I).

(O) FARRELL
(*Ó Fearghail*)

Ticknevin, Kilpatrick, Co. Kildare (I).

(O) FARRELLY
(*Ó Faircheallaigh*)

Bailieborough, Co. Cavan (I).

FAY
(*de Fae – Ó Fiaich*)

Scurlockstown, Clonarney, Co. Westmeath (N).

(O) FENNELLY
(*Ó Fionnghalaigh*)

Kilbraghan, Kilmanagh, Co. Kilkenny (I).

(O) FINNEGAN
(*Ó Fionnagáin*)

Clonmellon, Killua, Co. Westmeath (I).

(Mac) FINNUCANE
(*Mac Fionnmhacáin*)

Fennor, Islandikane, Co. Waterford (I): *Guide* 82, *Sloinnte* 528.

FITZMAURICE
(*Mac Muiris*)

Duagh, Co. Kerry (N).

FITZSIMONS
(*Mac Síomóin*)

Cashel, Slane, Co. Meath (A1, 13th century).

(O) FLANAGAN
(*Ó Flannagáin*)

Coolavin, Kilcoleman, Co. Sligo (I).

Birr, Co. Offaly (I).

(O) FLYNN
(*Ó Floinn*)

Sooey, Ballynakill, Co. Sligo (I).

(O) FOGARTY
(*Ó Fógartaigh*)

Aughrim, Ballykine, Co. Wicklow (I).

FOX
Shunny (*Ó Sionnaigh*)

Kilcash, Co. Tipperary (I).

(Mac) GAFFEY
(*Mac Gaibhidh*)

Cam, Fuerty, Co. Roscommon (I).

GAFFNEY
(*Mag Fhachtna?*)

Crossreagh, Mullagh, Co. Cavan
(I): *Guide* 87.

(O) GAHAN
(*Ó Gaoithín?*)

Mullaunreagh, Monamolin, Co.
Wexford (I); *MIF* 105.

(O) GALLAGHER
(*Ó Gallchobhair*)

Cam, Fuerty, Co. Roscommon
(I).

(O) GALLEN
(*Ó Gaillín*)

Termonamongen Parish, Co.
Tyrone (I).

(O) GALLIGAN
(*Ó Gealagáin*)

Tullytrasna, Templeport, Co.
Cavan (I).

(Mac) GANNON
(*Mag Fhionnáin*)

Rathdowney, Co. Laois (I).

(Mac) GARGAN
(*Garrigan — Mac Geargáin*)

Tierworker, Co. Cavan (I).

(Mac) GAVIGAN
(*Mag Cochagáin?*)

Tyrellspass, Clonfad, Co. Westmeath (I).

(Mac) GERAGHTY
(*Mag Oireachtaigh*)

Kilteevan, Co. Roscommon (I).

(Mac) GILL
(*Mac an Ghoill*)

Rathmore, Co. Westmeath (I or N).

Ballinlug, Rathconrath, Co. Westmeath (I or N); *IF* 233.

(Mac) GILMORE
(*Mac Giolla Mhuire*)

Sheepstown, Clonarney, Co.
Westmeath (I).

GRAHAM
(*Ó Greacháin?*)

Blacklion, Killinagh, Co. Cavan
(S? or I?).

GRIFFITH
(*Ó Gríobhtha*)

Ballymackeogh, Balla, Co. Mayo
(I or W).

(O) HANLON
(*Ó hAnnluain*)

Nemestown, Kilmore, Co. Wexford (I).

Ballyshane, Lea, Co. Offaly (I).

(O) HANLEY
(*Ó hÁinle*)

Tibohine, Co. Roscommon (I).

(O) HARTNETT
(*Ó hAirtnéada*)

Dromtrasna (Hartnett), Abbey-feale, Co. Limerick (I).

(O) HAYDEN
(*Ó hÉideáin*)

Morett, Coolbanagher, Co. Laois (I).

Fuerty Parish, Athlone, Co. Roscommon (I).

(O) HAYES
(*Ó hAodha*)

Ballynakill, Beagh, Co. Galway (I).

Paróiste na Dromad, Co. Kerry (I); *Guide* 110, *IF* 176.

(O) HEGARTY
(*Ó hÉigeartaigh*)

Killenbrack, Killare, Co. West-meath (I).

HOLMES
(*Mac Thomáis*)

Ballyvelly, Co. Westmeath (E or S); *Guide* 116, *Sloinnte* 96, 411.

HUSSEY
(*de Hosey — Húsae*)

Dingle, Co. Kerry (N).

JORDAN
(*Mac Siúrtáin —
Jordan D'Exeter*)

Tibohine, Co. Roscommon (N); cf. *Guide* 122, *Sloinnte* 407.

JUDGE
(*Breheny — Mac an
Bhreitheamhnaigh*)

Ticknevin, Kilpatrick, Co. Kildare (I).

KAVANAGH
(*Caomhánach*)

Ballyvourney, Co. Cork (I); *IF* 189.

(Mac) KEANE
(*Mac Catháin*)

Ennis, Drumcliffe, Co. Clare (I).

Mac KEANY
(*Mac Éanna?*)

Rosclogher, Rosinver, Co. Leitrim (I); *Guide* 123.

KEATING
(*Céitinn*)

Kilcarn, Co. Meath (N).

Rathsallagh, Tullamain, Co. Tipperary (N).

(Mac / O) KEEGAN
(*Mac Aodhagáin*)

Morett, Bannagher, Co. Laois (I).

Rathcoffey, Balraheen, Co. Kildare (I).

(O) KELLY
(*Ó Ceallaigh*)

Cam, Fuerty, Co. Roscommon (I).

(O) KENNEDY
(*Ó Cinnéide*)

Crinkell, Birr, Co. Offaly (I).

Ballyshane, Lea, Co. Offaly (I).

(Mac) KENNY
(*Mac Cionaoith*)

Tyrellspass, Clonfad, Co. Westmeath (I).

(Mac) KEOGH
(*Mac Eochaidh*)

Morett, Coolbanagher, Co. Laois (I).

LACEY
(*Ó Laitheasa – de Lascy*)

Aughrim, Ballykine, Co. Wicklow (I or N): *Guide* 133, *IF* 204.

LAWLESS
(*Laighléis*)

Toberpatrick, Kilpipe, Co. Wicklow (N): *MIF* 223.

(Mac) LEE
(*Mac an Leagha?*)

Virginia, Co. Cavan (I).

(O) LENIHAN
(*Ó Leannacháin*)

Ellenstown, Castletowndelvin, Co. Westmeath (I).

(O) LENNON
(*Ó Leannáin*)

Cam, Fuerty, Co. Roscommon (I).

(MAC) LOUGHLIN
(*Mac Lochlainn*)

Dromahaire, Inishmagrath, Co. Leitrim (I).

LÚISÉID
(Lucid)

Lispole area, Kinard, Co. Kerry (I); *Guide* 141, *Sloinnte* 304.

(O) LUNNEY
(*Ó Luinigh*)

Ballyconnell, Tomregan, Co. Cavan (I).

(O) LYNCH
(*Ó Loingsigh*)

Coolmeen, Killfiddane, Co. Clare (I).

Bailieborough, Co. Cavan (I).

Cavantimahon, Knockbride, Co. Cavan (I).

Kilnacor, Denn, Co. Cavan (I).

LYSTER (*de Leastar?*)	Kilteevan Parish, Co. Roscommon (?); *Guide* 143, *Sloinnte* 109, 264.
(O) MADDEN (*Ó Madáin*)	Scrabby, Co. Cavan (I).
(Mac) MAGUIRE (*Maguidhir*)	Kinawley, Co. Fermanagh (I). Blacklion, Killinagh, Co. Cavan (I).
(O) MALONE (*Ó Maoileoin*)	Moate area, Kilcleagh, Co. West-meath (I).
(O) MANNING (*Ó Mainnín*)	Athboy, Co. Meath (I).
(O) MANNION (*Ó Mainnín*)	Cam Fuerty, Co. Roscommon (I).
MARTIN (*Ó Mártain?*)	Ballinlug, Rathconrath, Co. West-meath (I or N); *Sloinnte* 134. Athboy, Co, Meath (I or N); *Sloinnte* 134.
(O) MEAGHER (*Ó Meachair*)	Cushenstown, Carnagh, Co. Wex-ford (I).
(O) MEEHAN (*Ó Miadhacháin*)	Rosclogher, Rossinver, Co. Leit-rim (I). Coolbawn, Coolcagh, Co. Tip-perary (I).
MILLER (*Muilleoir?*)	Mohill, Co. Leitrim (E); *Sloinnte*, 136,430.
(O) MONAGHAN (*Ó Manachain*)	Clonmellon, Killua, Co. West-meath (I).
(O) MOORE (*Ó Mórdha*)	Old Leighlin, Co. Carlow (I).
(O) MORAN (*Ó Móráin*)	Old Leighlin, Co. Carlow (I). Cam, Fuerty, Co. Roscommon (I).

(O) MORONEY
(*Ó Maolruanaidh*)

Ballingarry, Co. Limerick (I).

(O) MORRISSEY
(*Ó Muirgheasa*)

Killosseragh, Dungarvan, Co. Waterford (I).

Ballyshane, Lea, Co. Offaly (I).

(O) *Muintir* MHUINEACHÁIN
(Monaghan)

Gallaun, Kilcummin, Co. Kerry (I).

(O) MULLEN
(*Ó Maoláin – Ó Meallaín?*)

Lisnaskea, Co. Fermanagh (I).

(O) MULLIGAN
(*Ó Maolagáin*)

Moyleroe, Castletowndelvin, Co. Westmeath (I).

(O) MURPHY
(*Ó Murchadha*)

Corramonaghan, Kinawley, Co. Fermanagh (I).

Delvin, Castletowndelvin, Co. Westmeath (I).

Old Leighlin, Co. Carlow (I).

Dunshaughlin, Co. Meath (I).

(O) MURRAY
(*Ó Muireadhaigh*)

Moate area, Kilcleagh, Co. Westmeath (I).

Delvin, Castletowndelvin, Co. Westmeath (I).

Ballinlug, Rathconrath, Co. Westmeath (I).

Corramonaghan, Kinawley, Co. Fermanagh (I).

Clifferna, Larah, Co. Cavan (I).

MacARDLE
(*Mac Ardghail*)

Courtbane, Creggan, Co. Louth (I).

MacAULEY
(*Mac Amhalghaidh*)

Moate area, Co. Westmeath (I).

MacBRIDE
(*Mac Giolla Bhrighde*)

Enniscoe, Crossmolina, Co. Mayo (I).

MacCABE
(*Mac Cába*)

Murmod, Lurgan, Co. Cavan (SG); *Guide* 36.

MacCAFFREY
(*Mac Gafraidh*)

Blacklion, Killinagh, Co. Cavan (I).

Virginia, Lurgan, Co. Cavan (I).

MacCARTHY
(*Mac Cárthaigh*)

Bantry, Kilmocomoge, Co. Cork (I).

New Ross, Co. Wexford (I).

Rowls, Clonfert, Co. Cork (I).

Clonmel, Co. Tipperary (I).

MacCORMACK
(*Mac Cormaic*)

Cam Fuerty, Co. Roscommon (I).

Kilcommon, Templebeg, Co. Tipperary (I).

Lisnaskea, Co. Fermanagh (I).

MacCRORY
(*Mac Rory – Mac Ruaidhri*)

Coneyglen, Lr. Bodoney, Co. Tyrone (I).

MacDERMOTT
(*Mac Diarmada*)

Fuerty Parish, Athlone, Co. Roscommon (I).

MacDONAGH
(*Mac Donnchadha*)

Sooey, Ballynakill, Co. Sligo (I).

MacDONNELL
(prob. *MacDomhnaill*
of Fermanagh)

Murmod, Lurgan, Co. Cavan (I).

Blacklion, Killinagh, Co. Cavan (I).

MacDONNELL
(*Mac Domhnaill*)

Shramore, Burrishole, Co. Mayo (I); *MIF* 217.

Belderg, Doonfeeny, Co. Mayo (I); *MIF* 217.

MacELLIGOTT
(*Mac Uileagóid*)

Ballyvelly area, Tralee, Co. Kerry (?): *MIF* 96.

MacENTEE
(*Mac an tSaoi*)

Killann, Bailieborough, Co. Cavan (I).

MacEVILLY
(*Mac an Mhíleadha –
Mac an Mhílidh?*)

Clonmel, Co. Tipperary (I or N):
Guide 77, *MIF* 194.

MacEVOY
(*Mac Fhíodhbhuidhe*)

Crinkell, Birr, Co. Offaly (I).

MacGOLDRICK
(*Mac Ualghairg*)

Drumquin, Longfield, Co. Tyrone
(I).

MacGOWAN
(*Mac an Ghabhann*)

Rosclogher, Rosinver, Co. Leitrim
(I).

MacGOWAN
(*Mac an Ghabhann,
Mac Gabhann*)

Lisnaskea, Co. Fermanagh (I).

MacGUINN
(*Mac Guinn*)

Fermoyle, Co. Sligo (I).

MacGUINNESS
(*Mag Aonghusa*)

Derrylin, Kinawley, Co. Fermanagh (I).

MacGUIRE
(*Maguidhir*)

Ballyconnell, Tomregan, Co. Cavan (I).

MacHUGH
(*Mac Aodha*)

Termonamongan Parish, Co. Tyrone (I).

Aghyaran, Termonamongan, Co. Tyrone (I).

Blacklion, Killinagh, Co. Cavan (I).

MacINTYRE
(*Mac Ateer – Mac an tSaoir*)

Skeagh, Killinagh, Co. Cavan (I).

MacKENNA
(*Mac Cionaoith*)

Mullagh, Co. Cavan (I).

Deanhill, Co. Meath (I).

MacKEON
(*Mac Eoin or Eoghain*)

Knockbride, Co. Cavan (I).

Moate area, Co. Westmeath (I).

MacLOUGHLIN
(prob. *Ó Melaghlin –
Ó Maoilsheachlainn*)

Ticknevin, Kilpatrick, Co. Kildare (I); *IF* 212.

Kilcock, Co. Kildare (I).

MacMAHON
(*Mac Mathghamhna*)

Ennistymon, Kilmanaheen, Co. Clare (I).

MacMANAMON
(*Mac Meanman*)

Shramore, Burrishole, Co. Mayo (I).

MacMANUS
(*Mac Maghnuis*)

Lisnaskea, Co. Fermanagh (I).

MacNABOE
(*Mac Anabadha*)

Tullyhunco Barony, Co. Cavan (I).

MacNALLY
(*Mac an Fhailghigh*)

Virginia, Co. Cavan (I).

Cloonmorris, Mohill, Co. Leitrim (I).

MacNAMARA
(*Mac Conmara*)

Ennistymon, Kilmanaheen, Co. Clare (I).

MacNIFF
(*MacCunniff – MacConduibh*)

Glangevlin, Templeport, Co. Cavan (I).

MacPARTLAN
(*Mac Parthaláin*)

Bailieborough, Co. Cavan (I).

NAGLE
(*de Angulos – de Nógla*)

Lemonfield, Knocknagaul, Co. Limerick (N).

(O) NAUGHTON
(*Ó Neachtain*)

Kilteevan Parish, Co. Roscommon (I).

NEVILLE
(*de Neville – de Nuibhíol*)

Cushenstown, Co. Wexford (N).

MacNEVIN
(*Mac Cnáimhín*)

Abbey, Abbeyknockmoy, Co. Galway (I).

(O) BRIEN
(*Ó Briain*)

Killaloe, Co. Clare (I).

Ballagh, Kilfenora, Co. Clare (I).

Ballygriffin, Monanimy, Co. Cork (I).

Kilworth, Co. Cork (I).

Rossclogher, Rosinver, Co. Leitrim (I).

Cragg area, Kilcomenty, Co. Tipperary (I).

Clonmel, Co. Tipperary (I).

O'CONNOR
(*Ó Conchubhair*)

Killan, Bailieborough, Co. Cavan (I).

Rowls, Clonfert, Co. Cork (I).

O'DOHERTY
(prob. *Ó Dubhartaigh*
in Munster)

Kilcommon area, Caher, Co. Tipperary (I); *MIF* 216.

O'DONNELL
(*Ó Domhnaill*)

Glangevlin, Templeport, Co. Cavan (I).

Shramore, Burrishole, Co. Mayo (I).

Kilcash, Co. Tipperary (I).

O'DONOGHUE
(*Ó Donnchadha*)

Glenflesk, Killarney, Co. Kerry (I).

O'DWYER
(*Ó Duibhir*)

Kilcommon area, Caher, Co. Tipperary (I).

Ó hIARFHLATHA
(O'Herlihy or Hurley)

Cullenagh, Castlehaven, Co. Cork (I).

O'KEEFFE
(*Ó Caoimh*)

Ballyre, Dangandonovan, Co. Cork (I).

Kilmurry, Co. Cork (I).

O'LEARY
(*Ó Laoghaire*)

Gurraun Lr., Rathnure, Co. Wexford (I).

O'MALLEY
(*Ó Máille*)

Shramore area, Burrishole, Co. Mayo (I).

Enniscoe, Crossmolina, Co. Mayo (I).

O'MEARA (*Ó Meádhra*)	Tibohine, Co. Roscommon (I).
O'NEILL (*Ó Néill*)	Glengavlin, Templeport, Co. Cavan (I). Barony of Tullyhunco, Co. Cavan (I). Delvin, Castletowndelvin, Co. Westmeath (I). Kilcash, Co. Tipperary (I). Clonmel, Co. Tipperary (I).
O'REGAN (*Ó Riagáin*)	Shanid, Kilmoylan, Co. Limerick (I). Belderg, Doonfeeny, Co. Mayo (I).
O'REILLY (*Ó Raghallaigh*)	Murmod, Lurgan, Co. Cavan (I). Scrabby, Co. Cavan (I). Kilcash, Co. Tipperary (I).
O'SHEA (*Ó Séaghda*)	Macreary, Kilmurry, Co. Tipperary (I).
Ó SIADHAIL (Shiel, Shields)	Ballynamona, Duniry, Co. Galway (I).
O'SULLIVAN (*Ó Súilleabháin*)	Rowls, Clonfert, Co. Cork (I).
O'TOOLE (*Ó Tuathail*)	Kilcommon area, Caher, Co. Tipperary (I).
POTTERTON	Ballintemple, Co. Cavan (E).
POWER (*le Poer – de Paor*)	Ballylaneen, Co. Waterford (N). Bunmahon, Ballylaneen, Co. Waterford (N). Rosegreen, Tullamain, Co. Tipperary (N).

(O) QUINN
(*Ó Cuinn*)

Ballyshane, Lea, Co. Offaly (I).

Kilmore, Co. Cavan (I).

Abbey, Abbeyknockmoy, Co. Galway (I).

(O) REILLY
(*Ó Raghallaigh*)

Larah, Co. Cavan (I).

Cloggy, Killashandra, Co. Cavan (I).

Rosduff, Columbkill, Co. Longford (I).

Mulhuddart area, Co. Dublin (I).

REYNOLDS
(*Mac Rannall —
Mac Raghnaill*)

Ballymoe, Drumatemple, Co. Galway (I).

RICE
(*Rhŷs — Rís*)

Dingle, Co. Kerry (W, 14th century); *IF*, 256.

ROCHE
(*de la Roche — de Róiste*)

Tyrrellspass, Clonfad, Co. Westmeath (N).

RYAN
(*Ó Riain*)

Rathdowney, Co. Laois (I).

(Mac) SCALLY
(*Mac Scalaidhe*)

Tibohine, Co. Roscommon (I).

SCOTT

Drumcrow, Killashandra, Co. Cavan (E).

(O) SEXTON
(*Ó Seasnáin*)

Greaghagibney, Larah, Co. Cavan (I).

SIGERSON
(*Mac Síoghair*)

Dungeagan, Grange, Co. Kerry (Norse); *Guide* 187.

(Mac) SHANAGHY
(*Mac Seanchaidhe*)

Kilmore, Co. Cavan (I).

Rosduff, Columbkille, Co. Longford (I).

(O) SHEEDY (*Ó Síoda*)	Croom, Co. Limerick (I).
(Mac) SHEEHY (*Mac Síthigh*)	Askeaton, Co. Limerick (SG); *Guide* 185.
(O) SHERIDAN (*Ó Sirideáin*)	Kilmore, Co. Cavan (I).
SHERLOCK (*Scurlóg*)	Kilcarn, Co. Meath (I).
SMITH (*Mac Gabhann*)	Bailieborough, Co. Cavan (I).
	Kilmore, Co. Cavan (I).
	Corradoa, Killenkere, Co. Cavan (I).
	Tanderagee, Bailieborough, Co. Cavan (I).
	Drumcree, Kilcummy, Co. Westmeath (I).
STAFFORD (Macastockers in Ulster — *Mac an Stocaire*)	Munterconnaght Parish, Co. Cavan (I).
STRONG (*Lawder* — *Láidir* — Strong)	Munterconnaght Parish, Co. Cavan (I).
Muintir SHÚILLEABHÁIN (O'Sullivan)	An Blascaod Mór, Co. Kerry (I).
Muintir SHÚILLEABHÁIN (O'Sullivan)	Cullenagh, Castlehaven, Co. Kerry (I).
(O) SULLIVAN (*Ó Súilleabháin*)	Turnaspidogy (Tír na Spideoige) Inchigeelagh, Co. Cork (I).
	Ticknevin, Kilpatrick, Co. Kildare (I).
(Mac) SWEENEY (*Mac Suibhne*)	Ballyvourney, Co. Cork (SG); *Guide* 192.

TOBIN
(*de St. Aubyn* – *Tóibín*)

Cahernaleague, Seskinen, Co.
Waterford (N).

TRANT
(*(de) Treant*)

Dingle Co. Kerry (?); *MIF* 204,
Sloinnte 280.

TUITE
(*de Tuite* – *de Tiúit* or
Mac Confhiacla)

Virginia, Lurgan, Co. Cavan (I or
N).

(Mac) TULLY
(*Mac an Tuile*)

Realtogue,   Brownstown,   Co.
Meath (I).

WALSH
(*Breatnach*)

Bawnreigh, Buolick, Co. Tipperary
(N).

Old Leighlin, Co. Carlow (N).

Kilcock, Co. Kildare (N).

Bealin, Ballyloughloe, Co. Westmeath (N).

Coom, Ballincushlane, Co. Kerry
(N).

WARD
(*Mac an Bháird*)

Bailieborough, Co. Cavan (I).

Co. Donegal (I).

WESTROPP

Lismehane or Maryfort, Tulla,
Co. Clare (A1, 17th century).

WHELAN
(*Ó Faoláin*)

Rathdangan, Kiltegan, Co. Wicklow (I).

b)

SUMMARY

	Families	*Surnames*
Total	334	222
Irish	267	180*
Norse	3	2
Norman	34	24
Scottish Gallowglass	3	3
Anglo-Irish	11	11
Old-French	1	1
Welsh	1	1

Families whose origins cannot be accurately determined from the source material: 14

*   81% of total

2.5   Questionnaire replies dealing with the position
           of members within families followed by the
           banshee, *badhb* etc.

Connaught:
Gal. 56, 63; Mayo 29, 30; Ros. 1, 16.
Total: 6
Leinster:
Dub. 15; Kild. 8; Kilk. 7, 15; Lao. 15, 17; Off. 1; Wmea. 4; Wex. 19.
Total: 9
Munster:
Cl. 24: Cork 38; Ker. 4, 7, 19, 28, 45; Tipp. 2, 15, 16, 18, 20.
Total: 12
Ulster:
Ant. 6; Arm. 8; Cav. 9, 29, 35; Der. 1; Don. 22, 23, 28.
Total: 9
Overall total: 36

APPENDIX 3

The Manifestations of the Supernatural Death-Messenger

3.1   A break-down of the records in the archival and printed
       source material dealing with the manifestations of the
       supernatural death-messenger, according to *genre*.

The *genre* to which each item approximates is indicated as follows:
bs = belief statement; m = memorate; l = local legend; ml = migratory
legend.

a) Aural manifestations at death

Connaught
Gal. 7bs, 8bs, 9bs, 14m, 33bs, 34bs, 37m, 45m, 47m, 48bs, 49m, 50m,
54bs, 56bs, 58bs, 59bs, 61m, 65m, 67m, 69m, 70bs, 71bs
       Total: 22; m = 10, bs = 12

Leit. 2m, 4m, 5bs, 6m, 9m, 10m, 11m, 13m, 14m, 15m, 16m
       Total: 11; m = 10, bs = 1

Mayo 1bs, 2bs, 6m, 7bs, 11bs, 17bs, 23bs, 24bs, 25bs, 28bs, 29bs, 30bs,
31m, 32bs, 33m, 34bs, 35m
       Total: 17; m = 4, bs = 13

Ros. 1m, 2bs, 4m, 6bs, 7m, 9bs, 10bs, 11bs, 12ml, 13bs, 14bs, 17bs, 18m,
19bs, 21m, 22m, 23m, 24m, 27m, 28m
       Total: 20; m = 10, bs = 9, ml = 1

Sli. 2m, 4ml, 5bs, 7bs, 10bs, 11bs, 14bs, 16bs.
       Total: 8; m = 1, bs = 6, ml = 1

Total for Connaught: 78 records, m = 35, bs = 41, ml = 2

Leinster
Car. 1bs, 3bs, 5bs, 6bs, 12m, 15bs, 16m, 17m
       Total: 8; m = 3, bs = 5

Dub. 1bs, 2bs, 3bs, 4bs, 7bs, 8m, 9m, 10bs, 12m, 14m, 15bs, 17bs
       Total: 12; m = 4, bs = 8

Kild. 2bs, 4bs, 7bs, 8bs, 9m, 12bs
       Total: 6; m = 1, bs = 5

Kilk. 1bs, 2bs, 6bs, 9m, 10m, 11bs, 12bs, 13ml, 17m, 22bs, 25m, 26bs,
27bs
       Total: 13; m = 4, bs = 8, ml = 1

Lao. 5m, 6bs, 10m, 14bs, 17m, 18m
    Total: 6; m = 4, bs = 2

Long. 1bs, 2bs, 3m, 4bs, 5m, 8bs, 9m, 10bs, 11m, 12m, 13m, 14bs, 17bs,
18m, 19m, 20m, 21bs, 22m, 24m, 25m, 26bs, 27bs, 29bs, 30bs, 31m, 32m,
33m, 34m
    Total: 28; m = 16, bs = 12

Lou. 2m, 3m, 4bs, 12bs
    Total: 4; m = 2, bs = 2

Mea. 4m, 8bs, 9m, 10m, 15m, 16bs, 18m, 20m
    Total: 8; m = 6, bs = 2

Off. 1bs, 2bs, 3m, 7bs, 9m, 12bs, 13m, 15m
    Total: 8; m = 4, bs = 4

Wmea. 1bs, 2bs, 5m, 6m, 7bs, 10m, 13m, 14bs, 17m, 19bs, 21bs
    Total: 11; m = 5; bs = 6.

Wex. 1bs, 2m, 4m, 6bs, 8m, 9m, 12bs, 15bs, 16bs, 19m, 21m, 39m,
40bs, 41m, 42m, 44m, 46m, 47bs, 48m, 52m, 53m, 60bs, 61bs
    Total: 24; m = 14, bs = 10

Wick. 4bs
    Total: 1; bs = 1

Total for Leinster: 129 records; m = 63, bs = 65, ml = 1

Munster
Cl. 5bs, 6bs, 7bs, 12bs, 13m, 15bs, 20m, 23m, 25m, 26bs, 27bs, 29m,
34bs, 35m
    Total: 14; m = 6, bs = 8

Cork 1m, 2m, 3bs, 5bs, 7m, 8m, 9m, 10m, 11bs, 12bs, 13m, 14m, 17bs, 23m,
24m, 25m, 27m, 29m, 32bs, 35bs, 36bs, 38bs, 39bs, 40bs, 41m, 42bs
    Total: 26; m = 14, bs = 12

Ker. 2bs, 4bs, 7bs, 8bs, 9bs, 11m, 13m, 14l, 17bs, 18m, 19bs, 22m, 23m,
25m, 26m, 27bs, 29bs, 30m, 31bs, 32m, 33bs, 35m, 37bs, 38m, 39bs,
40bs, 41bs, 43bs, 45bs, 46m
    Total: 30; m = 12, bs = 17, l = 1

Lim. 1m, 2bs, 3bs, 4m, 6m, 7m, 9bs, 10m, 13bs, 15bs, 16m, 17m, 21l,
22m, 23m, 24bs, 25m, 28m, 30bs, 31m, 33bs, 34bs, 35bs, 37m
    Total: 24; m = 13, bs = 10, l = 1

Tipp. 1m, 11m, 13bs, 14bs, 17bs, 18m, 19bs, 20bs, 22m, 23m, 24bs, 26bs,

28bs, 35m, 38m, 41bs, 44m, 46m
  Total: 18; m = 9, bs = 9

Wat. 2m, 5bs, 7bs, 8m, 12bs, 13ml, 16m, 17m, 18bs, 23bs, 30m, 31bs, 34bs, 37ml, 38m, 44bs, 46ml, 49bs
  Total: 18; m = 6, bs = 9, ml = 3

Total for Munster: 130 records; m = 60, bs = 65, ml = 3, l = 2

Ulster
Ant. 1bs, 2m, 3m, 6bs, 12m
  Total: 5; m = 3 bs = 2

Arm: 1m, 2m, 6m, 8bs
  Total: 4; m = 3, bs = 1

Cav. 1.16 (p.445)m, 2m, 3bs, 4m, 6l, 8bs, 9bs, 13bs, 14m, 15m, 17bs, 18bs, 19m, 20m, 21m, 22bs, 23bs, 24bs, 25m, 26m, 27bs, 28bs, 29m, 32m, 33bs, 35bs, 36bs, 40bs, 41bs, 42bs, 43bs, 44m
  Total: 32; m = 13, bs = 18, l = 1

Der. 1bs
  Total: 1; bs = 1

Don. 4m, 6bs, 8bs, 9m, 9bs, 11bs, 12m, 14m, 16bs, 17bs, 21bs, 22bs, 23m, 24ml, 26m, 27bs, 29m
  Total: 17; m = 7, bs = 9, ml = 1

Down 1m, 4m, 6m, 7m, 11m
  Total: 5; m = 5

Fer. 1m, 2bs, 3bs, 4bs, 5bs
  Total: 5; m = 1, bs = 4

Mon. 1m, 2bs, 4bs, 5bs, 6m, 7l, 9m, 11m
  Total: 8; m = 4, bs = 3, l = 1

Tyr: 2bs, 3m, 4bs, 5m, 6bs, 9bs
  Total: 6; m = 2, bs = 4

Total for Ulster: 83 records; m = 38, bs = 42, l = 2, ml = 1

Overall total: 420 records (from 32 counties); m = 196, bs = 213, l = 4. ml = 7

(b) Aural and visual manifestations at death

Connaught

Gal. 13m, 18m, 23bs, 39m, 40m, 51l, 53m, 60m, 65m, 65bs, 66m
    Total: 11; m = 8, bs = 2, l = 1

Leit. 1m, 3m, 7ml, 8bs
    Total: 4; m = 2, bs = 1, ml = 1

Mayo 9m, 20bs, 28m
    Total: 3; m = 2, bs = 1

Ros. 1bs, 12m, 16bs
    Total: 3; m = 1, bs = 2

Sli. 1m, 6m, 13m, 17bs
    Total: 4; m = 3, bs = 1

Total for Connaught: 25 records; m = 16, bs = 7, l = 1, ml = 1

Leinster

Car. 7m, 8bs, 13m, 17m, 19m
    Total: 5; m = 4, bs = 1

Dub. 5m, 16m
    Total: 2; m = 2

Kild. 1bs, 3m, 6bs, 10m, 13m
    Total: 5; m = 3, bs = 2

Kilk. 10bs, 17m, 18bs, 26bs, 13m
    Total: 5; m = 2, bs = 3

Lao. 4m, 8l, 21m
    Total: 3; m = 2, l = 1

Long. 7m, 18m, 29m
    Total: 3; m = 3

Lou. 10m
    Total: 1; m = 1

Mea. 7m, 11m, 12bs, 17m, 21m, 25m
    Total: 6; m = 5, bs = 1

Off. 6m, 12bs
    Total: 2; m = 1, bs = 1

Wmea. 4bs, 5m, 6m, 8m, 11m
    Total: 5; m = 4, bs = 1

Wex. 5m, 10m, 13m, 18m, 19m, 24m, 28m, 29m, 32m, 33m, 36m, 38m, 43bs, 44bs, 45bs, 48bs
Total: 16; m = 12, bs = 4

Wick. 2bs, 3m, 4bs, 7bs, 8bs, 9bs
Total: 6; m = 1, bs = 5

Total for Leinster: 59 records; m = 40, bs = 18, l = 1

Munster
Cl. 8m, 19bs, 24m, 37bs
Total: 4; m = 2, bs = 2

Cork 26 and 31 are literary inventions.

Ker. no records

Lim. 8m, 12bs, 29m, 31m
Total: 4; bs = 1, m = 3

Tipp. 8m, 15bs, 16bs, 37m, 41bs, 44m
Total: 6; m = 3; bs = 3

Wat. 1m, 4m, 14bs, 15m, 21m, 22m, 24bs, 28m, 29l, 32bs, 35m, 39bs, 41m, 48l
Total: 14; m = 8, bs = 4, l = 2

Total for Munster: 28 records; m = 16, bs = 10, l = 2

Ulster
Ant. 4m, 13l
Total: 2; m = 1, l = 1

Cav. 5m, 7m, 18bs, 30m, 35m, 38m, 39m
Total: 7; m = 6, bs = 1

Don. no records

Down 13m
Total: 1; m = 1
Fer. no records
Mon. 8m, 10m
Total: 2; m = 2
Tyr. 1bs
Total: 1; bs = 1

Total for Ulster: 13 records; m = 10, bs = 2, l = 1

Overall Total: 125 records (from 27 counties); m = 82, bs = 37, l = 5, ml = 1

(c) Visual manifestations only — no death association

Connaught
Gal. 6l, 10m, 15l, 16l, 17l, 18l, 19l, 20l, 21l, 22l, 24ml, 25l, 26l, 27l,
28l, 30ml, 36ml, 39ml, 40l, 44ml, 50l, 52m, 53l, 55l, 56m, 60l, 62l
        Total: 27; m = 3, l = 19, ml = 5

Mayo 18ml, 27ml
        Total: 2; ml = 2

Ros. 3l, 5l, 7m, 13m, 23ml
        Total: 5; m = 2, l = 2, ml = 1

Sli. 9ml
        Total: 1; ml = 1

Total for Connaught: 35 records; m = 5, l = 21, ml = 9

Leinster
Car. 4m, 10ml, 11ml
        Total: 3; m = 1, ml = 2
Dub. 9m, 13l
        Total: 2; m = 1, l = 1

Kild. 1bs, 2l, 9ml, 13ml
        Total: 4; bs = 1, l = 1, ml = 2

Kilk. 4ml, 5ml, 7ml, 12ml, 14ml, 15ml, 16ml, 18ml, 19ml
        Total: 9; ml = 9

Lao. 1ml, 3m, 7ml, 11ml, 12ml, 15ml, 17ml, 19ml, 20ml
        Total: 9; m = 1, ml = 8

Long. 4ml, 6ml, 15l
        Total: 3; l = 1, ml = 2

Lou. 4m
        Total: 1; m = 1

Mea. 1l, 2m, 5m, 16m
        Total: 4; m = 3, l = 1

Off. 4ml, 5m, 8ml, 10ml, 11ml
        Total: 5; m = 1, ml = 4

Wmea. 3ml, 9ml, 12ml, 16ml
    Total: 4; ml = 4

Wex. 4ml, 6bs, 7ml, 12bs, 13m, 26m, 27l, 35ml, 37ml, 40ml, 43ml, 50ml,
51ml, 54m, 58l, 59l, 61bs
    Total: 17; m = 3, bs = 3, l = 3, ml = 8

Wick. 4m, 6bs, 12ml, 13ml
    Total: 4; m = 1, bs = 1, ml = 2

Total for Leinster: 65 records; m = 12, bs = 5, l = 7, ml = 41

Munster
Cl. 3l, 22l, 30l, 33l, 36bs
    Total: 5; bs = 1, l = 4

Lim. 14l
    Total: 1; l = 1

Tipp. 2ml, 3ml, 9ml, 10m, 18bs, 19bs, 29ml, 32ml, 34ml, 39ml, 42ml,
44ml, 45l
    Total: 13; bs = 2, m = 1, l = 1, ml = 9

Wat. 10ml, 19ml, 25ml, 26ml, 27ml, 33l, 36l, 40ml, 43m, 50ml
    Total: 10; m = 1, l = 2, ml = 7

Total for Munster: 29 records; bs = 3, m = 2, l = 8, ml = 16

Ulster
Ant. 6m, 11m
    Total: 2; m = 2

Cav. 12ml, 18bs
    Total: 2; bs = 1, ml = 1

Total for Ulster: 4 records; m = 2, bs = 1, ml = 1

*Overall Total: 133 records (from 16 counties); m = 21, bs = 9, l = 36,
ml = 67*

3.2 Aural Manifestations

1(a)   Terms used to denote the aural manifestations of the supernatural death-messenger

Cry

Connaught
Gal. 10, 18, 22, 25, 38, 39, 49, 58, 59, 60, 63; Leit. 1, 4, 7, 10, 11, 15, 16; Mayo 1, 6, 9, 16, 27; Ros. 1, 2, 4, 5, 6, 7, 11, 12, 17, 21, 22, 25; Sli. 1, 2, 4, 6, 9, 10
Total: 41

Leinster
Car. 6, 8, 15, 18; Dub. 2, 3, 5, 7, 10, 12, 15, 16, 17; Kild. 2, 3, 4, 8, 10, 13; Kilk. 1, 2, 4, 5, 11, 18, 28; Laois 1, 5, 6, 8, 11, 14, 15, 17, 18, 19, 20; Long. 1, 3, 4, 8-14, 16-22, 25, 26, 30-33; Lou. 2, 3, 4, 6, 10; Mea. 2, 3, 4, 8, 12, 14, 17, 20, 21; Off. 1, 7, 8, 9, 11, 12, 13; Wmea. 1, 2, 3, 4, 5, 9, 10, 11, 19; Wex. 4, 5, 8, 9, 13, 14, 18, 22, 40, 41, 44, 45, 48, 51, 54, 55; Wick. 2, 6, 8, 12
Total: 110

Munster
Cl. 1, 13, 17, 22, 23, 25; Cork 2, 3, 8, 9, 10, 11, 23, 24, 27, 30, 32, 38; Ker. 2, 3, 4, 6, 8, 18, 19, 23, 25, 27, 43, 45; Lim. 2, 6, 8, 10, 12, 13, 21, 25, 31, 32, 33, 37; Tipp. 1, 2, 7, 8, 15, 18, 19, 20, 23, 38, 40, 42, 44, 46; Wat. 2, 3, 5, 34, 58
Total: 61

Ulster
Ant. 1, 4, 11; Arm. 6, 8; Cav. 1.21 (p.444), 4, 5, 6, 8, 9, 14, 16, 18, 19, 21, 25, 26, 27, 29, 30, 33, 36, 37, 38, 40, 41, 42; Der. 1; Don. 1, 9, 11, 12, 16, 22, 24; Down 6, 11, 16; Fer. 1, 3, 4, 5; Mon. 2, 5, 6, 7, 8, 9, 10, 11; Tyr. 3, 5, 6
Total: 54

Overall Total: 266 records

Gol (cry)

Munster
Cork 5, 21; Ker 9, 14, 17, 30, 31, 33, 38, 41, 46; Wat. 32

Overall Total: 12 records

Wail

Connaught
Mayo 6, 21, 25; Ros. 10, 14, 18
Total: 6

Leinster
Car. 12; Dub. 1, 8, 15; Kild. 6, 8; Kilk. 11, 15, 16, 19; Lao. 5; Long. 28;
Mea. 4; Off. 2, 9; Wex. 4, 16, 50; Wmea. 21
Total: 19

Munster
Cl. 13, 14, 35; Cork 17, 23, 24, 25, 38, 42; Ker. 2, 6, 28, 35; Lim. 1, 16,
23; Tipp. 17; Wat. 24, 45
Total: 19

Ulster
Arm. 2; Cav. 2, 27; Don. 10, 13, 22, 27; Down 9; Fer. 4; Tyr. 1, 6
Total: 11

Overall Total: 55 records

Lament

Munster
Tipp. 15, 18, 19
Total: 3

Leinster
Car. 1; Kild. 6; Mea. 25; Off. 11; Wmea. 4
Total: 5

Ulster
Ant. 4, 10; Der. 1; Don. 23; Down 9; Fer. 4
Total: 6

Overall Total: 14 records

Olagón (wail, lament)

Munster
Cork 36; Ker. 13, 30, 32;
Total: 4

Ulster
Don. 21.
Total: 1

Overall Total: 5 records

Ochón

Munster
Wat. 41
Total: 1

Overall Total: 1 record

Lóg (wail, lament)

Connaught
Gal. 45 *(Lógóireacht)*
Total: 1

Munster
Wat. 20, 22, 46, 47
Total: 4

Overall Total: 5 records

Caoineadh (keen, lament)

Connaught
Gal. 9, 13, 14, 18, 45, 47, 48, 54; Mayo 7, 29
Total: 10

Leinster
Kilk. 7; Lao. 4; Wex. 19; Wick. 4
Total: 4

Munster
Cork 1, 11, 13, 27, 29, 39; Ker. 26, 29, 34, 39; Tipp. 41; Wat. 8, 31
Total: 13

Ulster
Don. 4, 6, 22, 28, 30
Total: 5

Overall Total: 32 records

Keen

Connaught
Leit. 8; Ros. 16; Sli. 3
Total: 3

Leinster
Car. 7; Kilk. 13, 22, 35; Long. 27; Off. 14; Wex. 1, 6, 21, 31, 44, 46.
Total: 12

Munster
Tipp. 42
Total: 1

Ulster
Mon. 4; Tyr. 4
Total: 2.

Overall Total: 18 records

Moan

Munster
Tipp. 9
Total: 1

Leinster
Lou. 4; Off. 6; Wex. 26
Total: 3

Ulster
Cav. 10; Down 1
Total: 2

Overall Total: 6 records

Roar

Leinster
Car. 16, 17; Lao. 17, 19; Wex. 4
Total: 5

Munster
Tipp. 35; Wat. 21, 23
Total: 3

Overall Total: 8 records

Scream

Leinster
Kilk. 26; Wex. 10, 19, 35, 52; Lao. 17
Total: 6

Munster
Wat. 24
Total: 1

Overall Total: 7 records

Shriek

Leinster
Mea. 4
Total: 1

Munster
Lim. 4; Tipp. 18, 42
Total: 3

Overall Total: 4 records

Screech

Leinster
Kild. 7
Total: 1

Overall Total: 1 record

Scréach (screech, moan, shriek)

Munster
Wat. 17
Total: 1

Overall Total: 1 record

Béic (shout, roar, cry out)

Munster
Wat. 36, 37, 38
Total: 3

Overall Total: 3 records

Call

Leinster
Car. 3
Total: 1

Munster
Ker. 22; Wat. 1
Total: 2

Overall Total: 3 records

Glaoch (call, shout, roar)

Munster
Wat. 30
Total: 1

Overall Total: 1 record

Liú (shout, yell)

Munster
Wat. 15, 16, 33
Total: 3

Overall Total: 3 records

(b) The variety of terms from each county denoting the aural manifestations of the death-messenger.

Ant.	cry, lament
Arm.	cry, wail
*Car.	cry, wail, lament, keen, roar, call
Cav.	cry, wail, moan
Cl.	cry, wail
Cork	cry, *gol*, wail, *olagón, caoineadh*
Der.	cry, lament
Don.	cry, wail, lament, *olagón, caoineadh*
Down	cry, wail, lament, moan
Dub.	cry, wail
Fer.	cry, wail, lament
Gal.	cry, *lógóireacht, caoineadh*
Ker.	cry, *gol*, wail, *olagón, caoineadh*, call
*Kild.	cry, wail, lament, keen, screech
*Kilk.	cry, wail, keen, *caoineadh*, scream
Lao.	cry, wail, *caoineadh*, roar, scream
Leit.	cry, keen
Lim.	cry, wail, shriek.
Long.	cry, wail, keen
Lou.	cry, moan.
Mayo	cry, wail, *caoineadh*
Mea.	cry, wail, lament, shriek
Mon.	cry, keen
Off.	cry, wail, lament, keen, moan
Ros.	cry, wail, keen
Sli.	cry, keen
*Tipp.	cry, wail, lament, keen, *caoineadh*, moan, roar, shriek
Tyr.	cry, wail, keen

*Wat.	cry, *gol,* wail, *lóg, ochón, caoineadh,* roar, *béic, liú,* call, *glaoch, scréach,* scream
Wmea.	cry, lament
*Wex.	cry, wail, keen, *caoineadh,* moan, roar, scream.
*Wick.	cry, *caoineadh*

*denotes counties in the *badhbh*-area

2. Alleged Notations of the Banshee's Wail from nineteenth-century literary sources.

(a) Mr. and Mrs. S.C. Hall appear to provide the earliest example in volume III of *Ireland: its Scenery, Character &c.,* London, 1843, p.106. The Halls describe the quality of the cry and then purport to give 'a correct notation of the wail of the Banshee' which they declare is 'the archetype of the Keen':

> This warning is given by a peculiarly mournful wail at night — a sound that resembles the melancholy sough of the wind, but having the tone of a human voice, and distinctly audible to a great distance. The following is a correct notation of the wail of the Banshee — the archtype of the Keen, as we have already had occasion to observe.

Plate 4

The Halls give no details of the source or provenance of their notation of the cry.

(b) W.B. Yeats reproduced Mr. and Mrs. Hall's notation of the cry in *Fairy and Folk Tales of the Irish Peasantry*, London, 1888, p. 321 (1st ed. Walter Scott).

(c) in 1888 also, D. R. McAnally in *Irish Wonders*, London, p. 110, includes a musical notation which he says is the 'Song of the Banshee by a Kerry Pishogue'

Plate 5   SONG OF THE BANSHEE.

By a KERRY PISHOGUE.

(d) In *Irish Fairy Tales*, London, n.d. [1892], 2nd impression children's ed., Appendix, p. 232, W.B. Yeats cites the case of an anthropologist who claimed he heard the banshee in Central America in 1867 on the death of his father. Yeats gives what he says is the anthropologist's notation of the cry, 'written down by him with the help of a Frenchman and a violin':

Plate 6

(e) But the most elaborate example of what purports to be a musical notation of the banshee's wail appeared in *The Dublin Penny Journal*, 27th February, 1903, p.613. It is attributed to the Lough Gur area, Co. Limerick and was 'musically noted by Mr. James Butler, Lough Gur'. It was submitted to the editor of the journal by Owen Bresnan. According to Bresnan 'The Wail is traditionally supposed to be caoined from the summit of Carrig na Galour at the time of the burial of the great

Irish Minstrel-bard, Thomas O'Connellan'. While Áine is not specifically named, no doubt she is the banshee in question.

Plate 7   ## THE   BANSHEE'S   WAIL.

MUSICALLY NOTED BY Mr. JAMES BUTLER, LOUGH GUR.

3. Descriptions of the aural manifestations

A mournful, sorrowful, lonely grieved sound

Connaught
Gal. 9, 14, 23, 54; Leit. 2, 9; Mayo 6, 9, 29, 30; Ros. 1, 2, 13, 23; Sli. 1
Total: 15

Leinster:
Dub. 12; Kild. 4; Kilk. 6; Lao. 5, 8; Long. 5, 9, 19, 29; Off. 9; Wex. 21, 55; Wick. 6
Total: 13

Munster
Cl. 14, 17, 24, 34; Cork 8, 9 , 10, 24, 27; Ker. 23, 30, 45; Lim. 1, 2, 12; Tipp. 8, 23, 42, 44; Wat. 14, 22, 30, 38
Total: 23

Ulster
Ant. 4; Arm. 1; Cav. 1.18 (p.469), 23, 41; Don. 4, 9
Total: 7

Overall total: 58 records

A frightening sound

Connaught
Gal. 50, 56; Leit. 2, 16; Mayo 30; Ros. 2, 18, 21
Total: 8

Leinster
Car. 1; Dub. 8, 12; Kilk. 7, 10, 15, 18; Lou. 7; Long. 1, 21; Mea. 4, 12; Off. 2, 13; Wmea. 2, 12, 17; Wex. 13, 19, 22, 48, 60; Wick. 4
Total: 23

Munster
Cl. 6; 14, 19; Cork 1, 9, 29; Ker. 7, 22; Lim. 4, 8; Tipp. 2, 18, 19, 20, 42, 44; Wat. 17, 21, 37
Total: 19

Ulster
Ant. 3; Arm. 8; Cav. 1.14 (p.461), 1.41 (p.469), 29, 31, 41; Don. 13, 14, 16, 20, 21, 22, 27; Down 7; Tyr. 6
Total: 16

Overall total: 66 records

3.3 Visual Manifestations

Distribution of aspects of the death-messenger's general appearance in the archival material.

(a)   Old Woman

Connaught
Mayo 3, 29, 32; Ros. 2, 16; Sli. 1, 8
Total: 7

Leinster:
Car. 17; Kild. 6; Lao 11; Long. 9; Mea. 12; Off. 1; Wmea. 2; Wex. 16, 32, 54; Wick. 6
Total: 11

Munster
Lim. 31; Tipp. 2, 15, 18, 20, 41
Total: 6

Ulster
Ant. 4; Arm. 8; Cav. 1.4 (p.461), 1.19 (p.462), 23, 26, 33, 35, 36; Don. 11, 18
Total: 11

Overall Total: 35 records

(b)   Small Stature

Connaught
Gal. 6, 38, 47, 58, 62, 63; Mayo 9, 28; Ros. 2, 23; Sli. 7, 13
Total: 12

Leinster
Car. 4; Kild. 5, 6; Lao. 15, 16, 17, 19, 21; Long. 5, 9, 12, 16, 18, 19, 20, 29; Lou. 4, 5, 6; Off. 1, 4, 12, 14; Wmea. 3, 12; Wex. 2, 5, 6, 11, 19, 38, 40, 42, 44, 45; Wick. 2, 3, 6, 9, 10
Total: 40

Munster
Lim. 11, 31; Tipp. 7, 19, 23, 34
Total: 6

Ulster
Ant. 4, 6, 13; Arm. 3, 8; Cav. 1.8 (p.462), 1.14 (p.463), 1.15 (p.463), 1.18 (p.463), 1.19 (p. 462), 1.21 (p.461), 1.24 (p.465), 1.28 (p.465), 1.41 (p.463), 9, 23, 30, 35, 36, 38; Don: 16
Total: 21

Overall Total: 79 records

(c)   Long Hair

Connaught
Gal. 46, 50, 54; Mayo 9, 17; Ros. 2, 23
Total: 7

Leinster
Car. 1, 3, 6, 17; Dub. 1 (indefinite provenance), 4, 5, 9; Kild. 6, 8, 10, 13;
Kilk. 10, 18, 19, 26; Lao. 4, 6, 8, 11, 20, 21; Long. 6, 29; Mea. 17; Off. 1, 4,
14; Wmea. 2, 4; Wex. 13, 16, 19, 22, 23, 26, 32, 36, 44, 48, 54; Wick. 2, 4, 7,
14
Total: 45
Munster
Cl. 19, 24, 34, 36; Lim. 2, 25; Tipp. 2, 3, 15, 16, 17, 18, 20, 23, 29, 31,
41; Wat. 1, 4, 5, 18, 24, 27, 28, 35, 36
Total: 26

Ulster
Arm. 8; Cav. 1.14 (p. 464), 1.37 (p. 458), 9, 16
Total: 5

Overall Total: 83 records

(d)   Combing Hair (excluding 32 references in The Comb Legend variants,
       p. 379-80).

Connaught
Gal. 10, 46, 47, 50, 54, 59; Mayo 9; Ros. 1, 12, 16
Total: 10

Leinster
Car. 1, 3, 4, 6, 12, 17; Dub. 1 (indefinite provenance), 5, 6, 9, 10; Kild.
4, 5, 6, 7, 8, 10, 11; Kilk. 1, 10, 26; Lao. 6, 9, 17, 21; Long. 23, 28, 29;
Mea. 7, 24; Off. 1, 4, 6, 10, 12, 14; Wmea. 2, 4, 11, 12; Wex. 1, 6, 10, 13,
16, 19, 23, 24, 32, 36, 38, 40, 42, 43, 45; Wick. 4, 5, 6, 7, 8, 9, 14
Total: 62

Munster
Cl. 19, 22, 24, 34; Lim. 1, 2, 24, 25; Tipp. 2, 7, 10, 15, 16, 18, 19, 20, 23,
24, 34, 37, 39, 41; Wat. 4, 5, 8, 18, 36, 42, 43, 45, 46
Total: 31

Ulster
Arm. 2, 3; Cav. 1.42, 1.43 (p.474), 9, 16, 21, 26, 29, 31
Total: 10

Overall Total: 113 records

(e)   White Clothes

Connaught
Gal. 39, 50, 58; Leit. 3; Mayo 17; Ros. 23; Sli. 7
Total: 7

Leinster
Car. 8; Dub. 4; Kild. 2, 13; Kilk. 1, 7, 13, 19, 26; Lao. 8, 15, 17, 18; Long. 9, 12, 14, 19, 29; Lou. 2, 5; Off. 4; Wmea. 10; Wex: 50; Wick. 5
Total: 24

Munster
Cl. 3, 36; Lim. 2; Tipp. 8, 9, 17, 32; Wat. 1, 5, 12, 14, 21, 22, 24, 27, 28, 33, 35, 40, 42
Total: 20

Ulster
Cav. 1.8 (p.462), 1.18 (pp.463, 450), 1.19 (p.463), 1.24 (p.465), 1.35 (p.458), 1.21 (p.461), 1.32 (p.466), 4, 5, 16, 17, 33, 38, 40; Down 9; Fer. 1
Total: 17

Overall Total: 67 records

3.4 Manifestation Situations

1. Records (545 = 59% in archival and printed source material stating that the supernatural death-messenger is connected with death.

Ant. 1-9; 11-13; Arm. 1-3, 6, 8; Car. 1, 3, 5-8, 12, 13, 15, 16, 17, 19; Cav. 1-9, 13-32, 35, 36, 38-43; Cl. 5-9, 12-17, 19-21, 23-27, 29, 34-37; Cork 1-3, 5, 7-14, 17, 23-27, 29-32, 35, 36, 38-42; Der. 1; Don. 1, 4, 6, 7-9, 11-14, 16-19, 21-24, 26-29; Down 1, 3, 4, 6, 7, 11-16; Dub. 1-5, 7-10, 12, 14, 15-17; Fer. 1-5; Gal. 7-10, 13, 14, 18, 23, 33-37, 39, 40, 45, 47-51, 53-54, 56, 58-61, 63, 65-70; Ker. 2, 4, 7, 8, 9-13, 14, 17, 18, 19, 22, 23, 25-27, 29, 30-33, 35, 37, 38-40, 41, 43, 45, 46; Kild. 1-4, 6-10, 12, 13; Kilk. 1, 2, 6, 9-13, 17, 18, 20, 22, 25, 26, 27; Lao. 4-6, 8, 10, 13, 16, 17, 18-20; Leit. 1-11, 13-16; Lim. 1-4, 6-10, 12, 13, 15-19, 21-25, 28, 29-35, 37; Long. 1-5, 7-14, 16-34; Lou. 2, 4, 5, 10, 12; Mayo 1-3, 6, 7, 9, 11, 17, 20, 23, 24, 27-34, 35; Mea. 4, 6-12, 14, 15-17, 18, 20, 21, 25; Mon. 1, 2, 4-7, 8-11; Off. 1-3, 5-7, 9, 12-14, 15; Ros. 1, 2, 4, 6, 7, 9-13, 15-18, 20-22, 24-28; Sli. 1, 2, 4-7, 10, 11, 13, 14, 16, 17; Tipp. 1, 7, 8, 11, 13-20, 22-24, 26, 28, 31, 35, 36, 37, 38, 41, 44; Tyr. 1-6, 8, 9; Wat. 1, 2, 4, 5, 7, 8, 12-18, 21-24, 28-32, 34, 35, 37-39, 41, 44, 46-49, 51-53; Wmea. 1, 2, 4-8, 9, 10, 11, 13, 14, 17, 19, 21; Wex. 1-6, 8-13, 15, 16, 18-24, 28, 29, 32, 33, 36, 38, 40-49, 52, 53, 55, 60, 61; Wick. 2-4, 6-9

Overall Total: 545 records

2.   Records indicating that the death-messenger manifests herself:

(a)   Before death

Connaught
Gal. 7, 9, 10, 14, 18, 23, 37, 39, 40, 45, 49, 50, 51, 53, 54, 56, 61, 63, 65-67, 69, 70; Leit. 1-11, 13-16; Mayo 1, 2, 3, 6, 7, 9, 11, 17, 28, 29-35; Ros. 1, 2, 4, 6, 7, 10-12, 14, 16-19, 21, 23, 27; Sli. 1, 2, 4, 5, 6, 10, 11, 12, 13, 15, 16
Total: 81

Leinster
Car. 1, 3, 7, 8, 12, 13, 15, 16, 17, 19; Dub. 1-5, 7-9, 10, 15-17; Kild. 2, 4, 7, 8, 10, 12; Kilk. 1, 2, 6, 9-13, 20, 22, 25-27; Lao. 4, 5, 6, 8, 14, 17, 19; Long. 1-5, 7-9, 11-14, 16-19, 21-25, 28-34; Lou. 2, 4, 5, 12; Mea. 4, 6-9, 10-12, 14, 17, 18; Off. 1, 2, 3, 6, 9, 12, 13, 15; Wmea. 2, 4-7, 9, 10, 11, 13, 17, 19; Wex. 1-5, 8-10, 13, 16, 19, 20-23, 29, 32, 36, 38, 40, 41-48, 52, 53, 55; Wick. 4, 6, 8, 9
Total: 146

Munster
Cl. 5, 6, 9, 12, 13, 14, 17, 19, 20, 21, 23, 24, 25, 26, 34; Cork 1, 8, 11-14, 17, 23-27, 30, 32, 36, 38, 40, 42; Ker. 4, 7, 8, 9, 13, 14, 18, 19, 22, 23, 25, 27, 29, 31, 32, 35, 37, 38, 40, 41, 43, 45, 46; Lim. 1, 2, 4, 6-10, 12,

15-17, 19, 21-24, 28, 30-35; Tipp. 7, 8, 11, 15, 19, 20, 22, 31, 35-37, 44; Wat. 1, 2, 4, 5, 8, 12, 13, 15, 16-18, 22-24, 28-31, 34, 37-39, 41, 46, 47, 51-53
Total: 120
Ulster
Ant. 2, 4, 6, 7, 8; Arm. 2, 3, 6, 8; Cav. 1, 1.6, 1.8 (pp. 437-438, 440), 1.21 (pp. 439, 440), 1.26 (p. 439), 1.32 (p. 439), 2, 3, 4, 6, 7, 8, 9, 14, 16, 17, 18, 21, 22, 23, 24, 25, 26, 27, 28, 29, 30, 31, 32, 35, 36, 38, 39, 41, 42; Der. 1; Don. 1, 4, 6, 9, 11-14, 16-19, 21, 23, 24, 26-28; Down 3, 6, 7, 13, 14, 15, 16; Fer. 1-5, 6; Mon. 2, 4-7, 8, 11; Tyr. 1-6, 8, 9
Total: 90

Overall Total: 437 (i.e. 80% of the 545 records that directly connect the death-messenger with death)

(b)   After death

Connaught:
Gal. 47(S); Mayo 20(S); Ros. 1(Q), 2(Q)
Total: 4

Leinster:
Dub. 12(L); Kild. 6(Q); Kilk. 18(S); Lao. 21(S); Long. 20(S); Mea. 23(S); Wex. 33(S); Wick. 3(S)
Total: 8

Munster
Cl. 29(S), 35 (S); Cork 9(S); Lim. 13(S), 25(S), 37(S); Tipp. 17(S), 23(S); Wat. 32(S), 48(M)
Total: 10

Ulster:
Cav. 19(Q), 20(Q)
Total: 2

Overall Total: 24 (i.e. 4% of the 545 records that directly connect the death-messenger with death)

(c)   At the moment of death

Ulster:
Ant. 3(L); Cork 8(M); Don. 22(Q); Down 11(M)

Overall Total: 4 (i.e. 1% of 545 records that directly connect the death-messenger with death)

(d)   Unspecified time in relation to death

Connaught:
Gal. 8(S), 13(M), 33(S), 34(M), 35(P), 36(M), 48(S), 58(S), 59(S), 60(S);
Mayo 24(S); Ros. 11(Q), 22(S); Sli. 7(S), 14(M)
Total: 15

Leinster:
Car. 5(M), 6(S); Dub. 14(L); Kild. 1(S), 3(S); Kilk. 17(S); Lao. 20(Q);
Long. 10(S), 26(S), 27(S); Lou. 10(P); Mea. 20(S); Off. 5(S), 7(S), 14(Q);
Wmea. 1(S), 14(S), 21(S); Wex. 11(M), 12(S), 15(P), 24(S), 60(M), 61(M);
Wick. 2(S), 7(S)
Total: 26

Munster:
Cl. 7(S), 36(S); Cork 2(S), 3(S), 5(S), 7(M), 10(S), 29(M), 31(P), 35(M),
39(M), 41(S); Ker. 2(Q), 17(S), 26(S), 33(M); Lim. 3(S), 18(S); Tipp.
16(M), 18(Q), 24(S), 26(S), 28(S), 38(S); Wat. 7(S), 14(M)
Total: 26

Ulster:
Ant. 1(M), 5(P), 9(P), 11(S), 12(Q), 13(P); Arm. 1(P); Cav. 5(S), 13(M),
40(S), 43(S); Don. 7(S), 8(S), 9(S); Down 1(M), 4(P), 12(M)
Total: 17

*Overall total: 84 (i.e. 15% of the 545 records that directly connect the
death-messenger with death)*

3. Records indicating manifestations is:

(a)   For a dying person

Connaught:
Gal. 7, 9, 10, 23, 40, 45, 49, 63, 69; Leit. 1-5, 7, 11, 14; Mayo 1, 9, 28-30,
32; Ros. 4, 6, 11, 12, 14, 21, 27; Sli. 11
Total: 31

Leinster:
Car. 1, 12, 15, 16, 17; Dub. 4, 5, 7, 8; Kild. 12; Kilk. 2, 9, 12, 13, 22; Lao.
4-6, 8; Long. 3-5, 9, 16, 18, 21, 25, 29, 30, 31, 34; Lou. 2, 4, 12; Mea. 9,
12, 17; Off. 1, 13, 15; Wmea. 2, 7, 9, 11, 13, 19; Wex. 4, 5, 8, 9, 10, 20,
21, 23, 29, 40, 41, 43-47, 52; Wick. 4, 6, 8
Total: 66

Munster:
Cl. 13, 17, 24, 26; Cork 8, 23, 25, 40; Ker. 13, 22, 25, 27, 37, 38, 46;
Lim. 2, 4, 6, 7-10, 12, 17, 23, 24, 28, 31; Tipp. 8, 19, 35, 37, 44; Wat. 2,
8, 16, 24, 30, 31, 34, 39, 41, 46, 47
Total: 44

Ulster
Ant. 2; Arm. 2, 8; Cav. 1(6), 3, 9, 14, 23-26, 29, 30, 36, 41, 42; Don. 4, 11, 13, 16; Down 7; Mon. 5
Total: 27

Overall Total: 168 (i.e. 31% of the 545 records that directly connect the death-messenger with death)

(b)   Very shortly before death

Connaught:
Gal. 14, 37, 39, 53, 65; Leit. 6, 7, 8, 10, 13, 16; Mayo 6, 7, 17; Ros. 19, 23; Sli. 1, 4, 5, 6, 16
Total: 21

Leinster:
Car. 8, 19; Dub. 9, 17; Kild. 4, 7; Long. 7, 11, 24, 32; Lou. 5; Mea. 4, 8, 18; Off. 3, 6, 9, 12; Wmea. 17; Wex. 3, 13, 19, 22, 32, 42, 53, 55
Total: 27

Munster:
Cl. 12, 23, 25; Cork 11, 32; Ker. 14, 18, 23, 35, 40; Lim. 1, 22, 34; Tipp. 31; Wat. 1, 4, 12, 13, 15, 17, 22, 23, 28, 29, 37, 38.
Total: 26

Ulster:
Ant. 6; Arm. 6; Cav. 1.37 (p.439), 3, 4, 25, 32, 33, 39; Don. 1, 9, 12, 21, 22, 26, 27, 28; Down 3, 6; Mon. 11; Tyr. 4
Total: 21

Overall Total: 95 (i.e. 17% of the 545 records that directly connect the death-messenger with death)

3.5 Times of Manifestations

In connection with death — archival records

(a)   Night-time — unspecified hour

Connaught:
Gal. 8, 13, 14, 23, 37, 45, 53, 54, 58, 61; Leit. 3, 4, 6, 7, 10, 13, 14, 16;
Mayo 7, 9, 17, 28, 34; Ros. 1, 2, 6, 11, 12, 17, 21, 22, 27; Sli. 1, 7, 13,
14, 16
Total: 37

Leinster:
Car. 8, 16, 19; Dub. 2, 3, 5, 8, 14, 16, 17; Kild. 6, 10; Kilk. 2, 6, 11, 20,
25, 26; Lao. 4, 5, 14, 17, 19, 20, 21; Long. 3, 11, 12, 13, 16, 18, 19, 20,
22, 24; Mea. 4, 9, 17, 25; Off. 1, 5, 9, 12, 15; Wmea. 2, 5, 11, 13; Wex.
10, 13, 22, 24, 29, 32, 44, 46, 47, 48, 52, 53, 56
Total: 61

Munster:
Cl. 6, 8, 12, 13, 17, 20, 29, 34, 35; Cork 1, 7, 8, 14, 21, 23, 27, 29, 36,
38, 40; Ker. 7, 9, 14, 43; Lim. 1, 4, 6, 8, 10, 15, 19, 22, 23, 25, 28, 29,
31, 37; Tipp. 8, 12, 20, 23, 28, 35, 37, 40, 42; Wat. 1, 2, 15, 16, 17, 23,
24, 25, 28, 29, 32, 37, 41
Total: 60

Ulster:
Ant. 3, 4, 10; Arm. 2, 7, 8; Cav. 1.37 (p.439), 4, 7, 8, 14, 15, 19, 20, 21, 23,
24, 26, 30, 33, 37, 39; Der. 1; Don. 1, 4, 8, 12, 23, 24, 26, 27, 29; Down 1,
4, 7, 11, 16; Fer. 1, 3, 5; Mon. 8; Tyr. 4, 6
Total: 43
*Overall Total: 201 records (i.e. 37% of the 545 records that directly
connect the death-messenger with death)*

(b)   Midnight
Connaught:
No records

Leinster:
Car. 17; Dub. 12; Kild. 7; Long. 33; Lou. 2; Mea. 8; Off. 9; Wex. 19;
Wick. 14

Munster:
Cl. 23, 24; Cork 11; Ker. 46; Lim. 2, 33; Wat. 5, 18, 22, 30

Ulster:
Cav. 2, 18, 41; Tyr. 5
*Overall Total: 23 records (i.e. 4% of the 545 records that directly connect
the death-messenger with death)*

3.6 Places of Manifestations

Records from archival and printed source material detailing the locations of the death-messenger manifestations in connection with deaths.

(a)   At or near the dying person's house.

Connaught:
Gal. 7, 8, 9, 37, 40, 45, 47, 50, 56, 63, 65, 67; Leit. 1, 2, 4, 5, 6, 7, 9, 10, 11, 13; Mayo 6, 9, 17, 20, 33; Ros. 1, 2, 4, 12, 16, 18; Sli. 1, 5, 13, 16
Total: 37

Leinster
Car. 1, 7, 13, 16, 17, 19; Dub. 5, 12, 15, 16; Kild. 2, 3, 4, 6, 8, 12; Kilk. 1, 2, 13, 18, 22, 26; Lao. 4, 5, 8, 14, 15, 16, 17, 19, 20; Long. 1, 2, 3, 5, 9, 11, 12, 21, 23, 31; Lou. 3, 4; Mea. 4, 7, 8, 9, 11, 12, 17, 20, 25; Off. 1, 9, 15; Wmea. 11; Wex. 4, 5, 6, 9, 17, 19, 22, 30, 33, 44-50, 55; Wick. 4, 6, 14.
Total: 76

Munster:
Cl. 12, 13, 14, 23, 24, 25, 26, 34, 35; Cork 1, 9, 17, 29, 38, 40, 42; Ker. 2, 4, 5, 19, 25, 27, 30, 39, 41, 45; Lim. 2, 4, 6, 8, 22, 23, 24, 25, 28, 34, 37; Tipp. 2, 7, 8, 16, 18, 19, 23, 37, 42; Wat. 15, 16, 17, 23, 32, 37, 41, 47, 48.
Total: 55

Ulster:
Ant. 2, 4, 6, 8; Arm. 6; Cav. 1.2 (p.470-471), 1.14 (p.471), 1.18 (p.450), 1.21 (p.471), 1.22, 1.41 (p.471), 1.43 (p.465), 2, 3, 7, 9, 14, 16, 17, 19, 22, 23, 25, 29, 33, 40, 41, 43; Der. 1; Don. 9, 11, 12, 16, 22, 23, 26, 27, 29; Down 3, 6, 7; Fer. 5; Mon. 1; Tyr. 4, 5, 6
Total 46

Total: 214 records (i.e. 77% of 'house manifestations')

(b)   At houses of relatives living at a distance from the dying person.

Connaught:
Leit. 14, 16; Ros. 2, 17, 23; Sli. 5, 6

Leinster:
Car. 19; Lao. 17; Off. 13; Wmea. 2, 5

Munster
Cl. 14; Cork 2, 10, 23, 32; Ker. 22, 35; Lim. 1; Wat. 1, 53

Ulster:
Ant. 3; Cav. 6; Down 1; Mon. 10; Tyr. 5, 6

Total: 28 records (i.e. 10% of 'house manifestations').

(c)   At houses of neighbours

Connaught:
No records

Leinster:
Wex. 52

Munster:
Cork. 1, 7, 8; Ker. 14, 23, 32; Lim. 17; Tipp. 35; Wat. 28, 38

Ulster:
Cav. 26.
Total: 12 records (i.e. 4% of 'house manifestations')

(d)   At old family home

Connaught:
Gal. 23, 54; Leit. 5, 10, 15; Ros. 2

Leinster:
Long. 34; Off. 1; Wmea. 8; Wex. 9, 16, 17

Munster:
Ker. 2, 26; Lim. 16

Ulster:
Cav. 6; Don. 22; Mon. 8

Total: 18 records (i.e. 7% of 'house manifestations')

(e)   Unspecified house

Leinster:
Kilk. 9, 10; Wick. 9

Ulster:
Arm. 8; Down 26.
Total: 5 records (i.e. 2% of 'house manifestations')

Overall Total for manifestations at or near a house = 277 records (i.e. 71% of records where the manifestation is localised).

(f)   At home in Ireland on the occasion of death abroad

Connaught:
Gal. 23 (America), 54 (America), 56 (America); Ros. 2(Q) (America), 22 (America); Sli. 6 (America).
Total: 6

Leinster:
Kild. 13 (America); Lao. 19 (England); Lou. 6(Q) (England); Off.1 (Q) (England), 13 (America); Wmea. 2(Q) (England or America), 5 (p.44) (West Indies), 5 (p.50) (America), 8 (America); Wex. 9 (Canada), 16 (America), 17 (America), 19(Q) (America).
Total: 13

Munster:
Cl. 13 (America); Cork 8 (America); Ker. 33 (America); Lim. 16 (America); Tipp. 2(Q) (Abroad); Wat. 1 (America).
Total: 6

Ulster:
Ant. 3(L) (abroad); Cav. 1.1 (p.456) (Australia), 6(P) (France), 24(Q) (America, Australia); Don. 11 (abroad), 22(Q) (America); Down 11 (Liverpool, England); Fer. 1(Q) (America), 5(Q) (America); Mon. 6 (abroad); Tyr. 2(Q) (England or America).
Total:11

Overall total: 36 records (References to: America, 24; England, 5; Canada, 1; Australia, 2; West Indies, 1; France, 1; Unspecified, 4)

(g)   At window of the house*

Connaught
Gal. 54; Ros. 1, 2, 23; Sli. 6
Total: 5

Leinster:
Car. 1, 13, 16; Kild. 3, 8; Kilk. 9, 10, 18; Lao. 19, 20, Long. 5, 21, 31; Mea. 12, 17, 20; Off. 1; Wmea: 2, 11; Wex. 5, 6, 9, 16, 17, 19, 33; Wick. 6, 9
Total: 28

Munster
Cl. 12, 14; Cork 1; Ker. 2; Lim. 2, 24; Tipp. 16, 42; Wat. 41
Total: 9

Ulster:
Ant. 6, 8; Arm. 8; Cav. 1.14 (p.471), 1.18 (p.450), 1.43 (p.465), 9, 16, 19, 33; Don. 11, 29; Down 7, 26 (indefinite provenance); Tyr. 6
Total: 15

Overall Total: 57 records (i.e. 21% of the records which indicate that the manifestation occurred at the house)

References to manifestation at the window in The Comb Legend when the object taken from the death-messenger is being sought by her and being returned to her are not included (Appendix 4).

3.7 The experiencers (in connection with deaths)

(a)   Members of the family and relatives

Connaught
Gal. 23, 45, 53, 59; Leit. 14; Mayo 7, 30, 33; Ros. 4, 22, 23, 25, 27;
Sli. 1, 6.
Total: 15

Leinster
Car. 1, 16; Dub. 4, 5, 9, 12, 14; Kild. 4, 8; Lao. 5, 19; Long. 3, 5, 11, 12,
18, 30, 32; Lou. 5; Mea. 7, 20, 25; Off. 1, 9, 13, 15; Wmea. 2, 4, 5, 7, 17;
Wex. 5, 9, 16, 24, 45
Total: 36

Munster
Cl. 12; Cork. 2, 10, 17, 32; Ker. 22, 32, 35, 38, 55; Lim. 1; Tipp. 2, 18,
20; Wat. 1, 15, 22, 24, 29, 53
Total: 20

Ulster
Cav. 1.1 (p. 456), 4, 6, 24; Ant. 2, 3, 46; Arm. 8; Don. 1, 20-23, 25, 27;
Fer. 1, 2, 5; Mon. 6, 8, 10; Tyr. 4
Total: 22

*Overall Total: 93 records (i.e. 17% of the 545 records that directly connect
the death-messenger with deaths)*

(b)   Neighbours

Connaught
Gal. 13, 14, 33, 37-40, 47-50, 65; Leit. 1, 2, 3-6, 9-11, 13, 15, 16; Mayo
2, 3, 6, 7, 9, 17, 23; Ros. 1, 2, 4, 6, 7, 12, 17, 18; Sli. 5, 7, 11
Total: 42

Leinster
Car. 7, 12, 15, 16, 17, 19; Dub. 8, 10; Kild. 3; Kilk. 2, 12, 13, 20, 26;
Lao. 4, 5, 14, 17, 19, 20, 21; Long. 1, 5, 7, 9, 12, 13, 16, 18-20, 22, 23,
25, 26, 29, 31-34; Lou. 2; Mea. 4, 8-10, 17, 18; Off. 1-3; Wmea. 4-6, 8-11,
13; Wex. 4, 10, 15, 19, 21, 41, 44, 48, 52, 53, 55, 61; Wick. 8, 9, 14
Total: 73

Munster
Cl. 5, 6-9, 13, 17, 20, 21, 23-27, 29, 34, 35; Cork 1, 5, 7, 8, 9, 11, 13, 14,
17, 23-25, 27, 29, 30, 36, 38, 40, 42; Ker. 4, 7, 9, 13, 14, 18, 25-27, 29,
32, 33, 37; Lim. 1, 3, 4, 6, 10, 15-17, 22, 23, 25, 28, 31, 33, 37; Tipp. 1,
2, 8, 11, 15, 18, 22, 23, 28, 35, 37, 38, 41; Wat. 2, 4, 7, 8, 12, 14, 16, 18,
24, 28, 30, 32, 34, 35, 37, 38, 39, 41, 47
Total: 96

Ulster
Ant. 6, 7, 13; Arm. 1, 2, 6, 7; Cav. 1, 2, 3, 8, 14-16, 18, 19, 20, 21, 22, 25, 26-32, 38, 40-42; Der. 1; Don. 8, 9, 11, 12, 14, 16, 25; Down 1, 3, 6, 7, 8, 11, 16, 17; Mon. 1, 7, 9, 11; Tyr. 2, 5, 6
Total: 54

Overall Total: 265 records (i.e. 49% of the 545 records that directly connect the death-messenger with death)

APPENDIX 4

The Insulted Supernatural Death-Messenger

4.1 The Comb Legend

(a)   A break-down of the versions of The Comb Legend according to province, county and type of source

Connaught
Gal. 24 (S), 32 (S), 37 (Q), 38 (S), 41 (M), 46 (L), 55 (M); Mayo 18 (S), 27 (S); Ros. 23 (Q); Sli. 9 (S)
Total: 11

Leinster:
Car. 10 (S), 11 (M), 13 (M); Dub. 6 (S); Kild. 2(Q), 9 (P), 13 (R); Kilk. 3 (S), 4 (S), 5 (S), 7 (Q), 12b (Q), 13 (S), 14 (S), 15 (Q), 16 (S), 18 (S), 19 (S); Lao. 1 (L), 5 (S), 7 (Q), 11 (S), 12 (R), 15 (R), 17 (R), 19 (R), 20 (Q), 22 (S); Long. 4 (M), 6 (S); Off. 4 (S), 8 (S), 10 (S), 11 (S); Wmea. 3 (M), 9 (S), 12 (P), 16 (L); Wex. 4 (M), 7 (S), 14 (S), 30 (S), 35 (P), 37 (P), 40 (Q), 43 (S), 50 (L), 51 (S); Wick. 12 (S), 13 (S)
Total: 50

Munster
Tipp. 2 (Q), 3 (S), 9 (S), 29 (S), 32 (S), 34 (S), 39 (S), 42 (Q), 43 (P), 44 (Q); Wat. 10 (S), 19 (M), 25 (S), 26 (S), 27 (S), 40 (M), 50 (S)
Total: 17

Ulster
Cav. 12 (S)
Total: 1

Unspecified Provenance: two published versions (a, b) in *Ireland's Own*, 27 November 1954, p. 15

Overall Total: 81; M = 9; S = 44; Q = 12; L = 4; R = 5; P = 7

(b)   Initial encounter versions − A redaction

Car. 11; Dub. 6; Gal. 24, 32, 37, 38, 41, 46, 55; Kild. 9; Kilk. 5, 7, 12, 13, 14, 18, 19; Lao. 1, 11, 22; Long. 4, 6; Mayo 18, 27; Off. 4, 8, 10, 11; Ros. 23; Sli. 9; Tipp. 3, 9, 29, 32, 34, 39, 42, 43; Wat. 19, 25, 27, 40, 50; Wmea. 3, 9, 12, 16; Wex. 4, 7, 14, 35, 37, 40, 43, 50, 51; Wick. 12, 13

Unspecified Provenance; 2
Total: 60 (i.e. 75% of The Comb Legend versions).

(c)   Comb, etc., taken forcibly

Car. 11; Dub. 6; Gal. 24, 37, 41, 46, 55; Kild. 9; Kilk. 5, 7, 12b, 13, 14; Lao. 1, 11, 22; Long. 4, 6; Mayo 27; Off. 8, 11; Tipp. 32, 34, 42; Wat. 19, 25, 40, 50; Wmea. 3, 12, 16; Wex. 4, 7, 14, 35, 37, 40, 43, 50, 51; Wick. 12, 13; Unspecified provenance: 2
Total: 44 records

(d)   Death-messenger leaves her comb after her

Gal. 32, 38; Kilk. 18, 19; Mayo 18; Off. 4, 10; Ros. 23; Sli. 9; Tipp. 3 9, 29, 39, 43; Wat. 27; Wmea. 9
Total: 16 records

(e)   No encounter versions: B - redaction

Car. 10 (S), 13 (M); Cav. 12 (S); Kild. 2 (Q), 13 (R); Kilk. 3 (S), 4 (S). 15 (Q), 16 (S); Lao. 5 (S), 7 (Q), 12 (R), 15 (R), 17 (R), 19 (R), 20 (Q); Tipp. 2 (Q), 44 (Q); Wat. 10 (S), 26 (S). Wex. 30 (S)
Total: 21 (i.e. 25% of The Comb Legend versions).

(f)   Identified or identifiable human actor

Car. 10, 11; Gal. 41; Kilk. 3, 7, 12(b), 14, 19; Lao; 1, 5, 11, 15; Mayo 18; Off. 4, 8, 10, 11; Ros. 23; Tipp. 9, 29, 34, 39, 42, 43; Wat. 10, 40; Wmea. 9, 16; Wex. 7, 14, 30, 35, 37, 43; Wick. 12
Total: 35

(g)   Unidentified or unidentifable human actor

Car. 13 (M); Cav. 12 (S); Dub. 6 (S); Gal. 24 (S), 32 (S), 37 (Q), 38 (S), 46 (L), 55 (M); Kild. 2 (Q), 9 (P), 13 (R); Kilk. 4 (S), 5 (S), 13 (S), 15 (Q), 16 (S), 18 (S); Lao 7 (Q), 12 (R), 17 (R), 19 (R), 20 (Q), 22 (S), Long. 4 (M), 6 (S); Mayo 27 (S); Sli. 9 (S); Tipp. 2 (Q), 3 (S), 32 (S), 44 (Q); Wat. 19 (M), 25 (S), 26 (S), 27 (S), 50 (S); Wmea. 3 (M), 12 (P); Wex. 4 (M), 40 (Q), 50 (L), 51 (S); Wick. 13 (S) and two versions in *Ireland's Own* (cf. (a) above)
Total: 46; M = 6; S = 22; Q = 8; L = 2; R = 4, P = 4

(h)   Variants where the death-messenger cries at the house for her comb etc.
Car. 10, 11; Dub. 6; Gal. 24, 32, 38, 46; Kild. 9, 13; Kilk. 3, 4, 5, 7, 12b, 13, 14, 15, 18, 19; Lao. 1, 5, 7, 11, 12, 15, 17, 19, 20; Long. 6; Mayo 18, 27; Off. 8, 11; Sli. 9; Tipp. 3, 9, 29, 32, 34, 39, 42, 43; Wat. 10, 25; Wmea 3, 12, 16; Wex. 4, 14, 30, 43, 50, 51; Wick. 12, 13
Total: 55

(i)   Comb, etc., returned through the window

Car. 13; Cav. 12; Gal; 32, 38; Kild. 9; Kilk. 3, 4, 5, 7, 13, 14, 15, 16; Lao. 1, 5, 7, 11, 12, 17, 20; Mayo 18, 27; Off. 8, 11; Sli. 9; Tipp. 2, 3, 9, 29, 32, 34, 42, 43, 44; Wat. 10, 25, 26, 27, 40, 50; Wmea. 3, 16; Wex. 4, 14, 43, 50, 51; Wick. 12, 13

Uncertain Provenance: 1 record (*Ireland's Own,* 27 Nov. 1954, p. 15 (b)
Total: 50 records

(j)   Tongs as Returning Implement

Car. 10, 11, 13; Cav. 12; Dub. 6; Gal. 38; Kild. 2, 9, 13; Kilk. 4, 5, 7, 13, 16, 19; Lao. 5, 7, 11, 12, 15, 17, 19, 20, 22; Long. 4; Off. 8; Tipp. 2, 9, 29, 34, 44; Wat. 25, 40; Wmea. 3, 16; Wex. 14, 35, 37, 40, 43, 50, 51; Wick. 12, 13

Uncertain Provenance: 1 record (*Ireland's Own,* 27 Nov. 1954, p. 15 (b))
Total: 45 records

(k)   Variants in which the implement used to return the comb, etc. is damaged

Car. 10, 11; Gal. 24, 37, 38, 41, 55; Kild. 2, 13; Kilk. 3, 4, 5, 7, 12b, 13, 15, 18, 19; Lao. 1, 5, 7, 11, 12, 15, 17, 19, 20, 22; Long. 4, 6; Mayo 27; Off. 8; Tipp. 2, 9, 29, 32, 39, 42, 44; Wat. 19, 26, 27, 40; Wex. 7, 14, 40, 43, 50, 51; Wick. 12, 13

Total: 51

4.2   The Imprint of the Banshee's Five Fingers Legend
— Versions

1. Scéal
Bhí an bhean sí ag ní éadaigh i dtubán uisce oíche amháin agus bhí fear ag
dul abhaile. Chonaic sé an bhean agus shíl sé gur bhean ón mbaile a bhí
ann. Chuaigh sé siar go dtí an áit ina raibh sí i ngan fhios di agus chuir sé a
dhá láimh timpeall uirthi. D'iompaigh an bhean sí thart agus bhuail sí buille
ar a leiceann lena lámh agus d'fhág sí marc a cúig méara ar a leiceann . . .

[The banshee was washing clothes in a tub of water one night when a man
was going home. He saw the woman and he thought that it was a woman
from the place who was there. He went over to where she was unknown to
her and he put his arms around her. The banshee turned around and
she gave him a clout on his cheek with her hand and she left the mark of
her five fingers on his cheek.] (Gal. 15)

2. An Bhean Sí
Tá an bhean sí le cloisteáil siar in Iarlatan freisin. Bean bheag is ea í agus bíonn
éadaigh dearg uirthi i gcónaí. Is í an bhean is measa a bhfaca tú ariamh. Tá
sí an-chrosta ar fad. Chuala mé go raibh fear síos i mBaile Bacach agus
chuaigh sé suas go dtí an bhean sí agus dúirt sé rud éigin léi. Bhuail sí é
agus d'fhág áit a cúig mhéar ar a aghaidh.

[The banshee is to be heard behind in Iarlatan also. She is a small woman
and she wears red clothes. She is the worst woman you ever saw. She is
very contrary altogether. I heard that there was a man below in Ballybacagh
and he went up to the banshee. He said something to her and she hit him
and she left the print of her five fingers on his face.] (Gal. 52)

3. There is a story told that when one of the Keegans died, during the
wake the banshee was heard wailing outside. Two men (names not known)
went out and tried to get rid of her. But as they came near the hedge
where she was she drew out and slapped one of the men across the face.
The marks of her fingers remained on that man's face until the day he
died. This story was given by Ned O'Neill who said he got it from his father
so it would be at least 110 years old. (Kild. 6 (Q))

4. The fourth version of the legend (Gal. 42) is included in Chapter 10, p.
182.

4.3   The Shirt Legend — Versions

a) An Bhean Sí
Cúpla bliain ó shin deirtear go raibh bean sí in Eochaill. Gach oíche bhíodh
sí ag ní éadaigh agus ag caoineadh. Oíche amháin, bhí tórramh in Eochaill.
Bhí fear ag dul chuig an tórramh agus chonaic sé an bhean sí ag ní éadaigh.
Dúirt sé go raibh a léine salach agus é a ní dó. Ní dúirt an bhean sí rud ar
bith. Nuair a bhí sé timpeall leathuair ag an tórramh tháinig an bhean sí
isteach agus thug sí a léine chuig an abhainn agus nigh sí é. Nuair a bhí sé
ag dul abhaile tháinig sí aríst leis an léine agus bhí sé go deas glan.

[A few years ago, it is said, there was a banshee in *Eochaill* (Waterdale).
Every night she used to be washing clothes and keening. One night there
was a wake in *Eochaill* (Waterdale). There was a man going to the wake
and he saw the banshee washing clothes. He said that his shirt was dirty
and to wash it for him. The banshee said nothing at all. When he was
about a half-hour at the wake she came in and took his shirt to the river
and washed it. When he was going home she came again with the shirt and
it was nice and clean.] (Gal. 16)

b) An Bhean Sí
Ins an tseanaimsir bhí fear ag dul ar tórramh. Ar a bhealach bhí abhainn
bheag ar thaobh an bhóthair. Amuigh i lár na habhann bhí cloch mhór.
Ba mhinic leis an mbean sí a bheith ag níochán éadaigh ar an gcloch seo.
Go tráthúil nuair a bhí an fear ag dul thart, chuala sé an torann. D'fhéach
sé amach ar an abhainn agus céard a chonaic sé amuigh ansin ina suí ar
an gcloch ach an bhean sí agus í ar a dícheall ag níochán éadaigh le slis.
Labhair sé léi agus dúirt 'Muise, a bhean chóir, ba cheart duit mo léine a ní
dom ó tharla go bhfuil tú ag ní'. Níor thaitin leis an mbean sí caidéis ar
bith a chur uirthi. Lean sí an fear agus marach chomh gar dó a bhí teach an
tórraimh, bheadh sé i ngreim aici. Rith an fear agus d'éirigh leis bheith
istigh insan teach sul má tháinig sí suas leis. Nuair a chuaigh sé isteach
bhuail sé a dhroim in aghaidh an dorais agus choinnigh sé brúite amach ina
h-aghaidh é. Nuair nár bhféad sí teacht isteach, chuir sí a lámh isteach ós
cionn an dorais agus rug sí ar ghruaig an fhir. B'éigin a ghruaig a ghearradh
agus lán a láimhe dá ghruaig a ligint léi, sin nó bheadh an bhaithis tar-
raingthe aici de.

[Long ago a man was going to a wake. On his way, there was a little river
at the side of the road. Out in the middle of the river there was a big stone.
The banshee was often washing clothes on this stone. Just as the man was
going by he heard the noise. He went out into the river and what did he
see out there sitting on the rock but the banshee and she washing clothes
with a beetle for all she was worth. He spoke to her and he said '*Muise*,
good woman, you should wash my shirt for me since you happen to be
washing'. The banshee did not like to be accosted at all. She followed the
man and only that the wake-house happened to be so near, she would have
got him. The man ran and he succeeded in being inside in the house before

she caught up with him. When he went in he put his back against the door and he kept it pushed out against her. When she was not able to come in, she put her hand in over the door and she caught the man's hair. His hair had to be cut and the full of her hand of his hair had to be let go with her, that, or she would have pulled the crown of his head off him] (Gal. 19).

c) An Bhean Sí ag Níochán
Bhí tórramh i mbaile fadó agus bhí fear ag dul ar an tórramh agus bhí sruthán uisce ann agus bhí bean sí amuigh sa sruthán ag níochán. 'Muise, a bhean chóir', ar sé, 'ó tharla tú ag níochán', ar sé, 'tá sé chomh maith duit', ar sé, 'mo léine-se a ní'. D'éirigh sí suas agus lean sí é agus murach chomh gar a bhí teach an tórraimh dhó, mharbhódh sí é. Is ar a dhul isteach dhó, is é an chéad áit a ndeachaigh sé leis an doras dúnta, ach chuir sí a lámh isteach sa bhfardoras agus rug sí ar ghruaig air. Agus b'éigean siosúr a fháil leis an ngruaig a ghearradh lena greim a scaradh.

[There was a wake in a place long ago and there was a man going to the wake and there was a stream of water there and there was a banshee out in the stream washing. '*Muise*, good woman', said he, 'you might as well', said he 'wash my shirt'. She arose and followed him and but for the wake-house was so close to him she would kill him. When he went in the first place he went was by the closed door, but she put her hand in over the door and she caught his hair and a scissors had to be got to cut the hair in order to remove her grip] (Gal. 20).

d) An Bhean Sí
Bhí fear ann fadó agus bhí sé ag dul ar thórramh duine muintearach dhó. Ar a bhealach go dtí teach an tórraimh bhí air a dhul le taobh abhainn bheag. Nuair a bhí sé ag dul thar an abhainn chonaic sé bean ina suí ar chloch amuigh i lár na habhann agus í ag níochán éadaigh le slis. Nuair a bhí sé ag dul thairsti dúirt sé, 'Muise a bhean chóir, ó tharla go bhfuil tú ag níochán ba cheart duit mo léine-se a ní freisin, agus bhéinn an-bhuíoch díot'. Ar an bpointe is a labhair sé d'éirigh an bhean agus lean sí é. Rith an fear agus níor stop sé go dtáinig sé go teach an tórraimh. Ar an bpointe is a ndeachaigh sé isteach dhún sé an doras agus chuir sé a dhroim leis. Ní túisce a bhí sé ina sheasamh leis an doras ná chuir an bhean sí a lámh isteach insan bhfardoras agus rug sí ar ghreim gruaige air. Chaith na daoine siosúr a fháil agus a chuid gruaige a ghearradh agus í a scaoileadh léi nó tharraingeodh sí an mullach dhó. Dúirt muintir an tí leis gur bhean sí a bhí inti agus dúirt siad leis gan labhairt le aon rud mar sin arís go deo, a d'fheicfeadh sé in am deireanach na hoíche.

[There was a man there long ago and he was going to a relative's wake. He had to go by a little river on his way to the wake-house. When he was crossing the river he saw a woman sitting on a stone out in the middle of the river and she was washing clothes with a beetle. When he was going past her he said '*Muise*, good woman, since you are washing, you should wash my shirt also and I would be very grateful to you'. The minute he spoke, the woman arose and she followed him. The man ran and he did not stop until he got to the wake-house. The minute he went in he closed door and he put his back to it. No sooner was he standing against the door than the banshee put her hand in over the door and she caught him by the hair. The people had to get a scissors and cut his hair and let it off with her or she would pull the top of his head off. The people of the house told him that she was a banshee and they told him not to talk again to anything like that he would see at the dead hour of night]. (Gal. 21)

e) An Bhean Sí agus an Fear a bhí ar an Tórramh
Bhí tórramh i mBaile Eochaille cúpla scór bliain ó shin. Ins an am sin théadh go leor, leor daoine go dtí tórramh agus bhíodh cleasa ar siúil da mba seanduine nó cailleach a bheadh ós cionn chláir. Ach da mba duine óg a bheadh caillte ní bheadh cleas ar bith ann, ach ag déanamh bróin agus ag gol. Bhíodh mná speisialta in gach uile bhaile a dtugtaí mná chaointe orthu mar gheall ar a nguth dolásach cráite a bhíodh acu. An oíche áirithe seo, is seanduine a bhí sínte, agus bhí an teach ag cur thar maoil le daoine, agus gach sórt pléaráca agus cleasaíochta ar bun, an droichead, harra, harra, díol choirce agus cleasa eile. Bhí cuid de na daoine leath-múchta sa teach agus chuadar amach san aer. Bhíodh an bhean sí ag bualadh slis tamall gearr ón áit chéanna agus bhí sí ag bualadh agus níochán an oíche áirithe seo. Chuala na daoine an slis á bualadh. Bhí fear amháin ann a raibh an tubaist ar a bhéal agus dúirt sé amach ina shean-bhéic leis an mbean sí 'Tá sé chomh maith duit mo léine-se a ní freisin ó thárla go bhfuil do lámh san obair'. Isteach leis i dtigh an tórraimh ansin, é féin agus a chompánaigh. Bhí sé ina shuí in aici an dorais, agus níor airigh sé ariamh go ndeachaigh an lámh síos taobh istigh dá chába agus tarraingíodh an léine dá dhroim agus marach gur scaoil duine éigin a bhóna thachtfaí é. Níor chualas ariamh an bhfuair sé an léine ar ais, ach creidim go raibh sé stróicthe is nárbh fhiú é a fhágáil ar ais.

[The Banshee and the Man who was at the Wake
A few score years ago there was a wake in the townland of *Eochaill* (Waterdale). At that time very many people used to go to wakes, and games used to be played, if it was an old man or woman, that was laid out. But if it was a young person that was dead there would not be a game at all there, but grieving and crying. There used to be particular women in every townland called keening women because of the sorrowful agonised voice they had. This particular night it was an old man who was laid out and the house was overflowing with people. There was every sort of high jinks and tricks in progress − the bridge, harra, harra, selling the corn and other games. Some of the people were half smothered in the house and they went out in the air. The banshee used to be beetling a short distance away from the same place, and she was beating the washing this particular night. The people heard the beetle being worked. There was one man there and he spoke very inadvisedly (but he had misfortune on his mouth) and he said in a great roar to the banshee, 'You might as well wash my shirt too since you have your hand

in the job'. Off with him then, into the wakehouse, himself and his companions. He was sitting near the door and he never sensed a thing until the hand went down inside his coat and the shirt was pulled off his back, and but for someone opened his collar he would have been choked. I never heard if he got the shirt back but I believe it was torn and it was not worth leaving back.] (Gal. 28)

f) An Bhean Sí
Bhí beirt fhear ag dul go teach tórraimh oíche. Bhí siad ag dul trasna abhann agus chonaic siad bean ag níochán éadaigh. Dúirt duine acu lena chuid ealaín mb'fhearr di a léine féin a ní freisin. D'imíodar leo ansin agus shuigh an fear ar chathaoir taobh istigh de dhoras tigh an tórraimh. Níor airigh sé ariamh gur sciobadh an léine dá dhroim. Ag teach abhaile dó agus é ag dul trasna na habhann chéanna, bualadh an léine san éadan air agus é nite. Bhí iomarca fad ar a theanga.

[The Banshee
Two men were going to a wake-house one night. They were going across a river and they saw a woman washing clothes. One of them with his antics said that it would be better for her to wash his own shirt too. They went on with themselves then and the man sat on a chair inside the wake-house door. He never sensed a thing until the shirt was grabbed from his back. When he was coming home and crossing the same river, the shirt was thrown in his face and it was washed. He was too loose with his talk.] (Gal. 57)

g) The seventh version of the legend (Gal. 17) is included in Chapter 11, pp. 187 - 8.

APPENDIX 5 – BASIC SOURCE MATERIAL

Manuscript material in the Department of Irish Folklore, University College Dublin (1928-1981) and Printed Works (c. 1800-1981).

Arrangement of the Material

1. The archival and printed source material of known provenance (apart from the material in American and Canadian sources, p. 362) is arranged according to the counties alphabetically. The province to which the county belongs is shown after the county name.* Within each county the material is arranged and numbered according to the baronies alphabetically which are determined by reference to the townland to which the information refers.** Where lack of details makes it impossible to assign the information to a particular townland within a county, it is placed towards the end of the list of sources for that county.

The material in the Main and Schools' Mss., with the notable exception of Cav. I (pp. 481-2) consists mainly of short accounts, mostly of one or two manuscript pages. In order to make the frequent references to these sources in the body of the work less cumbersome, each account in the Main and Schools' Mss. and printed sources is given a separate source number. Each letter and Banshee Questionnaire reply is also given a separate source number (with the exception of Down 18-25 and Tyr. 7) even though the questionnaire replies tend to be somewhat longer than the other manuscript sources.

The source items (with the exception of Tyr. 7) are therefore listed as follows: (a) source number, (b) in the case of the *archival* material, the manuscript collection to which it belongs, e.g. Main Mss. *(IFC)*, Schools' Mss. *(IFCS)* or Schools' Copybooks *(IFCS Copybooks)†*, and with regard to *printed* material, the book, journal, periodical or newspaper in which it is found, (c) manuscript volume number and page references for the *archival*

---

* See frontispiece (xiv) for a map of Ireland showing province and county boundaries.

** See frontispiece (xiii) for a map of Ireland showing the baronies. In the relatively few instances in the Schools' Mss. where it was not possible from the text or the context to determine the townland to which the information referred, the townland in which the school submitting the Mss. is situated is used. In many cases these two townlands would be the same, and in most cases they would be contiguous even where children crossed county boundaries to attend school, or where their informants lived in a neighbouring county, as children did not really travel long distances to school before the fairly recent closure of some small rural schools and the introduction of school transport. Thus, by using the school townland area no appreciable distortion in distribution patterns should occur.

material and author, book title, journal, periodical or newspaper title with volume number — where applicable — and page references for the *printed* material, (d) date of collection (where known) of the *archival* material†† (where the data was recently obtained as a result of the Banshee Questionnaire, 1976, letters, tape recordings, personal communications or from the Ulster Folk and Transport Museum Archive (UFTM), or from some other source e.g. the Dialects Archive, UCD (Tipp. 21), or if it has already appeared in print, e.g. in *Béaloideas*, this is also indicated) and date of publication of the *printed* material, (e) barony, parish and townland (the latter in capital letters since it is the key to the arrangement of the material) and its Ordnance Survey Sheet number, (f) in Cav. I, the informant's name follows and in Down 18-25 further relevant information about the material is given, (g) the letter I (Irish) or E (English) denoting the language in which the material was collected.

(The material in Tyr. 7 does not warrant separate listing of all the survey areas involved).

Where the same items of death-messenger traditions, or references to them, have appeared in different books or journals, these are also listed where known (e.g. Ant. 9, 14, Cav. 6, Cl. 8, Cork 30, Dub. 16, Ker. 47, Lao. 9, 23, Mayo 34, Ros. 20, Tipp. 48).

The barony, parish and townland names are in the anglicised forms found in the *General Alphabetical Index to the Townlands, Towns, Parishes and Baronies of Ireland, 1851*. These forms are preferred to those given by the collector or informant where there is a divergence of information. Confusion often arises between civil and ecclesiastical parishes or where the informant lives on the boundary of two parishes or baronies.

2. The material in American sources (p. 362) which consists of letters and Banshee Questionnaire replies, a tape recording and one printed item, is arranged and numbered according to the States alphabetically. The Canadian material consists of one printed source, the exact provenance of which cannot now be determined.

3. Relevant material of unknown provenance found only in some printed sources is listed separately according to author in section 3.

1. Traditional material of definite provenance
(with the exception of American and Canadian sources)

Antrim (Ant.), Ulster

1   IFC 1365: 169 (1954), Cary, Culfeightrin, RATHLIN ISLAND O.S. 1 (E).
2   IFC 1365: 218 (1954), Cary, Culfeightrin, RATHLIN ISLAND O.S.I. (E)
3   IFC 2110: 10 (1976, Letter), Cary, Ramoan, BALLYCASTLE O.S. (E)
4   IFC 2110: 15-18 (1976, *Banshee* Questionnaire), Cary, Ramoan, BALLYCASTLE O.S. 8 (E)
5   Jeanne Cooper Foster, *Ulster Folklore*, p. 17, (1951), Cary, Ramoan, BALLYCASTLE O.S. 8 (E)
6   IFC 2110: 22-25 (1976, *Banshee* Questionnaire), Kilconway, RASHARKIN O.S. 26 (E)
7   IFC 2111: 285 (c. 1960, UFTM notebook), Lwr Antrim, Racavan, BROUGHSHANE O.S. 33 (E)
8   IFC 2111: 295 (1961, UFTM notebook), Lwr Belfast, Inver, LARNE O.S. 40 (E)
9   The banshee of Dunluce Castle is referred to in: (a) Walter Thornbury, *Cross Country*, pp. 127, 196-202 (1861); (b) *Ireland's Own* XI, No. 286, p. 12, 13 May 1908, and p. 2, 24 Dec. 1955; (c) Rev. Hugh Forde, *Sketches of Olden Days in Northern Ireland*, p. 29 (1923); (d) Sheila St. Clair, *Folklore of the Ulster People*, p 20 (1971), Lower Dunluce, Dunluce, DUNLUCE O.S. 2, 6
10 IFC 1386: 13 (1955), Lwr. Glenarm, Ticmacrevan, GLENGARRIFF O.S. 20, 25 (E)
11 IFC 1878:292-3; Irish Life Folklore Competition for Schools 1976. Entry by Billy Healy and Frank Thomas in group project by St. Paul's Secondary School, Beechmount Parade, Belfast. Upper Belfast, Shankill, BELFAST O.S. 61 (E).
12 IFC 2110: 27-31 (1976, *Banshee* Questionnaire), Upr Belfast, Shankill, BELFAST O.S. 61 (E)
13 *Ulster Folklife* VI (1960), p. 41, Upr Toome, Drummaul, MILLTOWN O.S. 49 (E)
14 The banshee of the O'Neills of Shane Castle is referred to in: (a) Mr. and Mrs. Hall, *Ireland: Its Scenery, Character &c*, III, pp. 104-105 (1843), (b) D. R. McAnally, *Irish Wonders*, p. 112 (1888), (c) Lady F. Wilde, *Ancient Cures, Charms and Usages of Ireland*, p. 84 (1890), (d) *Ireland's Own* XIII, No. 322, p. 12, 20 Jan. 1909, (e) Sheila St. Clair, *Folklore of the Ulster People*, pp. 20-21 (1971), Toome, Drummaul, SHANE'S CASTLE O.S. 49 (E)
15 *Ulster Journal of Archaeology*, 3rd ser. I, 1938, p. 211, 'Ballycastle to Belfast, Larne to Lough Neagh' (E)
16 The Banshee of Lough Neagh referred to in *Ireland's Own* LIX, No.

1539, p. 695, 28 May 1932 (E)
17   Sheila St. Clair, *Psychic Phenomena in Ireland*, p. 52 (1972), *Folklore of the Ulster People*, pp. 20-22 (1971) (E)

Armagh (Arm.), Ulster

1   T. G. F. Paterson, *Country Cracks: Old Tales from the County of Armagh*, p. 75 (1945, 1st. ed. 1939), Fews Lwr, Lisnadill, SEAGHAN O.S. 16 (E).
2   IFC 2110: 32-34 (1976, Banshee Questionnaire), Lwr. Orior, Ballymore, POYNTZPASS O.S. 18 (E)
3   Michael J. Murphy, *At Slieve Gullion's Foot*, p. 76 (1975, 1st ed. 1940), Orior Upr, Forkill, SLIEVE GUILLON O.S. 28, 29 (E)
4   IFC 1753: 43 (1968), Orior Upr, Forkill, FORKILL O.S. 31 (E)
5   IFC 1786: 14, (1971), Orior Upr, Forkill, FORKILL O.S. 31 (E)
6   IFC 2110: 42-46 (1977, *Banshee Questionnaire* 1976), Orior Upr, Forkill, CARRICKNAGAVNA O.S. 25, 28 (E)
7   IFC 2110: 36, 38, 42, 44, 45 (1977, Banshee Questionnaire, 1976), Orior Upr., Killevy, ANNACLOGHMULLIN O.S. 25, 26 (E)
8   IFC 2110: 47-49 (1976, *Banshee* Questionnaire), Orior Upr. Killevy, MEIGH O.S. 29 (E)

Carlow (Car.), Leinster

1   IFC 2112: 10-11 (1976, *Banshee* Questionnaire), Carlow, Carlow, CARLOW O.S. 7 (E).
2   *Irisleabhar na Gaedhilge* XII, 1902, p. 62, Carlow, Carlow, CARLOW O.S. 7 (E)
3   IFC 94: 34 (c. 1928), Carlow, Carlow, CARLOW O.S. 7 (E)
4   IFCS 907: 482-483, Carlow, Tullowmagimma, TINRILAND O.S. 7, 12 (E)
5   IFC 462: 376 (1937-1938), Carlow, Tullowmagimma, TINRILAND O.S. 7, 12 (E).
6   IFCS 910: 107, Forth, Ardoyne, ARDATTIN 13, 14 (E)
7   IFCS 905: 302-303, Forth, Myshall, STRADUFF O.S. 17 (E)
8   *Béaloideas* IV, No. 1, 1933, p. 21, Rathvilly, Fennagh, CASTLEMORE O.S. 8, 13 (E)
9   IFC 954: 20 (1943, *Bogey* Questionnaire), Idrone East, Clonygoose, BALLYMARTIN O.S. 19 (E)
10   IFCS 904: 353, Idrone East, Kiltennel, KILCOLTRIM O.S. 22 (E)
11   IFC 412: 44-45 (1936), Idrone East, Fennagh, FENNAGH O.S. 16 -17 (E)
12   IFC 2112: 13-16 (1976, *Banshee* Questionnaire), Idrone West, Old Leighlin, OLD LEIGHLIN O.S. 11 (E)
13   IFC 265: 405-407, *Béaloideas* VII, 1937, p. 90, No. 13, Rathvilly, Hacketstown, HACKETSTOWN O.S. 4 (E)

14   Donn Piatt, *Dialects in east and mid-Leinster Gaelic Survivals*, p. 23 (1933), Rathvilly, Hacketstown, HACKETSTOWN O.S. 4 (E)

15   *Béaloideas* IV, 1933-1934 (1934), p. 5, Rathvilly, Rathvilly, PAT-RICKSWELL O.S. 4 (E)

16   IFCS 908: 170-171, Rathvilly, Clonmore, BALLYDUFF O.S. 9 (E)

17   IFCS 908: 172-173, Rathvilly, Clonmore, BELLSHILL O.S. 9, 10 (E)

18   James Murphy, *The House in the Rath*, pp. 7, 289 (1886), St. Mullin's Lwr, GLYNN O.S. 26 (E)

19   IFC 580: 11 (1938), St. Mullin's Upr, Moyacomb, BALLYRED-MOND O.S. 18 (E)

20   *Études Celtiques* VIII, 1957-1958, p. 408 (E)

Cavan (Cav.), Ulster

1   IFC 1209: 409-478. Banshee material collected by the part-time collector, P. J. Gaynor, Bailiborough, Co. Cavan, 2-27 July 1951, in the baronies of Castlerahan and Clankee. It is arranged according to the baronies alphabetically, and within the baronies according to the contributors alphabetically in order to distinguish the individual contributions.*

1.1   IFC 1209: 455-457, Castlerahan, Killenkere, CARRICKGORMAN O.S. 33, 34 (Matthew Cooney) (E)

1.2   IFC 1209: 415-417, 432, 434, 438-439, 466, 470. 472, 473, 474, Castlerahan, Mullagh, MULLAGH O.S. 41, 44 (John Gibney)(E)

1.3   IFC 1209: 431-432, 465-466, 474, Castlerahan, Mullagh, LISNAH-EDERNA O.S. 33, 34, 39, 40 (Peter Glennon) (E)

1.4   IFC 1209: 421-423, 434, 442, 462, 469, 470, Castlerahan, Lurgan MURMOD O.S. 39 (Charles King)(E)

1.5   IFC 1209: 455, Castlerahan, Killinkere, BILLIS O.S. 33 (William Martin)(E)

1.6   IFC 1209: 439, Castlerahan, Mullagh, CORRYROURKE O.S. 40 (John Osborne)(E)

1.7   IFC 1209: 445, Castlerahan, Lurgan, COPPANAGH O.S. 39 (James Tackney) (E)

1.8   IFC 1209: 410-412, 429-431, 432, 433, 437-438, 440, 443, 450-451, 462, 466-467, 468, 471, 472-473, 476, 477, Clankee, Bailieborough, GALBOLIE O'S. 28, 34 (James Argue) (E)

1.9   IFC 1209: 455, Clankee, Bailieborough, BAILIEBOROUGH O.S. 34 (Thomas Barron) (E)

1.10 IFC 1209: 448, Clankee, Bailiborough, CORKISK O.S. 28, 34 (Barney Barry)(E)

* *It is necessary to arrange the material in this way in view of its quantity and the fact that P. J. Gaynor collected data on each aspect of the banshee belief specified in the* Handbook, *pp. 490-491, from each of his informants with the result that data from several contributors on the same aspect may be found in each manuscript page.*

1.11 IFC 1209: 428, 471, Clankee, Bailieborough, CORKISH O.S. 28, 34 (James Bird)(E)

1.12 IFC 1209: 437, 442, Clankee, Bailieborough, LISNALEA O.S. 34 (Matthew Carolan) (E)

1.13 IFC 1209: 441-442, Clankee, Bailieborough, LISNALEA O.S. 34 (Mrs. Matthew Carolan) (E)

1.14 IFC 1209: 424-427, 431, 434-435, 463-465, 469, 471, 475-476, Clankee, Bailieborough, DROMORE O.S. 33, 34 (Mrs. Annie Clarke) (E)

1.15 IFC 1209: 463, Clankee, Bailieborough, URCHER O.S. 34 (Peter Clarke) (E)

1.16 IFC 1209: 429, 431, 442-443, 445, Clankee, Bailieborough, LISNALEA O.S. 34 (Terence Clarke) (E)

1.17 IFC 1209: 417-418, Clankee, Bailieborough, BAILIEBOROUGH O.S. 34 (William Clarke) (E)

1.18 IFC 1209: 450, 463, 469, 473, Clankee, Knockbride, KILNACREW O.S. 22 (Thomas Connolly)(E)

1.19 IFC 1209: 419-420, 442, 443, 462-463, 468, Clankee, Moybolgue, BALLYNAMONA O.S. 34 (John Coyle)(E)

1.20 IFC 1209: 427-428, Clankee, Moybolgue, BLACKHILLS O.S. 34 (John Cooney)(E)

1.21 IFC 1209: 412-415, 429, 431, 432, 439, 440-441, 443-445, 467, 468, 469-470, 473, 474, 476-477, Clankee, Bailieborough, TANDERAGEE O.S. 34 (John Cullen) (E)

1.22 IFC 1209: 452-453, Clankee, Eniskeen, CORRAWEELIS O.S. 34, 35 (Hugh Curtis) (E)

1.23 IFC 1209: 451, 467-468, Clankee, Bailieborough, GALBOLIE O.S. 28, 34 (James Cusack) (E)

1.24 IFC 1209: 453-454, 465, Clankee, Moybolgue, BLACKHILLS O.S. 34 (James Donnelly)(E)

1.25 IFC 1209: 459-461, Clankee, Bailieborough, LEAR O.S. 28 (John Gibson) (E)

1.26 IFC 1209: 431-432, 433, 439, 465-466, Clankee, Enniskeen, LISNAHEDERNA O.S. 35 (Peter Glennon)(E)

1.27 IFC 1209: 448-450, Clankee, Bailieborough, BAILIEBOROUGH O.S. 34 (Michael Heeney) (E)

1.28 IFC 1209: 451-452, 465, Clankee, Bailieborough, BAILIEBOROUGH O.S. 34 (Charles Lynch) (E)

1.29 IFC 1209: 419, 462, 466, 469, Clankee, Enniskeen, CORNASAUS O.S. 34, 35, John Lynch) (E)

1.30 IFC 1209: 457-458, 467, 477, Clankee, Bailieborough, DRUMBANNAN O.S. 28, 34 (Mrs. Susan McCluskey) (E)

1.31 IFC 1209: 435-437, Clankee, Bailieborough, BAILIEBOROUGH O.S. 34 (Mrs. Catherine McGuirk) (E)

1.32 IFC 1209: 417, 439, 466, 470, Clankee, Bailieborough, RAKEEVAN O.S. 34 (Michael Moore)(E)

1.33 IFC 1209: 420-421, Clankee, Shercock, CROSSMAKEELAN O.S. 28 (James Reilly)(E)

1.34 IFC 1209: 418, 470, Clankee, Bailieborough, GALBOLIE O.S. 28,

34 (Owen Reilly) (E).

1.35   IFC 1209: 453, Clankee, Bailieborough, URCHER O.S. 34 (Peter Reilly) (E).

1.36   IFC 1209: 421, 433, Clankee, Moybolgue, LEITRIM O.S. 34 (Andrew Smith)(E)

1.37   IFC 1209: 458-459, Clankee, Bailieborough, LEAR O.S. 28 (Mrs. Mary Smith and John Smith) (E).

1.38   IFC 1209: 427, Clankee, Bailieborough, CORNISH O.S. 28, 34 (Matthew Smith) (E).

1.39   IFC 1209: 423-424, 445, 461-462, 469, Clankee, Bailieborough, GALBOLIE O.S. 28, 34 (James Soden)(E)

1.40   IFC 1209: 423, 445, 469, 471, 475, Clankee, GALBOLIE O.S. 28, 34 (Mrs. Soden)(E)

1.41   IFC 1209: 418-419, 434, 463, 468-469, Clankee, Bailieborough, URCHER O.S. 34 (Thomas Tinnelly)(E)

1.42   IFC 1209: 474, provenance uncertain, (Michael Ward) (E)

1.43   IFC 1209: 465, Clankee, Bailieborough, TANDERAGEE O.S. 34 (Mrs. Ward)(E)

2   IFCS 999: 262, Castlerahan, Lurgan, CORREAGH School O.S. 39 (E)

3   IFC 830: 323-324 (1942), Castlerahan, Lurgan, VIRGINIA O.S. 39 (E)

4   IFCS 1003: 187-188, Castlerahan, Mullagh, MULLAGH O.S. 40, 44 (E)

5   IFCS 1003: 202-203, Castlerahan, Mullagh, MULLAGH O.S. 40, 44 (E)

6   'The Banshee of the Sheridans' in Alicia Lefanu, *Memoirs of the Life and Writings of Mrs. Frances Sheridan*, note pp. 32-33 (1824). This account also appears in T. Crofton Croker, *Fairy Legends and Traditions of the South of Ireland*, pp. 232-233 (1826) and in *The Shamrock* XI, No. 390, April 4, 1874, p. 440. Castlerahan, Mullagh, CUILCAGH O.S. 39, 40 (E)

7   IFCS 998: 74, Castlerahan, Munterconnaght, KNOCKTEMPLE O.S. 43 (E)

8   IFCS 998: 168, Castlerahan, Munterconnaght, KNOCKTEMPLE School O.S. 43 (E)

9   IFC 2110: 50-52 (1976, *Banshee* Questionnaire), Castlerahan, Munterconnaght, KNOCKTEMPLE O.S. 43 (E)

10   IFCS 1012: 90, Clankee, Bailieborough, BAILIEBOROUGH O.S. 34 (E).

11   IFCS 1011: 165, Clankee, Bailieborough, BAILIEBOROUGH O.S. 34 (E)

12   IFCS 1014: 404, Clankee, Bailieborough, BAILIEBOROUGH O.S. 34 (E).

13   IFC 832: 414-415 (1942), Clankee, Bailieborough, BAILIEBOROUGH O.S. 34 (E).

328   *The Banshee*

14   IFC 815: 436-437 (1942), Clankee, Enniskeen, BIRRAGH O.S. 35 (E)
15   IFC 832: 454 (1942), Clankee, Moybolgue, BALLYNAMONA O.S. 34 (E)
16   IFCS 1018: 115, Tullygarvey, Drumgoon, NEWGROVE School O.S. 17 (E)
17   IFCS 1022: 336-337, Tullygarvey, Drung, GORTSKEAGH O.S. 16, 21 (E)
18   IFCS 1022: 362-363, Tullygarvey, Drung, DRUNG O.S. 21 (E)
19   IFC 2110: 53 (1977, *Banshee* Questionnaire 1976), Tullyhaw, Killinagh, BLACKLION O.S. 3 (E)
20   IFC 2110: 54-57 (1977, *Banshee* Questionnaire 1976), Tullyhaw, Killinagh, BLACKLION O.S. 3 (E)
21   IFC 2110: 60-62 (1977, *Banshee* Questionnaire 1976), Tullyhaw, Killinagh, BLACKLION O.S. 3 (E)
22   IFCS 968: 420-421, Tullyhaw, Templeport, BRACKLEY O.S. 9 (E).
23   IFC 2110: 63-79 (1976, *Banshee* Questionnaire), Tullyhaw, Killinagh, BLACKLION O.S. 3 (E)
24   IFC 2110: 80-93 (1976, *Banshee* Questionnaire), Tullyhaw, Killinagh, BLACKLION O.S. 3 (E)
25   IFC 1861: 287-288 (1974), Tullyhaw, Killinagh, BLACKLION O.S. 3 (E)
26   IFC 2110: 94-100 (1977, *Banshee* Questionnaire 1976), Tullyhaw, Killinagh, CARRICKNAGROW O.S. 3 (E)
27   IFC 2110: 101-105 (1976, *Banshee* Questionnaire), Tullyhaw, Killinagh, DOWRA O.S. 5 (E)
28   IFC 968: 15, Tullyhaw, Tomregan, BALLYCONNEL O.S. 10 (E)
29   IFC 2110: 107-110 (1976, *Banshee* Questionnaire), Tullyhaw, Kinawley, SWANLINBAR O.S. 7 (E)
30   IFCS 963: 33-35, Tullyhaw, Templeport, TULLYBRACK O.S. 9 (E)
31   IFC 2110: 112-114 (1976, *Banshee* Questionnaire), Tullyhaw, Templeport, GLENGAVLIN O.S. 6 (E)
32   IFC 2110: 117-119 (1976, *Banshee* Questionnaire), Tullyhaw, Templeport, TEMPLEPORT O.S. 9, 13 (E)
33   IFCS 982: 143, Tullyhunco, Killashandra, DRUMCROW School O.S. 24 (E)
34   IFCS 982: 309, Tullyhunco, Killashandra, CORR O.S. 24 (E)
35   IFC 2110: 115-116 (1976, *Banshee* Questionnaire), Tullyhunco, Scrabby, SCRABBY O.S. 30 (E)
36   IFCS 986: 89, Tullyhunco, Scrabby, GOWNA School O.S. 36 (E)
37   IFCS 973: 109, Upr Loughtee, Castleterra, BALLYHAISE O.S. 16, (E)
38   IFCS 973: 111, Upr Loughtee, Castleterra, BALLYHAISE O.S. 16 (E)
39   IFCS 973: 113, Upr Loughtee, Castleterra, BALLYHAISE O.S. 16 (E)
40   IFCS 978: 123-124, Upr Loughtee, Denn, CROSSKEYS O.S. 32 (E)

41 IFCS 977: 5-6, Upr Loughtee, Kilmore, DRUMCOR School O.S. 25 (E)
42 IFCS 977: 254, Upr Loughtee, Denn, CROSSKEYS School O.S. 32 (E)
43 IFCS 980: 39, Upr Loughtee, Lavey, DRUMMANBANE O.S. 32 (E)
44 IFC 1196: 104 (1950), Provenance uncertain (E)

Clare (Cl.), Munster

1 *Folk-Lore* XXI, 1910, p. 191, Bunratty Lwr, Tomfinlough, NEW-MARKET-ON-FERGUS O.S. 51 (E)
2 IFC 2113: 14-15 (1976, *Banshee* Questionnaire), Bunratty Upr, Doora, BALLAGHBOY O.S. 33, 34 (E)
3 IFCS 594: 66 (cf. *Béaloideas* XLII-XLIV, 1974-1976 [1977], p. 99), Bunratty Upper, Doora, DOORA O.S. 34 (E)
4 IFC 433: 132-142, Bunratty Upr, Inchicronan, DRUMSALLAGH O.S. 18, 26 (E)
5 *Folk-Lore* XXI, 1910, p. 191, Bunratty Upr, Quin, BALLYMAR-KAHAN O.S. 42, 43 (E)
6 IFC 2113: 21-24 (1976, *Banshee* Questionnaire), Clonderlaw, Kilfiddane, COOLMEEN O.S. 59, 69 (I and E)
7 IFCS 603: 272-273, Clonderlaw, Kilfiddane, COOLMEEN School O.S. 59, 69 (I)
8 (a) *Folk-Lore* XXI, 1910, pp. 189-190; (b) St. J. D. Seymour and H. L. Nelligan, *True Irish Ghost Stories*, pp. 201-2 (1926), Clonderlaw, Kilchreest, BALLYNACALLY O.S. 50 (E)
9 *North Munster Antiquarian Journal* IX, 1962-1965, p. 182, Clonderlaw, Kilchreest, BALLYNACALLY O.S. 50 (E)
10 IFCS 620: 359, Corcomroe, Clooney, CAHERSHERKIN School O.S. 16 (E)
11 IFCS 620: 350-351 (cf. *Béaloideas* XLII-XLIV, 1974-1976 (1977), p. 114), Corcomroe, Kilmanaheen, CLOONEY O.S. 23 (E)
12 IFCS 620: 358-359, Corcomroe, Clooney, CAHERSERKIN School O.S. 16 (E)
13 IFCS 620: 361-364 (cf. *Béaloideas* XLII-XLIV, 1974-1976 (1977), pp. 97-98, 104), Corcomroe, Kilfineora, BALLAGH O.S. 16 (E).
14 IFC 2113: 25-28 (1976, *Banshee* Questionnaire), Corcomroe, Kilmanaheen, LAHINCH O.S.15, 23 (E).
15 *Folk-Lore* XXI, 1910, p. 191, Corcomroe, Kilfenora, CAHERMIN-NAUN O.S. 9, 16; Corcomroe, Kilmacrehy, DOUGH O.S. 15, 23 (E)
16 IFCS 623: 144-145, Ibrickan, Kilmurry, KNOCKNAHILLA O.S. 10 (E)
17 IFCS 625: 149, Ibrickan, Kilmurry, DOOLOUGH School O.S. 39 (E)
18 *Ireland's Own* LXXIV, No. 1973, p. 14, 16 Aug. 1941, Ibrickan, Kilfarboy, MILLTOWN MALBAY O.S. 30 (E)
19 IFC 2113: 29 (1976, *Banshee* Questionnaire), Inchiquin, Killinaboy, COROFIN O.S. 17 (E)

20   *Folk-Lore* XXI, 1910, p. 191, Inchiquin, Ruan, RUAN O.S. 25 (E).
21   *Folk-Lore* XXI, 1910, p. 191, Inchiquin, Killinaboy, COROFIN O.S. 17 (E)
22   IFCS 594: 69-70, Islands, Clareabbey, MANUS O.S. 42 (E)
23   IFCS 594: 74-75, Islands, Clareabbey, MANUS O.S. 42 (E)
24   IFC 2113: 31-34 (1976, *Banshee* Questionnaire), Islands, Drumcliff, ENNIS O.S. 33 (E)
25   IFC S608: 273, Islands, Kilmaley, KILMALEY School O.S. 32, 33, 40, 41 (E)
26   IFC 93: 42 (1931), Islands, Clondagad, LISCASEY O.S. 40, 49 (E).
27   *Folk-Lore* XXI, 1910, p. 191, Islands, Drumcliff, ENNIS O.S. 33 (E)
28   IFC 1358: 365 (1954), Moyarta, Kilrush, SCATTERY ISLAND O.S. 67 (E)
29   IFCS 631: 70-71, Moyarta, Kilmacduane, BRISLA O.S. 57 (I)
30   IFCS 630: 31 (cf. *Béaloideas* XII-XLIV, 1974-76 (1977), p. 114), Moyarta, Kilrush, KILRUSH O.S. 67 (E)
31   IFC 1358: 371 (1954), Moyarta, Kilrush, SCATTERY ISLAND, O.S. 67, (E)
32   IFC 2113: 35-39 (1976, *Banshee* Questionnaire), Tulla Lwr, Killaloe, KILLALOE O.S. 45 (E)
33   IFCS 538: 66, Tulla Lwr., Killaloe, KILLALOE, O. S. 45 (E)
34   IFCS 590: 167 (cf. *Béaloideas* XLII-XLIV, 1974-1976 (1977), p. 99), Tulla Upr, Tulla, GLANDREE School O.S. 19, 27 (E)
35   IFC S590: 174, Tulla Upr, Tulla, GLANDREE School O.S. 19, 27 (E)
36   IFCS 589: 67 (cf. *Béaloideas* XLII-XLIV, 1974-1976 (1977), p. 99), Tulla Upr, Inishcaltra, CLONTY O.S. 29 (E)
37   IFC 2111: 99-106 (passim) (1976, *Banshee* Questionnaire), Tulla Upr, Tulla, TULLA O.S. 35 (E)

Cork (Cork), Munster

1   IFCS 2113: 40-42 (1976, *Banshee Questionnaire*), Cork, CORK City (E)
2   IFCS 282: 144-145, Bantry, Kilmocomogue, BORLINN O.S. 118 (E)
3   IFCS 389: 103, Barretts, Grenagh, BALLYFADEEN O.S. 51, 62 (E)
4   IFC 955: 59 (1943, *Bogey* Questionnaire), Barrymore, Dungourney, DUNGOURNEY O.S. 66 (E)
5   IFCS 279: 475-477, Bear, Kilcaskan, TOOREENNAGRENA O.S. 104 (I)
6   IFCS 274: 26, Bear, Kilnamanagh, DURSEY ISLAND O.S. 126 (E)
7   IFC 579: 41 (1935), Condons & Clangibbon, Leitrim, LEITRIM O.S. 28, 36 (E)
8   IFC 128: 114-118 (1935) (cf. *Béaloideas* XLII-XLIV, 1974-1976 (1977), pp. 102-103), Condons & Clangibbon, Macroney, COOLANEAGUE O.S. 20, 28 (E)

9   IFCS 378: 117 (1938), Condons & Clangibbon, Fermoy, FERMOY
     O.S. 35 (E)
10   IFCS 378: 118 (1938), Condons & Clangibbon, Fermoy, FERMOY
     O.S. 35 (E)
11   IFCS 378: 119-120, Condons & Clangibbon, Fermoy, FERMOY
     O.S. 35 (E)
12   IFC 54: 140 (1934-1935), Condons & Clangibbon, Kilworth, KIL-
     WORTH O.S. 27, 28 (E)
13   St. J. D. Seymour and H. L. Neligan, *True Irish Ghost Stories*, pp.
     203-204 (1926), Cork, St. Finbar's, BLACKROCK O.S. 74 (E)
14   Mr. and Mrs. S. C. Hall, *Ireland: its Scenery, Character &c*, III, p.
     106 (1843), Cork, Kilmacomoge, BANTRY O.S. 118 (E)
15   *Journal of the Cork Historical and Archaeological Society* XLIX,
     2nd ser. 1944, p. 38, Cork, CORK City O.S. 74 (E)
16   IFCS 361: 425-427, Dunhallow, Clonmeen, LYRE O.S. 40 (E)
17   IFCS 350: 79, Duhallow, Clonfert, ROWLS O.S. 5, 14 (E)
18   IFCS 350: 249, Duhallow, Clonfert, ROWLS O.S. 5, 14 (E)
19   IFCS 351: 198, Duhallow, Clonfert, LYRANEAG O.S. 4 (E)
20   IFCS 356: 110-111, Duhallow, Castlemanger, CECILSTOWN
     O.S. 24 (I)
21   IFCS 305: 134-136, East Carbery W.D., Kilmichael, KILNADUR
     O.S. 93-94 (E)
22   IFC 2113: 44-45 (1976, *Banshee* Questionnaire), East Carbery W.D.,
     Ross, ROSSCARBERY O.S. 143 (E)
23   IFCS 345: 378, East Muskerry, Athnowen, CASTLEINCH O.S. 72,
     73 (E)
24   IFCS 345: 378-379, East Muskerry, Desertmore, CLASHANAF-
     FRIN O.S. 84, 85 (E)
25   IFCS 370: 250-251, Fermoy, Monanimy, KILLAVULLEN School
     O.S. 34 (E)
26   *Ireland's Own* XLV, No. 1154, 14 Jan. 1925, p. 25, Fermoy, Doner-
     aile, KILCOLEMAN O.S. 17 (E)
27   IFCS 397: 7-8, Imokilly, Dangandonovan, BALLYRE O.S. 55, 56
     (E)
28   IFCS 320: 116, Kinsale, Kinsale, KINSALE O.S. 112, 125 (E)
29   IFC 462: 225-227 (1937), Kinalmeaky, Desertserges, KILCOLMAN
     O.S. 109 (E)
30   The Bunworth Banshee in T. Crofton Croker, 'Legends of the Ban-
     shee', *Fairy Legends and Traditions of the South of Ireland*, pp. 197-
     204 (1826). This story is summarised in S. Baring-Gould, *Curious
     Myths of the Middle Ages*, pp. 490-493 (1876), and in *Ireland's Own*
     IV, No. 104, p. 3, 16 Nov 1904. It appears in translation in *Irländska
     Folksagor*, pp. 81-86, ed. Stockholm, 1839, in W.-E. Peuckert, ed.,
     Irische Elfenmärchen der Brüder Grimm [1826], pp.112-116 (1980)
     Orrery and Kilmore, Buttevant, BUTTEVANT O.S. 16, 17
31   *An Sguab* I, Uimh. 12, 1923, p. 242, Orrery and Kilmore, Rath-
     goggan, CHARLEVILLE O.S. 2, 3 (I)
32   IFCS 367: 344, Orrery & Kilmore, Shandrum, DROMINA School
     O.S. 7 (E)

33   IFCS 367: 401, Orrery & Kilmore, Churchtown, CHURCHTOWN
     O.S. 16 (E)
34   IFC 42: 146 (1928), Orrery & Kilmore, Rathgoggan, CHARLE-
     VILLE O.S. 2, 3 (E)
35   IFC 412: 263 (1937), West Carbery, Castlehaven, CULLENAGH
     O.S. 133 (E)
36   IFC 1262: 95 (c. 1943), West Carbery (E.D.), Myross, MYROSS
     O.S. 142, 151 (I)
37   IFCS 299: 113-114, West Carbery (E.D.), Kilmacabea, Skibbereen
     O.S. 141 (I)
38   IFC 2113: 47-54 (1976, *Banshee* Questionnaire), West Carbery
     (E.D.), Dromdaleague, DRUMDALEAGUE O.S. 119, 120 (E)
39   IFC 842: 121, 123 (1941), West Carbery, Clear Island, CLEAR
     ISLAND O.S. 153 (I)
40   IFC 2113: 55-57 (1976, *Banshee* Questionnaire), West Muskerry,
     Kilmurry, KILMURRY O.S. 83 (I)
41   IFCS 342: 203, West Muskerry, Macroom, MACROOM O.S. 70, 71
     (E)
42   IFCS 337: 84-85, West Muskerry, Kilnamartry, DUNAREIRKE O.S.
     70, 71 (E)

Derry (Der.), Ulster

1   IFC 2110: 120-122 (1976, *Banshee* Questionnaire), IFC 1840: 279-
     298, Tirkeeran, Clondermot, CLOGHORE O.S. 20, 21 (E)

Donegal (Don.), Ulster

1   IFCS 155: 535-540, Banagh, Killybegs Upr, KILLYBEGS O.S. 97
     (E)
2   *Béaloideas* XIII, 1943 (1944), p. 237, Banagh, Inishkeel, MEENA-
     CURRIN O.S. 72, 78, 81, 82 (I)
3   IFCS 1036: 75, Banagh, Killymard, GREENAN O.S. 85, 94 (E)
4   IFC 185: 150-151 (1936), Boylagh, Inishkeel, MEENATAWEY O.S.
     66, 67 (I)
5   IFC 2110: 125 (1976, *Banshee* Questionnaire), Boylagh, Inishkeel, NARIN &
     PORTNOO O.S. 64 (E)
6   IFC 2110: 126-129 (1976, *Banshee* Questionnaire), Boylagh,
     Templecrone, ROSSES O.S. 40, 41 (I)
7   IFCS 1050: 547, Boylagh, Inishkeel, MEENADOAN O.S. 58, 59
     (E)
8   IFCS 1114: 122, Inishowen East, Donagh, CARNDONAGH O.S. 29
     (E)
9   IFCS 1114: 143-144, Inishowen East, Donagh, CARNDONAGH
     O.S. 29 (E)
10   IFCS 1123: 503-504, Inishowen East, Culdaff, CULDAFF O.S. 5
     (E)

11   IFC 2110: 130-132 (1976, *Banshee* Questionnaire), Inishowen East, Culdaff (Clonca), CULDAFF, CLONCA O.S. 4, 5, 11, 12 (E)
12   IFCS 1090: 450-451, Kilmacrennan, Clondavaddog, TAMNEY O.S. 17 (E)
13   IFC 2110: 133-136 (1976, *Banshee* Questionnaire), Kilmacrennan, Conwal, LETTERKENNY O.S. 53 (E)
14   IFC 2110: 137-139 (1976, *Banshee* Questionnaire), Kilmacrennan, Conwal, LETTERKENNY O.S. 53 (E)
15   IFC 2110: 141 (1976, *Banshee* Questionnaire), Kilmacrennan, Tullaghobegly, FALCARRAGH O.S. 25 (E)
16   IFC 2110: 142-145 (1976, *Banshee* Questionnaire), Kilmacrennan, Tullyfern, KERRYKEEL O.S. 27 (E)
17   IFCS 1086: 32, Kilmacrennan, Aughnish, GLENALLA O.S. 28, 37 (E)
18   *The Cornhill Magazine* XXXV, 1877, p. 177, Kilmacrennan, Killygarvan, RATHMULLAN O.S. (E)
19   *Ulster Folklife* III, 1, 1957, p. 39, Kilmacrennan, Clondavaddog, GLENVAR VALLEY O.S. 8, 9 (E)
20   IFC 2110: 146-149 (1976, *Banshee* Questionnaire), Raphoe, Donaghmore, LISMULLYDUFF O.S. 78, 87 (E)
21   IFC 2110: 150-154 (1976, *Banshee* Questionnaire), Raphoe, Kilteevogue, CLOGHAN O.S. 68 (I)
22   IFC 2100: 156-158 (1976, *Banshee* Questionnaire), Raphoe, Kilteevogue, CLOGHAN O.S. 68 (E)
23   IFC 2110: 159-161 (1976, *Banshee* Questionnaire), Raphoe, Kilteevogue, CLOGHAN O.S. 68 (E)
24   IFCS 1106: 192, Raphoe, Taughboyne, ALTASKIN O.S. 55, 63 (I)
25   IFCS 1106: 267, Raphoe, Taughboyne, ARDAGH O.S. 63 (E)
26   IFCS 1106: 196, Raphoe, Taughboyne, CASTLETHIRD O.S. 55 (E)
27   IFC 2110: 162-166 (1976, *Banshee* Questionnaire), Tirhugh, Donegal, DONEGAL O.S. 94 (I)
28   IFC 2110: 167 (1976, *Banshee* Questionnaire), Tirhugh, Donegal, DONEGAL O.S. 94 (E)
29   IFC 171: 376 (1936), Tirhugh, Donegal, GOLADOO O.S. 85 (I).
30   Elizabeth Andrews, *Ulster Folklore*, p. 56 (1913), Lough Sessiagh area (E)

Down (Down), Ulster

1   IFC 1036: 395-399 (1948), Ards Upr, Slane, DOOEY O.S. 25, 32 (E)
2   IFC 2110: 172 (1976, *Banshee* Questionnaire), Castlereagh Lwr, Hollywood, HOLLYWOOD O.S. 1, 5 (E), negative reply.
3   IFC 2111: 302 (c. 1960, UFTM notebook), Kinelarty, Loughinisland, SEAFORDE O.S. 37 (E)
4   *Ulster Folklife* II, 1956, p. 48, Lecale Lwr, Kilclief, KILCLIEF O.S. 32, 38, 39 (E)

5   IFC 954: 163 (1943, *Bogey* Questionnaire), Lwr Iveagh, Upr Pt., Hillsborough, HILLSBOROUGH O.S. 14 (E)

6   IFC 1120: 93, Upr Iveagh, Lwr Pt., Clonduff, HILLTOWN O.S. 48 (E)

7   IFC 2111: 305 (1954, UFTM notebook), Upr Iveagh, Upr Pt., Clonallon, AGHAVILLY O.S. 51 (E)

8   IFC 2111: 305 (1954, UFTM notebook), Upr Iveagh, Upr Pt., Kilbroney, KNOCKBARRAGH O.S. 51 (E)

9   IFC 1470: 300 (1956), Upr Iveagh, Upr Pt., Clonallan, BURREN O.S. 51 (E).

10   IFC 1483: 305 (1957), Upr Iveagh, Upr Pt., Clonallan, BURREN O.S. 51 (E).

11   IFC 1567: 93 (1959-1960), Upr Iveagh, Upr Pt., Clonallan, LURGANCANTY O.S. 51 (E)

12   IFC 1691: 52 (1964), Upr Iveagh, Upr Pt., Warrenpoint, WARRENPOINT O.S. 54 (E)

13   IFC 1786: 291-297 (1971), Upr Iveagh, Upr Pt., Drumgath, RATHFRYLAND O.S. 41 (E)

14   IFC 2110: 173-175 (1976, *Banshee* Questionnaire), Upr Iveagh, Upr Pt., Drumgath, ANNACLONE O.S. 41 (E)

15   IFC 2110: 177-178 (1976, *Banshee* Questionnaire), Upr Iveagh, Upr Pt., Warrenpoint, WARRENPOINT O.S. 54 (E)

16   IFC 1020: 451-454 (1948), Upr Iveagh, Upr Pt., Kilcoe, NEWCASTLE O.S. 49 (E)

17   Sheila St. Clair, *Psychic Phenomena in Ireland*, pp, 53-54 (1972), Co. Down (E)

18   IFC 2111: 114-193 (1979), Upr Belfast, Shankill, BELFAST O.S. 61 (35 questionnaire replies relating to the Belfast area by school children in the Sacred Heart of Mary Grammar School, Hollywood, Co. Down) (E).

19   IFC 2111: 194-237 (1979), Ards Lwr, Bangor, BANGOR O.S. 2 (20 questionnaire replies relating to the Bangor area from school children in the Sacred Heart of Mary Grammar School, Hollywood, Co. Down) (E)

20   IFC 2111: 238-345 (1979), Castlereagh Lwr, Comber, COMBER O.S. 10 (3 questionnaire replies relating to the Comber area from the school children in the Sacred Heart of Mary Grammar School, Hollywood, Co. Down) (E)

21   IFC 2111: 246-250 (1979), Ards Lwr, Bangor, CONLIG O.S. 2, 6 (2 questionnaire replies relating to the Conlig area from school children in the Sacred Heart of Mary Grammar School, Hollywood, Co. Down (E)

22   IFC 2111: 251-254 (1979), Castlereagh Upr, Dundonald, DUNDONALD O.S. 5 (1 questionnaire reply relating to the Dundonald area from a school child in the Sacred Heart of Mary Grammar School, Hollywood, Co. Down) (E)

23   IFC 2111: 255-271 (1979), Castlereagh Lwr, Hollywood, HOLLYWOOD O.S. 1 (8 questionnaire replies relating to the Hollywood area from school children in the Sacred Heart of Mary Grammar

School, Hollywood, Co. Down) (E)
24 IFC 2111: 272-277 (1979), Ards Lwr/Castlereagh Lwr, Newtown-ards, NEWTOWNARDS O.S. 5, 6 (4 questionnaire replies relating to the Newtownards area from school children in the Sacred Heart of Mary Grammar School, Hollywood, Co. Down) (E)
25 IFC 2111: 278 (1979), Castlereagh Upr, Knockbreda, NEWTOWN-BREDA O.S. 9 (1 questionnaire reply relating to the Newtownards area from a school child in the Sacred Heart of Mary Grammar School, Hollywood, Co. Down) (E).
26 IFC 2111: 287 (1959, UFTM notebook), Co. Down

Dublin (Dub.), Leinster

1 *Béaloideas* XIV, 1944 (1945), p. 164, Southwest Co. Dublin (E)
2 IFC 2112: 17 (1976, *Banshee* Questionnaire), Castleknock, Finglas, FINGLAS WEST O.S. 14 (E)
3 IFC 2112: 18 (1976, *Banshee* Questionnaire), Castleknock, Finglas, FINGLAS WEST O.S. 14 (E)
4 IFCS 790: 112-113, Castleknock, Mulhuddart, MULHUDDART O.S. 13 (E)
5 IFC 2112: 19-20 (1976, Letter), Coolock, Artane, ARTANE O.S. 14, 15 (E)
6 IFCS 792: 285-287, Coolock, Santry, COULTRY O.S. 14 (E).
7 IFCS 789: 323, Nethercross, Donabate, DONABATE Girls' School O.S. 12 (E)
8 IFC 2112: 22-25 (1976, *Banshee* Questionnaire), Nethercross, Dona-bate, CORBALLIS O.S. 12 (E)
9 IFC 2112: 26-27 (1976, Letter), Swords, Co. Dublin, SWORDS O.S. 12 (E)
10 IFCS 794: 13, Lucan, Newcastle, LUCAN O.S. 10 (E)
11 IFC 2112: 28-30 (1976, *Banshee* Questionnaire), Newcastle, New-castle, PEAMOUNT O.S. 21 (E)
12 IFC 2112: 31-33 (1976, Letter), from Glenageary, Co. Dublin, but provenance of material uncertain (E)
13 IFCS Copybooks, Rathdown, Whitechurch, KILMASHOGUE O.S. 22, 25 (E).
14 IFC 2112: 34-36 (1976, Letter), Uppercross, St. Peter's, RATH-MINES O.S. 18, 22 (E)
15 ICS 2112: 37-38 (1976, *Banshee* Questionnaire), Dublin area (E)
16 John Todhunter, 'How Thomas Connolly met the Banshee', *The Dublin University Review*, Sept. 1885, pp. 149-155. This story appears in W.B.Yeats, (ed.), *Fairy and Folk Tales of the Irish Peasant-ry*, pp. 108-112 (1888), and in subsequent editions of the book, e.g. in *Irish Fairy and Folk Tales*, pp. 108-112, n.d., *Irish Folk Stories and Fairy Tales*, pp. 102-104, n.d. and *Fairy and Folk Tales of Ire-land*, pp. 100-105, (1973). It appears in translation in Frederik Het-man, ed., *Irische Gespenstergeschichten*, pp. 37-39 (1976)
17 Eilís Brady, *All In! All In!*, pp. 1, 23 (1975) (E)

Fermanagh (Fer.), Ulster

1   IFC 2110: 179-189 (1976, *Banshee* Questionnaire), Clanawley, Cleenish, HOLYWELL O.S. 25 (E)
2   IFC 2111: 308 (1958, UFTM notebook), Clanawley, Cleenish, BELLANALECK O.S. 27 (E).
3   IFC 1695: 93 (1950, *Fermanagh Herald*, Sat Jan. 7th), Clanawley, Kinawley, KINAWLEY O.S. 33 (E)
4   IFC 2110: 190-191 (1976, *Banshee* Questionnaire), Magherasta-phana, Aghalurcher, LISNASKEA O.S. 34 (E)
5   IFC 2110: 192-194 (1976, *Banshee* Questionnaire), Magherasta-phana, Aghalurcher, LISNASKEA O.S. 34 (E)
6   IFC 1696: 220 (1966), Magherastaphana, Aghavea, TRASNA ISLAND O.S. 23 (E)

Galway (Gal.), Connaught

1   IFC 2111: 10-12 (1981, Letter), Árann, Inis Oirr, INIS OIRR O.S. 119, 120 (I, negative reply)
2   *Proceedings of the Belfast Natural History and Philosophical Society*, 1896, pp. 33-34, Aran, Inishmaan, INISHMAAN O.S. 119 (E, negative)
3   IFC 2111: 13 (1976, *Banshee* Questionnaire), Aran, Inishmore. INISHMORE O.S. 110, 111, 119 (I), negative reply.
4   IFC 2111: 14-16 (1976, *Banshee* Questionnaire), Aran, Inishmore, INISHMORE O.S. 110, 111, 119 (I), negative reply.
5   Personal communication (1980), Aran, Inishmore, INISHMORE O.S. 110, 111, 119 (I), negative reply.
6   IFCS 34: 425, Athenry, Kiltullagh, CARNAKELLY O.S. 85 (E)
7   IFC 925: 175 (1943-1944), Ballymoe, Drumatemple, BALLYMOE O.S. 2 (E)
8   IFCS 37: 221, Ballymoe, Dunmore, DUNMORE O.S. 17 (E).
9   IFCS 18: 197-198, Ballymoe, Boyounagh, CLOONMINDA O.S. 6 (E).
10 IFC 1607: 208 Ballynahinch, Moyrus, AILLENACALLY O.S. 50 (E)
11 IFC 202: 145-149 (1933)(cf. *Béaloideas* XLII-XLIV, 1974-1976 (1977), pp. 99-101), Ballynahinch, Moyrus, ARDMORE O.S. 77 (I)
12 IFC 2114: 179 (1983), Ballynahinch, Omey, INISHTURK SOUTH O.S. 21, 34 (I)
13 IFC 1778: 126-127 (1970), Ballynahinch, Moyrus, MOYRUS 63, 76 (I)
14 IFC 1780: 49-52 (1971), Ballynahinch, Moyrus, MOYRUS O.S. 63, 76 (I)
15 IFCS 20: 31-32, Clare, Annaghdown, CAHERLEA O.S. 69 (I)
16 IFC S19: 113-118, Clare, Claregalway, WATERDALE (Eochaill) O.S. 69, 70 (E)
17 IFC 1402: 21 (1954), Clare, Claregalway, WATERDALE O.S. 69, 70 (I)

18   IFCS 30: 436-437, Clare, Claregalway, KINISKA O.S. 70, 83 (E)
19   IFCS 32: 37-38, Clare, Claregalway, MONTIAGH O.S. 69 (I)
20   IFC 349: 321-322 (1937), Clare, Claregalway, MONTIAGH O.S. 69 (I)
21   IFC 489: 210-211 (1937), Clare, Claregalway, MONTIAGH O.S. 69 (I)
22   IFCS 22: 625, Clare, Donaghpatrick, CAHERLUSTRAUN O.S. 42 (I)
23   IFCS 21: 254-255, Clare, Kilmoylan, BRACKLOON 57, 58 (E)
24   IFCS 20: 29, Clare, Lackagh, MONARD O.S. 70 (I)
25   IFCS 27: 182, Clare, Tuam, TUAM O.S. 29, 43 (E)
26   IFCS 27: 185, Clare, Killererin, GARRAUN (Coyle) O.S. 44 (E).
27   IFCS 27: 228, Clare, Tuam, CLOONDARONE O.S. 43 (E)
28   IFC 79: 190 (1928-1929), Clare, Annaghdown, BAUNMORE O.S. 70 (I).
29   IFCS 29: 65, Clonmacnowen, Kilcloony, BALLINASLOE O.S. 87, 88 (E)
30   IFC 1635: 206-207 (1960), Dunkellin, Claregalway, CARNMORE O.S. 83 (I)
31   IFCS 32: 403-404, Dunkellin, Oranmore, GLENNASCAUL O.S. 83 (E)
32   IFCS 32: 407, Dunkellin, Oranmore, ORANMORE O.S. 95 (E)
33   IFCS 38: 309-311, Dunmore, Dunmore, LISDUFF O.S. 5 (E)
34   IFC 1840: 337. Information from *Tomáis Laighléis*, Dialects Archive index cards, University College, Dublin, Galway, Oranmore, MEN-LOUGH O.S. 82 (I)
35   Tomás de Bhaldraithe, *Seanchas Thomáis Laighléis*, p. 204, 1977, Galway, Oranmore, MENLOUGH O.S. 82 (I)
36   IFC 1833: 34-36 (1973), Galway, Galway, GALWAY O.S. 82, 94 (I)
37   IFC 2111: 17-18 (1976, *Banshee* Questionnaire), Kilconnell, Aughrim, AUGHRIM O.S. 87 (E)
38   IFCS 34: 488, Kilconnell, Killimordaly, KILLIMOR O.S. 85 (E).
39   IFCS 15: 113-114, 181-182, Killian, Athleague, COALPITS O.S. 19, 20 (E)
40   IFCS 36: 255, Kiltartan, Ardrahan, CAHERGLASSAUN O.S. 113, 122 (E)
41   IFC 404: 108-114 (1937)(cf. *Béaloideas* XLII-XVIV, 1974-1976 (1977), pp. 116-118), Kiltartan, Beagh, KILLEEN O.S. 129, 133 (E)
42   IFC 405: 4-5 (1937), Kiltartan, Beagh, KILLEEN O.S. 129, 133 (E)
43   IFC 405: 137-141 (1973), Kiltartan, Beagh, BALLYNAKILL O.S. 129 (E)
44   IFC 405: 146-148 (1937), Kiltartan, Beagh, BALLYNAKILL O.S. 129 (E)
45   IFC 389: 481-485 (1937)(cf. *Béaloideas* XLII-XLIV, 1974-1976 (1977) pp. 107-109, Kiltartan, Kilbecanty, TONRANNY O.S. 129, 133 (I)

46   IFC2111:19-22(1976, Letter), Kiltartan, Kilbeacanty, KILBEACAN-
     TY O.S. 122, 123 (E)
47   IFCS 48: 125-126, Kiltartan, Kinvarradoorus, NORTHAMPTON
     O.S. 113 (I)
48   IFCS 53: 241-242, Leitrim, Duniry, BALLYNAMONA O.S. 116 (E).
49   IFCS 56: 115, Longford, Clonfert, BALLYNAKILL O.S. 108, 109
     (E)
50   IFCS 55: 194-196, Longford, Clonfert, LAURENCETOWN O.S. 100
     (E)
51   IFCS 55: 282-283, Longford, Meelick, KILMACHUGH O.S. 108,
     109 (E)
52   IFCS 59: 31, Loughrea, Ardrahan, CASTLEDALY School O.S. 114
     (E)
53   IFCS 59: 330-331, Loughrea, Killeenadeema, SONNAGH O.S. 115
     (E)
54   IFCS 60: 185, Loughrea, Loughrea, LOUGHREA O.S. 105 (I)
55   IFC 605: 326-328, Moycullen, Kilcummin, GLENGOWLA O.S. 53,
     54 (I)
56   IFC 2111: 23-30 (1976, *Banshee* Questionnaire), Moycullen, Kil-
     cummin, CARROWROE O.S. 78 (E)
57   IFCS 75: 127, Ross, Ross, TEERNAKILL O.S. 25, 38 (I)
58   IFCS 52: 99, Tiaquin, Abbeyknockmoy, ABBEY O.S. 116, 117,
     125 (E)
59   IFCS 52: 278-279, Tiaquin, Abbeyknockmoy, ABBEY O.S. 116,
     117, 125 (E)
60   IFCS 52: 397-398, Tiaquin, Abbeyknockmoy, ABBEY O.S. 116,
     117, 125 (E)
61   IFCS 78: 168, Tiaquin, Clonkeen, COLMANSTOWN O.S. 59, 72
     (E)
62   IFCS 59: 49, Tiaquin, Killoscobe, BALLYARA O.S. 59, 60 (E)
63   IFC 2111: 32-34 (1976, *Banshee* Questionnaire), Tiaquin, Killoso-
     lan, CALTRA O.S. 46, 60 (E)
64   IFCS 79: 65 (cf. *Béaloideas* XLII-XLIV, 1974-1976 (1977), p.96), Tia-
     quin, Monivea, MONIVEA O.S. 71 (E)
65   Augusta Gregory: *Visions and Beliefs*, pp. 170-179, 1970 (1st ed.
     1920, 2 vols). Mainly the baronies of Kiltartan, Loughrea and Athen-
     ry (E)
66   St. John D. Seymour and H. L. Neligan, *True Irish Ghost Stories*, p.
     199 (1926), Co. Galway (E)
67   'The O'Flaherty Banshee': referred to in (a) D. R. McAnally, *Irish
     Wonders*, pp. 112-114, 1888 and (b) E. O'Donnell, *The Banshee*, pp.
     22-24, (c. 1920), Co. Galway (E)
68   Aroon, *White Heather*, pp 13-37, 1903, Co. Galway (E)
69   Walter Thornbury, *'Cross Country*, pp. 119, 121, 126, 127, 1861,
     Co. Galway (E)
70   Mary Teresa Henaghan, *From the Brown Wastes of Connaught*, p. 5
     (n.d.), Co. Galway (E)
71   Seán Mac Giollarnáth, *Loinnir Mac Leabhair*, p. 203, *sub éist*, (1936),
     Iorrus Aithneach (I)

Kerry (Ker.), Munster

1   IFC 2113: 80 (1976, *Banshee* Questionnaire), Clanmaurice, Bally-
    heige, BALLYHEIGE O.S. 14 (E)
2   IFC 2113: 81-91 (1976, *Banshee* Questionnaire), Clanmaurice,
    Duagh, DUAGH O.S. 13 (E)
3   IFCS 440: 311-313, Clanmaurice, Kilflyn, KNOCKBRACK O.S. 20
    (E)
4   IFC 2113: 92-99 (1976, *Banshee* Questionnaire), Clanmaurice,
    Killury, CAUSEWAY O.S. 15 (E)
5   IFCS 407: 491, Clanmaurice, Duagh, MEENSCOVANE O.S. 17, 23
    (E)
6   IFCS 412: 229-231, Clanmaurice, Kilflyn, KILFLYN School O.S.
    21 (E)
7   IFC 2113: 100-106 (1976, *Banshee* Questionnaire), Clanmaurice,
    Ratoo, BALLYDUFF O.S. 9 (E)
8   IFC 782: 244 (1941), Corkaguiny, Ballynacourty, ANASCAUL O.S.
    44 (E)
9   IFCS 429: 650, Corkaguiny, Cloghane, BALLYDEENEY O.S. 26
    (I)
10 IFC 2113: 107 (1976, *Banshee* Questionnaire), Corkaguiny, Killiney,
    CASTLEGREGORY O.S. 27 (I), (negative reply).
11 IFC 1577: 365, Corkaguiny, Garfinny, GARFINNY O.S. 53 (I).
12 IFCS 8: 56 (1930-1935), Corkaguiny, Dingle, DINGLE O.S. 43, 53
    (I)
13 IFC 1505: 210 (1957-1958), Corkaguiny, Kilmalkedar, CAHER-
    SCULLIBEEN O.S. 33, 34.
14 *Béaloideas* IX (1939), pp. 276-277, Corkaguiny, Dingle, DINGLE
    O.S. 43 (I)
15 IFC 201: 260 (1936), Corkaguiny, Dunquinn, GREAT BLASKET
    O.S. 51, 61 (I)
16 IFC 8: 274-276 (1930-1935), Corkaguiny, Kinard, LISPOLE O.S. 40
    (I) (cf. 17).
17 IFCS 456: 18-20, Corkaguiny, Kinard, LISPOLE O.S. 40 (I)
18 IFC 2113: 108-110 (1977, Letter), Dunkerron North, Knockane,
    BEAUFORT O.S. 65 (E)
19 IFC 2113: 111-111a (1977, *Banshee* Questionnaire, 1976), Dun-
    kerron North, Knockane, BEAUFORT O.S. 65 (E)
20 IFC 26: 141 (c. 1926), Dunkerron South, Kilcrohane, CAHER-
    DANIEL O.S. 106 (I)
21 IFCS 462: 214-215, Glanarought, Tuosist, LEHID O.S. 100, 101
    108, 109 (I)
22 IFCS 461: 416-417 (1939), Glanarought, Kilgarvan, CAHER O.S.
    85, 94 (E)
23 IFCS 461: 422-423, Glanarought, Kenmare, KENMARE O.S.
    95 (E)
24 IFCS 461: 448, Glanarought, Kenmare, KENMARE O.S. 95 (E)
25 IFCS 461: 553, Glanarough, Kenmare, KENMARE O.S. 100, 101
    (E)

26   IFCS 464: 218-219, Glanarought, Tuosist, COORNAGILLAGH
      School O.S. 101 (E)
27   IFC 2113: 112-118 (1976, *Banshee* Questionnaire), Iraghticonnor,
      Kilconly, BEAL O.S. 1, 2 (E)
28   IFC 2113: 119-122 (1976, *Banshee* Questionnaire), Iraghticonnor,
      Killehenny, BALLYBUNION O.S. 4 (E)
29   IFC 699: 229-230 (1940), Iveragh, Dromod, MAULIN O.S. 80-89

30   IFC 462: 100-101 (1938), Iveragh, Glenbehy, GLENBEHY O.S. 63
      (I)
31   IFC 1312: 446 (1952), Iveragh, Grange, DUNGEAGAN O.S. 97 (I)
32   IFC 1312: 246-248, Iveragh, Killinane, KELLS O.S. 70 (I)
33   IFC 1052: 20-22 (1948), Iveragh, Prior, SUSSA O.S. 88 (I).
34   IFC 2113: 124-125 (1976, *Banshee* Questionnaire), Magunihy, Kil-
      cummin, COOM O.S. 60 (E)
35   IFCS 461: 365, Magunihy, Killaha, ANNAGH MORE O.S. 75, 76
      (E)
36   *Ireland's Own* LXIII, No. 1627, 3 Feb. 1934, p. 129 and *Irish Bits*
      IV, No. 93, p. 486, 1898. Magunihy, Killarney, KILLARNEY O.S.
      66 (E)
37   IFC S451: 365-366 = 388-389, Magunihy, Kilcummin, GALLAUN
      O.S. 60 (I).
38   IFCS 451: 405-406, Magunihy, Kilcummin, GALLAUN O.S. 60 (E)
39   IFCS 449: 16, Trughanacmy, Castleisland, DOOLAIG O.S. 30, 39
      (E)
40   IFCS 449: 20-21, Magunihy, Molahiffe, BALLYBANE O.S. 48 (E)
41   IFCS 449: 22, Trughanacmy, Ballincuslane, KILMURRY Girls'
      School O.S. 40 (E)
42   IFCS 449: 74-76, Trughanacmy, Ballincuslane, KILCUSNAUN
      O.S. 31-40 (E)
43   IFCS 442: 113-114, Trughanacmy, Ballyseedy, LISSARDBOOLA
      O.S. 38 (E)
44   IFC 1167: 181 (1948), Trughanacmy, Kiltallagh, CASTLEMAINE
      O.S. 47 (I)
45   IFC 2113: 126-133 (1976, *Banshee* Questionnaire), Trughanacmy,
      Tralee, BALLYVELLY O.S. 29 (E)
46   *An Claidheamh Soluis agus Fáinne an Lae*, 17 Lúnasa 1901, pp. 356-
      357, Trughanacmy, Killorglan, KILLORGLAN O.S. 56 (I)
47   An tAth Pádraig Ua Duinnín, eag., 'mo throchadh is mo shaoth rem
      ló thú', *Dánta Phiarais Feiritéir*, pp. 2-3, lines 13-36, 1903. John
      O'Brien, *Focalóir Gaoidhilge - Sax - Bhéarla* (1768, *s.v. Síth-Bhrog*,
      includes without translation a quatrain of Feiritéir's elegy for
      Maurice Fitzgerald corresponding to lines 25-28 in Ua Duinnín's
      edition of the Irish text of the elegy and the quatrain is reprinted by
      T. Crofton Croker, *Fairy Legends and Traditions of the South of
      Ireland*, Part 1, pp. 205-206, 1826 ed., and in translation, by Lady
      Chatterton in *Rambles in the South of Ireland during the year 1838*,
      1, p. 270, 1839. This verse is part of Lady Chatterton's
      selection of verses from Croker's then unpublished English

translation of the Irish text of Feiritéir's elegy for Fitzgerald — see Croker (1844) below. Mr. and Mrs. S.C. Hall, *Ireland: Its Scenery, Character &c.* III, p. 106, 1843, include with translation the quatrain corresponding to lines 25-28 in Ua Duinnín. T. Crofton Croker's 'Keen on Maurice Fitzgerald, Knight of Kerry' appeared in *The Keen of the South of Ireland*, pp. 15-20 (1844). (These verses, including lines 25-28 in Ua Duinnín, are part of Croker's translation from Irish of Feiritéir's elegy.) John O'Donovan: 'Elegy of the Death of the Rev. Edmond Kavanagh, by The Rev. James O'Lalor', *The Journal of Kilkenny and South-East of Ireland Archaeological Society*, 1856-1857, pp. 122-123, also includes with translation the quatrain corresponding to lines, 25-28 in Ua Duinnín, while Patrick Kennedy, *The Fireside Stories of Ireland*, p. 144, 1870, has an English translation only of it and W. G. Wood-Martin, *Traces of the Elder Faiths of Ireland*, I, pp. 368-369, 1902, has the Irish quatrain and Croker's English rendering of it. James Clarence Mangan's 'A Lamentation for the Death of Sir Maurice Fitzgerald, Knight of Kerry, *Poems by James Clarence Mangan*, pp. 347-348, (1859), described as 'An Abridged Translation from the Irish of Pierce Feiritéir' includes the quatrain in question and is reprinted in W. B. Yeats, *Fairy and Folk Tales of the Irish Peasantry*, pp. 112-113, 1888, and in subsequent re-issues of the book under various titles (cf. Bibliography). *Journal of the Cork Historical and Archaeological Society* V, 2nd series, 1899, pp. 228-229, contains a selection of verses from Croker, 1844, pp. 13-35, including lines 25-28 in Ua Duinnín above.

48   *Kerry Archaeological Magazine* I, No. 6, April 1911, p. 348 (E)

Kildare (Kild.), Leinster

1   IFCS 771: 80, Carbury, Ardkill, DERRINTURN School O.S. 8 (E)

2   IFC 2112: 39-41 (1976, *Banshee* Questionnaire), Carbury, Kilpatrick, TICKNEVIN O.S. 8, 12 (E)

3   IFCS 775: 1, Connell, Kilmeage, GRANGECLARE West O.S. 13, 18 (E)

4   IFCS 775: 15, Connell, Kilmeage, GRANGECLARE West O.S. 13, 18 (E)

5   IFCS 775: 42, Connell, Kilmeage, ALLENWOOD School O.S. 12, 13 (E)

6   IFC 2112: 42-43, (1976, *Banshee* Questionnaire), Ikeathy and Oughterany, Balraheen, RATHCOFFEY O.S. 10 (E)

7   IFC 1497: 23a, Ikeathy and Oughterany, Kilcock, KILCOCK O.S. 5 (E)

8   IFC 2112: 45-49 (1976, *Banshee* Questionnaire), Kilkea and Moon, Castledermot, CASTLEDERMOT O.S. 38, 40 (E)

9   *Journal of the County Kildare Archaeological Society and Surrounding Districts* VI, 2, 1909, p. 174, Kilkea and Moon, Dunmanoge, MAGANEY O.S. 37, 39 (E)

888888

10   IFCS 778: 99-100, Offaly East, Rathangan, RATHANGAN O.S. 17 (E)
11   IFCS 778: 44, Offaly East, Rathangan, COOLELAN O.S. 16 (E)
12   IFCS 780: 182, Offaly West, Kildangan Boys' School O.S. 27 (E)
13   IFC 2114: 116-128 (1978, *Banshee* Questionnaire 1976), Offaly West, Lackagh, O.S. 22 (E)

Kilkenny (Kilk.), Leinster

1   IFCS 854: 11, Callan, Callan, CALLAN O.S. 26 (E)
2   IFCS 854: 37, Crannagh, Kilmanagh, KILBRAGHAN O.S. 22 (E)
3   IFCS 866: 447, Crannagh, Odagh, THREECASTLES O.S. 14 (E)
4   IFCS 861: 3, Gowran, Gowran, CLIFDEN O.S. 20 (E)
5   IFCS 861: 19, Gowran, Gowran, GOWRAN O.S. 20 (E)
6   J. and M. Banim, *Tales, By The O'Hara Family*, vol. 1, p. 64 (1825), Gowran, CLARAGH parish, O.S. 15, 20 (E)
7   IFC 2112: 53-58 (1976, *Banshee* Questionnaire), Gowran, Inistioge, INISTIOGE O.S. 32 (E)
8   IFC 2114: 197 (1978), Gowran, Grangesilvia, GORESBRIDGE O.S. 21 (E)
9   IFC 2112: 59-61 (1978, *Banshee* Questionnaire 1976), Gowran, Kilmadum, BALLYFOYLE O.S. 14, 15 (E)
10   IFC 2112: 59-61 (1978, *Banshee* Questionnaire, 1976), Gowran, Kilmadum, BALLYFOYLE O.S. 14, 15 (E)
11   IFCS 856: 112-115, Gowran, St. John's GREENRIDGE O.S. 14, 15, 19 (E)
12   (a) IFCS 859: 425, Gowran, Tiscoffin, GRANGEHILL O.S. 20 (E)
     (b) IFC 2112: 22 (1976, *Bahshee* Questionnaire), Gowran, Graiguenamanagh, GRAIGUENAMANAGH O.S. 29 (E)
13   IFCS 847: 304-305, Ida, The Rower, COOLHILL O.S. 33 (E)
14   IFCS 846: 217, Ida, Shanbogh, SHANBOGH O.S. 37 (E)
15   IFC 2112: 64-69 (1976, *Banshee* Questionnaire), Ida, Kilcoan/Kilmaceevogue, GLENMORE O.S. 40, 41 (E)
16   IFCS 845: 342, Iverk, Kilmacow, KILMACOW O.S. 43 (E)
17   IFCS 843: 149-150, Iverk, Kilmacow, DANGAN O.S. 40, 43 (E)
18   IFCS 843: 132, Iverk, Kilmacow, BALLYNEARLA O.S. 42, 43 (E)
19   IFCS 843: 135-136, Iverk, Kilmacow, BALLYDAW O.S. 40, 43 (E)
20   IFCS 840: 157, Iverk, Pollrone, CLOGGA School O.S. 39, 42 (E)
21   IFCS 851: 304-306, Kells, Killamery, GARRYRICKEN O.S. 26, 30 (E)
22   IFCS 852: 220, Kells, Tullahought, KILMACOLIVER School O.S. 39 (E)
23   IFC 954: 35 (1943, *Bogey* Questionnaire), Kells, Tullahought, KILMACOLIVER O.S. 20 (E)
24   *Études Celtiques* VIII, 1957-1958, p. 411, Knocktopher, Jerpoint, GLENPIPE O.S. 36 (E)
25   IFCS 848: 252-253, Knocktopher, Derrynahinch, CASTLE-

GANNON School O.S. 35, 36 (E)

26   IFCS 854: 224. Shillelogher, Danesfort, DANESFORT O.S. 23 (E).
27   IFCS 854: 226, Shillelogher, Danesfort, DUNDARYARK O.S. 23 (E)
28   *Irisleabhar na Gaedhilge* XI, 1901, p. 93 (I)
29   *Old Kilkenny Review* VII, 1954, p. 50 (E)
30   R. B. Breatnach, *Gaedhilg Chonndae Chille Coinnigh*, unpublished M.A. Thesis, University College Dublin, 1939, p. 30 (I)

Laois (Lao.) Leinster

1   IFC 2112: 73-75 (1976, Letter), Ballyadams, Killabban, BALLYNAN O.S. 26 (E)
2   IFC 36: 201-202 (c. 1929), Ballyadams, Ballyadams, BALLYADAMS O.S. 19 (E)
3   IFC 2112: 79 (1976, *Banshee* Questionnaire), Clandonagh, Aghaboe, BALLYBROPHY O.S. 22 (E)
4   IFCS 829: 268, Clandonagh, Kyle, BALLAGHMORE O.S. 15, 21 (E)
5   IFCS 828: 201-202, Clandonagh, Rathdowney, Rathdowney, O.S. 28 (E)
6   IFC 954: 54 (1943, *Bogey* Questionnaire), Clarmallagh, Aghaboe, BORRIS-IN-OSSORY O.S. 21, 22 (E)
7   IFC 2112: 80-81 (1978, *Banshee* Questionnaire, 1976), Clarmallagh, Aghamacart, DERREEN O.S. 29, 35 (E)
8   IFCS 832: 61-62, Cullenagh, Abbeyleix, ABBEYLEIX Convent School, O.S. 23.
9   John Keegan 'Legends and Tales of the Queen's County Peasantry. No. I — The Banshee', *The Dublin University Magazine*, 1839, pp. 366-374. This story is reprinted in Very Rev. J. Canon O'Hanlon ed., *Legends and Poems by John Keegan*, pp. 123-143 (1907) and in *Weird Tales. By Irish Writers*, pp. 153-171 (n.d.), Maryborough West, Clonenagh & Clonagheen, MOUNTRATH O.S. 17 (E)
10   IFC 2112: 82-83 (1976 Letter), Maryborough West, Clonenagh & Clonagheen, BALLYLUSK O.S. 12 (E)
11   IFCS 834: 326-328, Maryborough West, Clonenagh & Clonagheen, CLONKEEN O.S. 12, 17 (E)
12   IFC 2114: 198-201 (1979), Maryborough West, Clonenagh and Clonagheen, BALLYFIN O.S. 7 (E)
13   *Études Celtiques*, VIII, 1957-1958, p. 411, Maryborough, Clonenagh and Clonagheen, TRUMERA O.S. 17 (E)
14   IFC 1840: 31-33 (1978), Portahinch/Tinnahinch, Ardea/Rosenallis, MOUNTMELLICK O.S. 8 (E)
15   IFC 1840: 104-113, 118-123 (1976, *Banshee* Questionnaire), Portnahinch/Tinnahinch, Ardea/Rosenallis, MOUNTMELLICK O.S. 8 (E)
16   IFC 1840: 339, 342-346 (1978), Portnahinch/Tinnahinch, Ardea/Rosenallis, MOUNTMELLICK O.S. 8 (E)
17   IFC 1840: 1-43, 217-222, 225-226 (1976, *Banshee* Questionnaire), Portnahinch/Tinnahinch, Ardea/Rosenallis, MOUNTMELLICK O.S. 8 (E)

18   IFC 1840: 189-201 (1976), Portnahinch/Tinnahinch, Ardea/ Rosenallis, MOUNTMELLICK O.S. 8 (E)
19   IFC 1840: 153-163 (1976), Portnahinch/Tinnahinch, Ardea/ Rosenallis, MOUNTMELLICK O.S. 8 (E)
20   IFC 2112: 87-96 (1976, *Banshee* Questionnaire), Portnahinch, Coolbanagher, EMO O.S. 8 (E)
21   IFCS 839: 230, Slievemargy, Killeshin, KILLESHIN School O.S. 32, 37 (E)
22   IFCS 826: 328, Upperwoods, Offerlane, DERRYLAHEN O.S. 15, 16 (E)
23   The Fitzpatrick Banshee 'Superstitions of the Irish Peasantry — No. I. The Banshee', *The Dublin and London Magazine*, 1825, pp. 31-34. This story also appears in *The Shamrock* XXIX, No. 1339,11 June 1892, p. 596 and in *Ireland's Own* IX, No. 233, 8 May 1907, p. 11 (E)

Leitrim (Leit), Connaught

1   IFCS 226: 132-133, Carrigallen, Oughteragh, BALLINAMORE O.S. 25 (E)
2   IFCS 229: 2-4, Carrigallen, Drumreilly, DRUMCONLEVAN O.S. 30 (E)
3   IFCS 229: 20, Carrigallen, Carrigallen, TULLYNORTH O.S. 26 (E)
4   IFCS 229: 21, Carrigallen, Carrigallen, NEWTOWNGORE School O.S. 26 (E)
5   IFC 1803: 23 (1972), Drumahaire, Cloonclare, MEENKEERAGH O.S. 12, 13 (E)
6   IFCS 202: 140-141, Drumahaire, Drumlease, DRUMAHAIRE O.S. 14 (E)
7   IFCS 204:201 (cf. *Béaloideas* XLII-XLIV, 1974-1976 (1977), p.98), Drumahaire, Inishmagrath, SHIVDILLAGH O.S. 28, 29 (E)
8   IFC 2111: 38-39 (1976, *Banshee* Questionnaire), Leitrim, Kiltoghert, CARRICK-ON-SHANNON O.S. 31 (E)
9   IFCS 210: 415, 519-20 (cf. *Béaloideas* XLII-XLIV, 1974-1976 (1977), p. 105), Leitrim, Kiltoghert, JAMESTOWN O.S. 31 (E)
10   IFC 1506: 352-353 (1958), Leitrim, Kiltoghert, DRUMSHAMBO O.S. 23 (E)
11   IFCS 197: 213, Mohill, Mohill, MOHILL O.S. 32 (E)
12   IFCS 218: 222, Mohill, Mohill, DRUMDOO. O.S. 32 (E)
13   IFCS 195: 21, Rosclogher, Cloonclare, KILTYCLOGHER O.S. 8 (E)
14   IFCS 195:21, Rosclogher, Cloonclare, KILTYCLOGHER O.S. 8 (E)
15   IFCS 195: 22, Rosclogher, Cloonclare, KILTYCLOGHER O.S. 8 (E)
16   IFCS 193: 357, Rosclogher, Cloonclare, CORRACLOONA School O.S. 8.9 (E)

Limerick (Lim.), Munster

1   IFC 2113: 137-142 (1976, *Banshee* Questionnaire), refers to the Parishes of St Mary, St Michael and St John, Limerick City, and to

parts of Co. Clare (E)

2   IFC 2113: 143-149 (1976, *Banshee* Questionnaire), Limerick City area (E)

3   IFCS 503: 165, Connello Lwr, Askeaton, ASKEATON School O.S. 11 (E)

4   IFC 575: 62-63 (1938), Connello Lwr., Rathkeale, RATHKEALE O.S. 29 (E)

5   IFCS 499: 200, Connello Upr, Ballingarry, BALLINGARRY O.S. 29 (I)

6   IFCS 500: 38, Connello Upr, Ballingarry, BALLYGUILE O.S. 38 (E)

7   IFCS 500: 39, Connello Upr, Ballingarry, BALLINGARRY O.S. 29 (E)

8   IFCS 498: 311, Connello Upr, Bruree, BRUREE School O.S. 39 (E)

9   IFC 1870: 218 (1972-1976), Coonagh, Toughcluggin, REASK O.S. 24 (E)

10   IFCS 518: 141, Coonagh, Pallasgrean, PALLASGREAN O.S. 24 (E)

11   IFCS 518: 127, Coonagh, Pallasgrean, PALLASGREAN O.S. 24 (E)

12   IFCS 509: 295, Coshlea, Particles, SUNVILLE UPR O.S. 48, 56 (E)

13   IFCS 509: 296, Coshlea, Ballingarry, MOUNTRUSSEL O.S. 55, 56 (E)

14   IFCS 505: 114-115, Coshma, Adare, ADARE O.S. 21 (E)

15   IFCS 507: 518-519 (cf. *Bealoideas*, XLII-XLIV, 1974-1976 (1977), p. III), Coshma, Croom, CROOM O.S. 30 (E)

16   IFCS 507: 519-521, Coshma, Croom, CROOM O.S. 30 (E)

17   IFCS 507: 521-522, Coshma, Croom, CROOM O.S. 30 (E)

18   IFCS 495: 61, Glenquin, Abbeyfeale, BALLAGHBEHY O.S. 42 (E)

19   *The Shamrock* XI, No. 378, 10 Jan. 1874, p.229, Glenquin, Abbeyfeale, ABBEYFEALE O.S. 42 (E)

20   IFC 629: 29-30 (1939), Glenquin, Monagay, GARRYDUFF O.S. 35, 36 (E)

21   IFCS 494: 85, Glenquin, Monagay, TULLIGOLINE O.S. 35, 43 (E)

22   IFC 2112; 150 (1976), Glenquin, Killeedy, BALLINTOBER O.S. 48 (E)

23   IFCS 504: 121, Kildimo, Kerry, KILDIMO O.S. 12 (E)

24   IFCS 520: 356, Owneybeg, Tough, CAPPAMORE O.S. 15 (E)

25   IFCS 521: 219-222, Owneybeg, Tuogh, CAPPAMORE O.S. 15 (E)

26   IFCS 519: 31, Owneybeg, Tuogh, PORTNARD O.S. 7, 15 (E)

27   IFCS 517:201, Pubblebrien, Ballycahane, KILDONNEL O.S. 22 (E)

28   IFCS 526: 100-101, Pubblebrien, Knocknagaul, LEMONFIELD O.S. 13 (E)

29   IFCS 527: 96, Pubblebrien, Mungret, LURRAGA School. O.S. 12 (E)

30   *Folk-Lore* XXI, 1910, p. 191, Pubblebrien, Killonohan, ATTYFLIN O.S. 12, 21 (E)

31   IFCS 484: 182, Shanid, Dunmoylan, MONEYMOHILL O.S. 18 (E)

32   IFCS 484: 193, Shanid, Dunmoylan, MONEYMOHILL O.S. 18 (E)

33   IFCS 486: 20, Shanid, Rathronan, ATHEA O.S. 34 (E)
34   IFCS 486: 45, Shanid, Rathronan, ATHEA O.S. 34 (E)
35   IFCS 486: 94, Shanid, Rathronan, ATHEA O.S. 34 (E)
36   IFC 955: 4 (1943, *Bogey* Questionnaire), Shanid, Rathronan, ATHEA O.S. 34 (E)
37   IFCS 488: 25-27, Shanid, Rathronan, GLENSHARROLD O.S. 18, 27, 28 (E)
38   IFCS 488: 8, Shanid, Rathronan, ARDAGH O.S. 28 (E)
39   *Irisleabhar na Gaedhilge* XII, p. 111, July 1902, Small County, Knockainy, LOUGHGUR O.S. 32 (I)
40   *The Dublin Penny Journal,* 7 Feb. 1903, p.613, Small County, Knockainy, LOUGHGUR O.S. 32 (E)

Longford (Long.), Leinster

1   IFC 1022: 389-390 (1947), Ardagh, Ardagh, ARDAGH O.S. 19 (E)
2   Maria Edgeworth, *Castle Rackrent,* note 1, p. 21 (1800) Ardagh, Mostrim, EDGEWORTHSTOWN O.S. 15, 20 (E)
3   IFC 1429: 87-88 (1955), Ardagh, Mostrim, EDGEWORTHSTOWN O.S. 15, 20 (E)
4   *Béaloideas* III, 1932, p. 302 (McKay I, 1946, pp. 354-355), Granard, Clonbroney, BALLINALEE O.S. 9 (E)
5   IFC 1506: 71-72 (1958), Granard, Columbkille, ROSSDUFF O.S. 3 (E)
6   IFCS 765: 67, Granard, Granard, COOLCOR O.S. 10 (E)
7   IFCS 765: 115-116, Granard, Granard, BUNLAHY School O.S. 10 (E)
8   IFC 1430: 24 (1955), Granard, Columbkille, SMEAR O.S. 2, 3 (E)
9   IFCS 764: 417, Granard, Granard, KILLASONA School O.S. 3 (E)
10   IFCS 766: 391, Granard, Killoe, MOYNE O.S. 2, 3 (E)
11   IFCS 766: 563, Granard, Killoe, MOYNE O.S. 2, 3 (E)
12   IFCS 766: 573, Granard, Killoe, MOYNE O.S. 2, 3 (E)
13   IFCS 766: 574, Granard, Killoe, AGHAGH O.S. 1, 3 (E)
14   IFCS 766: 575, Granard, Killoe, MOYNE O.S. 2, 3 (E)
15   IFCS 766: 578, Granard, Killoe, BALLYDUFFY O.S. 1, 2, 3 (E)
16   IFCS 766: 576, Granard, Killoe, BALLYDUFFY O.S. 1, 2, 3 (E)
17   IFCS 766: 576-577, Granard, Killoe, BALLYDUFFY O.S. 1, 2, 3 (E)
18   IFCS 766: 569, Longford, Killoe, LEGGA O.S. 2, 3 (E)
19   IFCS 766: 570, Longford, Killoe, LEGGA O.S. 2, 3 (E)
20   IFCS 766: 571, Longford, Killoe, LEGGA O.S. 2, 3 (E)
21   IFC 2112: 97-104 (1976 *Banshee* Questionnaire), Longford, Killoe, DOOROC O.S. 5, 9 (E)
22   IFC 1858: 77-78 (1964), Longford, Killoe, BALLINAMUCK 2, 5 (E)
23   Matthew Archdeacon, *Legends of Connaught,* pp. 166-180, (1839), Longford, Killoe, GLENMORE O.S. 5, 6 (E)
24   IFC 1902: 169-171 (1977-1978), Moydow, Moydow, CLOON-MUCKER O.S. 18 (E)
25   IFCS 755: 175, Moydow, Killashee, CLOONKEEL O.S. 12 (E)
26   IFCS 751: 154-155, Rathcline, Shrule, DAROGE O.S. 26 (E)

27   IFCS 755: 29-30, Rathcline, Rathcline, CLOONFORE 17, 18 (E)
28   IFC 2112:105 (1976, *Banshee* Questionnaire), Rathcline, Cashel, NEWTOWNCASHEL O.S. 21 (E)
29   IFC 2112: 106-111, (1976, *Banshee* Questionnaire), Rathcline, Rathcline, LANESBORO O.S. Long. 17/Ros. 37 (E)
30   IFCS 750: 353-354, Shrule, Forgney, CLOONCALLOW O.S. 27 (E)
31   IFCS 750: 354, Shrule, Forgney, FORGNEY O.S. 27 (E)
32   IFCS 750: 355, Shrule, Forgney, FORGNEY O.S. 27 (E)
33   IFCS 750: 355-356, Shrule, Forgney, FORGNEY O.S. 27, (E)

Louth (Lou.), Leinster

1   IFC 2112: 112-115 (1976, *Banshee* Questionnaire), Ardee, Ardee, ARDEE O.S. 17 (E)
2   IFC 2112: 118-119 (1976, *Banshee* Questionnaire), Ardee, Ardee, RIVERSTOWN O.S. 14 (E)
3   IFCS 680: 465-467, Drogheda, St. Mary's, DROGHEDA O.S. 24 (E)
4   IFC 2112: 122-123 (1976, *Banshee* Questionnaire), Drogheda, Drogheda, DROGHEDA, O.S. 24 (E)
5   IFCS 675: 141, Ferrard, Termonfeckin, BETAGHSTOWN, O.S. 22 (E)
6   IFC 2112: 116-118 (1976, *Banshee* Questionnaire), Lwr Dundalk, Carlingford, OMEATH O.S. 5 (E)
7   IFC 2112: 120-121 (1976, *Banshee* Questionnaire), Lwr Dundalk, Carlingford, BALLAGAN O.S. 9 (E)
8   IFC 1502: 186 (1957), Lwr Dundalk, Carlingford, BALLINTESKIN O.S. 5 (E)
9   IFC 1502: 187-188, Lwr Dundalk, Carlingford, ARDAGHY O.S. 4, 5 (E)
10   *The Shamrock* III, No. 57, Sat. Nov. 2, 1867, pp 68-70, Upr Dundalk, Castletown, CASTLETOWN O.S. 7 (E)
11   IFCS 664: 152, Upr Dundalk, Creggan, COURTBANE School O.S. 3 (E)
12   IFCS 661: 157, Upr Dundalk, Dundalk, DUNDALK School O.S. 7 (E)
13   *Folk-Lore* X, 1899, pp. 119, 121 (8), 123 (8), Upr Dundalk, Ballymascanlan, KILCURRY O.S. 4 (E)

Mayo (Mayo), Connaught

1   IFCS 87: 125, Burrishoole, Burrishoole, SRAHMORE O.S. 45, 57 (E)
2   IFCS 95: 203-204, Clanmorris, Balla, BALLA O.S. 90 (E)
3   IFC 2111: 43-46, (1976, *Banshee* Questionnaire), Clanmorris, Kilvine, KNOCKADOON O.S. 112 (E)
4   IFCS 107: 235-236, Costello, Annagh, BALLYHAUNIS O.S. 93 (E)
5   IFCS 129: 249, Erris, Kilcommon, TALLAGH O.S. 43, 44 (E)

6   IFC 1242: 55-68 (1940-1941) (cf. *Béaloideas* XLII-XLIV, 1974-1976 (1977), p. 104), Erris, Kilcommon, ROSSPORT O.S. 4 (E)
7   IFC 1586: 76-79 (1961), Erris, Kilcommon, ROSSPORT O.S. 4 (I)
8   IFC 1229: 236 (1952), Erris, Kilcommon, AGHOOS O.S. 11 (I)
9   IFC 1840: 304-322 (1976), Erris, Kilcommon, BELLANABOY O.S. 11 (E)
10   IFC 1208: 190-191 (1951), Erris, Kilcommon, KILGALLIGAN O.S. 3, 4 (I)
11   IFC 804: 334-335 (1942), Erris, Kilcommon, KNOCKMOYLEEN O.S. 34, 35, 44 (I)
12   IFCS 131: 638, Erris, Kilcommon, SRAH O.S. 17, 25 (E)
13   IFCS 123: 55, Gallen, Kilconduff, CLOONAGHBOY O.S. 62 (E)
14   IFC 117: 93 (1935), Gallen, Killasser, CLOONFINISH O.S. 61, 62 (E)
15   IFC 227: 102-103 (1936), Gallen, Killasser, CLOONFINISH O.S. 61, 62 (E)
16   IFCS 127: 422 (1938) (cf. *Béaloideas* XLII-XLIV, 1974-1976 (1977), p. 97), Gallen, Attymas, KILGELLIA O.S. 40, 49 (E)
17   IFCS 118: 33-34 (cf. *Béaloideas* XLII-XLIV, 1974-1976 (1977), p.99), Gallen, Kilconduff, BALLYGLASS O.S. 71 (E)
18   IFCS 124: 242, Gallen, Toomore, FOXFORD O.S. 60, 61 (I)
19   IFCS 103: 52, Kilmaine, Kilmolara, The NEALE Boys' School O.S. 121 (E)
20   IFCS 103: 360, Kilmaine, Ballinchalla, INISHMAINE O.S. 117 (E)
21   IFCS 103: 404, Kilmaine, Kilmolara, THE NEALE O.S. 121 (E)
22   IFCS 102: 177, Kilmaine, Shrule, SHRULE O.S. 123 (E)
23   IFCS 102: 183 Kilmaine, Shrule, SHRULE O.S. 123 (E)
24   IFC 1253: 208 (1950, *River Fords* Questionnaire), Kilmaine, Kilcommon, CLOGHAN'S HILL O.S. 119, 122 (E)
25   IFC 955: 251-252, (1943, *Bogey* Questionnaire), Murrisk, Kilgeever, CLOONCARRABAUN O.S. 86 (E)
26   IFC 955: 236 (1943, *Bogey* Questionnaire), Tirawley, Kilmoremoy, BALLINA O.S. 30 (E)
27   IFCS 145: 16 (cf. *Béaloideas* XLII-XLIV, 1974-1976 (1977) p. 104), Tirawley, Ballysakeery, NEWTOWNWHITE O.S. 22 (E)
28   IFCS 153: 87-88 (cf. *Béaloideas* XLII-XLIV, 1974-1976 (1977) p.99), Tirawley, Crossmolina, INISHCOE O.S. 38 (E)
29   IFC 2111: 47-53, (1976, *Banshee* Questionnaire), Tirawley, Doonfeeny, BEALDERG O.S. 6 (E)
30   IFC 2111: 55-58, (1976, *Banshee* Questionnaire), Tirawley, Ballina, BALLINA O.S. 30 (E)
31   *Folk-Lore* XXIX, 1918, pp. 308-310, information refers to the areas of Portacloy, Belmullet, and to Clare Island and Inishbofin (E)
32   W.H. Maxwell, *Wild Sports of the West*, I, pp. 67, 294, 1832 (2nd ed. 1850, reprint 1973, pp 36-37), Co. Mayo (E)
33   *Mayo Magazine*, No. 8; 17 Mar 1966, pp. 65-66, Co. Mayo (E) (E)

34   The Mayo Banshee. Referred to in (a) D.R. McAnally *Irish Wonders*, p.114 (1888), (b) E. O'Donnell *The Banshee*, pp. 36-37 (c. 1920), (c) *Ireland's Own* XII, No. 312, 11 Nov 1908, p. 4 and (d) Mary McGarry, ed., *Best Irish Ghostly Tales*, pp. 39-40 (n.d.), Co. Mayo (E)

35   *Proceedings of the Royal Irish Academy*, 3rd Ser., III, No. 4, p. 630, 1895, The Mullet, Inishkea Islands, and Portacloy (E)

Meath (Mea.), Leinster

1   IFCS 717: 301, Fore, Killeagh, BALLINACREE O.S. 8 (E)
2   IFCS 717: 383, Fore, Killeagh, MOATE O.S. 8 (E)
3   IFCS 717: 384, Fore, Oldcastle, OLDCASTLE O.S. 9 (E)
4   IFCS 684: 217-220, Lwr Duleek, Julianstown, SMITHSTOWN O.S. 20, 21, 27, 28 (E)
5   IFC 1209: 446-448 (1951), Lwr Kells, Kilmainham, BOYNAGH O.S. 5 (E)
6   IFC 1209: 462 (1951), Lwr Kells, Kilmainham, EDENGROVE O.S. 2 (E)
7   IFCS 706: 523-524, Lwr Kells, Moynalty, CARRIGAGH O.S. 1, 4 (E)
8   IFCS 706: 524, Lwr Kells, Moynalty, Maio School, O.S. 4 (E)
9   IFCS 706: 525, Lwr Kells, Moybolgue, LOSSET O.S. 4, 5 (E)
10   IFC 1840: 263-274 (1978), Lwr Navan, Donaghmore, RATHALDRON O.S. 25 (E)
11   IFCS 689: 288, Lwr Moyfenrath, Upper Navan, TRIM O.S. 36 (E)
12   IFC 2112: 132-133, (1976, *Banshee* Questionnaire), Lwr Navan/Skreen, Donaghmore/Navan, NAVAN O.S. 25 (E)
13   IFCS 702: 96, Lwr Navan, Ardbraccan/Mantry, BOHERMEEN O.S. 24 (E)
14   IFCS 696: 247, Lune, Athboy, ATHBOY O.S. 29 (E)
15   IFC 2112: 134-136 (1976, Letter), Ratoath, Dunshaughlin, DUNSHAUGHLIN O.S. 44 (E)
16   IFCS 687: 242, Ratoath, Dunshaughlin, DUNSHAUGHLIN School O.S. 44 (E)
17   IFCS 687: 164, Skreen, Athlumney, JOHNSTOWN O.S. 25 (E)
18   IFCS 687: 175, Skreen, Kilcarn, KILCARN O.S. 25 (E)
19   IFC 954: 77 (1943, *Bogey* Questionnaire), Skreen, Monkstown, WALTERSTOWN O.S. 32 (E)
20   IFCS 689: 421, Upr Dease, Gallow, GARRADICE O.S. 49 (E)
21   IFCS 689: 288, Upr Deece, Kilmore, KILMORE O.S. 43, (E)
22   IFC 2112: 141-142 (1976, Letter), Upr Duleek, Ardcath, ARDCATH O.S. 33 (E)
23   IFCS 685: 54, Upr Duleek, Duleek, BELLEWSTOWN O.S. 27 (E)
24   IFCS 714: 96-97, Upr Slane, Gernonstown, GERNONSTOWN O.S. 18, 19 (E)

Monaghan (Mon.), Ulster

1   IFC 2110: 195 (1976, Letter), Cremorne, Aghnamullen, GARRY-BANE O.S. 23, 24 (E)
2   IFCS 937: 92, Cremorne, Clontibret, CORDERRYDUFF O.S. 19, 24 (E)
3   IFCS 943: 160, Cremorne, Muckno, DRUMLEEK SOUTH O.S. 20 (E)
4   *Clogher Record* V, 1965, p.362, Dartree, Aghabog, AGHABOG O.S. 17 (E)
5   IFCS 932: 8-9 , Farney, Donaghmoyne, RAHANS O.S. 28, 31 (E)
6   IFC 2110: 196-199 (1976, *Banshee* Questionnaire), Farney, Inniskeen, INNISKEEN O.S. 29 (E)
7   IFCS 956: 321, Monaghan, Monaghan, MONAGHAN O.S. 9 (E)
8   IFCS 956: 336, Monaghan, Monaghan, MONAGHAN O.S. 9 (E)
9   IFC 1619: 24 (1960), Monaghan, TEDAVNET O.S. 6 (E)
      6 (E)
10   IFCS 955: 42, Monaghan, Tedavnet, TULLYCROMAN O.S. 9 (E)
11   IFCS 957: 382, Monaghan, Monaghan, KILLYMARLEY O.S. 9, 10 (E)
12   *Ireland's Own* LXXI, No. 3017, p. 4, Oct. 26th, 1946, Co. Monaghan (E)

Offaly (Off.), Leinster

1   IFC 2112: 146-151 (1976, *Banshee* Questionnaire), Ballybritt, Birr, CRINKILL O.S. 35 (E)
2   IFCS 821: 344, Ballybrit, Serkieran, GRANGE O.S. 39 (E)
3   IFCS 821: 347, Ballybrit, Serkieran, CLAREEN School O.S. 36 (E)
4   IFCS 805: 454-455, Ballycowan, Rahan, BALLINA O.S. 8, 16 (E)
5   IFCS 805: 455-456 Ballycowan, Rahan, CASTLETOWN O.S. 7, 8, 15 (E)
6   IFCS 819: 258-259, Clonlisk, Kilcomin, GLASSHOUSE O.S. 42, 44, 45 (E)
7   IFCS 800: 68, Coolestown, Clonsast, BALLYSHANE O.S. 28 (E)
8   IFCS 778: 46-47 Coolestown, Clonsast, CLONBRIN O.S. 28 (E)
9   IFC 2112: 152-153 (1976, *Banshee* Questionnaire), Coolestown, Monasteroris, KILLAN O.S. 12 (E)
10   IFCS 821: 122-123, Eglish, Drumcullen, RATHGIBBON O.S. 36 (E)
11   IFCS 811: 189-191, Carrycastle, Clonmacnoise, MAGHERAMORE O.S. 5, 6 (E)
12   IFC 1677: 346-347 (1964), Garrycastle, Tissarain, LISSDUFF O.S. 14 (E)
13   IFC 1677: 389 (1964), Garrycastle, Wheera, BALLYDALY O.S. 15 (E)
14   IFC 2112: 155-157 (1976, *Banshee* Questionnaire), Geashill, Geashill, KILLEIGH O.S. 25 (E)
15   IFCS 803: 46, Upr Philipstown, Clonyhurk, GARRYHINCH O.S. 33 (E)

Roscommon (Ros.), Connaught

1   IFC 2111: 67-70   (1976, *Banshee* Questionnaire), Athlone, Cam, CURRAGHBOY O.S. 45, 48 (E)
2   IFC 2111: 71-76 (1976, *Banshee* Questionnaire), Athlone, Cam, GRANGE O.S. 44, 45 (E)
3   IFC 1575: 73 (1961), (cf. *Béaloideas* XLII-XLIV, 1974-1976 (1977), p. 115), Athlone, Cam, GRANGE O.S. 44, 45 (E)
4   IFC 1677: 193 (1963), Athlone, Cam, GRANGE O.S. 44, 45, (E)
5   IFCS 269: 73, Athlone, Kiltoom, CORNASEER O.S. 48, 49 (E)
6   IFCS 269: 171, Athlone, Dysart, BALLINTHLEVA O.S. 45, 48 (E)
7   IFC 1639: 66-67 (1962), Athlone, Drum, NURE O.S. 52 (E)
8   IFCS 271: 49, Athlone, Drum, CORNAFULLA O.S. 51, 52, 55 (E)
9   IFCS 263: 302, Athlone, Fuerty, CLOVER HILL O.S. 39 (E)
10   IFC 2111: 78-9 (1976, *Banshee* Questionnaire), Ballintober South, Cloontuskert, LANESBORO O.S. (Ros. 37/Long. 17) (E)
11   IFC 2111: 80 (1976 *Banshee* Questionnaire), Ballintober South, Kilbride, LISGOBBAN O.S. 36, 40 (E)
12   IFCS 260: 95, Ballintober South, Kilteevan, KILTEEVAN O.S. 40 (E)
13   IFC 2111: 59-66 (1981), Ballintober South, Kilgefin, BALLAGH O.S. 36 (E)
14   IFC 2111: 81-82 (1976 *Banshee* Questionnaire), Ballintober South, Roscommon, ROSCOMMON O.S. 39 (E)
15   IFC 1399: 573-574 (1955), Ballintober North, Termonbarry, BALLYTOOHEY O.S. 30 (E)
16   IFC 2111: 84-86 (1976, *Banshee* Questionnaire), Ballymoe, Clooney-gormican, BALLYMACURLY O.S. 35 (E)
17   IFC 2111: 87-89 (1976 *Banshee* Questionnaire), Boyle, Boyle, DRUMDOE O.S. 3 (E)
18   IFC 2111: 90 (1976, *Banshee* Questionnaire), Boyle, Boyle, GORROW O.S. 5, 6 (E)
19   IFCS 237: 47, Boyle, Killukin, CORTOBER School O.S. 11 (E)
20   The O'Connor Banshee by J.L.L. in P.D. Hardy, ed., *Pic-Nics from the Dublin Penny Journal* . . . pp. 310-328 (1836). This story also appears in *Our Girls* II, Dec. 1932, pp. 306-309, 316 and in the *Irish Independent* 30 Dec. 1932 (Irish translation by S.O.C.). Castlereagh, Ballintober, BALLINTOBER O.S. 27, 34 (E)
21   IFC 2111: 92-95 (1976, *Banshee* Questionnaire), Frenchpark, Tibohine, FAIRYMOUNT O.S. 15 (E)
22   IFCS 239: 205-206, Frenchpark, Tibohine, FAIRYMOUNT O.S. 15 (E)
23   IFC 2111: 96-98 (1976, *Banshee* Questionnaire), Moycarn, Drum, OLDTOWN KILCASHEL O.S. 54 (E)
24   IFC 1640: 372 (1963), Moycarn, Moore, NEWTOWN KILCASHEL O.S. 54 (E)

25 IFC 1639: 252 (1962), Moycarn, Moore, AMERICA O.S. 54, 56 (E)
26 IFCS 253: 37, Roscommon, Lissonuffy, COGGAL (Caggle) O.S. 29 (E)
27 IFCS 255: 422-423, Roscommon, Kilglass, CLOONEEN (Hartland) O.S. 23 (E)
28 IFCS 255: 423, Roscommon, Kiltrustan, STROKESTOWN O.S. 23 (E)

Sligo (Sli.), Connaught

1   IFC 2111: 107-108 (1976, *Banshee* Questionnaire), Carbury, Calry, CARROWLUSTIA O.S. 39 (E)
2   IFC 1765: 32-33 (1964), Carbury, Ahamlish, INISHMURRAY O. S. 1 (E)
3   IFCS 157: 199, Carbury, Drumcliff, DRUM EAST O.S. 8, 9 (E)
4   IFCS 159: 77-78, Carbury, Killaspugbrone, STRANDHILL O.S. 14 (E)
5   IFCS 188: 146-147, Coolavin, Killaraght, CLOONCURRY O.S. 46, 47 (E)
6   IFCS 183: 512-513 (cf. *Béaloideas*, XLII-XLIV, 1974-1976 (1977), p.104), Corran, Kilmorgan, KNOCKMOYNAGH O.S. 33, 34 (E)
7   IFCS 165: 36, Tireragh, Easkey, EASKEY O.S. 11 (E)
8   IFCS 163: 87, Tineragh, Castleconnor, ARDVALLEY O.S. 27 (E)
9   IFCS 179: 541, Tirerril, Drumcolumb, RIVERSTOWN O.S 27 (E)
10 IFC 2107: 188 (1978, *Death Customs* Questionnaire), Tirerril, Aghanagh, BALLINAFAD O.S. 40 (E)
11 IFC 1757: 228 (1969), Tirerril, Ballynakill, SOOEY O.S. 27 (E)
12 IFC 1782: 91-92 (1969), Tirerril, Ballynakill, SOOEY O.S. 27 (E)
13 IFCS 182: 335, Tirerril, Kilmactranny, LOUGH ARROW School O.S. 41 (E)
14 IFC 485: 124-126 (1938), Tirerril, Kilmacullen, CORLISHEEN O.S. 34 (E)
15 IFC 485: 71 (1938), Tirerril, Kilmacullen, DRUMSHINAGH O.S. 34 (E)
16 IFCS 163: 87, Tirreril, Castleconnor, CORBALLY School, O.S. 22 (E)
17 *Folk-Lore* X, 1899, p.123, Tirreril, Ballysadare, BALLYSADARE O.S. 20 (E)

Tipperary (Tipp.), Munster

1   IFCS 581: 204 (cf. *Béaloideas*, XLII-XLIV, 1974-1976 (1977), p. 104), Clanwilliam, Clonbeg, GLENCOSHABINNA O.S. 74, 80 (E)
2   IFC 2113: 152-158 (1976, *Banshee* Questionnaire), Eliogarty, Thurles, THURLES O.S. 41 (E)
3   IFCS 507: 40-42, Eliogarty, Twomileborris, TWOMILEBORRIS O.S. 42 (E)
4   IFCS 506: 301, Eliogarty, Twomileborris, TWOMILEBORRIS O.S.

42 (E)

5   IFCS 573: 307, Iffa and Offa West, Burncourt, BALLYPOREEN School O.S. 86 (E)

6   IFC 955: 139 (1943, *Bogey* Questionnaire), Iffa and Offa West, Caher, CAHER O.S. 81 (E)

7   IFC 2113: 159-160 (1976, *Banshee* Questionnaire), Iffa and Offa West, Caher, CAHER O.S. 81 (E)

8   IFCS 571: 84-85, Iffa and Offa West, Neddans, NEDDANS O.S. 88 (E)

9   IFCS 571: 85, Iffa and Offa West, Derrygrath, GRANGE O.S 81, 82 (E)

10 IFCS 571: 86, Iffa and Offa West, Derrygrath, GRANGE O.S. 81, 82 (E)

11 IFCS 555: 173-175, Clanwilliam, Relickmurry and Athassel, GOLDEN O.S. 60 (E)

12 *Ireland's Own* LXV, No. 1698, 22 June 1935, p.805, Iffa and Offa West, Shanrahan, CLOGHEEN O.S. 87 (E)

13 IFC 1608: 39, 220-221 (1960), Iffa and Offa East, Carrick, CARRICK ON SUIR O.S. 85 (E)

14 IFC 1608: 210 (1960), Iffa and Offa East, SLIEVENAMAN area O.S. 78 (E)

15 IFC 2113: 161-163 (1976, *Banshee* Questionnaire), Iffa and Offa East, Kilcash, KILCASH O.S. 78 (E)

16 IFC 2113: 164-167 (1976, *Banshee* Questionnaire), Iffa and Offa East, Kilcash, KILCASH O.S. 78 (E)

17 IFCS 567: 15-16, Iffa and Offa East, St Mary's, CLONMEL O.S. 83 (E)

18 IFC 2113: 168-171 (1976, *Banshee* Questionnaire), Iffa and Offa East, St Mary's, CLONMEL O.S. 83 (E)

19 IFC 2113: 172-174 (1976, *Banshee* Questionnaire), Iffa and Offa East, St Mary's, CLONMEL O.S. 83 (E)

20 IFC 2113: 175-178 (1976, *Banshee* Questionnaire), Iffa and Offa East, St Mary's, CLONMEL O.S. 83 (E)

21 IFC 1840: 337. Information from Séan Ó Maolchathaigh. Dialects Archive index cards, University College, Dublin, Iffa and Offa East, St Mary's, CLONMEL O.S. 83 (I)

22 Mr and Mrs S.C. Hall, *Ireland: its Scenery, Character &c.*, III, London (1843) p.105, Iffa and Offa East, St. Mary's, CLONMEL O.S. 83 (E)

23 IFCS 829: 266-267, Ikerrin, Corbally, KNOCK O.S. 18 (E)

24 IFCS 582: 166, Kilnamanagh Lwr, Ballintemple, DUNDRUM O.S. 51, 52, 59, 60 (E)

25 *Ireland's Own* LXXIV, 16 Aug. 1941, p.14 Kilnamanagh Lwr, Ballintemple, DUNDRUM O.S. 51, 52, 59, 60 (E)

26 IFCS 583: 210-211 (cf. *Béaloideas* XLII-XLIV, 1974-1976 (1977), p.96), Kilnamanagh, Clonoulty, BALLAGH O.S. 52 (E)

27 IFC 266: 18 (1935), Kilnamanagh Lwr, Clonoulty, BALLAGH O.S. 52 (E)

28 IFCS 542: 373, Kilnamanagh Upr, Templebeg, KILCOMMON O.S.

39 (E)

29 IFCS 543: 234, Kilnamanagh Upr, Upperchurch, UPPERCHURCH O.S. 40 (E)

30 St. J. D. Seymour & H.L. Neligan, *True Irish Ghost Stories*, p.198 (1926), Kilnamanagh Upr, Toem, CAPPAWHITE O.S. 51 (E)

31 *"Lageniensis"*, (Canon John O'Hanlon), *Irish Folk Lore*, p. 64-68, 1870, Lwr Ormond, Terryglass, TERRYGLASS O.S. 6 (E)

32 IFCS 555: 10, Middlethird, Magorban, COLERAINE O.S. 61 (E)

33 IFCS 554: 209, Middlethird, Fethard, FETHARD O.S. 70 and CASHEL O.S. 61 (E)

34 IFCS 556: 27, Middlethird, Cashel, CASHEL O.S. 61 (E)

35 IFCS 556: 29, Middlethird, Cashel, CASHEL O.S. 61 (E)

36 IFCS 539: 56-57 (1938), Owney and Arra, Kilcomenty, BIRDHILL O.S. 25, 31 (E)

37 IFCS 539: 126 (1938), Owney and Arra, Kilcomenty, BIRDHILL O.S. 25, 31 (E)

38 IFCS 539: 129 (1938), Owney and Arra, Kilcomenty, CRAGG O.S. 31 (E)

39 IFCS 540: 129-130, Owney and Arra, Kilnarath, FIDDANE O.S. 31, 32 (E)

40 IFCS 540: 159-160, Owney and Arra, Kilnarath, KNOCKFUNE O.S. 32, 38 (E)

41 IFC 2113: 179-183 (1976, Letter), Slieveardagh, Buolick, BAWN-REIGH O.S. 42, 48 (E)

42 IFC 2113: 184-191 (1976, *Banshee* Questionnaire), Slieveardagh, Buolick, GORTNAHOE O.S. 43 (E)

43 *Ireland's Own* LXIV, No. 1671, 15 Dec. 1934, p. 14, Slieveardagh, Graystown, BALLINURE O.S. 53 (E)

44 IFC 2113: 193-196 (1976, *Banshee* Questionnaire), Slieveardagh, Killenaule, KILLENAULE O.S. 54 (E)

45 IFC 2113: 196-197, Upr Kilnamanagh, Toem, BROWNBOG O.S. 51 (E)

46 IFC 2113: 204-205 (1976, Letter), Upr Ormond, Templederry, DAWSONBOG O.S. 33 (E)

47 'The Banshee of the Branleys', *Ireland's Own*, 16 Aug. 1947, p.4, Co. Tipperary.

48 The MacCarthy Banshee, in T. Crofton Croker, 'Legends of the Banshee', *Fairy Legends and Traditions of the South of Ireland*, pp. 208-237 (1826). This story also appears in W.B. Yeats, ed., *Fairy and Folk Tales of the Irish Peasantry*, p. 113-127 (1888) and in subsequent editions of the book, e.g. in *Irish Fairy and Folk Tales*, pp. 113-127 (n.d.), *Irish Folk Stories and Fairy Tales*, pp. 101-118 (n.d.), *Fairy and Folk Tales of Ireland*, pp. 104-115 (1973) and in *Weird Tales. By Irish Writers*, pp. 172-192 (n.d.). It appears in translation in *Irländska Folksagor*, pp. 87-97, Stockholm, 1839. W.-E. Peuchert, ed., *Gebrüder Grimm. Irische Elfenmärchen* [1826], pp. 120-134, (1948) and in Fritz Krog, ed., *Irische Elfenmärchen der Brüder Grimm*, [1826], pp. 117-132 (1980).

Tyrone (Tyr.) Ulster

1   IFC 2111: 297 (1960, UFTM notebook), Clogher, Clogher, CLOGHER O.S. 58, 59, 64, 65 (E)

2   IFC 2110: 204-205 (1976, *Banshee* Questionnaire), Omagh East, Drumragh, OMAGH O.S. 34 (E)

3   IFC 1842: 225-226 (1976), Omagh East, Dromore, CORRASHESKIN O.S. 42, 50 (E)

4   IFC 1842: 288-290 (1976), Omagh West, Longfield, DRUMQUIN O.S. 33 (E)

5   IFC 2110: 206 (1976, *Banshee* Questionnaire), Omagh East, Urney, CASTLEDERG O.S. 16 (E)

6   IFC 2110: 208-210 (1976, *Banshee* Questionnaire), Omagh West, Termonamongan, AGHYARAN O.S. 23 (E)

7   *Ulster Folklife* VI, 1960, p.40, Strabane, Ardstraw, DRUMCLAMPH O.S. 16, 24 (E)

8   IFC 2110: 211-239, a comparative survey of Banshees in Mid-and West-Tyrone submitted by Form 1T (31 pupils) of St Patrick's Secondary Intermediate School, Omagh, as their entry for Feis Thír Eoghain 1977. Survey areas: Arvalee, Carrickamulkin, Carrickmore, Cashel, Cloughfin, Coneyglen, Crock Cullion, Derryvard, Dooish, Dregish, Dromore, Drumlea, Drumquin, Eskra, Formil, Glenhull, Gortin, Greencastle, Killadroy, Killybrack, Killyclogher, Knockmoyle, Limavaddy (Co. Derry), Mullaslin, Omagh, Seskinore, Sheskinsale, Sixmilecross, Slatequarry (East Tyrone), Tattyreagh, Tybane (E)

9   Jeanne Copper Foster, *Ulster Folklore*, p. 16 (1951). Cf. also Sheila St. Clair, *Folklore of the Ulster People*, p. 20 (1971), Clogher Valley (E)

Waterford (Wat), Munster

1   IFC 2113: 219 (1977, Letter), Coshmore & Coshbride, Lismore & Mocollop, BALLYDUFF O.S. 20 (E)

2   IFC 2113: 220 (1977, Letter), Coshmore & Coshbride, Lismore & Mocollop, BALLYSAGGART O.S. 21, 21 (E)

3   IFCS 638: 235-236, Coshmore & Coshbride, Tallow, TALLOW O.S. 28 (E)

4   IFCS 640: 316 (1939), Decies within Drum, Clashmore, BALLY-CURRANE O.S. 35, 38 (E)

5   IFCS 640: 351, Decies within Drum, Clashmore, ARDSALLAGH O.S. 37 (E)

6   Very Rev. P. Canon Power, *The Place-Names of Decies*, p. 55, 1952, Coshmore & Coshbride, Lismore & Moycollop, ROSGRILLA O.S. 29 (E).

7   IFCS 643: 174, Decies within Drum, Ardmore, MOUNTSTUART O.S. 35 (E)

8   IFCS 643: 175, Decies within Drum, Ardmore, MOUNTSTUART O.S. 35 (E)
9   Very Rev. P. Canon Power, *The Place-Names of Decies*, p. 80, (1952), Decies within Drum, Ardmore, FARRANGARRIT O.S. 40 (E)
10   IFCS 643: 99-100, Decies within Drum, Aglish, VILLIERSTOWN O.S. 29 (E)
11   IFC 955: 172 (1943, *Bogey* Questionnaire), Decies within Drum, Ringagonagh, RING O.S. 36 (I)
12   IFC 259: 518 (1936), Decies within Drum; Ballymacart, REAMANAGH O.S. 36 (I)
13   IFC 259: 616 (1936), Decies within Drum, Dungarvan, GLASMORE O.S. 37 (I)
14   IFC 150: 477 (1935), Decies within Drum, Ringagonagh, BALLY— NAGAUL O.S. 36 (I)
15   IFCS 642: 222, Decies within Drum, Ringagonagh, MWEELAHORNA O.S. 36 (I)
16   IFCS 642: 237 (cf. *Béaloideas* XLII-XLIV, 1974-1976 (1977) p.107), Decies within Drum, Ringagonagh, BALLYNACOURTY O.S. 36 (I)
17   IFCS 642: 437, Decies within Drum, Grange, GRANGE O.S. 38 (I)
18   IFCS 641: 124-126, Decies within Drum, Ardmore, BARRANA- STOOK O.S. 36, 39 (I)
19   IFC 1710: 436-437 (1928), Decies without Drum, Ballylaneen, BALLYGARRAN O.S. 24 (E)
20   R.B. Breatnach, ed., *Seana-Chaint na nDéise* II, pp.35, 277, 1961, Decies within Drum, Ringagonagh, KNOCKANPOWER O.S. 36 (I)
21   IFC 259: 488 (1936), Decies without Drum, Dungarvan, DUN- GAVAN O.S. 31 (E)
22   IFC 84: 293-294 (1932), (*Béaloideas* VI, 1936, p. 220, no. 108), Decies without Drum, Seskinan, BLEANTASOUR O.S. 13, 14 (I)
23   IFCS 648: 60, Decies without Drum, Kilrossanty, KILROSSANTY O.S. 23 (E)
24   IFCS 648: 211, Decies without Drum, Ballylaneen, BUNMAHON O.S. 24, 25 (E)
25   IFCS 648: 225-226, Decies without Drum, Ballylaneen, BUNMAHON O.S. 24, 25 (E)
26   IFCS 648: 230, Decies without Drum, Ballylaneen, BUNMAHON O.S. 24, 25 (E)
27   IFCS 648: 245-246, Decies without Drum, Ballylaneen, BUNMAHON O.S. 24, 25 (E)
28   IFCS 648: 322, Decies without Drum, Ballylaneen, BUNMAHON O.S. 24, 25 (E)
29   IFCS 648: 327-328, Decies without Drum, Ballylaneen, BUNMAHON O.S. 24, 25 (E)
30   IFCS 645: 57-58 (cf. *Béaloideas* XLII-XLIV, 1974-1976 (1977), p.104), Decies without Drum, Dungarvan, DUNGARVAN O.S. 31 (I)

31 IFCS 645: 246, Decies without Drum, Dungarvan, DUNGARVAN O.S. 31 (I)
32 IFCS 645: 70-71 (cf. *Béaloideas* XLII-XLIV, 1974-1976 (1977), pp.99, 107), Drum, Dungarvan, DUNGARVAN O.S. 31 (I)
33 *Béaloideas* XIV, 1944 (1945), p.109, Decies without Drum, Modelligo MODELLIGO O.S. 22 (I)
34 *Transactions of the Ossianic Society* 11, 1854 (1855), pp. 104-5, 109-110, Decies without Drum, Modelligo, MOUNTAIN CASTLE O.S. 22 (E)
35 IFC 2113: 221-224 (1976 *Banshee* Questionnaire), Decies without Drum, Rossmire, KILMOYLIN O.S. 15, 16, 24 (E)
36 IFCS 644: 101 (cf. *Béaloideas* XLII-XLIV, 1974-1976 (1977),p.99), Seskinan, CAHERNALEAGUE, O.S. 13 (I)
37 IFCS 644: 102-103, Decies without Drum, Seskinan, CAHERNA-LEAGUE O.S. 13 (I)
38 IFCS 644: 104, Decies without Drum, Seskinan, CAHERNALEAGUE O.S. 13 (I)
39 IFC 372: 354 (1937), Decies without Drum, Stradbally, STRAD-BALLY O.S. 24, 32 (I)
40 IFC 696: 233-236 (1940), Gaultiere, St. Johns Without, BALLY-TRUCKLE O.S. 9 (E)
41 IFC 33: 68-69 (1933), (cf.*Béaloideas* IX, 1939, pp. 39-40), Gaultiere, Kilea, DUNMORE O.S. 27 (I)
42 IFC 33: 69 (1933) (cf. *Béaloideas* IX, 1939, p.39), Gaultiere, Kilea, DUNMORE O.S. 27 (I)
43 IFC 33: 69-70 (1933) (cf. *Béaloideas* IX, 1939, p.39), Gaultiere, Kilea, DUNMORE O.S. 27 (I)
44 IFC 33: 70 (1933), Gaultiere, Kilea, DUNMORE O.S. 27 (I)
45 IFC 955: 169 (1943, *Bogey* Questionnaire), Gaultiere, Kill St. Nicholas, PASSAGE EAST O.S. 18 (E)
46 IFC 85: 238-239 (1931), (cf.*Béaloideas* III, 1932, p.283), Glenahiry, Kilronan, BALLYMACARBRY O.S. 5 (I)
47 IFC 2133: 225-229 (1976, *Banshee* Questionnaire), Sliabh gCua area (I)
48 IFC 84: 40-41 (1932), Middlethird, Islandikane, FENNOR O.S. 25, 26 (I)
49 IFC 372: 369 (1937), Upperthird, Mothel, KILCLOONEY O.S. 6, 7, 14, 15 (I)
50 IFCS 655: 173-174 (cf. *Béaloideas* XLII-XLIV, 1974-1976 (1977), p. 96), Upr Third, Rathgormack, RATHGORMACK O.S. 3 (E)
51 *(Ireland's Own* IX, No. 225, 13 Mar 1907, p. 31, Upr Third, Clona-gam, CURRAGHMORE O.S. 3, 4, 7, 8 (E)
52 Mr and Mrs S.C. Hall, *Ireland, Its Scenery, Character &c.* III, p. 107, Co. Waterford (E)
53 *Folk-Lore* XXV,1914, pp. 109-111, 121, Decies without Drum, Co. Waterford (E)

Westmeath (Wmea.), Leinster

1 IFCS 746: 259, Clonlonan, Ballyloughloe, BEALIN O.S. 29, 30, (E)
2 IFC 2112: 158-162 (1976, *Banshee* Questionnaire), Clonlonan, Kilcleagh, MOATE O.S. 30 (E)
3 IFC 1677: 559-560, 562-565 (1964) (cf. *Béaloideas* XLII-XLIV, 1974-1976 (1977), p.95), Clonlonan, Kilcleagh, BALLINLASSY O.S. 35, 36 (E)
4 IFC 2112: 165-168 (1976, *Banshee* Questionnaire), Delvin, Castletowndelvin, Delvin O.S. 14 (E)
5 IFC 1890: 42-50; (a) Delvin, Castletowndelvin, MOYLEROE O.S. 9, 14, pp.42, 43, 50, (b) Delvin, Castletowndelvin, DELVIN O.S. 14, pp.43-45, (c) Delvin, Killua, CLONMELLON O.S. 9, p.44 (E)
6 IFCS 724: 121 (cf. *Béaloideas* XLII-XLIV, 1974-1976 (1977), p.98), Delvin, Castletowndelvin, MOYLEROE O.S. 8, 9, 14 (E)
7 IFCS 724: 122, Delvin, Castletowndelvin, MOYLEROE O.S. 8, 9, 14 (E)
8 IFCS 724: 123-124, Delvin, Castletowndelvin, MOYLEROE O.S. 8, 9, 14 (E)
9 IFCS 725: 340-341, Delvin, Castletowndelvin, ROSMEAD O.S. 9, 14 (E)
10 IFC 1840: 333-335 (1978), Farbill, Killucan, KINNEGAD O.S. 27, 28 (E)
11 IFC 1840: 323-332 (1978), Farbill, Killucan, KINNEGAD O.S. 27, 28 (E)
12 Patrick Bardan, *The Dead-Watchers, And Other Folk-Lore Tales of Westmeath*, pp. 18, 52, 82, (1891), Farbill, Kilcullan, CORALSTOWN, O.S. 27 (E)
13 IFCS 727: 3-4, Farbill, Killucan, RIVERDALE O.S. 21, 28 (E)
14 IFCS 731: 525, Fartullagh, Clonfad, TYRRELSPASS O.S. 39 (E)
15 IFCS 721: 199-200, Fore, RATHGARVE, CASTLEPOLLARD School O.S. 3, 7, (from Patrick Bardan's *The Dead-Watchers, And Other Folk-Lore Tales of Westmeath*, cf. 12 above) (E)
16 IFC 2112: 169-171 (1976, Letter), Kilkenny West, Noughaval, CLONKEEN O.S. 15, 16, (E)
17 IFC 1888: 143 (1974, *Wellerisms* Questionnaire), Moyashel and Magheradernon, MULLINGAR O.S. 19 (E)
18 IFC 954: 92 (1943, *Bogey* Questionnaire), Moycashel, Kilbeggan, KILBEGGAN O.S. 38 (E)
19 IFCS 741: 195-196, Moygoish, Russagh, RUSSAGH O.S. 6 (E)
20 IFC 741: 196, Moygoish, Kilmacnevin, EMPER O.S. 10 (E)
21 IFCS 744: 43-44, Rathconrath, Killara, KILLEENBRACK O.S. 34 (E)

Wexford (Wex.), Leinster

1 IFC 96: 275 (1928), Ballaghkeen, Kilmackilloge, GOREY O.S. 6, 7 (E)

2   IFCS 887: 162, Ballaghkeen, Kilmuckridge, KILMUCKRIDGE School O.S. 22 (E)
3   IFC 544: 339-340 (1938), Bantry, Carnagh, CUSHENSTOWN O.S. 30, 35 (E)
4   IFC 544: 207-212 (1938), Bantry, Carnagh, CUSHENSTOWN O.S. 30, 35 (E)
5   IFC 544: 328-329 (1938), Bantry, Carnagh, CUSHENSTOWN O.S. 30, 35 (E)
6   IFCS 902: 245, Bantry, Clonmore, BREE O.S. 25, 31 (E)
7   IFCS 902: 251, Bantry, Clonmore, BREE O.S. 25, 31 (E)
8   IFC 1796: 432-434 (1973), Bantry, Killann, RATHNURE 18, 24 (E)
9   IFC 1796: 434-436 (1973), Bantry, Killann, RATHNURE O.S. 18, 24 (E)
10   IFCS 897: 151-152, Bantry, St Mary's, NEW ROSS O.S. 29 (E)
11   IFC 1840: 336-337 (1980), Bantry, St. Mary's, NEW ROSS O.S. 29 (E)
12   IFCS 901: 60, Bantry, Templeludigan, TEMPLELUDIGAN O.S. 24 (E)
13   IFC 107: 27-29 (1935), Bargy, Ambrosetown, KNOCKBINE O.S. 41, 46 (E)
14   IFCS 876: 41, Bargy, Bannow, BANNOW O.S. 45, 50 (E)
15   *Éigse* V, 1945-1947, 103, 104, Bargy, Bannow, BANNOW, O.S. 45, 46 50 (I)
16   IFC 2112: 173 (1976, Letter), Bargy, Duncormick, DUNCORMICK O.S. 46 (E)
17   IFC 2112: 174-175 (1976, *Banshee* Questionnaire, Welsh reply). Bargy, Duncormick, DUNCORMICK O.S. 46 (E)
18   IFC 54: 177 (1935), Bargy, Duncormick, DUNCORMICK O.S. 46 (E)
19   a) IFC 2112: 179-185 (1976, *Banshee* Questionnaire), Bargy, Kilmore, Nemestown O.S. 52, Mrs Elizabth Jefferies
      b) Notebook of Mrs Jefferies containing dialect words in the baronies of Forth and Bargy, dated 28 Feb. 1968, pp.40-41 (E)
20   IFC 96: 317 (1928), = IFC 94: 45. Forth, Carn, BALLYFANE O.S. 53 (E)
21   IFCS 897: 210-211, Forth, Kilscoran, TAGOAT O.S. 48 (E)
22   IFC 2112: 186-187 (1976 *Banshee* Questionnaire) Forth, Wexford, WEXFORD O.S. 37 (E)
23   IFC 2112: 187-192 (1976 *Banshee* Questionnaire), Forth, St Michael's, BALLYKNOCKAN O.S. 48 (E)
24   IFCS 881: 343, Forth, St. John's WEXFORD O.S. 37 (E)
25   IFCS 880: 334, Forth, Wexford, WEXFORD Christian Brothers' School O.S. 37 (E)
26   IFCS 880: 335, Forth, St Margaret's, DRINAGH O.S. 48, 53 (E)
27   IFCS 880: 336, Forth, Wexford, WEXFORD O.S. 37 (E)
28   IFCS 880: 337-338, Forth, Wexford, WEXFORD O.S. 37 (E)
29   IFCS 880: 339, Forth, Wexford, WEXFORD O.S. 37 (E)
30   IFCS 880: 339, Forth, Wexford, WEXFORD O.S. 37 (E)
31   IFCS 880: 340, Forth, Wexford, WEXFORD O.S. 37 (E)
32   IFCS 880: 340-341, Forth, Wexford, WEXFORD O.S. 37 (E)

33   IFCS 880: 342, Forth, Wexford, WEXFORD O.S. 37 (E)
34   *Enniscorthy Guardian*, Sat. 29 May 1965, (Pat O'Leary Column), Forth, Wexford, WEXFORD, O.S. 37
35   *Enniscorthy Guardian*, Sat. 14 Oct. 1967 (Pat O'Leary Column), Forth, Wexford, WEXFORD, O.S. 37.
36   *Wexford People*, 9 July 1976, (Pat O'Leary Column), Forth, Wexford, WEXFORD, O.S. 37
37   *Wexford People*, Fri. 16 July 1967, (Pat O'Leary Column), Forth, Wexford, WEXFORD, O.S. 37
38   IFC 2112: 200-203 (1976, *Banshee* Questionnaire), Forth, Wexford, WEXFORD O.S. 37 (E)
39   IFC 2112; 204-205 (1976, *Banshee* Questionnaire), Forth, Maudlintown, MULGANNON O.S. 37, 42 (E)
40   IFC 2112: 209-210 (1976, *Banshee* Questionnaire), Gorey, Kilcormick, BALLYTRACEY O.S. 16, 21 (E)
41   IFC 2112: 210-212 (1976, Banshee Questionnaire), Gorey, Kilcormick, BOLEYVOGUE O.S. 16, 21 (E)
42   IFC 1903, 147-154 (1977), Gorey, Ballycanew, BALLINCLARE O.S. 16, 17 (E)
43   IFCS 889: 73-74, Gorey, Kilnahue, MONASEED O.S. 2, 6 (E)
44   IFC 889: 200-203, Gorey, Ballycanew, BOLINREADY O.S. 16 (E)
45   IFC 1059: 70-72 (1939), Gorey, Kilcormick, BOLEYVOGUE O.S. 16, 21 (E)
46   IFC 1059: 72 (1939), Gorey, Kilcormick, CARRIGEEN O.S. 15, 16 (E)
47   IFCS 890: 116, Gorey, Kilcormick, BALLYTRACEY O.S 16, 21 (E)
48   IFC 2112: 214-215 (1976, *Banshee* Questionnaire), Scarawalsh, Kilbride, CLOLOGE O.S. 16 (E)
49   IFCS 896: 150, Scarawalsh, Kilbride, BALLYMORE O.S. 16 (E)
50   IFC 2112: 216-220 (1976, Letter), Shelburne, Ballybrazil, GARRAGHDUFF O.S. 34, 39 (E)
51   IFCS 870: 137, Shelburne, Templetown, TEMPLETOWN O.S. 49, 50 (E)
52   IFCS 871: 10, Shelburne, Tintern, BALLYCULLANE School O.S. 40, (E)
53   IFCS 871: 63, Shelburne, Tintern, SALTMILLS O.S. 45 (E)
54   IFCS 885: 180, Shelmaliere East, Ardcavan, CASTLEBRIDGE O.S. 32, 37 (E)
55   IFCS 885: 181, Shelmaliere East, Ardcavan, CASTLEBRIDGE O.S. 32, 37 (E)
56   IFC 544: 432 (1938), Shelmaliere East, Ballynaslaney, BALLYNASLANEY O.S. 32 (E)
57   IFC 460: 262 (1938), (cf. *Béaloideas* XLII-XLIV, 1974-1976 (1977), p. 96), Shelmaliere West, Ballymitty, BALLYMITTY O.S. 41 (E)
58   IFC 544: 25-26 (1938), Shelmaliere West, Clongeen, CLONGEEN O.S. 40 (E)
59   IFC 544: 75 (1938), Shelmaliere West, Clongeen, CLONGEEN O.S. 40 (E)

60   IFC 437: 29-30 (1937), Shelmaliere East, Artamon, GALYBALLY
O.S. 37 (E)
61   IFC 437: 188 (1937), Shelmaliere West, Kilgarvan, KILGARVAN
O.S. 36 (E)
62   *The Past* VIII, 1970, pp.46-47 (E)

WICKLOW (Wick.), Leinster

1   IFCS 924: 53, Arklow, Arklow, ARKLOW O.S. 40, 45 (E)
2   IFC Schools' Copybooks, Box 925B. Arklow, Castlemacadam,
KILMACOO O.S. 35 (E)
3   IFC Schools' Copybooks, Box 925B, Arknlow, Castlemacadam,
KILMACOO O.S. 35 (E)
4   IFC Schools' Copybooks, Box 925B, Arklow, Castlemacadam,
KILMACOO O.S. 35 (E)
5   IFC Schools' Copybooks, Box 925B, Arklow, Castlemacadam,
KILMACOO O.S. 35 (E)
6   IFC Schools' Copybooks, Box 925B, Arklow, Castlemacadam,
KILMACOO O.S. 35 (E)
7   IFC Schools's Copybooks, Box 925B, Arklow, Castlemacadam,
TEMPLELUSK O.S. 35, 40 (E)
8   IFCS 921: 154, Ballinacor South, Ballykine, Aughrim O.S. 34,
39 (E)
9   IFC 2112: 221-222 (1976, *Banshee* Questionnaire) 'Carlow-Wicklow
Border' Rathvilly and Ballinacor, Hacketstown-Killaveney O.S. Co.
Carlow, 415, Co. Wicklow, 4, 38, 39, 43, 44 (E)
10   IFCS 888: 200, Ballinacor South, Kilpipe, KILLAVENEY O.S. 38,
39, 43, 44 (E)
11   IFC 1840: 275-279 (1976), Rathdown, Powerscourt, ENNISKERRY
area O.S. 7, (E)
12   IFCS 924: 74, Upr Talbotstown, Freynestown, FREYNESTOWN
O.S. 21 (E)
13   IFCS 924: 75-76, Upr Talbotstown, Ballymure, GRANGECON
O.S. 20 (E)
14   IFC Schools' Copybooks. Upr Talbotstown, Kiltegan, RATHDAN-
GAN O.S. 28 (E)
15   *Irisleabhar na Gaedhilge* XII, 1902, p. 96, Upr Talbotstown, Baltin-
glass, KILMURRY O.S. 27 (E)

2. Traditional material in American and Canadian Scources

USA

1   IFC 2112: 223 (1977, Letter), Iowa, Rockwell City
2   IFC 2112: 224-229 (1977, Letter, *Banshee* Questionnaire), 1976
     Massachusetts, Agawan
3   IFC 2114: 190-196 (1982, USA Tape no. 3 by Séamus Ó Catháin
     Leo Corduff), Massachusetts, Northampton
4   IFC 2112: 230-232 (1977, Letter *Banshee* Questionnaire 1976),
     New Jersey, Irvington
5   IFC 2112: 232-234 (1977, *Banshee* Questionnaire 1976), Pennsyl-
     vania N.E.
6   IFC 2112: 235-242 (1977, Letter, *Banshee* Questionnaire 1976),
     Pennsylvania, Philadelphia
7   IFC 2112: 243 (1977, Letter), Washington, Bainbridge Island
8   'The Banshee of the Sheridans', *The Irish Packet* VII, no. 176, Feb.
     9, 1907, p. 473, Nebraska.

Canada

1   [The Banshee of the O'Grady's], Lady Wilde, *Ancient Legends,
     Mystic Charms and Supersititions of Ireland,* p. 260, 1887

3. Traditional material of indefinite provenance in printed works

William Allingham, *Poems by William Allingham*, selected and arranged by Helen Allingham, 'The Ban-Shee', pp. 43-46

S. Baring-Gould, *Curious Myths of the Middle Ages*, pp.488-493

J. Benwick, *Irish Druids and Old Irish Religion*, p.91

Mary E. Braddon, *Joshua Haggard's Daughter* I, p.67

E. Cobham Brewer, The Reader's *Handbook of Allusions, References, Plots and Stories*, p.76

K. Briggs *The Anatomy of Puck*, Appendix 1, p. 184

K. Briggs, *A Dictionary of Fairies*, pp.14, 15, 20, 61

Pádraic Colum, ed., *A Treasury of Irish Folklore*, pp. 396-397

T. Crofton Croker, *Researches in the South of Ireland*, p.91

T. Crofton Croker, *Fairy Legends and Traditions of the South of Ireland*, III, 1828, p.10

Alice Dease, *Mother Erin*, pp.73-76

Funk and Wagnalls *Standard Dictionary of Folklore, Mythology and Legend*, pp. 31, 133, 202, ed., Leach, Maria

George Laurence Gomme, ed., *English Traditions and Foreign Customs*, pp.15-17

Gerald Griffin, *Tales of the Munster Festivals*, II p.90

[P. D. Hardy], ed., *Characteristic Sketches of Ireland and the Irish*, p. 207

E. Hayes, ed., *The Ballads of Ireland* II, pp.113-114

W. Henderson, *Notes on the Folk-Lore of the Northern Counties of England and the Borders*, p. 344

Herbert F. Hore, 'Origin of the Irish Superstitions Regarding Banshees and Fairies', *Journal of the Royal Society of Antiquaries of Ireland* XXV, 1895, pp.115-129

Eleanor Hull, *Folklore of the British Isles*, pp.59-60

Douglas Hyde, 'An Bhean-Sidhe', *The Irish Packet*, I, No. 7, Oct. 1903, p. 24, VII, No. 176, Feb. 9, 1907, p. 437

Ireland's Own II, No. 34, 15 July 1903, p. 31; IV, No. 104, 16 Nov. 1904, p.3; XII, No. 312, 11 Nov. 1908, p.4; XLII, No. 1080, 15 Aug. 1923, p. 106; LXXIV, No. 1974, 23 Aug. 1941, p.3; LXXXI, No. 3015, 28 Sept. 1946, p. 16

Irish Independent, 30 December 1932

Journal of the Cork Historical and Archaeological Society III, May 1894, No. 29, pp. 133-135

P.W. Joyce, *A Social History of Ancient Ireland*, I, p. 264

Thomas Keightley, *The Fairy Mythology* II, p.179

G.H. Kinahan, 'Notes on Irish Folk-Lore', *Folk-Lore Record*, IV, 1881, pp.121-122

Rev. Michael P. Mahon, *Ireland's Fairy Lore*, pp.26, 27

Brinsley MacNamara, *The Valley of the Squinting Windows*, pp.100-101

Samuel McSkimin, *The History of Antiquities of the County of the town of Carrickfergus*, p. 258

The Banshee

Pádraig Ó Canainn, *eag., Filidheacht na nGaedheal, Uimh.* 95, pp. 116-117

Elliot O'Donnell, *The Banshee, c. 1920*

John O'Donovan ed., 'Elegy on the Death of the Rev. Edmond Kavanagh, by the Rev. James O'Lalor', *The Journal of the Kilkenny and South-East of Ireland Archaeological Society,* I, new ser., 1856-1857, Dublin 1858, pp 118-143.

John O'Neill, *Handerahan, the Irish Fairyman and Legends of Carrick,* with an introduction by Mrs. S.C. Hall, pp.6-7

Thomas Pennant, *A Tour in Scotland,* 1769, p.186

Sir Walter Scott, 'The Lady of the Lake', Canto III, *'The Poetical Works of Sir Walter Scott,* Logie, R.J., ed., p. 231 and notes p. 291-292

Sir Walter Scott, letter to Crofton Croker, 27th April, 1825, included in Preface of *Fairy Legends and Traditions of the South of Ireland,* 2nd ed. London, 1826, pp. VII-VIII.

Sir Walter Scott, *Letters on Demonology and Witchcraft,* p. 184, The Family Library Edition No. XVI

St. J.D. Seymour and H.L. Neligan, *True Irish Ghost Stories,* pp.202, 204, 2nd. ed.

The Shamrock XI, No. 390, April 4, 1874, p. 440

Sheila St. Clair, *Psychic Phenomena in Ireland,* pp. 58-59

John Todhunter, *The Banshee and other Poems,* pp.3-7

W.Y. Evans Wentz, *The Fairy Faith in Celtic Countries,* pp.283-307

Lady Wilde, *Ancient Legends, Mystic Charms and Superstitions of Ireland,* I, pp. 259-263

W.G. Wood-Martin, *Traces of the Elder Faiths in Ireland* I, pp.364-369

W.B. Yeats: *Fairy and Folk Tales of the Irish Peasantry,* pp. 109-127, and subsequent re-issues under various titles (see Bibliography)

For additional information on printed sources see bibliography.

Notes and References

Introduction

1   See Lysaght, 1974-6, 1978, 1979, 1985, 1986, 1996 and Sorlin 1991, and cf. Lysaght, 1990, 1994 ('Traditional beliefs ...'), 1995 ('Visible Death ...'), Connolly, 1991, Ó hÓgáin, 1994, pp. 45-6 and Bodley 1996 and note 2 below. The variety of approaches and interpretation from different disciplines is indicative of the richness of the death-messenger tradition.

2   The fact that the composer Seóirse Bodley in his poetic text for music (*The Banshee: Poetic Text for Music* published in full in *Sinsear* 8, 1996, pp. 111-117, excerpts from which appeared on the dust-jacket of the first edition of the present study — *The Banshee* (1986)), has drawn on, and has been inspired by, some of the extracts from the folklore manuscripts, is an indication of the benefit of the liberal use of quotations.

3   For some reason these collections have been afforded only complementary status in Sorlin (1991, p. 12)

4   The earliest volumes of the Main Manuscripts were brought together as a result of the efforts of *An Cumann le Béaloideas Éireann* (The Folklore of Ireland Society 1927-), *Institiúd Bhéaloideasa Éireann* (Irish Folklore Institute 1930-1935), and *An Coimisiún Béaloideas Éireann* (the Irish Folklore Commission, 1935-1971); subsequent volumes have been added since the Commission was replaced by the Department of Irish Folklore in 1971, and now number 2238.
In this study, however, death-messenger material received after 1980 (except replies to the Banshee Questionnaire (cf. 9 below), is not included in this work unless it is of particular significance.

5   Of the 222 accounts 173 are in English and 49 are in Irish. The majority (29) of the records in Irish are from Munster (Cork: 2; Kerry: 13; Waterford: 14), while Connaught has 17 (Galway: 13; Mayo: 4) and Ulster has 3 (all from Donegal). There are no Irish-language accounts from Leinster.

6   Of these 392 items, 364 are in English and 28 are in Irish. Most of the records in Irish (20) stem from Munster (Clare 2; Cork 3; Kerry 4; Limerick 1; Waterford 10). In Connaught there are seven (Galway 6; Mayo 1); there is one from Donegal in Ulster and there are none from Leinster.

7   These records are now bound in manuscript 2111, pp. 279-323, in the manuscript archive of The Department of Irish Folklore, University College Dublin. Linda-May Ballard, Ulster Folk and Transport Museum, is to be thanked for supplying these references. As the exact provenance of one reference (Down 26) is unclear, it does not appear on Map 1.

8   The questionnaire was also used by a group of school-children in Omagh, Co. Tyrone, in a survey of banshee traditions in mid- and west-Tyrone (Tyrone 7), and by another group in Holywood, Co. Down (Down 18 to 25). The geographical distribution of these questionnaire replies is shown on Map 1. It is evident, however, that the children were unable to handle such a detailed inquiry, and owing to their poor source value these replies are not used in the body of the text.

9   The requests for the Banshee Questionnaire from America arose from a short article called 'Hunting the Elusive Banshee' in Dúchas, July-Aug, 1977 (publication of the Irish-American Cultural Institute, St. Paul, Minnesota, USA). The Welsh request arose from newspaper items about the *bow* (see Chapter 1 for this name for the banshee) by Nicholas Furlong (alias Pat O'Leary) in the *Wexford People*, 9-16, July 1976, (cf. Apendix 5, Wex. 36-37). Nearly all the replies to the initial circulation of the questionnaire were received by 1979. Occasional replies received after 1 January 1980 — often as a result of individual interest in the subject — are not included unless they contain additional significant material.

10   Of the 132 questionnaire replies from Ireland only seven were in Irish — three from Galway in Connaught, one each from Cork, Kerry and Waterford in Munster, and the remaining one from Donegal in Ulster. There were no replies in Irish from Leinster. Four of the 132 replies were negative (Down 2; Galway 3, 4; Kerry 10).

11   Cf. note 9 above.

12   Full-time collectors were and are salaried, full-time collectors in the field. Special collectors were people who were employed on a part-time salaried basis as collectors in their own home areas. The Irish Folklore Commission 1935-1970 used the services of four special collectors; Seán Ó Dubhda (Dingle Peninsula, Co. Kerry, 1 April 1954 — 31 Jan 1962), Pádraig Ó Moghráin (west-Mayo, 1 April 1954 — 31 March 1956), Micheál Mac Éinrí (west-Mayo, 1 April 1954-31 Dec 1964) and Prionnsias de Búrca (Connemara and south-Mayo, 1 Jan 1953 — 1 Oct 1964).

13   Part-time collectors were, and are, unsalaried people who in their spare time collect what they can, usually in their home areas, and are paid a certain agreed fee depending on the quality of their work, per standard notebook.

14   The original school copy-books in which the material collected by the children was written in the first instance are preserved in the manuscript archive of the Department of Irish Folklore, University College Dublin, and are arranged according to the participating schools. It is obvious from even a summary perusal of these that what was re-written into the official notebooks was not the total material collected. Due to the quantity of this copy-book material and its unindexed state it has not been possible for me to use it in full, although I have included it on a few occasions, e.g., Wick. 2-7.

15 The booklet consisting of fifty-five topics and entitled *Irish Folklore and Tradition* (37 pp.)/ *Béaloideas Éireann* (38 pp.) was prepared in 1937 by Seán Ó Súilleabháin, Archivist in the Irish Folklore Commission, 1935-1970, and The Department of Irish Folklore, 1971-1974.

16 Tracking down references to the death-messenger in printed sources, including popular nineteenth- and twentieth-century magazines, was facilitated by reference to the subject index (section J, *sub bean sí*) in the archive of the Department of Irish Folklore, as well as to the bibliography in Ó Súilleabháin and Christiansen, *The Types of the Irish Folktale*, 1963, 1968, and to *A Bibliography of Irish Ethnology and Folk Tradition* (1978) by C. Ó Danachair.

17 *An Claidheamh Soluis and Fáinne ,an Lae,* 17 *Lúnasa* 1901, pp. 356-357; Douglas Hyde, *The Irish Packet*, 3 Oct. 1903, p. 24; Laoide, (1915), p. 20; *Irish Independent,* 30th Dec. 1932; Mac Giollarnáth, 1936, p. 203; de Bhaldraithe, 1977, pp. 204.

18 Ant. 5, 9, 13, 14, 16; Arm. 1, 3; Car. 2, 14, 18; Cav. 6; Cl. 1, 8, 9, 15, 18, 21, 27; Cork 13, 14, 15, 30, 31; Don. 18, 19, 30; Down 4, 17; Fer. 3; Gal. 2. 35; Ker. 36, 46, 47; Kild. 9; Kilk. 6, 24; Laois 9, 13; Lim. 30, 39, 40; Long. 2; Lou. 10, 13; Mayo 31, 35; Mon. 4; Ros. 20; Tipp. 22, 30, 31; Tyr. 9; Wat. 6, 9, 20, 34, 51; Wmeat. 12, 20; Wex. 15, 34, 35, 36, 37; Wick. 15. Total: 66
In a further 25 records it has been possible only to determine the counties to which the material refers:
Ant. 15. 17; Dub. 16, 17; Gal. 65-71; Ker. 48; Kilk. 28, 29, 30; Laois 23; Mayo 32, 33, 34; Mon. 12; Tipp. 47, 48; Wat. 52, 53; Wex. 62. Total: 25
The remaining 56 records do not provide the information necessary to locate them in specific areas: see Appendix 5.3 'Traditional material of indefinite provenance in printed works', pp. 363-4.

19 Information concerning the supernatural washerwoman of Scottish Gaelic tradition is derived from the nineteenth and twentieth century printed sources (see note, 49, pp. 387-8) and is used for comparative purposes in this work.

20 Michael O'Malley, The Pier, Murrisk, Westport, Co. Mayo, who came to live on the mainland in the late 1970's (information from Anne O'Dowd 9 Oct. 1979). As to Achill Island, Co. Mayo, only one inconclusive reference to the banshee is to hand. Writing from Mullingar, Co. Westmeath, on the 21st September 1904, to his son Jack, Robert McKinstry describes his recent visit to Achill Island and states (p. 25) 'Mr. Tuite's guide gave me a lot of information about giants, fairies, banshees and pirates' (National Library of Ireland Ms. No. 24,956). Cf note 3, p. 368.

21 According to material collected there in the 1950's by full-time collector Seán Mac Craith — (see M 1358: 371-4).

22 For definition of the terms *memorate, folk belief, belief statement, legend* and *fabulate*, see von Sydow, 1948, pp. 60-88, Honko, 1962. 1964, and Pentikäinen, 1968, 1978.

Chapter 1

1   e.g., the variety of names for 'dead-child beings' (Pentikäinen, 1968, pp. 125-33) and supernatural milk-stealing creatures (Wall, J., 1977, pp. 185-96; 1978, pp. 6-69) in Scandanavia which have no correspondence in Ireland.

2   For the problems connected with the interplay of folklore and philology see Pentikäinen, J., 1968, passim, and Almqvist, 1971, pp. 69 ff.

3   For north-Inishturk, and the inconclusive evidence for Achill Island, Co. Mayo and Scattery Island, Co. Clare, see notes 21,22, p. 367. Negative 19th-century data for Inishmaan, Aran Islands (Gal. 2) is complemented by recent questionnaire replies from Inishmore indicating that the term *bean sí* is an import from 'mainland' tradition.

4   Croker, T.C., 1828, p. 12.

5   Ua Duinnín, 1934, p. 131.

6   See Chp. 12, p. 193.

7   1977-8, pp. 137-155.

8   MacDougall and Calder, 1910, p. 214.

9   See Ó Súilleabháin, S., 1977, pp. 89-92.

10   'The Semantics of 'Síd', *Éigse* XVII, Part 2, 1977-8, p. 149.

11   Cf. Chp. 12, pp. 193-7.

12   1839, note, p. 368.

13   MacCana, P., 1973, pp. 86, 123-4.

14   This is in Seymour, St. J.D., and Neligan, H.L., 1926, p. 198, spelled Bankēentha.

15   Ó Dónaill, N., 1977, s.v. *cáineadh*.

16   The same qualities occur in relation to the Scottish Gaelic *caointeach*; cf. MacLagan, 1914, p. 84, Carmichael, Vol. II, 1928, pp. 244-5, and MacDougall and Calder 1910, pp. 214-15.

17   This spelling *badhbh* is also found in Nicholas O'Kearney's introduction to *Feis Tighe Chonáin*, 1855, p. 110 with reference to the Parish of Modeligo, Co. Waterford. O'Kearney is here clearly using the standard spelling of the dictionaries; cf. p. 35 above.

18   Wat. 4, 11, 12-14, 18, 21-23, 33, 36-44, 46-50. Moylan (1996, p. 24) has further noted the term for Mooncoin, which he renders phonetically [*bōlb*].

19   1957-8, p. 408.

20   In regard to the south-Kerry material, P.L. Henry states in a letter (Sept. 1978) '. . . . the term in question turned up in Glencar, Kerry, in connection with questions about fairies and bogeymen'. I have

been unable to trace this Glencar reference in the manuscripts in the archives of the Dept. of Irish Folklore. In view of note 50 below, one might expect to find *badhb* used in the sense of 'scold' or 'bogey' rather than 'supernatural death-messenger' in this area of Munster. Also, the description of the being given by Henry, 1957-8, p. 408 ('tall woman in white seen combing her long hair, or heard uttering three wails . . . ') clearly belongs to the *badhbh*-area (see Map 3) and especially to Co. Waterford (see Chps. 4 and 5).

21   1961, pp. 35, 277.

22   Power, P., 1952, pp. 47, 55, 80, 204, 215.

23   While the term *badhb* with various meanings is found in O'Clery's Glossary, 1643 (Miller, A.W.K., 1879-80, p. 368; 1881-83, p. 54, *s.v badhb, tethra*), in Plunkett R., *Vocabularium Latinum et Hibernum*, 1662,(*s.v. manerium*), in Lluyd *Archaeologica Brittanica*, 1707, (*s.v. badhb*), it is in O'Brien's dictionary, 1768, that it is first encountered glossed also in the meaning 'supernatural death-messenger'. Even though O'Brien was a native of Cork – he was born in Ballyvoddy, Natlash Parish, and was consecrated bishop of Cloyne in south-east Cork in 1747 (see Crone, 1928, p. 174) – on the evidence of the archival material (pp. 34, 36), it is unlikely that the term with the meaning 'supernatural death-messenger' applied to Cork. It is probable that O'Brien was familiar with the Waterford *badhb* and with its 'supernatural death-messenger' meaning.

On the other hand, his entry *babhb*, glossed as 'a scold', 'a quarrelsome woman', undoubtedly reflected local usage in Cork (see note 50).

24   Wex. 1-6, 17, 19, 22, 25-33, 38-40, 43, 45, 46, 57-59, 61 (archival records).

25   Car. 3, 7, 9, 12, 15, 19 (archival records).

26   The form *badhbh* appears in the Kildare questionnaire reply, but the correspondent said in the course of a telephone coversation on 17th Jan. 1978, (cf. M 2114: 197) that the local pronunciation was 'bow'.

27   Ó Scanláin, R.A., 1945-7; p. 104.

28   Piatt, D., 1933, p. 23.

29   de Brún, 1970, pp. 43-51, esp. p. 46, par. 2.

30   1957-8, p. 408.

31   Kilk. 9, 10, 23; Tipp. 3, 4, 16, 42, and also Fethard (oral communication from Sr. Kevins, Fordham University, New York, a native of Fethard, Co. Tipperary). Literary evidence in support of the archival material from Tipperary is found in Seymour St. J.D., and Neligan H. (1926, p. 198) where the form *bohëëntha* is given. As regards Tipp. 14, the collector Patrick C. Power has given the form *bean*

chaointe in the IFC manuscript. It is clear, however, from a letter dated 24 June 1980 from Power (cf. M 2113: 151 a, b) that the term actually used by his informant was *bo chaointe* and which he pronounced *bohynta/boheenta*. Power writes, 'about twenty years aso I met a man named Cooney in the Heathview area, east of Kilcash, who used the word *bohynta/boheenta* for the banshee . . . For further examples of *bo-chaointe* for Kilkenny see Moylan, 1996, p. 24

32   1957-8, p. 411.

33   1939, p. 30.

34   1954, p. 50.

35   1964, II, p. 61, points 6, 6a.

36   *Gaedhilg Chonndae Chille Coinigh*, 1939, p. 30. Professor Breatnach writes *'Is ait an focal atá ag muintir Ch. Ch. ar an mbean-sidhe, "bó chaointe"* . . . Pádraig de Brún, 1970, p. 46, note 24, has also noticed that the expression has been mistakenly placed under "Bé (?)' by H. Wagner.

37   *Tales, By the O'Hara Family*, I, London, 1825.

38   Crone, J.S., 1928, p. 8.

39   1856-7, p. 122.

40   Crone, J.S., 1928, p. 185.

41   1855, pp. 109-110.

42   O'Donoghue, D.J., 1912, p. 327.

43   1886, p. 289.

44   *ibid*, p 7.

45   Recent enquiry (June 1980) in the Kilcash, Carrick-on-Suir, and Clonmel areas of south-Tipperary yielded no further examples of the term. (Letters from Patrick C. Power (see note 31), and Pádraig Ó Cearbhail formerly of Clonmel (27 June 1980), (M2113: 134), who stated, *'Níor chualas an téarma úd 'boheentach' riamh'* ('I never heard that term *bóheentach'*).Cf *badhbhsánaí* [bəu 'sa:nI] Moylan (1996, p. 24)

46   1957-8, p. 411. See Moylan (1996, p. 24) for further examples.

47   de Fréine, 1977, p. 79.

48   Cf. *fadhbh, fadhb* in Dinneen, Rev. P.S., 1975.

49   See O'Rahilly C., 1976, pp. 182-183.

50   *Badhb (badhbh)* 'a scold', 'a quarrelsome woman' is found in O'Brien 1768. *Badhb* [bəib] 'scolding woman', 'scold', is attested from the following counties: Clare: MacClúin, 1940, p. 55; Cork: Ó Cuív, B., 1944, Index, s.v. *badhbh* and oral communications to the same effect from Donncha Ó Cróinín and Aindrias Ó Muimhneacháin; Kerry: oral communication from Pádraig ua Maoileoin.

For examples of *badhbh* as the basic element in *bobogha* / *bobodha* = bogeyman, see *bobhomh (s.v. lamia)* and *bobómha* / *bobhobha (s.v. maniae)*, in Plunkett, R., 1662: *bovova (s.v. maniae)* in Lhuyd, 1707, *bobodha* in de Bhaldraithe, T., 1959, and *badhbh, badhbh* in Ó Dónaill, N., 1977. See also the replies to the IFC Bogie Question-aire, 1943, M 954, M 955, M 1135 in the manuscript archive of the Dept. of Irish Folklore, University College Dublin, word lists, dialect studies, philological works etc., which show that: (a) the form *bobogha* / *bobau* / = 'bogeyman' is recorded from the following counties: Donegal: (M 954: 198) and oral communication from Niall Ó Dónaill; Kerry: (M 955: 24) and oral communication from Donncha Ó Cróinín and Pádraig Ó Fiannachta: Galway: (M 955: 270, 271, 272, 282, 283), de Bhaldraithe, T., 1943-1944, p. 211, 1945, p. 63, 1980, p. 8, Ó Fátharta, P., 1929, p. 8 and oral communication from Seán Ó Curraoin; Mayo: (M 955: 254, 266), Stockman, G., 1974, p. 4; Sligo: (M 955: 183); Westmeath: cf. Henry, P.L., 1957-1958, p. 409, *Éigse* IV, 1943-1944, p. 211; Wexford:cf Henry, P.L., 1957-1958, p. 409.

(b) The form *boghabogha* (also written *bau-wau* / *bow-wow* / *boubou* / in the IFC manuscripts) = bogeyman, is recorded from the following counties: Cavan: (M1209: 429); Cork: (M955: 83); Galway: (M955: 279, 315); Mayo: (M955: 259); Waterford and Wexford, (Henry, P.L., 1957-8, p. 409).

(c) *Bádhb* is recorded from Meath, (*Irisleabhar na Gaedhilge* XI, 1901, p. 154 and Henry, P.L., 1957-8, p. 410).

51 *Dictionary of the Irish Language (DIL) badb*; Henry, 1957-8, p. 407.

52 Breatnach 1939, p. 30; Henry 1957-8, p. 411. For the phonetic development of Early *bodb, badb* see Henry *ibid.* pp. 409-411.

53 Mann, 1984-87: *bhodhuos*, 'battle', Pokorny, 1927: bhaut- (?): bhut- 'schlagen, stoßen', pp. 126-7; Henry, 1957-8, pp. 407-8. Cf. also Cornish *bod y guerni* 'bussard' (Henry, *ibid.* p. 407).

54 Cf. Cross, 1952, Motifs: A 485.1, A 132.6.2*, D 1812.5.1.1.7.*, M 301.6.1*

55 Cf. Map 12. In the single doubtful reference to the death-messenger washing in the *badhbh*-area (Kilk. 15) she is called *bean sí*. Cf. n. 49, pp. 387-8 for the washing activities of *bean-nighe* and *caointeachán* of Scottish Gaelic tradition.

56 Cf. however, the connection of the *badhbh*-figure in *Caithréim Thoirdhealbhaigh* wich the O'Brien clan, in Chp. 12, pp. 200-1.

57 Cf. Chp. 12, pp. 197-202.

58 Cf. Chp. 12, p. 193.

59 Cf. p. 35.

60 O'Brien, J., 1768.

61 Cf. esp. pp. 198-200 and note 54 above. Cf. also note 58 above and note 98.

Chapter 2

1   cf. Hultkrantz, Å., *The Supernatural Owners of Nature* (1961).

2   Thompson, S., 1955-8, Motif D 113.1.1; see also Funk and Wagnalls *Standard Dictionary of Folklore Mythology and Legend, s.v. werwolf.*

3   For the beliefs and legends associated with the hag in hare-form in Ireland, cf. Ó Súilleabháin, S., 1942, pp. 484-5 and Ní Dhuibhne 1993. For the *mjölkhare* in Scandinavian tradition cf. Wall, J., 1977, pp. 185-96 passim; 1978, pp. 16-29.

4   The Guntram Legend (ML 4000) is one of the many stories which has grown around this nucleus of belief; see Lixfeld, H., 1972, pp. 60-107, and Almqvist, B., 1979, pp. 1-22.

5   Thompson, S., 1955-8, Motif E 723.2. Also Funk and Wagnalls . . . *op. cit. s.v. fetch, fylgja;* Turville-Petre, E.O.G., 1964, pp. 221-30 and *Kulturhistoriskt Lexicon för nordisk medeltid,* V, *s.v. fylgja.*

6   See Ó Súilleabháin, S., 1942, 'The Return of the Dead', pp. 244-50.

7   Ó Súilleabháin, S., 1977, pp. 92-94.

8   Thompson, S., 1955-8, Motif V 236.1. See also Christiansen, R.Th., 1971-3, pp. 96-7; Ó Duilearga, S., 1977, p. 291; Ó hEochaidh, S., Ní Néill, M., Ó Catháin, S., 1977, pp. 35-6 and O'Sullivan, S., 1977, pp. 44-5.

9   Ó Súilleabháin, S., 1942, 'Abduction by fairies', pp. 470-5. See also Ó Duilearga, S., 1977, p. 291 (*An Slua Sí*), and his notes and references to other works on this subject, p. 435.

10   Christiansen, R. Th., 1958, p. 75. See also Ó Duilearga, S., 1977, p. 315 and his notes and references to other printed versions, p. 438.

11   Motif C 611, Forbidden chamber, Thompson, S., 1955-8.

12   S 448: 275-6.

13   cf. note 7.

14   For the position of the restless dead children in Nordic tradition, see Pentikäinen, J., 1968; for their position in Irish tradition, see O'Connor, A., 1978, 86pp., 1979, pp. 33-41, 1981, 180pp.

15   e.g., S1:400 (Galway) and S 571:86 (Tipperary).

16   'The O'Brien Banshee' in Fanshawe, Lady, 1830, pp. 90-3; *ibid.* p. 38
      and notes 16-20, p. XXXVIII and Baring-Gould, S., 1876, pp. 489-90.
      'The Fitzpatrick Banshee' in *The Dublin and London Magazine*, 1825,
      p. 31; *The Shamrock* XXIX, No. 1339, 1892, p. 596; *Ireland's Own*
      IX, No. 233, 8 May 1907, p. 11. 'The Mayo Banshee' in McAnally,
      D.R., 1888, p. 114; O'Donnell, E., c. 1920, p. 36; *Ireland's Own* XII
      No. 312, 11 Nov. 1908, p. 4 and McGarry, M., ed., n.d., pp. 39-40.

17   Will O' the Wisp - see Thompson, S., 1955-8 Motif F 491; Ó Súilleabháin,
      S., 1942, p. 498; cf. also Aarne, A., Thompson, S., 1973, Types 330,
      332. For the Irish material in these two tale-types, see Ó Súilleabháin
      S., and Christiansen, R.Th., 1963.

18   Ó Súilleabháin, S., 1967, pp. 130-145.

19   A further example is: M 227: 380-381).   See also for this McClintock
      1876, p. 607; 'This yearning of the people after a little knowledge of
      what is unrevealed, has given birth to many strange fancies; among
      others the idea that the souls of the dead, made restless by the tears
      and regrets of survivors, are unable to get to heaven, and hover near
      the earth, sometimes appearing to reprove their relatives for their ex-
      cessive grief. The writer has frequently heard widows and mothers
      remonstrated with, by well-meaning neighbours in the following terms:

> "Dinna be crying an' lamenting that way,
> or you'll keep him frae his rest;"

and has seen the mourners forthwith struggle to restrain their tears
thus impelled by the strongest motive that could be presented to them.
A further example is: S 459:25 (Cork). References to the same belief
in Breton tradition are found in, Whitehead, A.E., n.d. pp. 164-9.

20   The reference here to Rachel may have come from Lady Gregory,
      Visions and Beliefs . . . 1970, p. 170.

21   cf. Lady Wilde, (1887, 1, pp. 259-60), 'sometimes the Banshee assumes
      the form of some sweet singing virgin of the family who died young,
      and has been given the mission by the invisible powers to become the
      harbinger of coming doom to her mortal kindred.'

22   1970, p. 172.

23   See also O'Kearney, N., ed., *The Battle of Gabhra*, 1855, note pp. 126-7
      on this point - 'The Bean Sighe was supposed to have been an ancestor
      of the person whose death she deigned to forewarn . . .' The banshee

of Dunluce Castle, Co. Antrim is said by some writers to be a relative
of the MacQuillan family, former owners of the now ruined castle ,
Forde, Rev. H., 1923, p. 29. See also Gregory, Lady A., 1962, p. 88,
where the banshee is said to be, 'of the nature of the McInerneys . . .'

Chapter 3

1   Cf. Introduction, note 22, p. 367.

2   Yeats, W.B., *Fairy and Folk Tales of the Irish Peasantry*, 1888, p. 108.

3   Cav. 8; Leit. 16; Long. 1, 5, 7, 24; Ros. 25; Wmea. 1, 6, 10.

4   See note 5, Chapter 2, p. 372.

5   This sentiment is expressed in Cav. 3: 'They say it follows the McCabe
     family, it follows all the McCabes everyplace the name is.'

6   The Mac and O records in the archival material are, Connaught: Gal. 4,
     54; Mayo 1, 9, 16, 28; Ros. 1, 11, 17, 18, 28. (Total: 11). Leinster:
     Car. 1, 12; Dub. 11, 15; Kild. 8; Kilk. 7, 10, 15; Lao. 3, 17, 19; Long.
     21, 29; Lou. 6; Mea. 7; Off. 1, 14; Wmea. 1, 2, 4; Wex. 10, 23. Wick. 9.
     (Total: 23). Munster: Cl. 12, 14, 34, 35, 36; Cork 11, 24, 27, 39; Ker.
     4, 7, 19, 45; Lim. 2, 8, 18, 23, 31; Tipp. 17, 18, 19, 20, 26, 42;
     Wat. 4, 18, 24, 30, 31, 32. (Total: 30). Ulster: Ant. 4, 6, 12; Arm. 2,
     8; Cav. 1.16 (pp. 442-3), 21, 26, 29, 31; Don. 9, 11, 16, 21, 27;
     Fer. 1, 4; Tyr. 2, 5, 6. (Total: 20).
     Overall Total: 84 archival records. Counties not represented in the
     material to hand: Derry, Down and Mon. in Ulster; Leit. and Sli. in
     Connaught.

7   Woulfe, Rev. P., 1923, p.xxiii. I have not been able to determine when
     or by whom these verses were composed, or which verse is the original
     one. On these points Dr. Edward MacLysaght states (letter to the writer
     22 July 1980), I have enquired of a number of people who might know
     about the 'Mac and O' rhyme, with which, in its form in English,
     everyone is familiar. I've seldom seen it in Latin. One and all said they
     didn't know where it made its first appearance. One secondary sugges-
     tion was, that to make it more impressive, someone translated it into
     Latin!'

8   *Ibid.* pp. xxiii-xxvii and Appendix 2.4 (a), p. 266 ((O) Doyle).

9   *Ibid.*, pp. xxv-xxxii and Appendix 2.4(a), p. 263 (Cody).

10   For indications of why the Mac and O prefixes were dropped and of

the periods at which the changes probably took place, see Woulfe, Rev. P., 1923, pp. xxxi-xxxiii and MacLysaght, E., 1957, p. 16.

11 Only two Anglo-Irish family names introduced into Ireland in the seventeenth century appear in the list, i.e., Darley, (cf. MacLysaght, E., 1982, p. 76) and Westropp (cf. MacLysaght, E., 1957, p. 303).

12 Both legend and verse were published in *Béaloideas* XLII-XLIV, 1974-6 (1977), pp. 112-3.

13 See Ó hÓgáin, D., 1979, pp. 239-41.

14 See *Béaloideas* XLII-XLIV, 1974-6 (1977), pp. 111-2, where full source references are given.

15 Woulfe, Rev. P., 1923, pp. xv-xx and MacLysaght, E., 1957, p. 14.

16 Connaught: Gal. 63; Mayo 30; Ros. 1, 16. Leinster: Dub. 15; Kilk. 7; Lao. 17; Off. 1; Wmea. 4; Wex. 19. Munster: Cl. 24; Ker. 7, 19, 27; Tipp. 2, 7, 20. Ulster: Ant. 6; Arm. 8; Cav. 9; Der. 1; Don. 22. Total: 22.

17 On the basis of his reassessment of the mortality data from 1840 in the 1841 *Census of Ireland,* Mokyr, J., 1985, pp. 37-8, 72-5, postulates an infant mortality rate of 224 per 1,000 births for the whole of Ireland (assuming an annual birth rate of 38.5 per 1000). Dr. Cormac Ó Gráda considers that this figure is too high (Ó Gráda, C., 'Poverty and Death in Pre-Famine Ireland,' - a lecture delivered to an economic history seminar in U.C.D., 16 Nov. 1983). Ó Gráda, in a lecture delivered to a postgraduate seminar in the Irish Dept. U.C.D., 11 Nov. 1983 ('Bochtaineacht, Beatha agus Bás'), showed an infant mortality rate in the first year of life, for the city of Dublin, for the two year period prior to the middle of 1841, of 200 per 1000 births (assuming an annual birth rate of 40 per 1,000). From Willis's enumeration of infant deaths in the first year of life, in Dublin, (1845, pp. 10-15) published just before the Famine of 1845, Ó Gráda showed a higher infant death rate of 230 per 1,000 births, but he pointed out that Willis's account referred to poor areas in the north side of the city only. Allowing, generally speaking, for a somewhat lower infant mortality rate in rural than in urban areas, Ó Gráda considered an overall infant mortality rate of about 200 per 1,000 births, or one child in five in the first year of life, as perhaps, a not too unrealistic assessment for mid-nineteenth century Ireland. For further assessment of pre-Famine infant mortality see Ó Gráda 1993, pp. 43-6.

18 Another factor which we must consider here is that other old and important families in an area may not be mentioned in connection with the death-messenger for the reason that they were believed to have other death-omens attached to them — the association of foxes with

the Preston family of Gormanstown Castle, for instance (see note 53, pp. 381-2). This problem cannot be solved, however, until a full study of death-omens in Irish tradition is undertaken.

19 For references to this tradition in Germany see, e.g., legend no. 272, *Die weisse Frau in Stuttgart*, in Petzoldt, L., ed., *Deutsche Volkssagen*, pp. 162-3 and his commentary on the legend, p. 407. In the course of his commentary on legend 271a (p. 407) he states: *In der feudalen Oberschicht kündet die Einscheinung der weissen Frau (Ahnfrau) Tod oder Kriegsgefahr an.* See also von der Leyen, F., 1933, no. 21, pp. 26-9 and notes, p. 143. Von Sydow refers to the Sweedish 'vit fru' in *Nordisk Kultur* XIX *Folktro*, 1935, p. 103. I wish to thank Professor Bo Almqvist for these references.

Chapter 4

1   Brackets are by the collector, Tadhg Ó Murchadha.

2   The nine counties from which *wail* has not been recorded are: Antrim, Derry, Galway, Leitrim, Louth, Monaghan, Sligo, Westmeath and Wicklow.

3   The term had not been recorded from Limerick where the appellation *bean chaointe* is found.

4   Ó Súilleabháin, 1967, pp. 136-43; Ó Muirithe, 1978, pp. 20-9.

5   This is no doubt, *A Mhurie, Mhuire!* (Mary, Mary! referring to the Blessed Virgin).

6   The term *call* could also, of course, be derived from the sound of an animal.

7   Croker, 1826, p. 201.

8   For examples of this death-omen in Irish folk tradition see M 96: 316-7; M 2110: 166. See also Barrington, 1827, p. 153. A more elaborate version of the omen is found in Njal's Saga (Magnusson and Pálsson, 1960, pp. 278-9), a late thirteenth-century Icelandic composition *(ibid.* p. 9). The names of the doomed men are called in series with a pause between each series. All the men subsequently die in the order in which they have been mentioned.
    Einar Ól. Sveinsson has shown (*Á Njálsbúd*, 1943, p. 171) that the episode in the *Njal's Saga* is based on a passage in the Dialogues of Pope Gregory in which Anastasius and his followers are called by

name in series and they all subsequently die in the order in which they have been called.

I wish to thank Professor Bo Almqvist for this reference.

9   Hall, 1843, p. 106; Yeats, 1888, p. 321, 1892, p. 232; McAnally, 1888, p. 110; *The Dublin Penny Journal,* 7 February, 1903, p. 613.

10   Ó Súilleabháin, 1967, p. 143.

11   See note 14, Chp. 2, p. 372.

12   R.B. Breatnach, 1961, p. 277

13   *An Claidheamh Soluis* VII, No. 9, 15 *Bealtaine,* 1905, p. 6.

14   Evans and Thomson, 1972, pp. 59-79.

15   See Armstrong, E. A., 1958, pp. 113-24.

16   Ó Dónaill, N. *eag.* 1977, *s.v. scréachóg.*

17   Dinneen, Rev. P.S., 1927, *s.v. gabhairín.*

18   Bruun, B., 1975, p. 118.

19   Hall, Mr. and Mrs. S.C., 1843, p. 106; Braddon, M.E., 1876, II, p. 67; Forbes, J., 1957, p. 39.

20   The volume or pitch of the cry is said by some nineteenth century writers to depend on the death-messenger's attitude towards the dying person and his family, or upon the circumstances surrounding the death. (Keegan, J., 1839, p. 368; MacAnally, D.R., 1888, pp. 114-7). There are no traces of a clear-cut distinction of this kind in the archival sources, however, and it would appear to be a literary invention.

21   There are also four records (Tipp. 20, 38; Wat. 2, 41) in which repetition of the sound is mentioned, though no specific number of times is given.

22   I have not found any examples of this characteristic attached to a female foreboder of death in Irish tradition apart from the archival material dealing with the supernatural death-messenger. We may, however, compare it with the references to three shouts of lamentation raised by the Fianna immediately on the death of Diarmaid Ó Duibhne and also by the households of Gráinne, and Aonghus from Brugh na Bóinne (Mac Cana 1973, p. 132), over the dead body of Diarmaid on Beann Gulban in the seventeenth century manuscript of *Tóruigheacht Dhiarmada agus Gráinne,* ed. Nessa Ní Shéaghdha, 1967, pp. 94, 99. This is the oldest extant copy of the *Tóruigheacht* (*ibid.,* p. xiv), but earlier literary references to the main features of

the tale show that it was well known in earlier centuries (*ibid.*, pp. x-xiv). It is possible, then, that the motif of the three shouts of lamentation at death was embodied in the tale in earlier times.

23 *Coisc! Coisc!*, 2nd person singular imperative mood of the verb *coisc* 'check', 'stop', 'prevent', 'restrain'. See Ó Dónaill, N. *eag.*, 1977, *s.v. coisc.*

24 *Éist!* be silent! whist!, Ó Dónaill, N. *eag.*, 1977, *s.v. éist.*

25 MacGiollarnáth, S., 1936, p. 203.

26 The position within the family of the experiencer will be discussed in Chp. 7, pp. 145-6.

28 For the effect of an encounter with a supernatural being on a dog, see de Bhaldraithe, 1977, p. 205 and M 1209:464.

29 For the power of horses to sense the presence of supernatural beings, see Ó hÓgáin, 1977-9, pp. 200-14.

Chapter 5

1 Eskeröd, A., 1947, p. 81.

2 1954, p. 396.

3 See *Béaloideas* 42-44, 1974-76, (1977) pp. 100-1. For another version of this legend *without* reference to the banshee etc., see M368: 362-3, from Carnmore, Claregalway, Co. Galway.

4 1888, p. 108: 1893, p. 108.

5 1976, p. 14; see also Briggs, K., 1959, p. 184.

6 Ó Giolláin, D., 1984, pp. 92-3.

7 e.g., the descriptions of Fedelm in *Táin Bó Cúailnge*, ed., O'Rahilly, C., The Stowe Version, 1978, p.7; The Book of Leinster Version, 1970, pp. 5-6, and Rescension 1, 1976, p. 2; the descriptions of Étaín in *Togail Bruidne Da Derga* in Dillon, M., *Early Irish Literature*, 1972, p. 25 and the descriptions of the *sí-bhean* in the Aisling poetry of Eoghan Rua Ó Súilleabháin, for example (Ua Duinnín, P., 1901, pp. 1-44).

8 Advances made by a mortal man to the banshee occur in interference legends where a man mistakes a banshee, *badhb* etc. for a mortal woman, in the dark, or in the distance (see pp. 182-6). Perhaps the

stealing of her comb from the banshee by a mortal man has underlying sexual connotations.

9 Although occurring in a schools' Ms., Wat. 36 was contributed by a
teacher.

10 1888, pp. 114-7.

11 cf. his speculation about several banshees appearing on the occasion of
the same death, pp. 113, 114.

12 A riddle according to the Oxford English Dictionary is a coarse-
meshed sieve used for separating chaff from corn, sand from gravel
etc.

13 1800, p. 21.

14 1888, p. 117.

15 See, however, Keegan, J., 1839, p. 368; Hall, Mr. and Mrs., 1843, p. 105;
McAnally, D.R., 1888, pp. 114, 117; 'Lageniensis', 1870, p. 64, and Wilde,
Lady, 1890, p. 83.

16 For example Edgeworth, M., 1800, p. 21; Keegan, J., 1839, p. 368.
Other examples include Lageniensis, 1870, p. 64 and Foster, J.
Cooper, 1951, p. 17.

17 Croker, T.C., 1826, p. 195; Hall, Mr. and Mrs., S.C., 1843, p. 105;
MacAnally, D.R., 1888, pp. 113, 115; cf. Yeats (W. Scott edn., pp. 122-3).

18 Scott, Sir W., 1913, p. 291 (first ed., 1810), Croker, T.C., 1826, pp.
201, 206, Keegan, J. 1839, p. 368, Hall, Mr. and Mrs. S.C., 1843, p.
105, Thornbury, W., 1861, p. 127, Lageniensis, A., 1870, p. 64,
Todhunter, J., 1885, p. 153, Murphy, J., 1886, p. 7, Seymour, St.
J.D., and Neligan, H.L., 1926, p. 199, Briggs, K., 1959, p. 184, 1976,
p. 14.

19 Mr. and Mrs. Hall's description of a keening woman at a wake of a
young man which they attended during their travels in Ireland (1825-
41), includes the detail — 'Her long black uncombed locks were
hanging about her shoulders;' (1841, p. 226). See also Partridge, A.,
1983, pp. 94-6, for further references to this characteristic of keening
and mourning women in Irish oral and literary traditions.

20 For Fedelm, see p. 203, for Clíona, see p. 196, for Étaín, see Dillon,
M., 1972, p. 25.

21 In 32 oral versions of The Comb Legend the banshee, *badhb* etc. is
depicted combing her hair: Car. 11, 13; Gal. 46; Kilk. 13, 14, 16, 18,

19; Lao. 11; Long. 6; Off. 8, 10, 11; Ros. 23; Sli. 9; Tipp. 3, 9, 29, 32, 34, 39, 43; Wat. 19, 25, 40; Wmea. 3, 9, 12, 16; Wex. 4, 43; Wick. 12.

22 Both are from the nineteenth century — Archdeacon, M., 1839, p. 176 and Lageniensis, 1870, p. 64. There are two further literary references to combing in nineteenth and twentieth century versions of The Comb Legend i.e. Bardan, 1891, p. 82 and *Journal of the County Kildare Archaeological Society and Surrounding Districts* VI, 2, 1909, p. 174.

23 Question 14:
    Is the banshee supposed to be seen combing her hair? Are there any particulars about special times or reasons for this?

24 1954, p. 397.

25 Sli. 9.

26 Long. 6; Ros. 23; Wex. 30.

27 Wat. 40.

28 Kilk. 12b; Leix. 17.

29 Kild. 2.

30 1885, p. 153.

31 1888, p. 110 and subsequent editions.

32 1959, p. 184, 1976, p. 14.

33 Breathnach, R.B., 1961, p. 35.

34 Croker, T.C., 1826, p. 226, 1828, p. 10; Keegan, J., 1839, p. 368; Hall, Mr. and Mrs. S.C., 1843, p. 104; Murphy, J., 1886, p. 7; Dease, A., 1910, p. 75.

35 1918, p. 310 ('dark cloaked').

36 See Ó Súilleabháin, S., 1942, pp. 426-7 and Wood-Martin, W.G., II, 1902, pp. 274-5.

37 Ó Danachair, C., 1967, p. 10.

38 It is also noteworthy that headgear of one type of another is often used to distinguish a particular type of supernatural being Ó Giolláin, 1984, p. 93, e.g., the *leipreachán's* hat.

39 Croker, T.C., 1826, p. 226, Todhunter, J., 1855, p. 153; Yeats, W.B., 1888, p.110 and in subsequent edns.; Briggs, K., 1959, p. 184. 1976, p. 14.

40 McClintock, H.F., 1943, Index, *s. v.* 'cloak'.

41 Lucas, A.T., 1951, pp. 114-6.

42 Lucas, A.T., 1956, pp. 352-7. Going barefoot was also a sign of mourning and was practiced by some men, women and children in Ireland on Good Friday (Danaher, K., 1972, p. 71). The characteristic is also attributed to the Virgin Mary in some traditional songs dealing with the Passion of Christ (Partridge, A., 1983, p. 94).

43 1976, p. 14.

44 Hennessy, W.M., 1870-2, p. 32ff.; *Dictionary of the Irish Language, sub badb.*

45 For the robin as an omen of death see, e.g., Ó Dochartaigh, L., pp. 183-9 and M 1840: 155; M 2110: 99-100; M 2113: 210.

46 Author's italics.

47 A curious and atypical reference (with an illustration) to the banshee in bird-shape but with 'the face of a person who died soon after' is found in Foster, J. Cooper, 1951, p. 16. The informant was a Belfast journalist.

48 Ó Súilleabháin, S., 1942, pp. 33, 337; Ní Dhuibhne, 1993, pp. 77-85. Scandinavian milk-stealing creatures are dealt with in Wall, J., 1977, 1978.

49 See especially Wex. 38 of Nicholas Furlong's material (Wex. 34-9) in Appendix 5.2, p. 360.

50 1832, I, pp. 67, 294.

51 Ó Súilleabháin, S., 1942, pp. 483-4.

52 1910, p. 75.

53 References to the Gormanston Foxes in the subject index in the manuscript archive of the Department of Irish Folklore under *An Madra Rua* (Section F) are the following: S680: 49, S682: 160, S685: 1, 54, 315, 318, S699: 121, M1379: 222-231. None of these accounts gives any explanation of the phenomeon. See also *New Ireland Review* xxix, 1908, pp. 123-7 and the Hole, C., 1961, p. 166.
The Preston family is a distinguished old English family established in Leinster since the end of the 13th century (MacLysaght, E., 1957, p.

299). They remained Catholic and were always on the Irish side. The connection of the family with foxes may well be the reason why such a prominent family was not believed to be followed by the banshee. It is also possible that the legend was already attached to the family when they came to Ireland and this may be the reason why the fox figures so prominently in the Gormanston coat of arms — see Burke's Peerage, 1959 ed., p. 961.

54   See note 4, Chp. 2, p. 372, on the Guntram Legend (ML 4000). In the Irish versions of the legend included in Ó Súilleabháin, S., and Christianson, R. Th., *The Types of the Irish Folktale*, 1963 under Type 1645A (cf. Lixfeld, 1972, pp. 101-2), and the additional versions adduced by Almqvist, B., 1979, pp. 8, 12, the soul-animal is a butterfly.

55   Thompson, S., 1955, Motif E 734. 1 'Soul in the form of a Butterfly' For further Irish examples of this belief see M34:83-4, M782:247 and Lady Wilde, 1887, Vol. 1, pp. 65-7. For some Scottish examples see Henderson, G., 1911, pp. 79-80.

Chapter 6

1   References to this custom are common in the IFC Mss. — see for example Schools' Mss. 30:538; 32:13; 118:51, 58; 122:92; 130:528; 134:353; 306:283; 315:27; 358:414; 937:222; 939:268. An early nineteenth century reference to this custom from Ballycarey, Co. Antrim, is found in *The Posthumous Works of James Orr*, Belfast, 1817, p. 74, v. 1, lines 7-8.

2   cf. the *mors repentina et improvisa* discussed by Ariès, P., 1983, pp. 10-13, 587.

3   Sir William Wilde referring to the city of Dublin for example, states in his 'Report upon the Tables of Deaths' pp. lxxii-lxxiv in the 1841 *Census of Ireland*, that the records of burial 'in the three great cemeteries in the vicinity of the city and some of the graveyards within the municipal boundary' (cf. p. lxx) showed on the average of two years (June 1839 — June 1841) a 'preponderence of deaths during the winter and spring seasons' (p. lxxiv).

4   Cl. 25(S); Don. 9 (S); Gal. 33(S), 50(S); Ker. 2, 13 (M), 18(L), 22(S), 23(S), 32(M), 33(M). Sli. 4(S); Wex. 9(M); Total: 13 (2% of records (545) directly connecting the death-messenger with death, (p. 303).

5   See Appendix 3.5 (a) and (b), p. 307.

6   Arm. 1; Cav. 32; Cork 8; Don. 27; Gal. 18, 40, 41, 44; Ker. 11, 26; Laois 17; Leit. 1; Long. 1, 7, 9, 10, 19, 21, 25, 26; Mayo 6; Mea. 7, 18; Ros. 1, 17; Total: 25 (4.5 % of records (545) connecting death-messenger with death).

7   Arm. 8; Cav. 29; Cork 2, 9; Gal. 39, 49; Leit. 11; Off. 11.
Total: 8 (1.46 of the records (545) directly connecting the death-messenger with death.)

8   cf. the Irish saying, *dhá dtrian galar na h-oíche*, 'a patient is doubly ill at night', (Ó Súilleabháin, S., 1977, p. 49, and M 2053: 92 in which the reply to a query on this point was, 'Oh! they're always worse by night, they are! '

9   e.g., M 1010:347; M 1402:2-4; M 2114: 277-8. For a discussion of the magical force of liminal areas and situation, see Hand, W., 1983, pp. 3-15 and Nagy, J.F. 1981-2, pp. 135-43.

10 I have made some efforts to collect material in the USA. The Banshee Questionnaire was circulated on a limited scale in America (Introduction, p. 19 and Appendix 5.2, p. 362). Question 9 (Appendix 1, p. 248) included the following query:
Are there any traditions of banshees appearing abroad (in America, for instance) on the occasion of deaths abroad?
A further item on the banshee was recorded by Dr. Séamus Ó Catháin and Mr. Leo Corduff of the Dept. Irish Folklore, U.C.D., in Northampton, Massachusetts, (USA 3, p. 362) in October 1982.

11 Some answers were triggered off by the query in question 9 (see note 10) about manifestations abroad on the occasions of deaths there.

12 Appendix 3.6 (f), p. 310.

13 Freeman, T.W., 1950, p. 125.

14 Johnston, J.H., 1967, pp. 97-112.

15 See Dudley, Edwards, R., 1973, pp. 146-7.

16 1888, p. 118.

17 1824, note, pp. 32-3.

18 Ua Duinnín, P., 1903, p. 1, line 13; 1934, p. 73, line 17.

19 e.g., 240 records (62% of localised manifestations (388, see note 51)) which clearly show that the person died in his own home parish. These include 214 records (Appendix 3.6 (a), p. 308) of manifestations at or near the dying person's house, 12 records of manifestations at his neighbours' house (Appendix 3.6 (c), p. 309, 5 records of manifestations at a hospital in the vicinity of the deceased (Arm. 6, Lim. 16, Tyr. 6, Wat. 30, Wex. 21), and 5 records of manifestations on land in the vicinity belonging to the dying person (Cav. 10, 26; Don. 22; Long. 29; Mea. 4).

20 von Sydow, C.W., 1926, pp. 53-70.

21 cf. also Wex. 40; "Hilly-Holly" and note 38 below.

22 cf. Wood-Martin, W.G., II, 1920, p. 251:
    Some curiously shaped masses of rock have been named by
    antiquaries "Druids' Chairs", "Brehon Chairs" and "Inaugurat-
    ion Chairs", according as it was imagined that they had been used
    by the Druids when giving instruction, by the Brehons when lay-
    ing down the law, or by chiefs when being installed in office.
    See also figures 79 (p. 252), 82 (p. 254), 83, 84 (p. 255). He also
    mentions: 'The Hag's Chair', (pp. 251-3 and fig. 80), 'St. Dabehoe's or
    St. Brigid's Chair', (pp. 253-4 and fig. 81) on the shore of Lough Derg,
    Co. Donegal. Cf. also 'Cathaoir-na-Callighe-Beurtha' in Borlase, 1897,
    iii, p. 838.

23 According to Marie Ní Néill (20 May, 1980), Corofin, Co. Clare. (M
    2113:30):
    The Bottles . . . . is well known to all the older people of Corofin.
    It is a spot about a quarter mile north of the village at an angle
    where the old road to Gort turns east from the modern main
    road, which from this point is of fairly recent making. There was
    a hollow between the two roads which was used as a dump for
    old bottles — (the Medical Dispensary is nearby) — etc., ... The
    place is said to be haunted, and strange music was heard at it. . . .

24 Connaught: Gal. 8bs, 13m, 22m, 23bs, 34bs, 40m, 45m, 56bs, 65bs;
    Leit. 8bs, 10m, Mayo 9m, 23bs, 24bs, 25bs; Ros. 1bs, 13bs, 16bs; Sli.
    17bs. Total: 19, m = 6, bs = 13.
    Leinster: Car. 1bs, 5bs, 12bs, 15bs; Dub. 4bs, 9bs, 16m; Kild. 1bs
    10m, 13bs x 3; Kilk. 10bs, 15m; Leix 4m, 7bs; Long. 7m, 24m,
    25m, 26bs, 29m, 30bs; Lou. 2m; Wmea. 4bs; Wex. 13(m), 38(m).
    Total: 25, m = 11; bs = 14.
    Munster: Cl 4bs, 15bs, 34bs, 36bs, 37bs; Ker. 2bs, 45bs; Lim. 33bs;
    Tipp. 11m, 14bs, 16bs, 44bs; Wat. 5m.
    Total: 13, m = 2; bs = 11.
    Ulster: Ant. 13bs; Cav. 1.21 (pp. 443-4)bs, 1.21 (p. 469)bs, 10bs,
    15m, 25m; Don. 6bs, 16bs, 21bs, 22bs; Down 13m; Fer. 1m.
    Total: 12, m = 4. bs = 8.
    Unspecified Provenance: 1 (Archdeacon, 1839, p. 176)bs;
    Overall Total: 70 records; m = 23; bs = 47.
    Closeness to water is also stressed in four versions of The Comb
    Legend (Gal. 41, 46; Kilk. 15; Lao. 5), in all versions of The Shirt
    Legend (Chapter 11, pp. 187-90, Appendix 4.3, pp. 317-20), in one
    version of The Imprint of the Banshee's Five Fingers Legend (Gal. 15,
    see Appendix 4.1 p. 316) and in one record from the USA (USA 3,
    p. 362).

25 Car. 1; Cl. 37; Don. 6, 16, 21, 22; Fer. 1; Gal. 56; Ker. 2, 45; Kilk. 10, 15; Leit. 8; Long. 29; Lou. 2; Ros. 1, 10, 16; Tipp. 16, 44; Wmea 4; Wex. 38.
Total: 22 Questionnaire replies.

26 See Appendix 1, pp. 247-54.

27 Lough Allen: Leitrim and north-east Roscommon. It is the first lake on the River Shannon.

28 Caherglassaun Lake: in the townland of Caherglassaun, Parish of Ardrahan, Galway (O.S. 113, 122).

29 Cloggagh Lough: in the townland of Aghnaclue, Parish of Moybolgue, Cavan (O.S. 34), and in the townland of Cormeen, Parish of Moynalty, Meath (O.S. 1).

30 Lough Derg: the third and largest lake on the River Shannon. It borders on Galway, Clare and Tipperary.

31 Lough Gowna: on the borders of Longford and Cavan.

32 Lough Hackett: in parts of the surrounding townlands of Bunnasillagh, Donaghpatrick, Lisdonagh and Oltore, in the parish of Donaghpatrick, Galway (O.S. 42).

33 Lough Macnean Upr: on the borders of Cavan, Leitrim and Fermanagh.

34 Teevurcher Lough: in parts of the surrounding townlands of Black-hills Lwr. and Carnans Lwr., Cavan (O.S. 34) and Teevurcher, Parish of Moybolgue, Meath (O.S. 1).

35 River Barrow: from its source in the Slieve Bloom Mountains in Laois, it flows through Laois, Kildare, Carlow and borders on Kilkenny and Wexford on its route to the sea through Wexford Harbour.

36 River Boyne: from its source in the Bog of Allen, Kildare, it flows through part of Kildare, borders on Offaly, flows through Meath and borders on Louth on its way to the sea at Drogheda.

37 The Daelagh: Thomas J. Westropp makes the following remarks about this river in *A Folklore Survery of Co. Clare*, 1910, p. 191.
    The stream which flows from Caherminnaun [Kilfenora Parish] to Dough [Kilmacrehy Parish] (the Daelach) was called the "Banshee's Brook", and when, as sometimes happens after an unusually dry summer, the water gets red from iron scum, everyone is on the alert to hear the rustling flight of the banshee . . . .

38 The Horse River: Nicholas Furlong, Drinagh Lodge, Wexford, has

supplied me with the following information about the Horse River
(see M 2112:199):

> The Horse River and the Bishopswater River are the same. It
> caused enormous flooding in Wexford for centuries until recently
> diverted underground. It flows down the Distillery Road and
> underneath Pierce's Foundry. However, as an open small river it
> flowed by or skirted Wexford's major site of Bow manifestation
> and midsummer night festivities, called Hilly Holly or Cornick's
> Bower, now in the grounds of Staffords of Cromwell's Fort. This
> was the area always, and still, associated with the Bow (never
> Banshee in Wexford). . . . There is still belief.

39 Millburn River: it flows through the village of Milltown, Parish of
Antrim, Antrim, into Lough Neagh (O.S. 49).

40 Multeen River: a tributary of the River Suir; it flows into the Suir
near Golden, Parishes of Relickmurry and Athassel, Tipperary.

41 River Shannon: this is Ireland's longest river; it rises in the Cuilcagh
Mountains, Cavan and flows through Cavan and Leitrim and borders
on Roscommon, Longford, Westmeath, Galway, Offaly, Tipperary,
Clare, Limerick and north-west Kerry, on its route to the Atlantic
Ocean.

42 Power, 1952, p. 80, translates *Tobar na Baidhbe* 'The Banshee's Well';
onomastic references (Wat. 6, 9) are not included in note 24.

43 cf. note 9.

44 1839, p. 176.

45 Connaught: Gal. 8bs, 22m, 23bs, 34bs, 56bs, 65bs; Mayo 23bs, 24bs;
Ros. 1bs, 16bs; Sli. 17bs
Total: 11 m = 1; bs = 10
Leinster: Kild. 13bs; Kilk. 15m; Long. 23bs, 29m; Lou. 2m; Wmea.
4bs.
Total: 6, m = 3; bs = 3.
Munster: Cl. 37bs; Tipp. 44bs.
Total: 2, m = 0; bs = 2.
Overall Total: 19 m = 4, bs = 15

46 App. 4.3, pp. 317-20; cf. also two Galway versions of The Comb Legend
(Gal. 24, 41), a version of The Imprint of the Banshee's Five Fingers
Legend (Gal. 15), p. 316, and Lou. 13, an abduction legend.

47 Gal. M 1546:26, M 1205:521, 522 (Claregalway parish), M 1739:205
(Carna parish), M 405:8-9 (Beagh parish), de Bhaldraithe, T., 1977,
pp. 204-5 (Oranmore parish), Mayo S 121: 11-12, and S 410:
187-8.

Not included in Map 12 are references from Galway (M 969: 187-9), Sligo (S 164: 310), Leitrim (S 214: 350-1, S 223: 300. S 225: 146, *Proceedings of the Royal Irish Academy*, 1908-9, p. 325), Cavan (M 1507:113-4) and Westmeath (S 746:89-90) to a washerwoman who hits (in the Cavan example) and kills (in other examples) with her beetle the enchanted black pig of the Schoolmaster legend, a legend about the schoolmaster who was changed into a black pig and chased across various parts of the country. Examples of this legend without the beetling woman motif are also found in Galway, Leitrim, Cavan and Westmeath and in Armagh, Donegal, Down, Kildare, Longford, Louth, Meath, Monaghan, Roscommon and Wicklow. (I wish to thank Fionnuala Williams and George McClafferty for this information).

48   See Map 12, which includes the following references from Clare, Cork and Kerry. Cl. M 39: 410-11, S 629: 112, *An Claidheamh Soluis* IV, 19 July 1902, p. 320. Cork: M 1158: 213-4, S 314: 119-20. Ker.: M 243:481, M 469:19, M 927:432, S 410:187-8, *Béaloideas* I, 1927-8, p. 204 = Ó Duilearga, S., 1977, no. 133, pp. 320-1.
A reference pertaining to Waterford states that beetling sounds commonly heard at streams and rivers at nightfall on summer evenings were attributed to the heron (M 1367:137), which brings to mind Yeats's reference to 'flapping herons' in his poem 'The Stolen Child' (*Collected Poems of W. B. Yeats*, 1891, p. 20).
For reference to female washing beings in France (esp. in Brittany), Spain, and even Korea, see Schoepperle, G., 1919, p. 65 and Jones, G., 1922, 105ff. For beetling women in Manx tradition see Gill, 1934, p. 107, (*sub, sladdhan* 'beetle'), and references to similar beings in Lithuanian tradition are found in pp. 7-13b of Jonas Balys's notes on Lithuanian folklore in M 1374: 138-41 in the manuscript archive of the Dept. of Irish Folklore, University College Dublin. Washing *weisse Frauen* in German tradition are referred to in Petzoldt, L. ed., legends 273 a, c, and 274, pp. 163-5 and commentary p. 407. They are also referred to in Peuckert, W.-E., 1962, no. 263, p. 148, and 1965, no. 235, pp. 134-5.

49   The following references to the *bean-nighe* of Scottish Gaelic tradition have been noted: Briggs, K., *Dictionary of Fairies*, 1976, pp. 19-20, 61, and works mentioned there; Campbell, J. F., *Leabhar na Féinne*, I, 1872, pp. 182, 191-2; *Popular Tales*, 3, 1892, pp. 320-5. Campbell, J.G., *The Fians*, 1891 (= *Waifs and Strays*, IV), pp. 32-4, 39-40: *Superstitions*, 1900, pp. 42-5; *Witchcraft and Second Sight*, 1902, pp. 111-9, Campbell, J. L., and Hall, T. H., *Strange Things*, 1968, pp. 283, 289; Carmichael, A., *Carmina Gadelica*, I, 1928, p. 30; II, 1928, pp. 227-9, 244-5; V, 1954, pp. 272-5; Dwelly, E., ed. *The Illustrated Gaelic - English Dictionary*, 1941, s.v. *bean-nighe*; Donaldson, M.E.M., *Wanderings in the Western Highlands and Islands*, 1923, p. 227; Grant, I.F., *Highland Folk Ways*, 1961, p. 186; Jones, G., 'A Washer at the Ford', *Aberystwyth Studies*, IV, 1922, p. 107; Mac Cormick, J., *The Island of Mull*, 1934, pp. 87-88; MacFarlane A.M., 'Myths Associated with Mountains, Springs and Lochs in the

Highlands', *Transactions of the Gaelic Society of Inverness* XXXIV, 1927-8, pp. 146-7; MacGregor, A.A., *The Peat - Fire Flame*, 1937, pp. 297-8; McKay, J.G. *More West Highland Tales*, I, 1940, Appendix 3, p. 501; MacLagan, R.C., '"The Keener" in the Scottish Highlands and Islands' *Folk-Lore* XXV, 1914, pp. 84-91, MacLean, C.I., *The Highlands*, 1975, p. 131; MacPhail, M. *'A' bhean-nighe.* (The Washerwoman), *Folk-Lore*, IX, 1898, pp. 91-2, Miller, H., *The Cruise of the Betsy*, 1858, p. 51, *Scenes and Legends*, 1869, p. 301; Schoepperle, G., 'The Washer of the Ford', *Journal of English and Germanic Philology* XVIII, 1919, pp. 63-4; *'A' Bhean Nighe or Loireag'*, I, *Guth na Bliadhna* IX, *Air.* 2, 1912, pp. 195-221; II, *Air.* 3, 1912, pp. 333-65, Watson, E.C., 'Highland Mythology', *Celtic Review* V, 1908-9, pp. 49-50.

50   The use of the term *léine* in what is termed The Shirt Legend in this work adds weight to the suggestion that the Irish and Scottish Gaelic traditions of the supernatural washerwoman foreboding death are generically related and thus of considerable age. In the context of the legend shirt corresponds to *léine* and the garment in question is an ordinary shirt. *Léine*, however, originally meant linen and linen cloth and it also came to mean 'a garment worn next the skin by both sexes, frequently made of linen, sometimes of silk, descending sometimes to the knee, sometimes to the ankle, smock or tunic' (*Dictionary of the Irish Language, s.v. léine*). According to Ó Danachair, 1967, p. 7, 'Fighting men wore a thick padded or quilted tunic reaching to about the knee: this protected the wearer's body against the chafing of his heavy chain-mail and helped to absorb the shock of blows in battle'. In an episode in *Táin Bó Cúailnge*, Rescension I, reference is made to the twenty-seven shirts, *secht cneslénti fichit* which Cúchulainn was credited with wearing tied to him with ropes and cords, going in to battle (O'Rahilly, C., ed., 1976, p. 123). It is thus possible that the *léine* would have been part of the *fadhbh*, 'spoils, generally of clothing or equipment taken from the dead,' and of the *earra* 'military equipment, dress', (*Dictionary of the Irish Language s.v. fadb, errad),* from which the Badb washed blood in the *badhbh*-texts discussed in Chapter 12: *fadhbh* is mentioned in *'Aided Con Culainn'*, (Van Hamel, A.G., ed., 1968, p. 96), in *Reicne Fothaid Canainne*, (Meyer, K., ed., 1910, p. 16, v. 42 and in *Da Choca's Hostel*, (Stokes, J., ed., 1900, v. 15, p. 156), while *earra* is referred in *'Aided Con Culainn'*, p. 96. In the Scottish Gaelic texts — *'Bas Osgair'* in Campbell, J.F., *Leabhar na Féinne*. 1872, pp. 182, 191-2 and *'Laoidh Osgair'* in Campbell, J.F., *Popular Tales,* III, 1892, p. 325, v. 6 — the *baobh* (Irish *badhbh*) washes *faobh (aobh),* 'spoil, booty, dead men's clothes' (Dwelly, E., 1941, *s.v. faobh*). The léine would also have been part of *an t-eudach* which the *baobh* washed in the Oscar texts just mentioned and in 'Cath Gabhra nó Laoidh Oscair' in Campbell, J.G., *The Fians,* 1891, p. 39. Turning back to the Irish material, reference is found in the fourteenth century *Caithréim Thoirdhealbhaigh* (O'Grady, S.H. *eag.,* I, 1929, p. 140) to *séimléinted srebnaide sídamail,* 'smooth, fine-

textured silken shirts (*ibid.*, 2, p. 124), which are among the items the *badhbh*-figure washes on the shores of Lough Riasc, Co. Clare.
In the nineteenth and twentieth century Scottish Gaelic folk tradition *léine* is sometimes used to denote the garment the *bean-nighe* washes, e.g., Carmichael, A., II, 1928, p. 228, V, 1954, pp. 272, 274, 276, 282-3; Campbell, J.G., 1902, p. 115; *Guth na Bliadhna* IX, *Air.* 3, pp. 344-9. (In Carmichael, A., V, 1954, p. 282, the being is named *Léinteag).* It is found in translation as 'shirt' in further texts, e.g., *Guth na Bliadhna* IX, *Air.* 2, p. 218, *Air.* 3, pp. 339-45; MacFarlane, A.M, 1927-8, p. 147, and Miller, H., 1869, p. 301. In the twentieth century Irish folk tradition the *bean sí* washes a *léine* in all versions of The Shirt Legend. From these references it is evident that the washing of the *bean sí* in Irish tradition and of the *bean-nighe* in Scottish Gaelic tradition is related to the pre-battle washing of Badb, goddess of war as exemplified in the Old, Middle and Early Modern Irish texts and in later Scottish Gaelic manuscript and oral versions of *Laoidh Oscair.* There is thus added support for the suggestion that there is a close generic relationship between the supernatural washerwoman connected with death in Irish tradition, the *bean-sí* especially in Galway, and the *bean-nighe* of Scottish Gaelic tradition, and that they both derived initially from a common heritage. In Irish (Dinneen, P.S., 1975, *s.v. léine)* and Scottish Gaelic (Dwelly, E., 1941, *s.v. léine) léine* has also the secondary meaning, 'shroud' 'winding sheet' and it is found in this sense in Scotland referring to the garment the *bean-nighe* washes, e.g., Campbell, J.L., and Hall, T.H., 1968, p. 289); Carmichael, A., II, 1928, p. 227; Donaldson, M.E.M., 1923, p. 227; *Guth na Bliadhna, Air* 3, 1912, pp. 335, 341; MacLagan, H., 1914, p. 87; Miller, E.C., 1858, p. 50 and Watson, E.C., 1908-9, p. 49. It also occurs as a translation of *léine/léineag* in Carmichael A., II 1928, pp. 227-9; V. 1954, p. 282. In view of this and also because of the archival references to shrouds (Gal. 56; Wmea. 4) and a winding sheet (Archdeacon, M., 1839, p. 176) being washed by the *bean sí* in Irish tradition, it is not improbable that *léine* as found in The Shirt Legend, in earlier times meant a shroud or winding sheet.
In the area of material culture, the Irish-Scottish connection has been referred to by McCourt, D., 1964, p. 70, in relation to the cruck trusses of some vernacular houses of north-west Ireland. He states:

> the similarity between the Irish and Scottish trusses is to be explained by links of longer standing than the seventeenth century, going back possibly to prehistoric times and embracing a single cultural region that reached from Connacht to the west of Scotland.

51 The manifestation locations (388) on occasions of death specified in the material are:
at or in the vicinity of a house — 277 records (Appendix 3.6, pp. 308-9; unusual nature formations, 8 records (Cl. 7, 19; Car. 15; Mon. 7; Wat. 34, 36; Wex. 38 (x2) — pp. 125-9; miscellaneous nature locations — 3 records (Cav. 30; Gal. 13; Ker. 35), at or near water — 70 records (cf. note 24); in the home parish of a person dying

abroad or far away in another part of Ireland — 25 records (Appendix 3.6 (f), consists of 36 records of manifestations of the death-messenger in Ireland and the occasion of deaths abroad; 11 of these records are, however, included in Appendix 3.6 (d) — manifestations at the old family home — and they are not, therefore, again included here); on land belonging to the dying person — 5 records (Cav. 10, 26; Don. 22; Long. 29; Mea. 4).

52   Appendix 3.6 (a), p. 308.

53   See Chp. 3, note 19.

54   1877, p. 177.

55   Edgeworth, M., 1800, p. 21; Croker, T.C., 1828, III, p. 10; Keegan, J., 1839, p. 370; McAnally, D.R., 1888, p. 118.

Chapter 7

1   Almqvist, B., 1974-6, (1977), pp. 1-40.

2   1861, p. 127.

3   Cav. 1.4 (pp. 421-2), 41; Kilk. 15; Leit. 7; Ros. 12; Wat. 37, 41, 46.

4   Further examples are: Don. 27(Q); Ker. 27(Q); Lao. 19(Q); Long. 29(Q); Tipp. 20(Q); Wmea. 4(Q).

5   1888, p. 112; '. . . the death notice being for the family rather than for the doomed individual.'

6   Further examples are: Cl. 26; Fer. 1; Ros. 2; Tipp. 26.

7   See also Cl. 24; Don. 11; Ker. 25; Tyr. 6.

8   Neighbours of the dying person figure as experiencers in 49% of the relevant records.

9   See 8 above.

10   Cf. Ker. 13.

11   This is indicated in Ros. 2(Q) which states that while the immediate family did not experience the death-messenger, nevertheless 'when all was over they were the people that were proud when they heard that the banshee cried after a member of their family.'

Chapter 8

1   1839, pp. 371, 373.

2   Similar beliefs about the *bean-nighe (Folk-Lore* IX, 1896, p. 91) and the *caointeachán (Folk-Lore* XXV, 1914, pp. 88-9) are found in Scottish-Gaelic tradition.

3   Ant. 6; Cav. 21; Cl. 14; Don. 6, 16; Ker. 4, 45; Kild. 6, 8, 13; Kilk. 15; Lao. 17; Long. 29; Wmea. 2, 4; Wex. 23, 38; Wick. 9.
Total: 18.

Chapter 9

1   These aspects of the belief are referred to in the following ten records: Car. 16; Cav. 21; Lao. 17; Wmea. 2, 4, 5 (a), p. 50; Wex. 42; Wick. 6, 7, 9. In folk tradition, the comb serves for warding off witchcraft and evil magic but it is also dangerous and unlucky (see *Handwörterbuch des Deutschen Aberglaubens,* IV, pp. 942). The magical properties of the comb in Scottish-Gaelic tradition and the serious consequences of being hit by one are referred to in McKay, J.G., I, 1940, pp. 352-3, note 3, and the idea is also enshrined in the saying, *Na tilg a' chír ach air do nàmhaid,* 'do not throw the comb except on your enemy'. (Henderson, G., 1911, p. 293) cf. Chp. 12, note 94.

2   For a possible older life history of The Comb Legend see Patricia Lysaght's further study of the legend, 1991, p. 79, note 9.

3   1909, p. 174; probably taken down by a 'Miss Greene of Millbrook [Maganey, Co. Kildare], from the narration of Tom Daly, gardiner.'

4   Question 14. See Appendix 1, p. 249.

5   See also Ker. 4, 7, 27 and Mayo 30.

6   1958, ML 4080.

7   Map 17 is based on seminar work in the Department of Irish Folklore 1974-5, and on further research by the author.

8   Cavan S 966: 353; Galway M 349: 304-8, S 24: 110-13, Leitrim S 189: 8

9   e.g., Ros. 23; Ros. 1 indicates influence from mermaid traditions.

10   *sliseog giúise* 'strip of bog-deal', cf Ó Dónaill, N., *eag.*, 1977.

11   *caisnín* 'splint-light', cf. Ó Dónaill, N., *eag.*, 1977.

12   'door-bar' (Ó Dónaill, 1977, *s.v. maide*). Ciarán Bairéad, former full-
     time collector, has the following description of the *maide éamainn*
     from John Flaherty, stone mason, *Gráinseach*, Co. Galway in M 1402:
     342-3:
     The doors of the houses in old times were made of hazel switches
     plaited. There was no hinges or anything on them and the *maide
     éamainn* was a stick to keep the door from falling in. It went across
     the back of the door from one door-post to the other. There was a
     strap in the middle of the door through which it passed'. cf. also
     Lucas, 1956, pp. 16-35 ('Wattle and Straw Mat Doors in Ireland').

13   In Gal. 37 (Q), it is unclear who took the object, and in Off. 4 (S);
     Tipp. 32 (S); Wmea. 16 (L) and Wex. 4 (M), it is taken by a female.

14   Cav. 12 (S); Kilk. 4 (S), 15 (Q); Laois 5 (S), 15 (R); Wex. 30 (S).

15   Lao. 17 (R); Tipp. 44 (Q).

16   e.g., Gal. 38 (party); Wat. 25 (dance); Mayo 18, Sli. 9, Tipp. 3 (card-
     playing); Gal. 55, Lao. 12, 22 (*cuaird*/rambling).

17   Kilk. 13; Wmea. 9.

18   Gal. 46; Lao. 11.

19   Night-time (unspecified hour) is mentioned in 29 variants Car. 11; Gal.
     24, 38, 41, 46, 55; Kilk. 5, 12, 13; Lao. 11, 12, 22; Long. 6; Mayo
     18; Sli. 9; Tipp. 34, 39, 42; Wat. 10, 25, 27, 40, 50; Wex. 4, 7, 50, 51;
     Wick. 12, 13. Midnight is specified in 3 variants (Gal. 32; Tipp. 9, 43),
     while evening-time is mentioned in Gal. 41; Lao. 5; Off. 8 and Wat.
     19. Only 2 variants (Off. 4, Ros. 23) mention day-time.

20   The encounter occurs in the vicinity of a house in 6 variants: the
     human actor's own house (Kilk. 12 (b); Lao. 1; Wat. 27; Wick. 13);
     the dying person's house (Kilk. 13; Wmea. 9).

21   Mayo 18; Off. 10; Wmea. 3.

22   Car. 11; Gal. 32, 38; Sli. 9; Tipp. 34, 43; Wmea. 16; Wick. 12.

23   Ros. 23; Tipp. 39.

24   Gal. 24, 41, 46, 55.

25   von Sydow, C.W., 1948, pp. 19, 74.

26 In 18 examples from 8 counties the being is heard crying at the window: Gal. 32; Kild. 9; Kilk. 4, 5, 16, 18; Lao. 5, 7, 11, 17; Off. 8; Sli. 9; Tipp. 3, 9, 34, 39, 42, 43; Wat. 27. The crying takes place at the door in five variants: Dub. 6; Gal. 24; Kilk. 7; Lao. 15; Mayo 27.

27 cf. motif C 543 'Tabu: picking up comb from ground. It belongs to fairy (witch) who will avenge insult', in Thompson, S., 1955-8. The Scottish attribution of this motif by Thompson is based on the motif-index in McKay, J.G., *More West Highland Tales* I, 1940, p. 526. However, the motif is, in fact, from Irish material published in *Béaloideas* III, p. 302, and quoted in McKay, I, 1940, pp. 354-5, note I.

28 For the position of the priest in Irish traditional society, see Ó Héalaí, P., 1977, pp. 109-31.

29 Object not taken into house: Wex. 35, 37; Long. 4; Gal. 55.
Object not returned to being: *Ireland's Own*, 27 Nov. 1954, p. 15 (a); Ros. 23 (hybrid with Man Marries Mermaid Legend (ML 4080); Off. 4 (S); 10 (S); Wmea. 9 (S).
Object left on window-sill; Kilk. 18 (S); Wex. 7 (S), 30 (S); Tipp. 39 (S).
Lack of details in source material: Gal. 37 (Q); Car. 10 (S); Kilk. 12b (Q), 19 (S); Lao. 19 (R), 22 (S); Wmea. 12 (P); Wex. 40 (Q).

30 Object thrown to pursuing death-messenger: Gal. 55, object not returned to being: see note 29.
Object thrown out to death-messenger: Sli. 9 (S); Kilk. 12b (Q); Off. 11 (S); Wat. 10 (S), 27 (S).
Object left outside on window-sill: Wex. 7 (S), 30 (S); Tipp. 39 (S).
Human actor hands object to death-messenger: Kilk. 15, 18 (Q); Wex. 4 (M); Tipp. 3 (S), 43 (P). Death-messenger seizes comb: Wat. 50 (S).
Lack of sufficient details in source material: Gal. 32 (S), 46 (S); Mayo 18 (S); Kilk. 14 (S); Long. 6 (S); Wmea. 12 (P).

31 In this connection, see Kennedy, P., 1886, pp. 151-3.

32 For an examination of beliefs and legends concerning changelings in Irish tradition see MacPhilib, S., 1980, especially p. 240 which deals with the banishment of the changeling by means of a red-hot plough-coulter.

33 Typological and distribution aspects of the spade in Ireland are dealt with by Ó Danchair, C., 1963, pp. 98-114 and Gailey, A., 1970., pp. 35-48.

34 MacPhilib, S., *op. cit.*, pp. 236, 239; cf. also Ó Súilleabháin, S., 1942, p. 476.

35 F 625, Strong Man: breaker of iron: Thompson, S., 1955-8.

36   ML 5010, Christiansen, R. Th., 1958, pp. 86-7; 1964, pp. 82-4.

37   Type 726 in Ó Súilleabháin, S., Christiansen, R.Th., *The Types of the Irish Folktale*, 1963.

38   In McPhail, 1896, p. 91, a basically similar saying: *As maith a' chur sin ruit* 'It is well for you it is so' is attributed to the supernatural washer-woman of Scottish-Gaelic tradition, the *bhean-nighe* in a dialogue between her and the man who molests her. A similar type saying occurs in some Cork legends dealing with evil female spirits, e.g., M49: 202 in which an evil female spirit says to the man who has given her a lift on his horse, *gur mhaith an bhail air gur thug sé an marcaíocht di*, 'that it was well for him that he gave her the lift'; M1015: 380 in which *Máire Gaelach*, also an evil spirit, says to the man who succeeded in closing the door of the house on her ''Twas well for you'.

Chapter 10

1   Motif E 542.1.2, Thompson, S., 1955-8.

2   M1158: 213-4.

3   Tape 25(I) B. Ó F., 14 October 1979. Collected by Bairbre Ó'Floinn from Steven Croghan, Roscommon, cf. also the legend entitled 'The Print of her Fingers' in M556: 332-3 from the parish of Glenbeigh, Co. Kerry, where a boy who had fallen asleep while minding his employer's cows, is slapped on the face by a dead female relation of the farmer. The print of the woman's hand remained on his face until the day he died.
      cf. also references to the imprint of five fingers left on objects like stones or rocks by ghosts (M 42; 219) or saints (St. Brigid: *Béaloideas* IV, p. 14 and St. Molaga, M132: 108). For references to other imprints left on similar objects by saints, supernatural beings or animals, see Section F, *Foirgnithe Nadúir* 'Nature Constructions', *Rian Duine ar Chlocha* 'Human trace on Stones', of the Subject Index in the manuscript archive of the Department of Irish Folklore, University College Dublin.

Chapter 11

1   cf. note 50, pp. 388-9.

2   Although Gal. 21 is from a Main Ms. it was contributed by a school-boy. It is part of a collection of 388 manuscript pages written by school children from the parishes of Annaghdown and Claregalway, Co. Galway, in 1937 (M489: 122-410). Then then archivist of the *Irish Folklore Commission*, Seán Ó Súilleabháin, made the following note about the material (p. 121):

'Sé Dónall Ó Dúnaí, Cigire Scoile, i gCo. na Gaillimhe do chuir go dtí an Coimisiún an t-abhar so leanas. Na leanaí scoile do scríobh an t-abhar. Bhíodar á scrúdú le haghaidh an dá phunt a thugann an Rialtas do leanaí as tithe go mbíonn an Ghaeilge á labhairt ionta de ghnáth. [It was Dónall Ó Dúnaí, School Inspector, in Co. Galway, who sent this material to the Commission. It was the schoolchildren who wrote it. They were being examined for the two pounds that the Government pays to children from houses where Irish is usually spoken.]

3 cf. Wilde, 1867, pp. 18-9 and accompanying end-map showing the navigation course. See also Semple, M., 1974 'Corrib Navigation', p. 21 ff., and 'Steamers on the Corrib', p. 41 ff.

Chapter 12

1 A similar type being in Welsh tradition — the Cyhiraeth — is considered by scholars to be an ancestress of the family she attends; cf. Rhŷs, J., Vol. 1, 1901, p. 545, II, 452-5; Croker, III, 1828, pp. 289-294.

2 1973, p. 94.

3 1955, p. 24.

4 Meid, W., ed., 1967, pp. ix, xi.

5 See pp. 9-10 of Meid's 1967 ed. of the Irish text and pp. 8, 9 of J. Carney's 1955 English translation.

6 See Mac Cana, P., 1973, pp. 33, 35.

7 See Ó Cadhlaigh, 1956, pp. 411, 412. Intensification in numbers is a persistent motif in Irish literary tradition, e.g., the *mná sí* lamenting in seventeenth and eighteenth century Irish poetry. In a lament composed for the poet Seán Ó Tuama (+ 1775) sixty *mná sí* are said to have keened him (Ua Duinnín, P., 1906, p. 90):
    Níl mothar ná mínleach coillte cumar ná céim gan seascad beantsidhe dá chaoineadh i ndoilbheas déar.

8 Todd, J.H., 1867, pp. xix-xxvii.

9 Todd, J.H., ed., 1867, p. 200.

10 Goedheer, A.J., 1938, pp. 23, 25.

11 Hennessy, W.M., ed., 1871, p. 8.

12 For Norse prognostications about the outcome of the Battle of Clontarf, see Goedheer, A.J., 1938, pp. 74 ff.

13 Ó hÓgáin, D., 1979, pp. 239-41.

14 This is a lament composed by Seán Clárach Mac Domhnaill on the death of Donnchadha Mac Sheaghán, Bishop of Cork, 1726. (Ua Duinnín, P., 1902, pp. 49-50). Line 1176 (p. 50) concerns us here because the use of the conditional tense *éagfadh* 'would die' shows that Clíona's crying and lamenting is for a death which will take place in the near future.

    Tuigim-sé ar uair uaithe go n-éagfadh tráth . . .

    [I understood from her immediately that soon would die . . .]
    The use of the word *tuar* in line 1180 (p. 50) also shows that the crying is an omen or foreboding of death:

    Mo thubaist an tuar duailseach do theacht in dháil

    [Alas that this sorrowful omen should come to me!]

15 By contrast, the sovereignty figure Mór Mumhan, is depicted as a keening, rather than a foreboding figure, (cf. Ó hÓgáin, 1990, p. 45.)

16 1870-2, pp. 32 ff.

17 There is a further reference to the Morrígan, i.e. Badb, washing in the tale commonly known as *The Second Battle of Magh Tuireadh*, but it is unclear from the text what the washing entails. Both W. Stokes' (1891), pp. 84, 85, and E.A. Gray's (1983), p. 240, interpretation of the passage in question is that the Morrígan is washing herself. Gray states: 'When the Dagda meets her, the Morrígan is bathing; her 'nine loosened tresses' suggest that she has just unbraided her hair to wash it.' Mac Cana, on the other hand, seems to take the view that the Morrígan in this passage is a 'Washer at the Ford' (Mac Cana, P., 1973, p. 66).

18 The three 'Washer at the Ford' texts here discussed are also dealt with by Schoepperle in relation to the Fiona Macleod writing of William Sharp (cf. note 41). See also Jones, G., 1922. The motif is numbered D 1812.5.1.1.7* 'Washer at the Ford' in Cross, T.P., 1952.

19 Van Hamel, A.G., ed., 1968, p. 96.

20 The oldest Ms. text of this version dates from the 16th century — *ibid.*, p. 70.

21 *Ibid.*, p. 69; for earlier reference to the 'Washer at the Ford' cf. p. 199.

22 *Ibid.*, pp. 95-6.

23 *Ibid.*, p. 96.

24 For the equasion of Badb and Morrígan in Irish literature, see Mac Cana, P., 1973, p. 86, and also the extracts from older texts quoted by Hennessy, W.M., ed., 1870-2, pp. 36-7.

25 O'Rahilly, C., 1976, p. 57; cf. Hennessy, 1870-2, pp. 45-6.

26 For the estimated date of the text see Meyer, K., 1910, p. 1.

27 Cf. *Dictionary of the Irish Language, s.v. mong.*

28 Mac Cana, P., 1980; the early version is mentioned in the 9th century (*ibid.* n. 41).

29 Stokes, W., ed., 1900, p. 156.

30 O'Davoren's Glossary defines *corrguinech* 'sorcery' as the process of making *glám dícinn*, a type of satire, on one foot, with one eye open, and using only one hand (Stokes, W., ed., 1904, p. 257 (383). See also *Dictionary of the Irish Language*, '*corrguinne*', '*corguinech*', and Joyce, P.W., I, 1903, pp. 240-242.

31 Stokes, W., ed., 1900, pp. 156-7.

32 Joynt, M., n.d., p. 111.

33 O'Grady, S.H., *eag.*, 1929, Vol. 1, pp. xiii-xiv.

34 *Ibid.*, p. 103-5; Vol. II, 93-4 (English translation).

35 For accounts of the battles of Corcomroe Abbey and Dysert O'Dea, see Hayes-McCoy, G. A, 1969, pp. 35-46 and works quoted on pp. 46-7 of that work.

36 O'Grady, S.H., 1929, Vol. 1, pp. 140-41; Vol. II, pp. 124-5.

37 O'Grady, Vol. 1, p. xiv.

38 *Ibid.*, p. 104.

39 O'Grady, S.H., *eag.*, 1929, Vol. 2, p. 93.

40 e.g., *Irisleabhar na Gaedhilge*, xvii, April 1907, p. 306. The motif however, was used creatively by some 19th-century writers in English. In his long poem *Congal* (1872), (Book iii, pp. 57-9). Sir Samuel Ferguson includes a powerful 'Washer at the Ford' episode, which he states (p. 206) is based on 'McCraith's "Wars of Turlough" (Ms., R.I.A.)' (i.e. *Caithréim Thoirdhealbhaigh*, O'Grady, (ed.), 1929, Vol. 1, pp. 103-5, 140-1). Abroad, the motif occurs in the 'Fiona MacLeod' writings of William Sharp (cf. *The Washer of the Ford: and Other Legendary Moralities* (1896).

Schoepperle (1919, pp. 60-65) maintains that Sharp's use of the motif springs from his knowledge of the Scottish-Gaelic traditions of the *bean-nighe.*

41   Tomás Laighléis's account (from Menlo (Gal. 34)) states that the woman was beetling under a bridge, while another Menlo version states that she was lamenting loudly in a bog-hole near the battlefield of Aughrim (Ó Broin, 1957, pp. 10-11).

42   Chp. 6, pp. 129-33.

43   Cf. note 49, Chp. 6.

44   Cf. Chp. 6, pp. 116-8, Chp. 7, pp. 141-2.

45   Cf. pp. 69-70.

46   See O'Rahilly, C., ed., 1970, p. ix.

47   O'Rahilly, C., ed., 1976, p. 2. *Imbas forosna,* 'divination which illuminates' is dealt with by N.K. Chadwick, 1935, pp. 97-135. See further O'Rahilly, 1946, pp. 339-40, and Joyce, I, 1903, pp. 242-5.

48   O'Rahilly, C., 1976, pp. 2-4.

49   Windisch, E., 1887, Vol. 2, p. 242. James Carey in his article 'Notes on the Irish War-Goddess', 1983, p. 265, refers to another lone woman riding in a chariot — 'the witch (*badb*) *símha',* in *Cath Maighe Léna,* ed. Jackson, K.H., 1938, p. 16.

50   O'Rahilly, C., ed., 1970, p. 5.

51   O'Rahilly, C., (ed.), 1978, 'Addenda', p. 283.

52   1938, p. 74.

53   See Goedheer, A.J., 1938, pp. 80-1.

54   As 50 above.

55   Cf. note 8, Chapter 4.

56   For earlier Norse contact with the Gaelic world, cf. Ó Corráin, D., 1972, p. 81.

57   O'Rahilly, C., ed., 1978, p. vii.

58   Book of Leinster versions, ed. O'Rahilly, C., 1970, p. 6, lines 197-205:

Forrécacha Medb furri. 'Ocus cid dogní-siu and sain innossa, a ingen?' for Medb. 'Ic tairdeilb I do lessa-su 7 do lítha. Ic teclaim 7 ic tinól cethri n-ollchóiced ñHérend lat-su i crích ñUlad ar cend Tána Bó Cúalnge.' 'Cid 'má ndénai-siu dam-sa sain?' ar Medb, 'Fail a mórabba dam. Banchumal dit muntir atamchomnaic.' 'Cóich dom muntir-sea tussa?' ar Medb. 'Ní handsa ém. Feidelm banfáid a Síd Chrúchna atamchomnaic-se.' 'Maith and sin,

> a Feidelm banfáid, cia facci ar slúag?'
> 'Atchíu forderg forro, atchíu rúad.'

cf. also The Stowe Version, ed., O'Rahilly, C., 1978, pp. 7-8, lines 197-236.

59 Mac Cana, P., 1973, p. 120.

60 Mac Cana, P., 1955-6, p. 88.

61 Mac Cana, P., 1973, p. 117.

62 For the effects of the Cromwellian and Williamite confiscations on the proportion of land owned by Catholics in Ireland see maps in Moody, T.W., and Martin, F.X., 1967, p. 201.

63 Mac Cana, P., 1973, p. 94.

64 See Carney, J., *The Irish Bardic Poet*, Dublin 1967; Bergin, O., *Irish Bardic Poetry*, Dublin, 1970, and Ó Cuív, B., *The Irish Bardic Duanaire or "Poem Book"*, Dublin 1973.

65 cf. notes 71-3 below.

66 cf. Chp. 1, pp. 29-30.

67 cf. Chp. 3.

68 O'Brien, J., 1768.

69 cf. note 50, Chapter 1.

70 cf. Chp. 6, p. 132.

71 Cf. Moody and Martin, 1967, Chps. 8-15, pp. 123-363.

72 cf. Chp. 1, p. 38, Chp. 5, pp. 106-9.

73 de Fréine, S., 1977, pp. 78-9.

74 Chp. 1, p. 29.

75 Modern Irish *cailleach, amaid,* see Ó Dónaill, N., *eag.,* 1977.

76 e.g., Bé Find and her retinue with the river Boyne (cf. p. 193), Aoibheall with Tobar Aoibhill, Clare (Joyce, P.W., 1869, p. 183), Áine with Lough Gur and the Camóg river, Limerick (p. 214 and note 92, below), and Clíona with Tonn Chlíona, Cork (Joyce, P.W., 1869, p. 182).

77 Cf. the reference to Étaín from the Síd of Brí Leith sitting by a well (p. 214, and n. 91 below), and to Áine in Lough Gur (she is also associated with the Camóg river — see note 76). The *spéirbhean* in Aisling poetry is also, sometimes, experienced by the poet near water. e.g., poems 2, 5, 6, 9, 13 and 14 in *Amhráin Eoghain Ruaidh Uí Shúilleabháin,* (ed., Ua Duinnín, P., 1901).

78 In the twelfth century Book of Leinster version of the Táin, Fedelm is described as being *a Síd Chrúachna* (cf. n. 58 above), and in Hennessy, 1870-2, the reference — *Badb Síde Femin* — occurrs (p. 41).

79 The washing motif and its connection with blood survived much stronger in Gaelic Scotland; perhaps the reason was that war continued much longer between the Gaelic clans there, e.g., England ruled through native clans with Gaelic culture such as the Campbells.

80 1839, p. 176.

81 Westropp, T. J., 1910, p. 189.

82 cf. pp. 122 ff.

83 Chp. 6, pp. 128-30.

84 Chp. 6, pp. 130-133.

85 pp. 197-201.

86 See Chp. 6, pp. 130-3, note 49 pp. 387-8, and also p. 197.

87 pp. 130-3.

88 e.g., through the sea, a lake, a river or a well. See Thompson, S., 1955-8, motif F 93 'water entrance to the Lower World', and Mac Cana, P., 1973, pp. 123-4.

89 1973, p. 94.

90 Knott, E., ed., 1936, p. 1. When Eochaidh Aireamh became King of Ireland his Kingship could not be ratified until he had a Queen. He then married Étaín — 'otherwise he would have been the supreme paradox of a king without sovereignty' (Mac Cana, P., 1973, p. 120).

For other examples see Mac Cana, P., 1955-6, p. 85 and works quoted there.

91 In a well known passage at the beginning of *Togail Bruidne Da Derga*, ('The Destruction of Da Derga's Hostel'), Étaín from the Síd of Brí Leith, as perceived by Etarscéle, is sitting at the edge of a well washing herself in a silver basin and she has also with her a *cír chuirrél airgit* Knott, E., ed., 1936, p. 1) which Dillon (1972, p. 25) translates as a 'silver comb'. The references in the Metrical (Gwynn, E., ed; 1909, p. 22, line 53) and Prose (Stokes, W., ed., 1894, p. 292) Dind-shenchas to the Comb of the Daghda's wife, one of a pair of mounds at *Brugh na Bóinne* (Newgrange), seem to suggest that the combing characteristic was also associated with Boann, goddess of the Boyne (cf. Hennessy, W.M., 1870-2, p. 55). The combing motif is also found in Arthurian Romance. In the twelfth century Lancelot tale of Chrétien de Troyes a comb belonging to King Arthur's wife, Guenievre is found on a stone basin encircling a spring and 'in it's teeth there was almost a handful of hair belonging to her who had used the comb' (de Troyes, 1965, p. 287. I wish to thank Dr. Yolanda de Pontfarcy-Sexton for this reference).

92 Nineteenth century folk tradition from Limerick depicts Áine comb-ing her hair on the bank of the Camóg river and also combing it mermaid-like in Lough Gur (Fitzgerald, D., 1879-80, pp. 187, 189). Apart from the mermaid tradition in which the combing of her hair is a very prominent trait (cf. pp. 160-63), examples of the motif are found in the traditions attached to other categories of supernatural beings. *Sprid na Bearnan* for example, an evil spirit in Limerick trad-ition, is depicted going by a stream combing her hair in a reference from Limerick (S 495:35) and it appears that Petticoat Loose, another evil spirit associated mainly with the Decies of Munster is, in a few references from Cork similarily depicted (I wish to thank Anne O'Connor for this information). The combing motif is also found attached to a penetential female being at a stream in a Cork record (S 312: 287) and to a 'foxy woman . . sitting on top of the [fairy fort] in a Kerry record (IFC 744: 171). It also occurs in some Donegal and Mayo versions of the Céadach tale (Bruford, 1969, pp. 125, 131) and in a version of Tale Type 302, 'The Orge's (Devil's) Heart in the Egg' (Aarne, A., and Thompson, S., 1973), from Clear Island, Cork (see *Béaloideas* V, 1935, p. 114). cf. Hyde, D., 1979, pp. 20, 126, for reference to an old woman seen sitting on the edge of a well combing her hair.
    In Scottish Gaelic tradition too, supernatural women are also often seen combing their hair (Campbell, 1893, p. 293), as in versions of the Céadach tale (Bruford, A., *op, cit.*) and according to Carmichael (II, 1928, p. 250) in the traditions of St. Bride (or Bridget). For further references to the combing of the hair in Scottish Gaelic tradition, see the index in Campbell, J.G., IV, 1893, under 'comb'. The motif is also found in Germany (see *Handwörterbuch des Deutschen*

Aberglaubens, IV, p. 951, in France (cf. Taylor, 1865), and in Indic tradition (motif F 324.1 in Thompson, S., and Balys, J., 1958).

93   e.g. Mac Cana, P., 1973, p. 123.

94   Apart from the connection of the comb with otherworld women associated with water (p. 215) and thus also with death, further indication of the possible connection of the comb with death is the occurrence in many cultures of the comb shape as a symbol of 'Heaven's Water'. In Ireland, the comb shape found on the central stone in the *Slieve na Caillí* tumulus, a megalithic burial chamber in Co. Meath, might also indicate a possible connection of the comb with death; see Streit, 1984, pp. 32-3 and also Borlase II, 1897, pp. 313-43.

95   Connaught: Gal. 10, 46, 59; Mayo 9; Ros. 12.
Leinster: Car. 4, 13; Dub. 6; Kild. 4, 6, 7, 10, 11; Kilk. 12b, 16, 18, 19, 26; Lao. 5, 11; Long. 23, 28; Off. 12; Wmea. 11; Wex. 1, 6, 10, 24, 32, 40, 43, 45; Wick. 6, 8, 9, 14.
Munster: Cl. 22, 34; Lim. 2; Tipp. 2, 7, 10, 19, 23, 41; Wat. 8.
Total: 48
cf. also Lim. 24 and Wex. 38 in which the banshee's wail is said to be the noise of the comb as she draws it through her hair.

96   The *badhbh* is depicted combing her hair in a lament in Irish for John Stafford, coadjutor bishop of Ferns, Wexford, who died in 1781 (de Brún, P., 1970, note, p. 47).

97   cf. Partridge, A., 1978, p. 72.

98   For the tracing of the epic (*Táin Bó Cúalnge*) back to the seventh century, and possibly the fourth century, cf. Jackson, K.H., 1964, p. 524-5; cf. O'Rahilly, C., 1970, pp. xii-xiv.

Chapter 13

1   The fear of being ridiculed is strong and is especially referred to in Cav. 9, 14; Der. 1; Ker. 28; Gal. 63; Ros. 1.

2   Honko, L., 1964, p. 10.

3   cf. pp. 73-5.

4   von Sydow, C.W., 1935, pp. 117 ff.

5   From the Irish word *cnoc,* 'hill' Ó Dónaill, N., *eag.,* 1977, *s.v. cnoc.*

6   cf. Chp. 5, 74.

7   1826, pp. 235-7.

8   In Der. 1 a similar type of prank which had the same result was perpetrated by the informant and a companion on a group of girls coming along the road at night. In Cav. 27 it is not clear what form the prank took.

9   Edgeworth, M., 1800, p. 21.

10   Croker, T.C, 1826, pp. 235-7.

11   Hall, 1845, p. 7 ('...even the wail of the banshee is heard no more...')

12   McAnally, 1888, p. 118.

13   Wood-Martin, W.G., 1, 1902, p. 370.

14   Ant. 4, 12; Arm. 8; Cav. 23; Cl. 14, 24; Cork 1; Der. 1; Don. 13, 14, 15, 27; Dub. 8, 15; Gal. 56; Ker. 2, 19, 27, 45; Kild. 6; Long. 21, 29; Lou. 1; Mea. 12; Off. 1; Ros. 11, 17; Tipp. 7, 16; Tyr. 2; Wmea 2, 4, Wex. 17, 41, 48; Wick. 9.
Total: 36 records

15   Arm. 6; Cav. 9, 24, 29; Don. 28; Gal. 63; Ker. 4; Kild. 8.
Total: 8 records

16   There are in fact five records which deal with death-messenger experiences by, or for, priests (Ker. 2; Leit. 14; Wmea. 5, 7; Wex. 4). See also p. 172.

17   Ó Súilleabháin, S., 1967, pp. 19-23, 138-43, 146-54.

18   For an account of the establishment and development of the primary and secondary (Intermediate) education systems in Ireland, see Coolahan, J., 1981, Chapters 2-3.

19   Honko, L., 1964, pp. 16-7.

20   For a description of the Irish Broadcasting Service 1926-66, see Gorham, M., 1967.

21   *Ibid,* p. 1 (Wireless Telegraphy Act, 1926).

22   In 1926 it was estimated that there were 25,000 receiving sets in use

(Gorham, M., 1967, p. 33); in 1949 there were 280,270 licensed radios (Gorham, p. 181); in 1951 there were 310,000 (Gorham, p. 202); in 1961 when the Irish Television Service started this figure had increased to 501,871 (Gorham, p. 325).

23 For the 1925 figure see *Statistical Abstract (Saorstát Éireann) 1931*, p. 158, Table 206. The 1984 figure is from the Department of the Environment. The totals refer to the number of private cars licensed in each County and County Borough of the Republic of Ireland.

24 *The Rural Electrification Scheme* got under way pursuant to the *Electricity (Supply) (Amendment) Act 1945*, Section 41 (Shiel, M., 1984, p. 29.) The large increases in the number of consumers occurred in the late 1940s and especially in the mid 1950s and early 1960s (Shiel, pp. 150-5).

25 For the 1926 figure, see *Census of Population of Ireland*, 1971, vol. I, p. xv, and also Vaughan, W.E., and Fitzpatrick, A.J., 1978, p. 27. For the 1981 figure, see *Census of Population of Ireland*, 1981, Table 8, p. 14, under heading: 'Percentage of Population in Aggregate Town Areas' (towns with a population of 1500 and over comprise the aggregate town areas – see *ibid.* p. VIII.). These figures refer to the twenty-six counties of Ireland and do not, therefore, take into account the rural versus urban population levels in counties Antrim, Armagh, Derry, Down, Fermanagh and Tyrone. According to Vaughan and Fitzpatrick (p. 27) the *Censuses of Population of Northern Ireland* show that in 1926, 50.6% of the population of these counties lived in towns and cities while the figure for 1971 was 55.6%. For references to the *Censuses of Population of Northern Ireland*, 1926-71, see the bibliography in Vaughan and Fitzpatrick, pp. 359-60.

26 See Ariès, p., 1981, Part V, 'The Invisible Death' and pp. 611-4.

27 Anne Hill had no knowledge of The Comb Legend (Chp. 9). It is known in Offaly, but apparently no examples of it from Edenderry have so far come to light.

28 See Chp. 6, p. 135.

29 Information from various schoolteachers.

30 For further discussion on this concept first mooted by Moser (1962), see Hörandner, E., and Lunzer, H., 1982.

31 *Banshee Journal* of Irish Women United, I, no. 1 (May 1975), published by Irishwomen United.

32 *The New Musical Express*, 26 Aug. 1978, pp. 28-9.

Bibliography

Aarne, A., and Thompson, S., *The Types of the Folktale*, FF Communications no. 184, Helsinki, 1973 (Second Revision)

Aberystwyth Studies IV, 1922, Aberystwyth

Allingham, W., *Poems by William Allingham*, Selected and arranged, Allingham, Helen, London, 1912

Almqvist, B., 'Folk Beliefs and Philology', *Arv* XXVII, 1971, pp. 69-120, Stockholm

Almqvist, B., 'The Death Forebodings of Saint Óláfr, King of Norway and Rögnvaldr Brúsason, Earl of Orkney', *Béaloideas* XLII-XLIV, 1974-76 (1977), pp. 1-40, Dublin

Almqvist, B., 'Dream and Reality', *Sinsear* I, 1979, pp. 1-22, Dublin

Almqvist, B., 'Of Mermaids and Marriages. Séamus Heaney's "Maighdean Mara" and Nuala Ní Dhomhnaill's "An Mhaighdean Mhara" in the light of folk tradition,' *Béaloideas* 58, 1990, pp.1-74

Andrews, E., *Ulster Folklore*, London, 1913

Archdeacon, M., *Legends of Connaught*, Dublin, 1839

Archiv für Celtische Lexikographie 1, no. 813, p. 271, 1990; 11, no. 375, p. 256, 1904, Halle

Ariès, P., *The Hour of Our Death*, trans. Weaver, H., London 1983 (Peregrine)

Armstrong, E.A., *The Folklore of Birds*, London, 1958

"Aroon", 'Our Banshee', *White Heather*, Dublin, 1903, pp. 13-37

Arv XXVII, 1971, pp. 69-120, Stockholm

Banim, M. and J., *Tales, By the O'Hara Family*, I-III, London, 1825

Banshee, Journal of Irish Women United 1, no. 1, May, 1975, p. 2, Dublin

Bardan, P., *The Dead-Watchers, And Other Folk-Lore Tales of Westmeath*, Mullingar, 1891

Baring-Gould, S., *Curious Myths of the Middle Ages*, London, 1876

Barrington, Sir Jonah, *Personal Sketches of His Own Times*, 2 vols., London 1827

Béaloideas 1, 1927-28, p. 204; III, 1932, pp. 283, 302; IV, 1933-4 (1934), pp. 5, 21; V, 1935, pp. 114, 144, 222; VI, 1936, p. 220; VII, 1937, p. 90; IX, 1939, pp. 39-40, 276-77; XIII, 1943 (1944), p. 237; XIV, 1944 (1945), pp. 109, 164; XXI, 1951-2 (1952); XXIV, 1955; XXXI, 1963, pp. 98-114; XXXIV, 1966 (1969); XXXIX-XLI, 1971-3, pp. 95-111; XLII-XLIV, 1974-6 (1977), pp. 1-40, 94-119; XLV-XLVII, 1977-9, pp. 164-243; LII, 1984, pp. 75-150; LIX, 1991, pp. 67-82, Dublin

Beck, J.C., 'The White Lady of Great Britain and Ireland', *Folklore* 81, 1970, pp. 292-306, London

Benwell, G., and Waugh, A., *Sea Enchantress: The Tale of the Mermaid and her Kin*, London, 1961

Benwick, J., *Irish Druids and Old Irish Religion*, London, 1894

Bergin, O., *Irish Bardic Poetry*, Dublin, 1970

Best, R.I., O'Brien, M.A., eds., *The Book of Leinster*, II, Dublin, 1956 (5 vols., 1954-1967)

Bhreathnach, M., The Sovereignty Goddess as Goddess of Death?', *Zeitschrift für Celtische Philologie* 39, 1982, pp. 243-60, Tübingen

Bødker, L., ed., *C.W. v. Sydow: Selected Papers on Folklore*, Copenhagen, 1948

Bødker, L., *International Dictionary of Regional European Ethnology and Folklore* II, *Folk Literature (Germanic)*, Copenhagen, 1965

Bodley, S., 'The Banshee. Poetic Text for Music,' *Sinsear*, 8, 1995, pp. 111-117, Dublin

Bonthrone, G.C., 'Childhood Memories of County Antrim', *Ulster Folklife* VI, 1960, pp. 32-42, Belfast

Borlase, W.C., *The Dolmens of Ireland*, I-III, London, 1897

Braddon, M.E., *Joshua Haggard's Daughter* I-III, London, 1876

Brady, E., *All in! All in!*, Dublin, 1975

Breatnach, R.A., *Gaedhilg Chonndae Chille Coinnigh*, unpublished M.A. thesis, University College Dublin, 1939

Breatnach, R.A., 'The Lady and the King: A Theme of Irish Literature', *Studies: An Irish Quarterly Review*, 42, 1953, pp. 321-36, Dublin

Breatnach, R.B., ed., *Seana-Chaint na nDéise* II, Dublin, 1961

Brednich, R.W., *Volkserzählungen und Volksglaube von der Schicksalfrauen*, FF Communications 193, Helsinki, 1964

Bresnan, O., 'The Banshee's Wail', *The Dublin Penny Journal*, 7 Feb 1903, p. 613, Dublin (New Series, Vol. I)

Brewer, E.C., *The Reader's Handbook of Allusions, References, Plots and Stories*, London, 1882

Briggs, K.M., *The Anatomy of Puck*, London, 1959

Briggs, K., *A Dictionary of Fairies*, London, 1976

Browne, C.R., 'The Ethnography of the Mullet, Inishkea Islands and Portacloy, Co. Mayo', *Proceedings of the Royal Irish Academy*, 3rd ser., III, no. 4, 1895, pp. 587-649, Dublin

Browne, H.T., 'Co. Antrim Folklore Today', *Ulster Journal of Archaeology*, 3rd ser., I, 1938, pp. 208-14, Belfast

Bruford, A., *Gaelic Folk-Tales and Medieval Romances*, Dublin, 1969 (*Béaloideas* XXXIV, 1966 (1969), Dublin)

Bruun, B., *Birds of Britain and Europe*, London, 1975

Buchanan, R., 'The Folklore of an Irish Townland', *Ulster Folklife* II, 1956, pp. 43-55, Belfast

Burke's Genealogical and Heraldic History of Peerage, Baronetage and Knightage, 102nd ed., London, 1959

Byrne, F.J., *Irish Kings and High Kings*, London, 1973

Campbell, J.F., *Leabhar na Féinne* I, Gaelic Texts, Heroic Gaelic Ballads collected in Scotland from 1512-1871 etc., London, 1872

Campbell, J.F., *Popular Tales of the West Highlands* I-IV, London, 1890-3

Campbell, J.G., *The Fians; or Stories, Poems & Traditions of Fionn and his Warrior Band*, 1891, vol. 4, *Waifs and Strays*, (5 vols.) London, 1888-95

Campbell, J.G., *Superstitions of the Highlands and Islands of Scotland*, Glasgow, 1900

Campbell, J.G., *Witchcraft and Second Sight in the Highlands and Islands of Scotland*, Glasgow, 1902

Campbell, J.L., and Hall, T.H., *Strange Things*, London, 1968

"Caoilte Mac Rónáin", 'Feis Laighean agus Midhe', no. 3 competition, *Irisleabhar na Gaedhilge* XII, 1902, p. 96, Dublin

Carleton, W., *Traits and Stories of the Irish Peasantry*, I-II, 11th ed., London n.d., first publ. 1830

Carey, J., 'Notes on the Irish War-Goddess', *Éigse* XIX, 2, 1983, pp. 263-75, Dublin

Carey, J., 'The Irish "Otherworld": Hiberno-Latin Perspectives', *Éigse* XXV, 1991, pp. 154-9, Dublin

Carmichael, A., *Carmina Gadelica*, 6 vols., Edinburgh, I-IV, 1928-41, V-VI, 1954-71

Carney, J., *Studies in Irish Literature and History*, Dublin, 1955

Carney, J., *The Irish Bardic Poet*, Dublin, 1967

The Celtic Review V, 1908-9, pp. 49-51, Edinburgh

Census of Ireland 1841, Dublin, 1843; 1851; 1971, 1, Dublin, 1972; 1981, 1, Dublin, 1982

Chadwick, N.K., 'Imbas Forosnai', *Scottish Gaelic Studies* IV, 2, 1935, pp. 97-135, London, Edinburgh, Glasgow

Chatterton, Lady, *Rambles in the South of Ireland during the year 1838* I-II, London, 1839

Christiansen, R. Th., *The Migratory Legends, A Proposed List of Types With a Systematic Catalogue of The Norwegian Variants*, FF Communications no. 175, Helsinki, 1958

Christiansen, R.Th., *Folktales of Norway*, London, 1964

Christiansen, R.Th., 'Some Notes On The Fairies And The Fairy Faith', *Béaloideas* XXXIX-XLI, 1971-73, pp. 95-111, Dublin

An Claidheamh Soluis agus Fáinne an Lae, 17 *Lúnasa* 1901, pp. 356-7; 19 *Iúil* 1902, p. 320; 15 *Bealtaine* 1905, p. 6, Dublin

Clogher Record V, no. 3, 1965, p. 362, Monaghan

Colum, P., ed., *A Treasury of Irish Folklore*, New York, 1954

Connolly, S., 'The Banshee', *How High the Moon*, Dublin, 1991, pp. 7-12

Coolahan, J., *Irish Education: Its History and Structure*, Dublin, 1981

The Cornhill Magazine XXXV, 1877, p. 177, London

Crane Bag, The, 4, 1, 1980, pp. 12-19, Dublin

Croker, T.C., *Researches in the South of Ireland*, London, 1824

Croker, T.C., *Fairy Legends and Traditions of the South of Ireland*, vol. 1, 2nd ed., London, 1826; Parts 2-3, London, 1828

Croker, T.C., *The Keen of the South of Ireland*, The Percy Society, London, 1844

Crone, J.S., *A Concise Dictionary of Irish Biography*, Dublin, 1928

Cross, T.P., Motif-Index of Early Irish Literature, Bloomington, Indiana, [1952]

Cussen, M.R., 'The Banshee of Kilcoleman', *Ireland's Own* XLV, no. 1154, 14 Jan 1925, p. 25, Dublin

Danaher, K., *The Year in Ireland*, Cork, 1972

Dease, A., *Mother Erin*, London, 1910

de Bhaldraithe, T., 'Cainteannaí as Cois Fhairrge', *Éigse* IV, 1943-4, pp. 210-19, Dublin

de Bhaldraithe, T., *'Nótaí ar an Aisling Fháithchiallaigh'*, *Measgra i gCuimhne Mhichíl Uí Chléirigh*, eag., Fr. S. O'Brien OFM, Dublin, 1944, pp. 210-19

de Bhaldraithe, T., *The Irish of Cois Fhairrge, Co. Galway: A Phonetic Study*, Dublin, 1945

de Bhaldraithe, T., ed., *English-Irish Dictionary*, Dublin, 1959

de Bhaldraithe, T., eag., *Seanchas Thomáis Laighléis*, Dublin, 1977

de Bhaldraithe, T., 'Foclóirí agus Foclóireacht na Gaeilge', *The Maynooth Review* VI, no. 1, May 1980, pp. 3-15, Maynooth

de Brún, P., 'A Lament in Irish for John Stafford, Coadjutor Bishop of Ferns', *The Past* VIII, 1970, pp. 43-51, Enniscorthy

de Fréine, S., 'The Dominance of the English Language in the Nineteenth Century', *The English Language in Ireland*, ed., D. Ó Muirithe, Cork and Dublin, 1977, pp. 71-87

de Troyes, Chrétien, *Arthurian Romances*, ed., W.W. Comfort, London, 1965, first publ. 1914

Dictionary of the Irish Language, Royal Irish Academy, Dublin, 1913-76

Dillon, M., *Early Irish Literature*, Chicago and London, 1972, first publ. Chicago, 1948

Dinneen, Rev P.S., eag., *Foclóir Gaedhilge agus Béarla*, Dublin, 1975, first publ. 1927

Dineen, Rev P.S., and O'Donoghue, T., *The Poems of Egan O'Rahilly*, London, 1911 (Irish Texts Society III, 1909). Revised edn.

Doan, J.E., *Sovereignty Aspects in the Roles of Women in Medieval Irish and Welsh Society*, Northeastern University Working Papers in Irish Studies, Boston, 1984

Donaldson, M.E.M., *Wanderings in the Western Highlands and Islands*, 2nd rev. ed., Paisley, 1923

The Dublin and London Magazine, 1825, pp. 31-4, London

The Dublin Penny Journal, 7 Feb 1903, p. 613, Dublin

The Dublin University Magazine XIV, Sept 1839, pp. 366-74, LXXXVIII, Nov 1876, p. 607, Dublin

The Dublin University Review, Sept 1885, pp. 149-55, Dublin

Dúchas, July-Aug 1977, St Paul, Minnesota

Dudley Edwards, R., *An Atlas of Irish History*, London, 1973

Dunne, T.J., 'The Gaelic Response to Conquest and Colonisation: The Evidence of Poetry', *Studia Hibernica*, No. 20, 1980, pp. 7-30, Dublin

Dwelly, E., *The Illustrated Gaelic-English Dictionary*, Glasgow, 1941

Edgeworth, Maria, *Castle Rackrent, an Hibernian Tale*, Dublin, 1800

Éigse II, 1940, pp. 123-36, 267-73; IV, 1943-4, p. 211; V, 1945-7, pp. 103, 257; XVII, 2, 1977-8, pp. 137-55; XVIII, 1, 1980, pp. 25-37, 2, 1981, pp. 183-209; XIX, 2, 1983, pp. 230-62, 263-75; XXV, 1991, pp. 154-9, Dublin

Éire-Ireland II, no. 3, 1967, pp. 5-11, St Paul, Minnesota

Enniscorthy Guardian, 29 May 1965, 14 Oct 1967, Wexford

Ériu 1, 1904, p. 190, Dublin

Eskeröd, A., *Årets Åring. Ethnologiska Studier I Skördens Och Julens Tro Och Sed*, Stockholm, 1947 (*Nordiska Museets Handlingar* XXVI)

Études Celtiques VII, 1955-6, pp. 76-114; VIII, 1957-8, pp. 407-11, 1958-9, pp. 59-65, Paris

Evans, G.E., and Thomson, D., *The Leaping Hare*, London, 1972

Fabula 13, 1972, pp. 60-107, Göttingen

Fanshawe, Lady, *Memories of Lady Fanshawe*, ed., Sir N.H. Nicolas, London, 1830

Ferguson, S., *Congal: A Poem in Five Books*, Dublin and London, 1872

Fermanagh Herald, 7 Jan 1950

Fitzgerald, D., 'Popular Tales of Ireland – VI: Gearóid Iarla and Áine N'Chliar', *Revue Celtique* IV, 1879-80, pp. 185-99, Paris

Fleming, A., 'The Banshee', *Ireland's Own* IV, no. 104, 16 Nov 1904, p. 3, Dublin

Folk-Liv XXVIII-XXIX, 1964-5, pp. 64-78

Folk-Lore IX, 1898, pp. 91-2; X, 1899, pp. 119-23; XXI, 1910, pp. 180-91; XXV, 1914, pp. 84-91, 121: XXIX, 1918, pp. 308-10; LXXXI, 1970, pp. 292-306, London

Folklore Fellows Communications no. 175, 1958; no. 184, 1961, 1973; no. 188, 1963; no. 193, 1964; no. 202, 1968; no. 219, 1978; no. 248, 1991; no. 249, 1991, Helsinki

Folk-Lore Record IV, 1881, pp. 121-2; London

Folkminnen och Folktankar XIII, 1926, pp. 53-70, Göteborg

Forbes, J., 'Folklore and Tradition in Glenvar, County Donegal', *Ulster Folklife* III, 1, 1957, pp. 37-41, Belfast

Forde, Rev Hugh, *Sketches of Olden Days in Northern Ireland*, Belfast, 1923

Foster, J. Cooper, *Ulster Folklore*, Belfast, 1951

Freeman, T.W., *Ireland; Its Physical, Historical, Social and Economic Geography*, London, 1950

Funk and Wagnall's *Standard Dictionary of Folklore, Mythology and Legend* I-II, ed., Maria Leach, New York, 1949

Furlong, N. (Pat O'Leary), *Wexford People*, 9, 16, July 1976; *Enniscorthy Guardian*, 29 May 1965, 14 Oct 1967, Wexford

Gailey, A., 'The Typology of the Irish Spade', *The Spade in Northern and Atlantic Europe*, eds., A. Gailey and A. Fenton, Belfast, 1970, pp. 35-48

'General Alphabetical Index to the Townlands and Towns, Parishes and Baronies of Ireland', *Census of Ireland 1851*, Dublin, 1861

Gill, W.W., *Manx Dialect*, London, 1934

Gimbutas, M., *The Goddesses and Gods of Old Europe 6500-3500 B.C. Myths and Cult Images*, London 1989. New and updated edition; first published 1974

Goedheer, A.J., *Irish and Norse Traditions about the Battle of Clontarf*, Haarlem, 1938

Gomme, G.L., ed., *English Traditions and Foreign Customs*, The Gentleman's Magazine Library, London, 1885

Gordon, Lady E., 'Some Kerry Fairies', *Kerry Archaeological Magazine* I, no. 6, April 1911, pp. 347-56, Tralee

Gorham, M., *Forty Years of Irish Broadcasting*, Dublin, 1967

Grant, I.F., *Highland Folk Ways*, London, 1961

Gray, E.A., 'Cath Muige Tuired', *Éigse* XVIII, 2, 1981, pp. 183-209; XIX, 2, 1983, pp. 230-62, Dublin

Gray, E.A., *Cath Maige Tuired*, Dublin, 1982

Green, M.J., *Symbol and Image in Celtic Religious Art*, London, New York, 1989

Green, M.J. *Dictionary of Celtic Myth and Legend*, London, 1992

Green, Miss, 'County Kildare Folk-Tales – The Banshee', *Journal of the County Kildare Archaeological Society and Surrounding Districts* VI, 1909-11, p. 174, Dublin

Gregory, Lady A., 'The Workhouse Ward', *Selected Plays*, chosen and introduced by Coxhead, Elizabeth, London, 1962

Gregory, Lady A., *Visions and Beliefs in the West of Ireland*, 2nd ed., New York, 1970; first publ., 2 vols., New York and London, 1920

Griffin, G., *Tales of the Munster Festivals* I-III, London, 1827

Guth na Bliadhna IX, 1912, *Air* 2, pp. 195-221; *Air* 3, pp. 333-366, Edinburgh

Gwynn, E., ed., *The Metrical Dindshenchas*, 2, Todd Lecture Series IX, Dublin, 1906

Gwynn, E. 'On the Idea of Fate in Irish Literature', *Journal of the Ivernian Society* II, 1910, pp. 152-165

Haddon, A.C., 'The Aran Islands, County Galway: A Study in Irish Ethnography', *The Irish Naturalist* II, no. 12, Dec 1893, pp. 300-308, Dublin

Hall, Mr and Mrs S.C., *Ireland: Its Scenery, Character &c.*, I-III, London, 1841-3 (I, 1841; II, 1842; III, 1843)

Hall, Mrs S.C., 'Introduction' in O'Neill, J., *Handerahan, the Irish Fairyman; and Legends of Carrick*, London, 1854

Hand, W., 'Boundaries, Portals, and Other Magical Spots in Folklore', *The Katharine Briggs Lecture 2*, Nov 1982, London

Hanley, W., 'Tales and Legends of the Banshee', *Ireland's Own* XII, no. 312, 11 Nov 1908, p. 4

[Hardy, P.D.], ed., *PIC-NICS from the Dublin Penny Journal ...* , Dublin, 1836

[Hardy, P.D.], ed., *Characteristic Sketches of Ireland and the Irish*, 4th ed., Dublin, 1842

Harris, K.M., 'Extracts from the Committee's Collections 2', *Ulster Folklife* VI, 1960, pp. 35-47, Belfast

Hartmann, H., *Der Totenkult in Irland*, Heidelberg, 1952

Hayes, E., ed., *The Ballads of Ireland* I-II, London, 1885

Hayes-McCoy, G.A., *Irish Battles*, London, 1969, Dublin, 1980

Henaghan, M.T., *From the Brown Wastes of Connaught*, privately publ., n.d.

Henderson, G., ed., *Fled Bricrend: The Feast of Bricriu*, Irish Texts Society II, London, 1899

Henderson, G., *Survivals in Belief among the Celts*, Glasgow, 1911

Henderson, W., *Notes on the Folk-Lore of the Northern Counties of England and the Borders*, Folk-Lore Society, London, 1879

Hennessy, W.M., 'The Ancient Irish Goddess of War', *Revue Celtique* I, 1870-2, pp. 32-57, Paris

Hennessy, W.M., ed., *The Annals of Loch Cé* I-II, London, 1871

Henry, P.L., 'The Goblin Group', *Études Celtiques* VIII, 1957-8, pp. 404-416, Paris

Herbert, M., 'Goddess and King: The Sacred Marriage in Early Ireland', in L.A. Fradenburg (ed.): *Women and Sovereignty*, Edinburgh, 1992, pp. 264-275, (*Cosmos, The Yearbook of the Traditional Cosmology Society*, Vol. 7)

Hetman, F., *Irische Gespenstergeschichten*, Frankfurt am Main, 1976

Hewson, M., 'A Word-List from South-West Clare', *North Munster Antiquarian Journal* IX, 1962-5, pp. 182-6, Limerick

Hickson, M.A., *Selections from Old Kerry Records*, London, 1872

Hoffman-Krayer, E., and Bächtold-Staüble, H., eds., *Handwörterbuch des Deutschen Aberglaubens*, Berlin and Leipzig, 1924-42

Hole, C., *Encyclopaedia of Superstitions*, London, 1961

Honko, L., *Geisterglaube in Ingermanland*, FF Communications no. 185, Helsinki, 1962

Honko, L., 'Memorates and the Study of Folk Beliefs', *Journal of the Folklore Institute* I, 1964, pp. 5-19, Bloomington, Indiana

Hörandner, E., and Lunzer, H., eds., *Folklorismus;* Neusiedl/See, 1982

Hore, H.F., 'Origin of the Irish Superstitions Regarding Banshees and Fairies', *Journal of Royal Society of Antiquaries of Ireland* XXV, 1895, pp. 115-29, Dublin

Hull, E., *Cuchulainn, The Hound of Ulster*, London, 1913

Hull, E., *Folklore of the British Isles*, London, 1928

Hultkrantz, Å, ed., *The Supernatural Owners of Nature*, Acta Universitatis Stockholmiensis I, Stockholm, 1961

Hyde, D., '*An Bhean-Sidhe*', *The Irish Packet* I, no. 7, 3 Oct 1903, p. 24

Hyde, D., *Legends of Saints and Sinners*, Talbot Press, Dublin n.d.

Hyde, D., *The Stone of Truth and Other Irish Folktales*, Dublin 1979

Institute of British Geographers, Transactions, no. 41, June 1967, pp. 97-112, London

Ireland's Own II, no. 34; 15 July 1903; IV, no. 104, 16 Nov 1904; IX, no. 225, 13 Mar 1907, no. 233, 8 May 1907; XI, no. 286, 13 May 1908; XII, no. 312, 11 Nov 1908; XIII, no. 332, 20 Jan 1909; XLII, no. 1080, 15 Aug 1923; XLV, no. 1154, 14 Jan 1925; LIX, no. 1539, 28 May 1932; LXIII, no. 1627, 3 Feb 1934; LXIV, no. 1671, 15 Dec 1934; LXV, no. 1698, 22 June 1935; LXXIV, no. 1973, 16 Aug 1941; no. 1974, 23 Aug 1941; LXXXI, no. 3015, 28 Sept 1946; no. 3017, 26 Oct 1946; 16 Aug 1947, 27 Nov 1954, 24 Dec 1955.

Irish Bits IV, no. 93, 1898, p. 486, Dublin

Irish Independent, 30 Dec 1932, Dublin

The Irish Naturalist II, no. 12, Dec 1893, p. 307, Dublin

The Irish Packet I, no. 7, 3 Oct 1903, p. 24; VII, no. 176, 9 Feb 1907, p. 473, Dublin

Irisleabhar na Gaedhilge XI, 1901, pp. 93, 154; XII, 1902, pp. 62, 96, III; XVII, 1907, p. 306, Dublin

Irländska Folksagor, Stockholm, 1839 (partial translation of Croker, T.C., *Fairy Legends and Traditions of the South of Ireland*)

Jackson, K.H., *Cath Maighe Léna*, Medieval and Modern Irish Series IX, Dublin, 1938

Jackson, K.H., *The Oldest Irish Tradition: A Window on the Iron Age*, Cambridge, 1964

J.L.L., 'The Banshee of the O'Connor's', *Our Girls* II, Dec 1932, pp. 306-9, 316, Dublin

Johnston, J.H., 'Harvest Migration from Nineteenth Century Ireland', *Institute of British Geographers, Transactions*, no. 41, June 1967, pp. 97-112, London

Jones, B.J., 'Traditions and Superstitions Collected at Kilcurry, Co. Louth, Ireland', *Folk-Lore* X, 1899, pp. 119-22, London

Jones, G., 'A Washer at the Ford', *Aberystwyth Studies* IV, 1922, pp. 105-9, Aberystwyth

Journal of the Cork Historical and Archaeological Society III, no. 29, 1894, pp. 133-35; V, 2nd ser., 1899, pp. 224-34; XLIX, 2nd ser., 1944, p. 38; LVI, 1951, pp. 104-119, Cork

Journal of the County Kildare Archaeological Society and Surrounding Districts, VI, 1909-11, p. 174, Dublin

Journal of the County Louth Archaeological Society XIII, no. 4, 1956, pp. 309-94, Dundalk

Journal of English and German Philology XVIII, 1919, pp. 60-6, Urbana, Illinois

Journal of the Folklore Institute I, 1964, pp. 5-19, Bloomington, Indiana

Journal of the Kilkenny and South-East of Ireland Archaeological Society I, new ser., 1856-7, pp. 118-43, Dublin

Journal of the Royal Society of Antiquaries of Ireland, XXV, 1895, pp. 115-29

Joyce, P.W., *The Origin and History of Irish Names of Places*, Dublin, 1869

Joyce, P.W., *Ancient Irish Music*, Dublin, 1873

Joyce, P.W., *A Social History of Ancient Ireland*, I-II, London, 1903

Joyce, P.W., *English as we Speak it in Ireland*, London, 1910

Joynt, M., *Golden Legends of the Gael*, Dublin and Cork, n.d.

[Keegan, J.], 'Legends and Tales of the Queen's County Peasantry', *The Dublin University Magazine* XIV, Sept 1839, pp. 366-74, Dublin

Keightley, T., *The Fairy Mythology*, I-II, London, 1833

Kennedy, P., *The Legendary Fictions of the Irish Celts*, London 1866

Kennedy, P., *The Fireside Stories of Ireland*, Dublin, 1870

Kent, N., 'Bansheed! What's in an Image?', *New Musical Express*, 26 Aug 1978, pp. 28-9, London

Kerry Archaeological Magazine I, no. 6, April 1911, p. 348, Tralee

Kinahan, G.H., 'Notes on Irish Folk-Lore – 'Banshee'. *Folk-Lore Record* IV, 1881, pp. 121-2, London

Knott, E., ed., *Togail Bruidne Da Derga*, Medieval and Modern Irish series VIII, Dublin, 1936

Knott, E., 'The Destruction of Dá Chóca's Hostel', *The Golden Legends of the Gael*, Dublin n.d.

Krog, F., ed., *Irische Elfenmärchen der Brüder Grimm*, Frankfurt, 1980

Kulturhistoriskt Lexicon for nördisk mediltid V, Malmö, 1960

"*Lageniensis*" (Canon John O'Hanlon), *Irish Folk Lore*, Glasgow/London, 1870

Laoide, S., *Tonn Tóime*, Dublin, 1915

Laoide, S., *Éan an Cheoil Bhinn agus Scéalta eile*, (*Imtheachta an Oireachtais* 1901, Book 2, Part 3), Dublin 1908

Laverty, M., 'The Banshee of Lough Neagh', *Ireland's Own* LIX, no. 1539, 28 May 1932, p. 695, Dublin

Leach, Maria, ed., Funk and Wagnall's *Standard Dictionary of Folklore, Mythology and Legend* I-II, New York, 1949

Le Braz, A., *La Légende de la Mort en Basse-Bretagne*, Paris, 1893

Léachtaí Cholm Cille VIII, 1977, pp. 109-31, Maynooth

Le Fanu, A., *Memoirs of the Life and Writings of Mrs Frances Sheridan*, London 1824

Lhuyd, E., *Archaeologia Britannica*, Oxford, 1707

Liston, M., 'The Banshee', *Ireland's Own* LXXIV, no. 1973, 16 Aug 1941, p. 14, Dublin

Lixfeld, H., *'Die Guntramsage'* (AT 1645A), *Fabula* 13, 1972, pp. 60-107, Göttingen

"Loch gCarmain", *'Feis Laighean agus Midhe'* 1901, no. 3 competition, *Irisleabhar na Gaedhilge* XII, 1902, pp. 61-3, Dublin

Logan, P., *The Old Gods: the Facts about Irish Fairies*, Belfast, 1981

Lucas, A.T., 'The Hooded Cloak in Ireland', *Journal of the Cork Historical and Archaeological Society* LVI, 1951, pp. 104-119, Cork

Lucas, A.T., 'Footwear in Ireland', *Journal of the County Louth Archaeological Society* XIII, no. 4, 1956, pp. 309-94, Dundalk

Lucas, A.T., 'Wattle and Straw Mat Doors in Ireland', *Studia Ethnographica Upsaliensia* II, 1956, pp. 16-35, Uppsala

Lynch, J.F., 'Lough Gur', *Irisleabhar na Gaedhilge* XII; July 1902, p. 111, Dublin

Lysaght, P., 'Irish Banshee Traditions', *Béaloideas* XLII-XLIV; 1974-6 (1977), pp. 94-119, Dublin

Lysaght, P., *'An Bhean Sí sa Bhéaloideas'*, *Gnéithe den Chaointeoireacht*, eag., Ó Madagáin, B., pp. 53-66, Dublin, 1978

Lysaght, P., *'An Bhean Chaointe:* The Supernatural Irish Keening Woman', *Éire-Ireland*, Winter 1979, pp. 7-29, St Paul; Minnesota

Lysaght, P., *The Banshee. The Irish Supernatural Death-Messenger*, Dublin 1986

Lysaght, P., 'A Tradition Bearer in Contemporary Ireland', in Röhrich, L., Wienker-Piepho, S., *Storytelling in Contemporary Societies*, Tübingen, 1990, pp. 199-214

Lysaght, P., 'Fairylore from the Midlands of Ireland', in Narváes, P., ed., *The Good People. New Folklore Essays*, New York, London, 1991, pp. 22-46

Lysaght, P., '"Is There Anyone Here to Serve My Mass?": the Legend of the Dead Priest's Midnight Mass in Ireland', *Arv, Scandinavian Yearbook of Folklore*, vol. 47, 1991, pp. 193-207, Uppsala

Lysaght, P., 'The Banshee's Comb (MLSIT 4026). The role of tellers and audiences in the shaping of redactions and variations,' *Béaloideas* 59, 1991, pp. 67-82, Dublin

Lysaght, P., 'Traditional Beliefs and Narratives of a Contemporary Irish Tradition Bearer', *Acta Ethnographica Hungarica*, 39 (3-4), pp. 419-441, 1994, Budapest

Lysaght, P., 'Women, Milk and Magic at the Boundary Festival of May', in Lysaght, P., ed., *Milk and Milk Products from Medieval to Modern Times*, Edinburgh, 1994, pp. 208-229

Lysaght, P., 'Caoineadh na Marbh: Die Totenklage in Irland', *Rheinisch-westfälische Zeitschrift für Volkskunde*, 40. Jahrgang 1995, pp. 163-214, Bonn/Münster

Lysaght, P., 'Visible Death: Attitudes to the Dying in Ireland', *Marvels and Tales*, vol. IX, no. 1, May 1995, pp. 27-60, pp. 85-100, Boulder, Colorado

Lysaght, P., 'Tänapäeva Iiri Pärimusekandja Traditsioonilised Uskumused Ja Juted', in: Hiiemäl, M., Kõiva, M., eds. *Rahvausund tänapäeval*, Tartu, 1995, pp. 242-257

Lysaght, P., 'Aspects of the Earth-Goddess in Traditions of the Banshee,' in Billington, S., Green, M., eds., *The Concept of the Goddess*, London/New York, 1996

McAnally, D.R., (Jnr), *Irish Wonders*, London 1888

MacBain, A., *An Etymological Dictionary of the Gaelic Language*, Stirling, 1911, first publ. 1896

Mac Cana, P., 'Aspects of the Theme of King and Goddess in Irish Literature', *Études Celtiques* VII, 1955-6, pp. 76-114, 356-413; VIII, 1958-9, pp. 59-65, Paris

Mac Cana, P., *Celtic Mythology*, London, 1973, first publ. 1970

Mac Cana, P., *The Learned Tales of Medieval Ireland*, Dublin, 1980

MacCarvill, Canon M., 'An Aghabog Glossary', *Clogher Record* V, no. 3, 1965, pp. 361-70, Monaghan

McClintock, H.F., *Old Irish and Highland Dress*, Dundalk, 1943

McClintock, L., 'Folk Lore of the County Donegal', *The Dublin University Magazine* LXXXVIII, Nov 1876, pp. 607-14, Dublin

McClintock, L., 'Folk-Lore of County Donegal', *The Cornhill Magazine* XXXV, 1877, pp. 177-81, London

Mac Clúin, An tAth S., *Caint an Chláir* I-II, Dublin, 1940

MacCormick, J., *The Island of Mull: Its History, Scenes and Legends*, Glasgow, 1934, first publ. 1928

McCourt, D., 'The Cruck Truss in Ireland and its West-European connections', *Folk-Liv* XXVIII-XXIX, 1964-5, pp. 64-78, Stockholm

MacCulloch, J.A., *The Religion of the Ancient Celts*, Edinburgh, 1911

MacDougall, J., Calder, G., *Folk Tales & Fairy Lore*, Edinburgh, 1910

Mac Erlean, J.C., *Duanaire Dháibhidh Uí Bhruadair*, 3 vols., (1910, 1913, 1917), London, (Irish Texts Society)

MacFarlane, Rev A.M., 'Myths Associated with Mountains, Springs, and Lochs in the Highlands', *Transactions of the Gaelic Society of Inverness* XXXIV, 1927-8 (1935), pp. 135-52, Inverness

McGarry, M., ed., *Best Irish Ghostly Tales*, London, n.d.

Mac Giollarnáth, S., *Loinnir Mac Leabhair*, Dublin, 1936

Mac Gréine, P., 'Further Notes on Tinkers' "Cant" ...', *Béaloideas* III, 1932, pp. 290-303, Dublin

McGregor, A.A., *The Peat-Fire Flame*, Edinburgh, 1937

McKay, J.G., *More West Highland Tales*, I-II, Edinburgh, I, 1940; II, 1960

MacLagan, R.C., '"The Keener" in the Scottish Highlands and Islands', *Folk-Lore* XXV, 1914, pp. 84-91, London

MacLean, C.I., *The Highlands*, Inverness, 1975, first publ. 1959

MacLeod, Fiona, *The Washer of the Ford: and Other Legendary Moralities*, The Celtic Library, Edinburgh and Chicago, 1896

MacLysaght, E., *Irish Families*, Dublin, 1957

MacLysaght, E., *A Guide to Irish Surnames*, Dublin, 1964

MacLysaght, E., *More Irish Families* ..., Dublin, 1982

MacLysaght, E., *Irish Life in the Seventeenth Century: After Cromwell*, Dublin and Cork, 1939

MacNamara, B., *The Valley of the Squinting Windows*, Tralee, 1973, pp. 100-1

MacPhail, M., '*A' bhean nighe* (The Washerwoman)', *Folk-Lore* IX, 1898, pp. 91-2, London

MacPhilib, S., *Iarlaisí, Símhalartú Páistí i mBéaloideas na hÉireann*, unpublished MA thesis, University College Dublin, 1980

McSkimin, S., *The History and Antiquities of the County of the town of Carrickfergus*, Belfast, 1823

Magnusson, M., and Pálsson, H., eds., *Njal's Saga*, Harmondsworth, 1960

Mahon, Rev M.P., *Ireland's Fairy Lore*, Boston, 1919

Mangan, J.C., *Poems*, New York, 1859

Mann, S.E., *An Indo-European Comparative Dictionary*, Hamburg, 1884-7

The Maynooth Review VI, no. 1, May 1980, pp. 3-15, Maynooth

Mayo Magazine, no. 8, 17 Mar 1966, pp. 65-6, Swinford

Maxwell, W.H., *Wild Sports of the West*, I-II, London, 1973, first publ. 1832

Meid, W., ed., *Táin Bó Fraích*, Medieval and Modern Irish Series XXII, Dublin, 1967

Meyer, K., ed., 'Macgnimartha Find', *Revue Celtique* V, 1881-3, pp. 195-204, Paris

Meyer, K., ed., '*Reicne Fothaid Canainne*', *Fianaigecht*, Royal Irish Academy Todd Lecture Series, vol. XVI, Dublin, 1910, pp. 1-21

Mhac an Fhailigh, E., 'A Westmeath Word-List', *Éigse* V, 1945-7, pp. 256-66

Miller, A.W.K., ed., 'O'Clery's Irish Glossary', *Revue Celtique* IV, 1879-80, pp. 349-428; V, 1881-3, pp. 1-69

Miller, H., *The Cruise of the Betsy*, Edinburgh, 1858

Miller, H., *Scenes and Legends of the North of Scotland*, Edinburgh, 1869

Milligan, S.F., 'Antiquities, Social Customs, and Folk Lore of Tory, Innismurray, and the South Islands of Aran', *Report and Proceedings of the Belfast Natural History and Philosophical Society*, 1896, pp. 27-36, Belfast

Mokyr, J., *Why Ireland Starved: A Quantitative and Analytical History of the Irish Economy, 1800-1850*, London 1985. Revised edition

Moody, T.W., and Martin, F.X., *The Course of Irish History*, Cork, 1967; (Rev. and enlarged ed. 1984)

Moser, H., 'Vom Folklorismus in unserer Zeit', *Zeitschrift für Volkskunde* LVIII, 1962, pp. 177-209, Stuttgart

Moylan, S., *The Language of Kilkenny*, Dublin, 1996

Murphy, G., *The Ossianic Lore and Romantic Tales of Medieval Ireland*, Dublin, 1961

Murphy, J., *The House in the Rath*, Dublin, 1886

Murphy, M.J., *At Slieve Gullion's Foot*, Dundalk, 1975, first publ. 1940

Nagy, J.F., 'Liminality and Knowledge in Irish Tradition', *Studia Celtica* XVI-XVII, 1981-2, pp. 135-43, Oxford

Nagy, J.F., *The Wisdom of the Outlaw. The Boyhood Deeds of Finn in Gaelic Narrative Tradition*, Berkeley, 1985

New Ireland Review XXIX, 1908, pp. 123-7, Dublin

New Musical Express, 26 Aug 1978, pp. 28-9, London

Nicholls, K., *Gaelic and Gaelicised Ireland in the Middle Ages*, Dublin, 1972

Ní Bhrolcháin, M., 1980: 'Women in Early Irish Myths and Sagas', *The Crane Bag*, 4, 1, 1980, 12-19, Dublin

Ní Dhuibhne, E., 'The Old Woman as Hare: Structure and Meaning in an Irish Legend,' *Folklore*, vol. 104, 1993, 77-85

Ní Shéaghdha, N., *Tóruigheacht Dhiarmada agus Gráinne*, Dublin, 1967 (Irish Texts Society XLVII)

Nic Dhonnchadha, L., ed., *Aided Muirchertaig meic Erca*, Dublin, 1964

Nordisk Kultur XIX, *Folktro*, 1935, pp. 95-159, Stockholm

Nordiska Museets Handlingar XXVI, 1947, Stockholm

North Munster Antiquarian Journal IX, 1962-5, p. 182, Limerick

O'Brien, J., *Focalóir Gaoidhilge-Sax-Bhéarla/An Irish-English Dictionary*, Paris, 1768, 2nd ed., Dublin 1832

Ó Broin, T., ed., *Scéaltaí Tíre. Bailiúchán Seanchais ó Ghaillimh*, Baile Átha Cliath, 1957 (= *Béaloideas* XXIV, 1955)

Ó Cadhain, M., 'Cnuasach Ó Chois-Fhairrge', *Béaloideas* V, 1935, pp. 219-72, Dublin

Ó Cadhlaigh, C., *An Rúraíocht*, Dublin, 1956

Ó Canainn, P., ed., *Filidheacht na nGaedheal*, Dublin, n.d.

Ó Cathasaigh, T., 'The Semantics of "Síd" ', *Éigse* XVII, 2, 1977-8, pp. 137-55, Dublin

Ó Ceallaigh, E., '*Liosta Focal Gaeilge atá meascaithe tríd an Béarla ag Muinntir Chill Chainnigh*', *Old Kilkenny Review*, VII, 1954, pp. 50-3, Kilkenny

O'Connell, P., 'The Banshee of the Branleys', *Ireland's Own*, 16 Aug 1947, p. 4, Dublin

O'Connor, A., *Unbaptised Children in Irish Tradition*, unpublished student essay, University College Dublin, 1978

O'Connor, A., 'The Placeless Dead', *Sinsear*, 1979, pp. 33-41, Dublin

O'Connor, A., *The Death and Burial of Unbaptised Children in Irish Folk Tradition*, unpublished MA thesis, University College Dublin, 1981

O'Connor, A., *Child Murderess and Dead Child Traditions. A Comparative Study*, FF Communications 249, Helsinki 1991

Ó Corráin, D., *Ireland before the Normans*, Dublin, 1972

Ó Cuív, B., *The Irish of West Muskerry, Co. Cork: A Phonetic Study*, Dublin, 1944

Ó Cuív, B., *The Irish Bardic Duanaire or "Poem-Book"*, Dublin, 1973

Ó Cuív, B., *Cath Muighe Tuireadh. The Second Battle of Magh Tuireadh*, Dublin, 1945

Ó Cuív, B., *Irish Dialects and Irish-Speaking Districts*, Dublin 1951

Ó Dálaigh, P., *File an Chomaraigh: Riobárd Bheldon*, Dublin, 1903

Ó Danachair, C., *A Bibliography of Irish Ethnology and Folk Tradition*, Dublin and Cork, 1978

Ó Danachair, C., 'The Dress of the Irish', *Éire-Ireland* II, no. 3, 1967, pp. 5-11, St Paul, Minnesota

Ó Danachair, C., 'The Spade in Ireland', *Béaloideas* XXXI, 1963, pp. 98-114, Dublin

Ó Dochartaigh, L., '*An Spideog i Seanchas na hÉireann*', *Béaloideas* XLV-XLVII, 1977-79, pp. 164-98, Dublin

Ó Dónaill, N., eag., *Foclóir Gaeilge-Béarla*, Dublin, 1977

O'Donnell, E., *The Banshee*, London, c.1920

O'Donoghue, D.J., *The Poets of Ireland*, Dublin/London, 1912

O'Donovan, J., ed., *The Banquet of Dun na N-Gedh and the Battle of Magh Rath*, Irish Archaeological Society, Dublin, 1842

O'Donovan, J., ed., 'Elegy on the Death of the Rev Edmond Kavanagh, by the Rev James O'Lalor', *The Journal of the Kilkenny and South-East of Ireland Archaeologial Society* I, new ser., 1856-7 (1858), pp. 118-43, Dublin

Ó Dubhda, S., '*Measgra Ó Dhuibhneachaibh*', *Béaloideas* IX, 1939, pp. 245-87, Dublin

420   *The Banshee*

Ó Duilearga, S., '*Measgra Sgéal Ó Uibh Ráthach*', *Béaloideas* I, 1927-8, pp. 199-204, Dublin

Ó Duilearga, S., eag., *Leabhar Sheáin Í Chonaill*, 3rd ed., Dublin, 1977, first publ. 1948; *Seán Ó Conaill's Book*, trans. MacNeill, Máire, Dublin, 1981

Ó Fátharta, P., '*Gluaiseanna*', *An Stoc*, 1929, Book 6, no. 7, p. 8, Galway

Ó Fionúsa, P., '*Measgra Dhéiseach*', *Béaloideas* III, 1932, pp. 283-9, Dublin

Ó Giolláin, D., 'The *Leipreachán* and Fairies, Dwarfs and the Household Familiar: A Comparative Study', *Béaloideas* LII, 1984, pp. 75-150, Dublin

Ó Glaisín, S., '*Béaloideas*', *Ireland's Own* LXV, no. 1698, 22 June 1935, p. 805, Dublin

Ó Gráda, C., *Ireland Before and After The Famine*, Manchester, 1993. New edition

O'Grady, S.H., ed., *Caithréim Thoirdhealbhaigh*, I-II, London 1929, (Irish Texts Society XXVI-XXVII) Engl. trans. vol. II

O'Hanlon, Rev J., Canon, ed., *Legends and Poems by John Keegan*, Dublin, 1907

Ó hAodha, M., '*Seannchas ós na Déisibh*', *Béaloideas* XIV, 1944, pp. 53-112, Dublin

Ó Héalaí, P., '*Cumhacht an tSagairt sa Bhéaloideas*', *Léachtaí Cholm Cille* VIII, 1977, pp. 109-31, Maynooth

Ó h-Éaluighthe, D., 'Irish Words in Cork Speech', *Journal of the Cork Historical and Archaeological Society*, XLIX, 2nd ser., 1944, pp. 33-48, Cork

Ó hEochaidh, S., Ní Néill, M., Ó Catháin, S., *Síscéalta Ó Thír Chonaill, Fairy Legends from Donegal*, Dublin, 1977

Ó hÓgáin, D., '*An Capall i mBéaloideas na hÉireann*', *Béaloideas* XLV-XLVII, 1977-9, pp. 199-243, Dublin

Ó hÓgáin, D., '*Gearóid Iarla agus an Draíocht*', *Scríobh* IV, 1979, pp. 234-59, Dublin

Ó hÓgáin, D., 'The Folklore of Castle Rackrent', in Owens, C., ed., *Family Chronicles: Maria Edgeworth's* Castle Rackrent, Dublin, 1987

Ó hÓgáin, D., *Myth, Legend and Romance*, London, 1990

[Ó hÓgáin, S.], '*Brisleach Mhór Mhaighe Mhuirtheimhne*', *Irisleabhar na Gaedhilge* XVII, 1907, pp. 305-8, Dublin

O'Kearney, N., ed., *The Battle of Gabhra*, Dublin, 1855 (*Transactions of the Ossianic Society for the Year 1853*, I)

O'Kearney, N., eag., *Feis Tighe Chonáin*, Dublin, 1855 (*Transactions of the Ossianic Society for the year 1854*, II)

Old Kilkenny Review VII, 1954, p. 50, Kilkenny

Ó Milléadha, P., '*Seanchas Sliabh gCua*', *Béaloideas* VI, 1936, pp. 169-256, Dublin

Ó Muirithe, D., 'An Chaointeoireacht in Éirinn – Tuairiscí na dTaistealaithe', *Gnéithe den Chaointeoireacht, eag.*, Ó Madagáin, B., Dublin, 1978, pp. 20-29

Ó Muirithe, D., ed., *The English Language in Ireland*, Cork and Dublin, 1977

O'Rahilly, C., ed., *The Stowe Version of Táin Bó Cuailnge*, Dublin, 1978, first publ. 1961

O'Rahilly, C., ed., *Táin Bó Cúalnge from the Book of Leinster*, Dublin, 1970

O'Rahilly, C., ed., *Táin Bó Cúalnge, Rescension 1*, Dublin, 1976

Ó Rathile, T., *eag.*, *Dánta Grádha*, Cork, 1926

O'Rahilly, T.F., *Early Irish History and Mythology*, Dublin, 1946

O'Rahilly, T.F., *Irish Dialects*, Dublin, 1976

O'Reilly, L., 'The Legend of Dunluce', *Ireland's Own* XI, no. 286, 13 May 1908, p. 12, Dublin

Orr, James, *The Posthumous Works of James Orr of Ballycarry*, Belfast, 1817

Ó Scannláin, R.A., 'Cnuasach Focal ó Loch Garman', *Éigse* V, 1945-7, pp. 102-7, Dublin

Ó Súilleabháin, S., 'Irish Folklore and Tradition', 'Béaloideas Éireann', Dublin, 1937

Ó Súilleabháin, S., 'Cnuasach Déiseach', *Béaloideas* IX, 1939, pp. 38-46, Dublin

Ó Súilleabháin, S., *A Handbook of Irish Folklore*, Dublin, 1942

Ó Súilleabháin, S., eag., *Scéalta Cráibhtheacha*, Dublin, 1952 (*Béaloideas* XXI, 1951-2, Dublin)

Ó Súilleabháin, S., and Christiansen, R. Th., *The Types of the Irish Folktale*, FF Communications no. 188, Helsinki, 1963; second printing 1968

Ó Súilleabháin, S., *Irish Folk Custom and Belief*, Dublin and Cork, 1977, first publ. Dublin, 1967

Ó Súilleabháin, S., *Irish Wake Amusements*, Cork, 1967 (trans. *Caitheamh Aimsire ar Thórraimh*, Dublin, 1961)

O'Sullivan, S., *Legends from Ireland*, London, 1977

O'Toole, E., 'The Holy Wells of County Carlow', *Béaloideas* IV, 1933-4 (1934), pp. 3-23, Dublin

Ó Tuathaill, P., 'Folk-Tales from Carlow and West Wicklow', *Béaloideas* VII, 1937, pp. 46-94, Dublin

Our Girls II, Dec 1932, pp. 306-9, 316, Dublin

Oxford English Dictionary, 3rd rev. ed.

Pakenham, T., *The Year of Liberty*, London, 1969

Partridge, A., 'Caoineadh na dTrí Muire agus an Chaointeoireacht', *Gnéithe den Chaointeoireacht, eag.*, Ó Madagáin, B., Dublin, 1978, pp. 67-81

Partridge, A., 'Wild Men and Wailing Women', *Éigse* XVIII: 1, 1980, pp. 25-37, Dublin

Partridge, A., *Caoineadh na dTrí Muire. Téama na Páise i bhFilíocht Bhéil na Gaeilge*, Dublin, 1983

The Past VIII 1970, pp. 43-51, Enniscorthy

Paterson, T.G.F., *Country Cracks. Old Tales from the County of Armagh*, Dundalk, 1939

Pennant, T., *A Tour in Scotland 1769*, 3rd ed., Warrington, 1774

Pentikäinen, J., *The Nordic Dead-Child Tradition. Nordic Dead Child Beings*, FF Communications no. 202, Helsinki, 1968

Pentikäinen, J., *Oral Repertoire and World View*, FF Communications no. 219, Helsinki, 1978

Petzoldt, L., ed., *Deutsche Volkssagen*, Munich, 1970

Peuckert, W.-E., ed., *Gebrüder Grimm. Irische Elfenmärchen*, Berlin, 1948

Peuckert, W.-E., ed., *Deutsche Sagen II. Mittel- und Oberdeutschland*, Berlin, 1962

Peuckert, W.-E., ed., *Westalpensagen. Europäische Sagen*, Band IV, Berlin, 1965

Philippson, E.A., *Germanisches Heidentum Bei Der Angelsachsen*, Leipzig, 1929

Piatt, D., *Dialects in east and mid-Leinster Gaelic Survivals*, Dublin, 1933

Plunkett, R., *Vocabularium Latinum et Hibernum 1662*, Mss. Z4.2.5 in Marsh's Library, Dublin

Pokorny, J., *Vergleichendes Wörterbuch der Indogermanischen Sprachen*, Berlin, II. Band, Leipzig, 1927

Power, Very Rev P. Canon, *The Place Names of Decies*, 2nd ed., Cork, 1952

Prendergast, F.J., ed., 'Ancient History of the Kingdom of Kerry by Friar O'Sullivan, of Muckross Abbey', *Journal of the Cork Historical and Archaeological Society* V, 2nd ser., 1899, pp. 224-31, Cork

Proceedings of the Royal Irish Academy, 3rd ser., III, no. 4, 1895, p. 630; 1908-9, p. 325, Dublin

Rees, A. and B., *Celtic Heritage*, London, 1961

Report and Proceedings of the Belfast Natural History and Philosophical Society 1896, pp. 32-4, Belfast

Report of the Commissioners appointed to take the Census of Ireland for the year 1841, Dublin, 1843

Revue Celtique I, 1870-2, pp. 32-55; IV, 1879-80, pp. 185-99, 369; V, 1881-3, p. 204; XII, 1891, pp. 52-130; XV, 1894, pp. 272-336; XXI, 1900, pp. 149-65; XXII, 1901, pp. 9-61, 105-215, 282-329, 390-437; XXIII, 1902, p. 88; XXIV, 1903, pp. 190-207, Paris

Rheinisch-wesfälische Zeitschrift für Volkskunde, 40. Jahrgang 1995, pp. 163-214

Rhŷs, J., *Celtic Folklore. Welsh and Manx*, I-II, Oxford, 1911

Ross, A., *Pagan Celtic Britain*, London, 1967 (Revised edn. 1992)

[Sargent, M.], 'A Family Legend', *New Ireland Review* XXIX, 1908, pp. 123-7, Dublin

Sergent, B., Cinq Études Sur Mélusine,' Premier partie: 1-3, *Mythologie Française*, No. 177, 2ème Trimestre 1995, p. 27-37

Schoepperle, G., 'The Washer of the Ford', *Journal of English and Germanic Philology* XVIII, 1919, pp. 60-6, Urbana, Illinois

Scott, Sir W., Letter to Thomas Crofton Croker, 27 April 1825, Croker, T.C., *Fairy Legends and Traditions of the South of Ireland*, Part 1, 2nd. ed., London 1826, Preface

Scott, Sir W., *Letters on Demonology and Witchcraft*, London, 1830

Scott, Sir W., 'The Lady of the Lake', *The Poetical Works of Sir Walter Scott*, ed., Robertson, J.L., London, 1913

Scottish Gaelic Studies IV, 2, 1935, pp. 97-135, London, Edinburgh, Glasgow

Scríobh IV, 1979, pp. 234-59, Dublin

"*Sean-Draoi*", 'Irish Words in the Spoken English of Leinster', *Irisleabhar na Gaedhilge* XI, 1901, pp. 93-94, Dublin

Sébillot, P., *Le Folk-Lore de France* I-IV, Paris, 1904-7

Sébillot, P., *Traditions et Superstitions de la Haute Bretagne* I-II, Paris, 1882

Semple, M., *Reflections on Lough Corrib*, Galway, 1974

Seymour, St John D., and Neligan, H.L., *True Irish Ghost Stories*, 2nd. ed., Dublin, 1926, first publ. 1914

An Sguab I, uimh. 12, 1923, p. 242, Dublin and Ring

The Shamrock III, no. 57, 2 Nov 1867, pp. 68-70; XI, no. 378, 10 Jan 1874, p. 229; no. 390, 4 April 1874, p. 440; XXIX, no. 1339, 11 June 1892, p. 596, Dublin

Sinsear, 1979, pp. 1-22; no. 8, 1995, pp. 111-118, Dublin

Sharkey, M., 'The Banshee', *Mayo Magazine*, no. 8, 17 Mar 1966, pp. 65-6, Swinford

Sheehan, Most Rev M., *Sean-Chaint na nDéise*, 2nd ed., Dublin, 1944

Shiel, M., *The Quiet Revolution: The Electrification of Rural Ireland 1946-1976*, Dublin, 1984

Sims-Williams, P., 'Some Celtic Otherworld Terms', in A.T.E. Matonis/Melia, D. F., eds., *Celtic Language, Celtic Culture: A Festschrift for Eric P. Hamp*, Van Nuys, California, 1990

Sjoestedt, M.-L., *Gods and Heroes of the Celts*, Berkeley, 1982 (Trans. by Myles Dillon of *Dieux et Héros des Celtes*, Paris, 1940)

Sorlin, É, *Cris De Vie, Cris De Mort. Les Fées Du Destin Dans Les Pays Celtiques*, FF. Communications no. 248, Helsinki, 1991

Statistical Abstracts (Saorstát Éireann), 1931, Dublin, 1931

St. Clair, S., *Folklore of the Ulster People*, Cork, 1971

St. Clair, S., *Psychic Phenomena in Ireland*, Cork and Dublin, 1972

An Stoc, leabhar 6, uimh. 7, 1929, p. 8, Galway

Stockman, G., *The Irish of Achill, Co. Mayo*, Belfast, 1974

Stokes, W., 'The Second Battle of Moytura', *Revue Celtique* XII, 1891, pp. 52-130, 306-8, Paris

Stokes, W., ed., 'Da Choca's Hostel', *Revue Celtique* XXI, 1900, pp. 149-65, 312-27, 388-402, Paris

Stokes, W., ed., 'The Prose Tales in the Rennes Dindšenchas', *Revue Celtique* XV, 1894, pp. 272-336, Paris

Stokes, W., ed., 'O'Mulconry's Glossary', *Archiv für Celtische Lexikographie* I, 1900, pp. 232-324, Halle

Stokes, W., ed., *The Destruction of Dá Derga's Hostel*, Paris, 1902 (Reprinted from *Revue Celtique* XXII 1901, pp. 9-61, 165-215, 282-329, 390-437; XXIII 1902, p. 88), Paris

Stokes, W., 'Echtra Mac Echach Muigmedoin', *Revue Celtique* XXIV, 1903, pp. 190-207, Paris

Stokes, W., ed., 'O'Davoren's Glossary', *Archiv für Celtische Lexikographie* II, 1904, p.197-504, Halle

Streit, J., *Sun and Cross*, Edinburgh, 1984 (German original, Stuttgart, 1977)

Studia Celtica XVI-XVII, 1981-2, pp. 135-43, Oxford

Studia Ethnographica Upsaliensia II, 1956, pp. 16-35; III, 1977; V, 1978, Uppsala

Studia Hibernica, No. 20, 1980, pp. 7-30, Dublin

Studies: An Irish Quarterly Review, 42, 1953, pp. 321-36, Dublin

Sveinsson, E. Ól., *Á Njálsbúd*, Reykjavik, 1943

Taylor, T., *Ballads and Songs of Brittany*, London, 1865

Thompson, S., *Motif-Index of Folk-Literature* I-IV, rev. ed., Copenhagen, 1955-8

Thompson, S., and Balys, J., *Motif Index of the Oral Tales of India*, Bloomington, Indiana, 1958

Thurneysen, R., *Die irische Helden- und Königsage bis zum siebzehnten Jahrhundert*, I-II, Halle (Saale), 1921

Thornbury, W., *'Cross Country*, London, 1861

Todd, J.H., ed., *Cogadh Gaedhel re Gallaibh*, London, 1867

Todhunter, J., 'How Thomas Connolly Met The Banshee', *The Dublin University Review*, Sept 1885, pp. 149-55, Dublin

Todhunter, J., *The Banshee and Other Poems*, London, 1888

Transactions of the Gaelic Society of Inverness XXXIV, 1927-8 (1935), pp. 146-7, Inverness

Transactions of the Ossianic Society I, 1853, pp. 126-7; II, 1854, pp. 109-10, Dublin

Turville-Petre, E.O.G., *Myth and Religion of the North*, London, 1964

Ua Broin, L., 'A South-West Dublin Glossary', *Béaloideas* XIV, 1944 (1945), pp. 162-86, Dublin

Ua Duinnín, An tAth, P., eag. *Amhráin Eoghain Ruaidh Uí Shúilleabhán*, Dublin, 1901

Ua Duinnín, An tAth. P., eag. *Dánta Phiarais Feiritéir*, Dublin, 1903, 2nd ed., 1934

Ua Duinnín, An tAth, P., eag., *Filidhe na Máighe*, Dublin, 1906

Ua Duinnín, An tAth. P. eag., *Amhráin Sheagháin Chláraigh Mhic Dhomhnaill*, Dublin, 1902

Ua Síothcháin, S., 'Focail Gaedhilge sa mBéarla', *An Sguab* I, uimh, 12, 1923, p. 242, Dublin and Ring

Ulster Folklife II, 1956, p. 48; III, 1, 1957, p. 39; VI, 1960, pp. 32-42, Belfast

Ulster Journal of Archaeology 3rd series, I, 1938, p. 211, Belfast

Ussher, E., 'Waterford Folk-Tales, I', *Folk-Lore*, XXV, 1914, pp. 109-21, London

Van Hamel, A.G., ed.,' Aided Con Culainn' in: *Compert Con Culainn*, Dublin, 1968

Vaughan, W.E., and Fitzpatrick, A.J., *Irish Historical Statistics, Population, 1821-1971*, Dublin, 1978

Verdier, Y., 'La femme qui aide et la Laveuse', *l'Homme*, 16, 1976, pp. 103-28

Verdier, Y., *Façons de Daire, Façons de Faire. La Laveuse, La Couterière, La Cuisinière*, Paris, 1979

von der Leyen, F., *Lesebuch der deutschen Volkssage*, Berlin, 1933

von Sydow, C.W., 'Det ovanligas betydelse i tro och sed', *Folkminnen och Folktanker* XIII, 1926, pp. 53-70, Göteborg

von Sydow, C.W., 'Övernaturliga väsen', *Nordisk Kultur* XIX, *Folktro*, 1935, pp. 91-159, Stockholm

von Sydow, C.W., *Selected Papers on Folklore*, ed., L. Bødker, Copenhagen, 1948

Wagner, H., *Linguistic Atlas and Survey of Irish Dialects*, Dublin, 1958-69

Wall, J., *Tjuvmjölkande väsen*, I-II, Studia Ethnologica Upsaliensia 3, 1977, 5, 1978, Uppsala

Watson, E.C., 'Highland Mythology', *The Celtic Review* V, 1908-9, pp. 48-70, Edinburgh

Weird Tales, By Irish Writers, London, n.d.

Wentz, W.Y. Evans, *The Fairy Faith in Celtic Countries,* Oxford, 1977, first publ. Oxford 1911

Westropp, T.J., 'A Folklore Survey of Co. Clare', *Folk-Lore* XXI, 2, 1910, pp. 180-91, London

Westropp, T.J., 'A Study of the Folklore on the Coast of Connaught, Ireland', *Folk-Lore* XXIX, 1918, pp. 305-19, London

Wexford People, 9 July 1976; 16 July 1976, Wexford

Whitehead, Mrs. A.E., *Dealings with the Dead,* Camden, n.d.

Wilde, Lady, *Ancient Legends, Mystic Charms, and Superstitions of Ireland,* I-II, London, 1887

Wilde, Lady, *Ancient Cures, Charms and Usages of Ireland,* London, 1890

Wilde, Sir, W.R., *Lough Corrib,* Dublin, 1867

Willis, T., *Facts connected with the social and sanitary condition of the working classes in the city of Dublin,* Dublin, 1845

Windisch, E., 'Táin Bó Regamna', *Irische Texte* II, Leipzig 1877, pp. 224-54

Wood-Martin, W.G., *Traces of the Elder Faiths of Ireland* I-II, London, 1902

Woulfe, Rev. P., *Sloinnte Gaedheal is Gall,* Dublin, 1923

Wright, J., *The English Dialect Dictionary* I-VI, London, 1898-1905

Yeats, W.B., ed., *Fairy and Folk Tales of the Irish Peasantry,* London, 1888

Yeats, W.B., ed., *Irish Fairy Tales,* 2nd impression, London, 1892

Yeats, W.B., ed., *Irish Fairy and Folk Tales,* Walter Scott, London, n.d.

Yeats, W.B., *Folk-Lore* X, 1899, pp. 119-22, London

Yeats, W.B., ed., *Irish Folk Stories and Fairy Tales,* Grosset's Universal Library, New York. n.d.

Yeats, W.B., ed., *Fairy and Folk Tales of Ireland,* Foreword, Raine, Kathleen, London, 1973

Yeats, W.B., *Collected Poems of W.B. Yeats,* London, 1981, first publ. 1933

Zeitschrift für Celtische Philologie, XXXIX, 1982, pp. 243-60, Tübingen

Zeitschrift für Volkskunde LVIII, 1962, pp. 178-209, Stuttgart

Index

Achill Island, 367, 368
age of death-messenger belief, 23, 29-30, 37, 39-40, 191 ff.
Aided Con Culainn, The Death of Cúchulainn, 198, 203, 215, 388-9
Ailill, 193
Áine, 45, 59, 124, 195, 196, 206, 214, 400, 410
Aisling Poetry, 196, 400
Alter ego, 41-2
Amhráin Eoghain Ruaidh Uí Shúilleabháin, 400
Anglo Norman, 57, 200, 206, 209
Á Njálsbúd, 376
Annals of Loch Cé, 194
Aoibheall (Fairy Queen), 194-5, 196, 202, 206, 400
Aonghus, 380
Aos sí, 31
appearance of death-messenger – solitary female being, small/tall, old/young, beautiful/ugly, clothes, barefoot, long hair, combing hair, colour of hair, see also bird shape, 87 ff, 214-5, 218
Aran Islands, 25, 368
Archaeologia Brittanica, 369
Ariès, P., 382, 404
Áth na Foraire, 198
attitude of tradition bearers to death-messenger belief, 22-23, 219 ff.
Aughrim, 201, 398
Badhbh-names, bow (*babha*), *badhb*, *bochaointe* (*bohaíonta, boheanter, bohinkey, bocheentha*), *bo chaointeach* (*boheentach, bogheentheagh*), *bochaointeacháin* (*bochaoideachán, boheentacán*) 34 ff.
badhbhsánaí, 370
Badhbh-stratum, 192, 197 ff., 216-17

banfháidh, see Fedelm
Bankeentha, see *bean chaointe*
Bán na mBadhb, 34
Bannim, Michael, 35
Banquet of Dun na N-Gedh and The Battle of Magh Ragh, 397
Banshee, The, Elliot O'Donnell, 15
Banshee's Brook, Clare, 385, see also Daelagh River
Banshee's Chair, 126 f, see also Corby Rock Mill
Banshee's Well, see *Tobar*
baobh, 388, see also *badhbh*
barefoot, as sign of mourning, 381
Barrow River, 129, 385
Battle of Clontarf, 194-5, 204, 396
Battle of Corcomroe Abbey, 200, 397
Battle of Dysert O'Dea, 200, 397
Battle of Gabhra, 388, see *Cath Gabhra*
Battle of Magh Ragh, see *Banquet of Dun na N-Gedh*
beadu, 37
bean an leasa, 30
bean chaointe, bean a' chaointe, bean chaoint', bean chaointe cháinte, 29, 32-3, 145-6, 210, 376, Bankeentha, 368
bean-nighe (Washerwoman), 133, 139, 202, 212, 368, 371, 387-9, 391, 394, 400, see also beetle, 'Washer at the Ford'
Bean-Shithe, 30
beetle, 130, 165, 166, 170, 187, 317-20, 387
Bé Find, 193, 194, 400
béic (shout), 67, 68-9, 77-9, 294, 295
ben síde, 30, 193, 205
  ben a sídib, banshídaige, 30
  mná síde, 193, 194
Bernadette Place, Wexford, 126

McClintock, L., 135, 373
McCourt, Desmond, 389
MacDomhnaill, Seán Clárach, 396
Mac Gearailt, Muiris, Mac Ridire
  Chiarraí, 29, 59, 124, 195
Mac Giollarnáth, S., 378
McGlynn, Jenny, 22, 23, 238-9
Mag na hEamna, 198
Magnusson, M., Pálsson, H., eds., 376
Magrath, John, see *Caithréim
  Thoirdhealbhaigh*, 201
maide éamainn, 392
Máire Gaelach, evil spirit, Cork, 394
Manerium, 369
manifestations of the death-messenger
  experiencers of; dying person, family,
    neighbours, 140-50
  for death; before, after, at moment of, for
    sudden deaths, 112-21, 238-40, 303-6
  locations; house of dying person, old
    family home, vicinity of house,
    window, window-sill, nature
    formations, near water, in Ireland for
    deaths abroad, abroad for deaths in
    Ireland, 121 ff, 308-10
  times, 119-21, 307
  types: aural, 65-6, 67 ff., 283-5, aural and
    visual, 66-7, 99, 286-7, visual only, 65,
    288-9
Medb, 193, 203, 204
Menlo, Co. Galway, 398
Mermaid, 41, 42, 45-6 (Seal Woman
  Legend ML 4080), 66, 97, 101, 160-3,
  172, 181, 401
milk-stealing creatures, 368, 372,
  see also butter stealing
Millburn River, 129, 386
moan, 67, 68
Mokyr, J., 375
mong, 199, 397
Morrígan, Morrigu, 106, 130, 198, 211,
  396, 397
Mulgannon, Wexford, 126

Multeen River, 129, 386
Motifs
  A 132.6.2* Goddess in form of bird, 371
  A 485.1, Goddess of War, 371
  C 543, *Tabu:* picking up comb from
    ground, 393
  C 611, Forbidden chamber, 46, 372
  D 113.1.1., Werwolf, 372
  D 1812.5.1.1.7*, Washer at the Ford, 371
  E 542.1.2, Ghost touches man's neck,
    leaves impression of hand on neck,
    185, 394
  E 723.2, Seeing one's wraith is a sign that
    person is to die shortly, 372
  E 734.1 Soul in form of butterfly, 382
  F 93, Water entrance to Lower World, 400
  F 324.1, Girl borrows comb and mirror
    from bonga (fairy): carried to
    fairyland when she returns them, 402
  F 491 Will O' the Wisp leads people
    astray, 373, see also Types of Folktale
  F 625; Strong man: breaker of iron, 393
  M 301.6.1*, Banshees as portents of
    misfortune, 371
  V 236.1, Fallen angels become fairies, 372
Neman, 106
Newgrange, see *Brugh na Bóinne*
Nét, war god, 38
Ní Shéaghdha, N., 377
Njal's Saga, 204, 376
Norman, see Anglo Norman
O'Brien's of Thomond, 194-5, 201, 371,
  see also Brian Boru
  O'Brien, Donnchadh, 200-1
  O'Brien, Turlough, 200-1
Ochón! 67, 68, 70, 292, 296
O'Clery's Glossary, 369
O'Connell, Peter (lexicographer), 38
O'Davoren's Glossary, 397
O'Donnell, Elliot, 15
O'Kearney, Nicholas, 35, 368, 373
olagón, 65, 67, 69, 291, 295, see also
  lament